# AFTER THE END

# AFTER THE END⸻⸻⸻⸻⸻

*Making U.S. Foreign Policy in the Post–Cold War World*

Edited by James M. Scott

Duke University Press   Durham and London   1998

© 1998 Duke University Press
All rights reserved
Printed in the United States of America on acid-free paper ⊛
Typeset in Trump Mediaeval by Tseng Information Systems, Inc.
Library of Congress Cataloging-in-Publication Data appear
on the last printed page of this book.
Second printing, 2000

For Meghan Rose and Michael James

# Contents

# List of Tables and Figures

# Preface

*James M. Scott*

The world has changed dramatically since the end of the cold war. So, too, has the role and purpose of the United States in the world. It seems clear that, while the post–cold war world may be a more benign environment for foreign policy choices, the world "after the end" is also more complex and is perhaps more difficult to address. The changes associated with the end of the cold war, and their consequences, raise important and intriguing questions concerning the making of U.S. foreign policy: how will post–cold war foreign policy be made? What will the role and influence of the White House, bureaucracy, Congress, and nongovernmental actors be? How will post–cold war foreign policy making compare to policy making in other periods?

This volume assesses the consequences of changes associated with the end of the cold war for both the processes and policies of the United States. To do so, it presents a collection of essays and case studies that explore the policy makers and processes responsible for U.S. foreign policy in the post–cold war period. A basic organizational framework provides coherence to the volume. Our purpose is to provide for scholars, teachers, and students of U.S. foreign policy a broad, but coherent, evaluation of U.S. foreign policy making in the post–cold war setting. Together we

- assess the landscape of the post–cold war policy-making environment by examining the international changes of the last decade and the broad American societal attitudes toward them and toward foreign policy in general;
- examine the elements of continuity and change with respect to the actors, groups, and institutions responsible for shaping the foreign policies of the United States, highlighting the central characteristics, structures, processes, roles and challenges in the post-cold war setting;
- probe, through case studies, key foreign policy problems of the post–cold war period;

- explore, in these cases, the shifting roles and relationships among the actors and institutions responsible for U.S. foreign policy choices; and
- synthesize key patterns in the shifting roles and relationships among the four circles of actors, weighing the resulting impact on foreign policy decisions.

The volume has four sections. First, the major features of the international and domestic landscape of the post–cold war world are assessed to provide the context of constraints and imperatives within which foreign policy decisions are made (chapter 1, on the international, societal, and institutional context). Second, the individual elements of the organizing framework—the White House, Congress, bureaucracy, and nongovernmental actors—are examined for distinguishing structures, processes, and roles, particularly in light of the end of the cold war (chapters 2–7, on the presidency, foreign policy bureaucracy, foreign economic bureaucracy, Congress, public opinion, and interest groups/media). Third, the interaction of these "players" is examined through case studies of specific foreign policies and decisions in the post–cold war environment (chapters 8–14). Fourth, "After the End" assesses the broad patterns of and insights into post–cold war U.S. foreign policy making.

Initial work on this project began in the spring of 1996. As the editor, I invited proposals for the various chapters, which were then evaluated for their fit with the overall purposes and themes of the volume. By December 1996, the contributors had submitted chapter drafts, which underwent two layers of peer review—by the volume's editor, and by a panel of anonymous reviewers. Comments, critiques, and suggestions for revisions were returned to the contributors, who addressed them in second drafts. The editor made another round of revisions to these second drafts, completing the manuscript which was submitted to Duke University Press, whose own anonymous peer reviews resulted in yet another round of revisions. Hence, the chapters in this volume have been carefully scrutinized through three layers of peer review, each of which has strengthened the overall manuscript and the individual chapters. All of the contributors wish to thank the anonymous reviewers—both the initial panel arranged by the editor, and those relied on by the publisher—for their helpful comments and suggestions.

This project has received generous support from a grant from the Research Services Council of the University of Nebraska at Kearney, additional funds from the graduate school at the University of Nebraska at Kearney, and further support from the College of Natural and Social Sciences at the University of Nebraska at Kearney, for which the editor and contributors wish to offer their sincerest gratitude. Additional thanks go to Valerie Millholland, our Duke Press editor, to Maura High, who copyedited the manuscript, and to Michele Steinbacher-Kemp, who carefully and competently prepared the index to this volume. In addition to being contributors to the volume, Ralph G. Carter, Peter J. Schraeder, Steven W. Hook, James M. McCormick, and John T. Rourke provided advice from the early stages of the project, without which the book would not have been completed. Finally, the editor extends his appreciation to his colleagues in the Department of Political Science at the University of Nebraska at Kearney for their aid, support, and encouragement throughout the project. In recognizing this assistance, the editor and contributors happily acknowledge that any errors of fact or interpretation are theirs alone.

# 1.

## Out of the Cold: The Post–Cold War Context

## of U.S. Foreign Policy

*James M. Scott and A. Lane Crothers*

"Gosh, I miss the Cold War." These words, uttered by President Bill Clinton in late 1993, are characteristic of a growing disillusionment regarding American foreign policy in the post–cold war world. At first glance, this regret seems misplaced. After all, during the cold war, two superpowers approached the brink of nuclear war, played dangerous games of "chicken" with their military forces, sought to subvert each other by overt and covert measures, and routinely referred to each other as "evil." What could possibly drive the nostalgia for such a setting?

The president's musing reflects a growing suspicion that the cold war was, in a sense, a simpler time in which to set a foreign policy course, in spite of the high stakes and costly "imperatives" imposed by the contest between the Soviet Union and the United States. The U.S.-Russian relationship has evolved from confrontation to cooperation, making the post–cold war world a more benign environment for foreign policy choices. For example, Americans helped Russian president Boris Yeltsin win reelection, the United States and the international community have provided substantial assistance to the Russian government, Russian troops serve under the tactical command of U.S. officers as Bosnian peacekeepers, and Russian foreign minister Yevgeny Primakov successfully brokered the reentry of U.S. weapons inspectors into Iraq to deal with that country's attempts to build an arsenal of destructive weaponry. Nevertheless, the emerging environment may also prove to be substantially more difficult to address.

The end of the cold war eliminated a number of reliable and well-recognized reference points from the landscape and established new, as yet ambiguous ones. Liberated from an overriding concern with the threat that the Soviet Union was understood to represent, policy makers are now required to think seriously about the roles, interests, and purposes of the United States in the twenty-first century. Since foreign policy may be conceptualized, at least in part, as adaptive behavior, it seems clear that the changing international context of the post–cold war environment requires adaptation to face the new issues and problems it raises.[1] Just how well have U.S. foreign policy makers adapted to this altered setting? As the remainder of this volume will indicate, the U.S. response has involved both attempts to grapple with the new issues and challenges of the post–cold war world and alterations in the process through which policy makers shape foreign policy. However, the process adjustments have complicated the policy adjustments. To return to President Clinton's reflection, it is in the context of these substantive changes and the procedural permutations they help to create that the former era seems a simpler world that U.S. policy makers could address through a simpler process.

This volume examines the characteristics and patterns of policy making that are emerging in response to the shift from cold war to post–cold war. By considering the actors and institutions and probing their behavior in a set of foreign policy cases, the authors shed light on the changes and adaptations that have (and have not) occurred. This chapter sets the stage for the analyses that follow by introducing the context of U.S. foreign policy making and discussing the changes associated with the end of the cold war. It concludes by raising a few considerations that will be explored more thoroughly in the volume's chapters and revisited in the conclusion.

### The U.S. Foreign Policy Context

Within the United States, the domestic context of U.S. foreign policy derives from societal forces and the institutional arrangements and structures established by the U.S. Constitution. This context makes societal forces—political culture, public opinion, and group interests and activity—a critical part of the U.S. foreign policy arena, and it establishes a complex set of fluctuating arrangements among the people and institutions of the government. Hence, understanding how U.S. foreign policy makers adapt to the issues and problems of the international environment first requires a grasp of the societal and institutional settings within which they act.

*The American Societal Context*
The institutions and actors that shape U.S. foreign policy do so in the context of multifaceted and complex societal setting. For definitional

purposes, this context may be understood as, first, the broad attitudes and orientations of the people of the United States and, second, some of the societal actors that affect policy making. The broad societal context, or political culture, is a set of shared ideas, ideals, concepts, stories, and myths that orient citizens within their political systems. Its relevance rests in large measure on several strands of influence. It influences "the manner in which members of society, including the state elite, define themselves and their place in the larger global setting." It also gives shape to the arena of possible actions (i.e., the kinds of policies and programs that the American people are likely to support) and helps to shape the perceptual maps of the policy makers themselves.[2]

The heart of the societal context within which U.S. foreign policy is made consists of a set of core dimensions or a "creed" through which Americans define themselves and politics.[3] Foremost among these dimensions is *democratic liberalism*. The U.S. society is liberal in that, politically, it emphasizes the individual and the rights and freedoms to which he or she is entitled, with a particular commitment "to individual liberty and the protection of private property; to limited government, the rule of law, natural rights, the perfectibility of human institutions, and the possibility of human progress."[4] Economically, liberalism means capitalism, an economic system based on markets, free enterprise, and private ownership. The U.S. is *democratic* in the sense of a commitment to (1) the principle that specific procedures must be followed for filling government positions (elections) and for making government decisions; (2) popular sovereignty, or the view that the citizens of the country are the source of government authority, and thus the government must be accountable to them; and (3) limited majority rule, or the idea that the majority of a nation's citizens ought to set the general direction for society so long as the majority respects and protects the rights of the minority. Democratic liberalism therefore calls for limited, accountable government that should be responsive to and formed with the participation of the citizens of the country.

Other elements of the societal context concern relations among individuals and groups in society, and between them and the government. For example, the United States is *egalitarian*, in the sense that there is broad agreement that citizens ought to have equal political standing and generally equal opportunities in society. While much of U.S. history has involved a struggle to define and apply these principles of equality (especially as regards racial, ethnic, and gender differences), in the main, the commitment has militated against various forms of social and class distinctions, preferences, and discrimination that have been more common and pronounced elsewhere. Additionally, the United States is *pluralist*, accepting decisions that result in the victory of one group over another, as long as individuals are free to associate with groups of their choice and there are no systematic barriers blocking the right of any group or individual to advocate for their preferences. Moreover, the United States is *legalist*. This means that it is a "law-oriented society": there is a societal preference for lawmaking to resolve conflict, and a broad belief that "ideas embodied in legal precepts are entitled to respect and obedience."[5]

Finally, a general *universalism/exceptionalism* underlies these preceding features, a sense that "the American way" is a model that all others would do well to emulate. Americans widely believe that values such as those outlined above are universal public goods to be maximized in other nations. Hence, universalism essentially means that commitments to democratic liberalism, constitutional government, and the like are superior preferences, suitable and desirable for all people and countries.

One way to simplify the complex connection between these aspects of culture and foreign affairs is to identify the *societal impulses* and *foreign policy orientations* the culture generates in the individuals of the society. These may be considered in terms of two continua. The societal impulse continuum ranges between *moralism/idealism* at one end and *pragmatism/realism* at the other. Moralism/idealism describes the impulse to promote certain values in foreign policy, rather than to defend various interests. Moralists/idealists argue that the United States should involve itself in international affairs "only for sufficient ethical reasons" (i.e., that foreign policy "should be motivated by moral principles").[6] Further, moralists/idealists tend to believe that a peaceful and prosperous world can be created according to universal (i.e., U.S.) moral principles, so that adherence to these (U.S.-defined) principles of right and wrong are as important as some conception of interests. At its extreme, moralism/idealism may become "messianism," or the "missionary urge to remake the world in the American image" in order to "save" it.[7] This type of moralism/idealism implies a sense of duty and destiny best defined as the "U.S. mission" to serve as "the custodian of the future of humanity."[8]

On the other hand the constellation of societal values in the United States also supports a sense of *pragmatism/realism*, or ad hoc problem solving that eschews broad moral, ideological, or doctrinal purposes in favor of a concern with concrete interests and a results-based standard of evaluation.[9] Values like democracy, which promotes open public debate, and pluralism, which encourages multiple groups and individuals to come together to come to mutually acceptable—and inevitably compromising—solutions to their problems, tend to support *pragmatic* approaches to problem solving, even in foreign policy. Within the broad parameters of U.S. values, the impulse toward pragmatism means a concern with interests and necessity, "case-by-case-ism," reactive approaches, and a focus on the short term rather than the long term.[10]

A *foreign policy orientation* continuum—based on broad attitudes toward U.S. policy—ranges between *isolationism,* on the one hand, and *internationalism,* on the other. Isolationism may be simply defined as the desire to keep the United States out of substantial political and military involvement with the world (especially Europe). It is, in short, a preference for a passive response to the world whereby the United States serves chiefly as an example, without assuming responsibility for the world, acting as agent to reform the world, or intervening in the affairs of others in the world. It is in this sense that John Winthrop's frequently repeated "city upon a hill" metaphor is most apt. An oft-cited example is found in an 1821 speech by Secretary of State John Quincy Adams: "Wherever the standard of freedom and independence has been or shall be unfurled, there will [America's] heart, her benedictions, and her prayers be. But she goes not abroad in search of monsters to destroy. She is the well-wisher to the freedom and independence of all. She is the champion and vindicator of her own. She will recommend the general cause by the countenance of her voice, and by the benignant sympathy of her example."[11]

In contrast, internationalism suggests that the United States should be actively involved in the world's political affairs in order to protect U.S. interests and provide necessary American leadership. According to this view the United States has interests and responsibilities that must be served through participation and leadership. In practice, internationalism includes the willingness to exercise power, to intervene—politically, militarily, and economically—in affairs around the world, to exercise leadership in world affairs, and even to transplant American values and institutions.[12] Statements illustrative of this view include those of President Harry Truman, who once argued that "the free peoples of the world look to us for support in maintaining their freedoms. . . . If we falter in our leadership, we may endanger the peace of the world—and we shall certainly endanger the welfare of our own nation."[13]

The seemingly uneasy coexistence of these apparently opposite orientations is misleading, for they spring from the same political culture. Not only do both orientations exist simultaneously (helping to generate a fundamental ambivalence among Americans toward world affairs),[14] but the orientations themselves are bound together by a common element: the sense of an American *mission* to lead the world into a better form of political, social, and economic relationships. In effect, the orientations divide over the proper method to achieve that mission: isolationists tend to argue that the United States should order its own affairs and lead the world only by example, while internationalists suggest that the United States cannot transform the world without being actively involved in the affairs of the world. Both depend on a unique sense of American duty and destiny; at issue is simply the best means to "spread" the values.

Political culture, in the end, is a factor in shaping the mode of international interactions the United States undertakes. It tends to limit policy flexibility by constraining the range of choices available to policy makers. However, it also provides concepts, ideas, ideals, and values through which foreign policies can be legitimated in a democratic polity. Additionally, the broad political culture is doubly important because the political system of the United States is constructed as it is— a pluralist democracy. As such, the actors and institutions of the government who make policy choices do so in the context of a circle of nongovernmental actors whose preferences, attitudes, and values constrain and influence their choices. The circle includes such elements as public opinion, which may act as a constraint, if not a guide, for government policy (see chapter 8, by Ole Holsti). The media may also affect policy by acting as a gatekeeper or framer of issues, a source of information, a watchdog, and an agenda setter, while interest groups of varying types may affect policy as well (see chapter 9, by James M. McCormick). Trade, ethnic, ideological, corporate, transnational, and foreign groups (government, business, or otherwise) may lobby, pressure, persuade, publicize, and endorse or oppose candidates for office in order to influence policy in their particular areas of interest. Moreover, a network of think tanks and research institutions affect foreign policy through actions such as policy studies, endorsements, and the provision of personnel for government positions. Finally, some private citizens may affect policy on the strength of their experiences, status, prestige, or relationships. Their views, advice, and ideas may be solicited or heeded by policy makers.

*The Institutional Context*
The institutional context of U.S. foreign policy derives from the U.S. Constitution. Without delving deeply into the constitutional distribu-

tion of powers and responsibilities over various aspects of foreign affairs,[15] several points should be noted. The Constitution provides for accountability and access on the part of the public, making U.S. foreign policy the legitimate target of public interest and pressure, and causing U.S. foreign policy makers to be rightfully concerned with public acceptance. Institutionally, the Constitution establishes the principles of separation of powers and checks and balances by which policy-making power is divided, distributed, and balanced among three branches. Furthermore, the Constitution does not assign to any branch "the foreign policy power"; indeed, neither the term nor its synonyms appears in the text. Instead, the Constitution breaks foreign policy power into pieces and assigns various portions to the Congress and to the executive, generally forcing a sharing of responsibility. Yet, the Constitution does not specify which branch is to lead in foreign policy, providing an "invitation to struggle" to the political branches.[16] In short, the provisions and ambiguities of the U.S. Constitution establish an institutional context that is messy and complex.

In spite of this ambiguous arena, it is common practice to refer to "the preeminence of presidents" over American foreign policy. In fact, the predominant model of American foreign policy making is a series of concentric circles beginning with the president and expanding outward to include advisors, bureaucracies, Congress, and the public (see figure 1.1). According to this "presidential preeminence" image, the influence and relevance of actors decreases with distance from the center of the circles. To the extent that this model suggests that the White House is central to the foreign policy process, it is generally useful. However, it is often taken to mean the White House is *always* the center of policy making, which is less accurate. As a former member of the National Security Council staff notes, policy making begins "before the decision memorandum reached the president's desk and continues after it has gone into the out-box."[17] In addition to the White House, it is possible for the bureaucracy or Congress to be at the center of foreign policy making or, at least, to exercise significant influence. Moreover, societal actors including public opinion, the media, and interest groups (as well as the even broader elements of political culture) may also play an important role.

Thus, a more accurate depiction of the institutional policy-making environment would posit a series of shifting constellations formed by three groups—the president and chief advisers (the White House), the foreign policy bureaucracy and Congress—who are embedded in and affected by both a societal circle (in which a variety of forces and non-

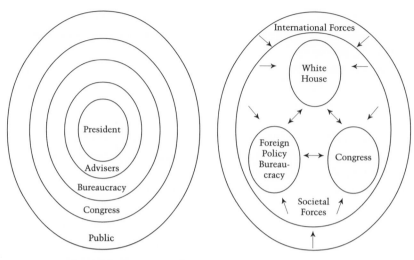

Figure 1.1 (left). The Presidential Preeminence Image
Figure 1.2 (right). The Shifting Constellations Image

governmental actors reside) and the international environment. Unlike the image depicted in figure 1.1, this "shifting constellations" image (see figure 1.2) indicates that foreign policy may emerge from shifting and uncertain interactions between the White House, Congress, bureaucratic agencies, and groups and individuals from the private sector. The White House *may* dominate, but it does not *necessarily* dominate. Therefore, the influence of the institutions that make American foreign policy will vary, and this variation will likely manifest itself on the micro-level (i.e., variation from policy to policy and from stage to stage in a given policy) and the macro-level (i.e., there may be different "default" or dominant constellations in different historical periods). Understanding this complex environment is central to explaining how American foreign policy makers will adjust policy to meet the challenges that emerge from the end of the cold war.[18]

Given the institutions established or authorized by the U.S. Constitution (and the ambiguity on their role), within this circle of societal forces, the shifting constellations image has a number of implications for U.S. foreign policy making. First, *policy emerges from the interaction of three circles of policy makers*—the White House, the foreign policy bureaucracy, and Congress.

*The White House.* The first institutional circle is the White House. The role of the president and top aides and advisers stems from the president's position as the chief executive. This circle commands the executive branch and thus has access to its expertise, information, and capabilities for implementing policy. Moreover, this group has the ability to set the agenda and seize the initiative, mobilize opinion, set the bureaucracy in motion, exert pressure on Congress, and force it to react, in addition to such powers as are bestowed on the commander in chief, chief executive, chief diplomat, and chief legislator of the U.S. government. This combination provides persistent opportunities to lead policy making (see chapter 3, by Jerel A. Rosati and Steven Twing).

*The Foreign Policy Bureaucracy.* The bureaucracy—or that part of the bureaucracy with foreign policy responsibility—is also a significant institutional player in American foreign policy making. This circle consists of the State Department, Defense Department, Central Intelligence Agency (see chapter 4, by Christopher Jones), and other economic agencies (see chapter 5, I. M. Destler), created to provide advice and implement policy decisions. The bureaucracy's expertise and control of information place it in a position to shape the formulation of policy by performing much of the generation and consideration of policy alternatives. Moreover, the various agencies of the foreign policy bureaucracy shape policy with their primary role in its implementation. In both of these roles, disagreements among different officials and agencies affect both the nature of the policy and the process by which it is formulated and implemented. Its policy behavior is affected by its fragmentation, disagreement, "turf wars," and organizational characteristics such as parochialism, risk avoidance, and routinization.

*Congress.* Congress also influences foreign policy. The congressional circle includes the leadership, committees, and individual members of both houses. While members and the institution are limited by many structural characteristics (including size, decentralization, procedures, segmentation of and limited access to information, and electoral constraints), the institution and its individual members have access to potentially potent avenues of influence. These include tools such as their ability to legislate, their constitutional and statutory authority to hold oversight hearings, require reports, and request briefings by executive branch officials, their advise-and-consent authority over treaties and appointments, and their "power of the purse." In addition, instruments such as threatening to legislate, expressing a "mood," issuing requests and warnings directly to executive branch personnel, or passing nonbinding resolutions also provide a means for congressional influence, as do the abilities to frame opinion and enact procedural legislation (see Ralph G. Carter's discussion of Congress in chapter 6).

In addition, the shifting constellations image implies that *the role and influence of each circle varies* within a policy, across different policies, and over different policy and historical settings. Thus, constellations change: leadership and influence among the governmental actors can shift, and societal actors may affect a given policy (i.e., presidential leadership is a variable, not a given). Among the factors that may account for these shifts are policy type (e.g., crisis, strategic, or structural); timing, policy stage, or policy cycle; issue area; situation (e.g., crisis or noncrisis); and policy instrument (e.g., aid, troop deployment, diplomacy). Taking into account these potential explanations, the shifting constellations image suggests that policy-making leadership may take at least five different forms, or constellations.

*White House Leadership.* This constellation supposes leadership by the president and his advisers, consistent with the tenets of the presidential preeminence image (figure 1.1). Foreign policy is seen as a product of presidential policy making and leadership; this constellation assumes that, after discussion and debate, the president decides on a course of action, which is then implemented. Since the White House is dominant, a small group of advisers (e.g., the National Security Council) and their personal characteristics, group dynamics, and policy preferences will be of great importance. While coherent, essentially rational, policy making may ensue, the potential for "groupthink" is also present, particularly if the group of advisers is characterized by a high level of homogeneity in ideological and attitudinal approach. The classic examples of this policy-making model derive from crisis policies such as the Cuban missile crisis and others, whose nature concentrates policy making in the White House. In addition, the capacity to structure an "interagency process" centered on the White House also strengthen presidential leadership, while providing opportunities to manage or channel some of the rivalries and processes inherent in "bureaucratic politics."

*Bureaucratic Leadership.* This constellation posits that some foreign policy is made and conducted primarily in the mid- to lower levels of the executive branch. This occurs because of the broad range and complexity of policy that must be attended to (i.e., literally countless decisions on foreign policy matters, in which the White House and Congress figure in relatively few), and because high-level officials in either branch are limited in their time and interest (i.e., with the scope of the political agenda, officials prioritize issues and focus on those at the top of the list). The bureaucracy may occasionally make policy without reference to upper-level officials, or interagency efforts may produce choices that high-level officials simply ratify. The most significant patterns of behavior from this constellation stem from the "multivoice" character of the foreign policy bureaucracy, which may cause compromise, bargaining, incrementalism, competition, and/or stalemate. The features of bureaucratic policy making—both intraagency features stemming from an organization's structure, process, and culture, and interagency features stemming from interaction, competition, conflict, and compromise between different units of the bureaucracy, which may produce policy that is cautious, noninventive, contradictory, ineffectual, and less than optimal for the given situation. Although bureaucratic politics occurs in many types of policies, bureaucratic leadership seems to be most prevalent in routine, noncrisis, and low-priority situations.[19]

*Interbranch Leadership.* This constellation has all three governmental circles sharing responsibility and nongovernmental actors playing supporting roles. Interbranch policy making may occur in one of at least four variants: *cooperation,* in which the circles work together to make policy; *constructive compromise,* in which members of the circles devise solutions that garner enough support for policy to proceed, although these sometimes satisfy no group completely and contain inherent contradictions; *institutional competition,* involving legislative-executive or interagency contention (actors may pursue parallel policy making, seeking to act independently of one another, or the members of each circle may forge alliances with like-minded members of the other circles to compete over policy); *confrontation and stalemate,* in which each circle, endowed with some "negative power," blocks the preferences of the others.[20] Examples of interbranch leadership may be found in many noncrisis situations, including foreign economic policy (see chapter 14), foreign aid policy (see chapters 9 and 12), and a wide variety of others.[21]

*Subgovernment Leadership.* Subgovernments are closed policy systems consisting of alliances between members of subcommittees in Congress, bureaucratic agencies, and relevant interest groups, nominally led by the legislative component. Within these systems, policy is made through bargaining and "log rolling" by actors with reinforcing objectives and interests without involvement of the upper levels of the executive branch or Congress. By closing off avenues of debate, and narrowing the circle of actors involved, subgovernment produces policy supported by all the elements of the closed policy system. However, multiple policy systems usually exist, and may clash over their "turf." In U.S. foreign policy, subgovernment constellations are most common in defense policies, budgeting, and procurement decisions.[22]

*Congressional Leadership.* Members of Congress may also legislate foreign policy. In this constellation, members of Congress formulate and select the option through the legislative process. Ultimately, policy is arrived at through voting procedures, in the subcommittees, committees, and floors of both houses, and through House-Senate conferences if necessary. As a result, the president is typically presented with legislation conveying Congress's policy. While the foreign policy bureaucracy is usually responsible for implementation, it is supervised and evaluated by members of Congress through the institution's oversight powers. Congressional leadership generally occurs only when consensus within the institution exists. In that case, Congress may legislate policy. This is particularly likely when agreement on the need for a policy exists but the president or executive branch has not acted (i.e., a policy vacuum), or when an administration adopts a policy that a substantial part of Congress rejects (i.e., a policy disagreement). In general, although it rarely occurs throughout a policy, congressional leadership occurs occasionally during certain periods or stages of a policy. Examples might include U.S. policy toward South Africa from 1985 to 1986 or U.S. policy toward Nicaragua between 1987 and 1989.[23]

A final implication of the shifting constellations image is that *rival alliances of different individuals from different circles may form in an attempt to shape U.S. foreign policy.* Many different individuals comprise the White House, the foreign policy bureaucracy, Congress, and the public. These individuals will have different policy views, so disagreements, disputes, and divisions will occur within each circle, as well as between them. This provides the opportunity for like-minded individuals from different circles to unite to force their preferences into policy. These factions may contend with one another to establish policy; once policy is determined, they may alternately conspire to undermine the existing policy or unite to preserve the status quo.[24]

The formation and manipulation of cross-branch alliances provide many advantages to their members. First, alliances expand access to and sharing of information. Second, the alliances help their constituents set the agenda, raise issues, and force consideration of certain options. Third, forming cross-branch alliances enhances the ability of each individual component to structure the terms of the debate, and apply pressure or persuasion, whether in policy deliberations, legislative efforts, or the framing of public opinion. Fourth, well-developed alliances with members in each circle acquire opportunities to act, allowing coordination and orchestration of efforts and sometimes providing openings to conduct their own policies. Fifth, alliances enhance the ability of their members to sustain preferred initiatives or to obstruct undesired policies by expanding the ranges of access points and policy instruments at their disposal. In sum, these networks increase the number of individuals who may influence policy, and expand the influence of specific individuals by enhancing their access to policy-making tools and procedures.

## Adapting to the Post–Cold War International Context

If, as the complex environment of the shifting constellations image suggests, patterns of involvement, influence, and leadership can vary across policies and time, what effect does the end of the cold war have on the pattern of constellation formation and constellation dominance? Answering this question requires a brief discussion of the cold war years, some review of the international changes associated with the end of the cold war, and an assessment of the impact of the end of the cold war on the societal and institutional context of U.S. foreign policy.

*White House Leadership and the Cold War Years*
In a number of respects, the cold war simplified U.S. foreign policy and the process by which it was formulated. Part of the explanation for this rests in the "shortcuts" provided by the cold war to U.S. foreign policy makers: they made it clearer what price to pay and when to pay it. Contending with a complex world was made easier by a "cold war consensus," which narrowed and simplified both problem interpretation and policy prescription. This consensus—a "set of beliefs, values, and premises about America's role in the world"[25]—included basic agreement on the nature of the world (bipolar), the nature of conflict in the world (zero-sum between the United States and the Soviet Union), the U.S. role in the world (leadership), and broad U.S. foreign policy (containment of the Soviet Union and communism and promotion of an open, multilateral economy). During the period in which this consensus was strongest, debate in the United States tended to be more about narrow policy tactics and less about broader strategy or purposes.

One need not minimize the policy disputes—often lively, if not heated—that occurred both within and between the political branches of the U.S. government during this so-called era of bipartisanship, to recognize the substantial agreement on role and purposes that existed during this time. Among the many consequences of this consensus, two stand out for the purposes of this volume. First, this consensus generated substantial societal support for an internationalist foreign policy orientation. In effect, the American public tended to support (or, at least, acquiesce in) U.S. leadership in the world, in part because it was predicated on a clear threat, substantial security concerns, and a sharply defined sense of moral purpose. Second, this consensus generated a much greater tendency toward executive branch (especially White House) leadership in the making of U.S. foreign policy than had been the case prior to the cold war era. While this presidential leadership was predicated on numerous factors, one central aspect was simple policy agreement.

In effect, the cold war consensus offered three essential shortcuts for foreign policy that dramatically simplified efforts to set a course of action: a definitive threat that required response; distinct priorities to guide policy decisions and the inevitable trade-offs that occur between competing goals; a basis for societal and institutional consensus that made forging policy a simpler process. As a result, most observers of U.S. foreign policy during the first two decades after World War II agree that the executive branch (and especially the White House) exercised policy leadership. While there were limits to "presidential preeminence," most observers expected White House leadership, as any perusal of foreign policy textbooks of the era clearly indicates. Hence, the cold war years effectively established a "dominant policy-making constellation" (White House leadership) and a dominant mode of foreign policy (internationalism).

Roughly two decades into the cold war, White House leadership began to erode. In particular, the Vietnam experience destroyed much of the cold war consensus, and the ensuing policy disagreements largely ended the era of bipartisanship, leading to two decades of thrashing about in search of a new basis for consensus.[26] During this time, even while the Soviet Union was a central issue in and reference point for U.S. foreign policy, societal support and institutional agreement over the role, purposes, and processes of U.S. foreign policy decayed. White House leadership came under increasing scrutiny as congressional assertiveness increased, and domestic pressures proliferated. The White House (and the broader executive branch) retained important leadership roles, but the breadth and scope of such leadership was increasingly challenged. It is in the context of this overall erosion that the end of the cold war occurred.

*The Changing International Environment*

Virtually every observer has recognized that the end of the cold war altered the international "playing field" of American foreign policy. What is perhaps less appreciated is the impact of this change on foreign policy making. In a sense, the end of the cold war completed a shift away from a dominant policy-making constellation (White House leadership) that had begun after the Vietnam War. Consider first the emerging landscape of the post–cold war world,[27] in which two features stand out as the most critical: changes in the distribution and composition of power in the international arena and changes in the types of relationships nations have with each other in the international system.

*The Changing Distribution and Composition of Power.* Since the end of the cold war, its bipolar distribution of military and other types of power has yielded to a world with different types of power more widely distributed among many actors. Military power seems to be unipolar, concentrated in the United States. Economic power, in contrast, is diffusing among more states—especially former U.S. allies such as Japan and Western Europe and rising powers such as China and the newly industrializing economies (NIES)—and nonstate actors (international organizations, transnational corporations, and nongovernmental organizations). Such a distribution can perhaps be best described as a layer cake: "[T]he top military layer is unipolar. . . . The economic middle layer is tripolar and has been for two decades. The bottom layer of transnational interdependence shows a diffusion of power."[28] In addition, with the demise of the cold war, the utility of some power resources has changed, and new resources and forms of power have emerged. Relevant forms of power tend to be less tangible and less coercive, and have more to do with economics, technology, agenda setting, and cooption (or "soft" power).[29] For the United States and other great powers, the end of the cold war and the disappearance of the Soviet threat effectively closes, at least for now, the era of the predominance of military power and security issues. Together, the diffusion and changing nature of power make its exercise more complex and less coercive and result in a greater significance for economic power. This shift may precipitate a period in which the most powerful states are chiefly concerned with economic prosperity and growth.

*Changing Relationships.* Obviously, the end of the cold war changed relationships between many countries. More elemental, however, are changes in the underlying dynamics that structure relations in the international arena. The most obvious of such changes include the dramatically reduced ideological divisions and rivalries among the world's leading powers.[30] Among the more advanced countries of the world, ideological consensus on the values of democracy and market economics has been deepening since World War II. The collapse of communism and the Soviet Union has accelerated and expanded this order, promoting integration and cooperation. Embedded in a "democratic peace" (which involves more variables than simply political democracy), these nations, which currently include the most significant great powers, "do not expect, or prepare for, the use of military force in their relations with each other."[31] Therefore, the end of the cold war has helped to expand a nascent "security community," which at present includes most of the world's leading countries. In part due to globalization, interdependence (see next paragraph), and ideological harmonization, this burgeoning security community ties its members together through a complex mix of societal linkages, policy practices, state and international institutions, and agreements. Although competition abounds, it may be "fanciful to think of [conflicts] deteriorating to the point that war is threatened."[32] This clearly affects the combination of interests, goals, threats, and issues facing U.S. policy makers.

Perhaps as important, the end of the cold war has helped to accelerate the twin forces of globalization and interdependence, although these are long-term trends driven by many factors like technological revolutions in information, communications, and transportation. Globalization shrinks the world into "one McWorld tied together by technology, ecology, communications, and commerce" through "the intensification of economic, political, social, and cultural relations across borders."[33] Interdependence signifies a basic interconnectedness such that there are mutual dependencies established among states and societies where actions in one place affect developments in others, and where decisions in one area are affected by and influential over actions and decisions taken in another area. Involving economic, social, ecological, and military dimensions, interdependence creates a web of linkages between international institutions, governments, economies, and societies that bind them together and reduce national autonomy.

A final aspect of the post–cold war world is the growing gap and often diverging directions between the members of the developed world and the members of the developing world. This *stratification* reinforces the dominant place of the members of the developed world (the liberal democratic community). While the developed world enjoys increasing security and prosperity (at least in aggregate terms), much of the developing world is mired in violence and economic stagnation. There is, then, a continually widening gap between the rich and poor of the international system. Moreover, serious political, ecological, and environmental problems seem to be concentrated in the developing world, including explosive ethnic conflict and violence, political instability, population pressures, and environmental and health problems with potentially serious consequences for the rest of the world. These forces of fragmentation and stratification have led other observers to classify the developing world as the "zone of turmoil, war, and development," in stark contrast to the developed world's "zone of peace, prosperity, and democracy."[34] This suggests a "world of tiers" in which a developed first tier exists alongside a developing second tier.[35] As in the case of the burgeoning ethnic conflicts, these are often a partial consequence of the end of the cold war. For U.S. policy makers, these relationships pose a myriad of challenges: promoting development and integration, responding to demands for independence, and coping with increasing turmoil and violence, all the while attempting to determine U.S. interests in a given situation.

Along with other developments, these two central elements of the post–cold war world have impacted both the participants and the issue agenda of international relations. In terms of participants, for example, there are, first, new and changing states with whom the United States must contend. Not only has Japan risen to "great power" status, but the collapse of the Soviet Union and the dismantling of the Warsaw Pact have introduced some two dozen states into world affairs (including a changing Russia), and the reunification of Germany restores that country to a more substantial position as a player in Europe. Also important, states are no longer the only significant actors of international relations; they must compete with nonstate actors in an increasingly large number of situations. This "power shift" away from states to nonstate actors involves subnational actors (e.g., individuals, groups, and nonstate national groups within a state), transnational actors (e.g., multinational corporations and nongovernmental organizations), and international/supranational actors (e.g., the United Nations, the World Trade Organization, and the European Union) whose rising influence cause power to be more diffused among new "players," suggesting that the "state-centric world" of previous decades is increasingly challenged by a "multicentric world" of state and nonstate actors.[36]

With respect to the issue agenda, the elements discussed above help to raise new issues alongside or above military security concerns. In particular, promoting economic growth and prosperity become more significant. This issue includes dealing with economic interdependence and competition with key economic rivals, including Japan, Europe, and rising economic challengers such as the new industrializing economies (South Korea, Taiwan, Hong Kong, and Singapore), China, and others. It also involves managing the complicated economic relationships with the developing world, where liberalization presents opportunities for exports and trade, but whose cheap labor sources threaten U.S. jobs, and whose need and demand for aid raises a host of difficulties. Moreover, the long-term trends toward interdependence and globalization have gradually eroded much of the distinction between domestic and international issues, especially as they involve economic, environmental, and humanitarian issues. The cold war's end accelerates this trend in part because it places economic affairs and other issues at the forefront of international relations. It is, therefore, less possible to make either domestic or foreign affairs "stop at the water's edge," and the United States and other countries have experienced the consequences of this, chiefly in the form of domestic political pressures in the arenas of foreign policy.[37]

Other important elements of the changing issue agenda include contending with the one or more of three difficult transitions facing a large number of countries: toward more advanced economies; from command economies to market economies; and from nondemocratic systems to democratic systems. Moreover, industrialization, globalization, and interdependence introduce a variety of "global issues" to the U.S. foreign policy agenda. Ecological and environmental concerns, population, and human rights issues, among others (e.g., sustainable development) have become increasingly important since the disappearance of the U.S.-Soviet security conflict. The rise of nongovernmental organizations with interests in such issues, and their increasingly complex and influential relationships with states and international organizations, with whom they have forged cooperative ties, create pressures on U.S. policy makers (and others) to address these issues. Finally, the end of the cold war has seen the reawakening of regional and intranational conflicts in many parts of the developing world and former Soviet bloc, conflicts long restricted or subsumed by the dynamics of the cold war. This resurgence of hypernationalism and ethnonationalism has been accompanied by a potential "clash of civilizations" between other cultures and "the West."[38]

*The Impact of the Post–Cold War World*
*on U.S. Foreign Policy Making*
It would appear, then, that the evolving environment of the post–cold war world complicates U.S. foreign policy. What then can be expected for U.S. foreign policy making in the post–cold war world? First, and most obviously, the policy agenda should change to take up the salient issues that arise after the end of the cold war. Second, the actors and in-

stitutions that shape foreign policy should also be expected to adapt to face the changing environment. Most important for this volume, however, the post–cold war environment should be expected to contribute to changes in the process by which U.S. foreign policy is determined. If the cold war era contributed to consensus and executive leadership, the post–cold war era should be expected to contribute to dissensus and greater fragmentation of leadership. As suggested by the preceding discussion, the combination of more voices from inside and outside government, less consensus, and more varied issues should be expected to lead to (or complete, as such a shift has been occurring since the Vietnam War) a constellation shift from White House leadership to inter-branch leadership.

Consider, for example, that, among other things, the post–cold war characteristics sketched out above have the following results for U.S. foreign policy making:

1. The ambiguity in the threat-interest-cost equation intensifies the tendency in the American public toward ambivalence (or reluctance) concerning international involvement.
2. Expanding globalization, interdependence, and transnationalism have raised the stakes for domestic interests, making foreign policy making more like domestic policy making—subject to conflict, bargaining, and persuasion among competing groups within and outside the government—in part due to the increasingly important link between domestic interests and international events, which has given rise to the expansion of "intermestic" issues.[39]
3. Agenda change (from traditional security to economic and others) has expanded the elements of the bureaucracy with foreign policy concerns (especially the "economic complex") and increased the scope of the intermestic arena (thereby prompting more activity by Congress and nongovernmental actors), making both White House management (of the bureaucracy) and leadership (of policy) more difficult.
4. The lack of consensus makes policy leadership by *any* element of the U.S. government more difficult, and encourages elements of many parts of the government to press for their policy preferences.

For U.S. foreign policy making, these and other developments are likely to reduce the instances of presidential preeminence or White House leadership. This is due to agenda change and the rise of inter-mestic issues, which reduce presidential control and open up foreign policy to more members of Congress and private citizens and groups. The obvious example of this is the area of foreign economic policy, an increasingly broad and important issue area especially among the major powers. Moreover, presidential preeminence depends as much on substantive agreement on the purposes and instruments of US foreign policy as it does on institutional powers and levers of influence. The lack of consensus, therefore, contributes to the diffusion of leadership ability. In addition, in times of relative peace, power and influence tend to flow from the White House to Congress, with the pattern reversed in times of relative conflict or war (see chapter 2). Moreover, post–cold war foreign policy is likely to be more heavily influenced by societal forces —or, more specifically, nongovernmental actors—than has been previously the case. As an observer has noted, "[P]olicy across a broad array of regional and functional issues is much more heavily affected by domestic factors. Many of these make it harder to shape coherent policies and to achieve cooperation with allies or even former adversaries."[40] Given the twin factors of competing agendas/fragmented interests and growing indifference in the American public, this will complicate the process of making foreign policy decisions.

This changing process should also make it more difficult to make the policy adjustments that seem to be required in the post–cold war world. This would seem to be especially true for attempts to establish broad policy initiatives or contend with less compelling problems (e.g., outside of traditionally central U.S. foreign policy arenas). At the same time, however, the more complex and subtle international context works against consensus on the proper role, important interests, and necessary actions of the United States in the world. This makes the process of adaptation more difficult. If, as the former director of the the Central Intelligence Agency James Woolsey has suggested, the cold war's dragon was slain, the snake-filled jungle that remains is perhaps even more difficult to negotiate. To push the analogy further, it is more difficult to see the snakes, tell whether they are poisonous, and know how to react to them. Thus, while the post–cold war presents a more benign face (in the sense of reduced strategic threat), it also introduces more threat ambiguity. This has had a particularly important impact on the willingness (reduced) of the American public to undertake (and pay for) leadership commitments in the world, given long-standing ambivalence toward international involvement unless "vital interests" are at stake. In the post–cold war period, indeed, in a growing trend since the shattering of the cold war consensus in the late 1960s and early

1970s, policy makers and the public are increasingly divided over foreign policy goals and instruments, and do not agree on even more basic issues such as the appropriate role of the United States in the world.

### Conclusion

Cumulatively, then, U.S. policy makers are required to cope with the changing distribution and composition of power and the changing underlying dynamics of international relations (and all they entail) in a context that brings more participants and more issues onto the stage. Furthermore, the end of the cold war has, in effect, removed the last vestiges of the "shortcuts" that made U.S. foreign policy during the cold war a simpler task. The post–cold war world lacks the "very things that gave structure and purpose to post–World War American foreign policy. . . . Now these guideposts, which had imposed a rough sense of order and discipline on the world, are gone"[41] and policy choices for the United States are more varied and less self-evident than before.[42] Role, interests, and priorities must be reconsidered and revised in light of the changing world. Specific strategies and policies must be developed to deal with the specific problem and issue agenda of the post–cold war world. And yet, all this must be done in the context of a more fragmented policy process, itself a partial consequence of the changes associated with the end of the cold war.

The chapters that follow take up these issues in detail. Chapters 2–7 examine the elements of the shifting constellations image (i.e., the presidency; the foreign policy and foreign economic bureaucracy; Congress; and the societal forces of the public, interest groups, and the media) with a particular focus on their role and adaptation to the post–cold war environment. Following that, chapters 8–14 present a series of cases in which the authors explore the processes through which U.S. foreign policy was made, reflecting the changing policy agenda of the post–cold war world. In these cases, the authors use the shifting constellations image as an organizing device and highlight the nature and characteristics of the role, behavior, and interactions of the various elements of that image. The final chapter offers some observations about the nature of the shifting constellations and the role and behavior of the elements of which they are composed in the post–cold war world.

## Notes

1  See, for example, James N. Rosenau, "Foreign Policy as Adaptive Behavior: Some Preliminary Notes for a Theoretical Model," *Comparative Politics* 2: 355–374.

2  Daniel Deudney and G. John Ikenberry, "The International Sources of Soviet Change," *International Security* 16, no. 3 (Fall 1991): 111. According to Aaron Wildavsky the notion of "interests," is deeply embedded in the political culture (see "Choosing Preferences by Constructing Institutions: A Cultural Theory of Preference Formation," in Arther Asa Berger, ed., *Political Culture and Public Opinion* (New Brunswick, N.J.: Transactions Publishers, 1989), pp. 21–46.

3  This is a synthesis of John Dumbrell, *The Making of U.S. Foreign Policy* (Manchester, U.K.: Manchester University Press, 1990); Edward S. Greenberg, *Capitalism and the American Political Ideal* (Armonk, N.Y.: M. E. Sharpe, 1985); Louis Hartz, *The Liberal Tradition in America* (New York: Harcourt, Brace, and World, 1955); Charles W. Kegley Jr. and Eugene R. Wittkopf, *American Foreign Policy: Pattern and Process*, 5th ed. (New York: St. Martin's Press, 1995); James M. McCormick, *American Foreign Policy and Process* (Itasca, Ill.: F. E. Peacock, 1992); Richard M. Merelman, *Making Something of Ourselves: On Culture and Politics in the United States* (Berkeley: University of California Press, 1984); John T. Rourke, Ralph G. Carter, and Mark A. Boyer, *Making American Foreign Policy*, 2nd ed. (Madison, Wisc.: Brown and Benchmark, 1996); and John Spanier and Steven W. Hook, *American Foreign Policy since World War II, 13th ed.* (Washington, D.C.: Congressional Quarterly Press, 1995).

4  Dumbrell, *The Making of U.S. Foreign Policy*, p. 6.

5  Cecil V. Crabb, *The Doctrines of American Foreign Policy: Their Meaning, Role, and Future* (Baton Rouge: Louisiana State University Press, 1982), p. 375.

6  See McCormick, *American Foreign Policy and Process*, ch. 1; Rourke, Carter, and Boyer, *Making American Foreign Policy*, ch. 4; and Spanier and Hook, *American Foreign Policy since World War II*, ch. 1.

7  Rourke, Carter, and Boyer, *Making American Foreign Policy*, p. 102.

8  Walt Whitman, quoted in Crabb, *The Doctrines of American Foreign Policy*, p. 378. On the idea of "mission," see Edward M. Burns, *The American Idea of Mission: Concepts of National Purpose and Destiny* (New Brunswick, N.J.: Rutgers University Press, 1957). Societal (and elite) values may also translate into an impulse toward paternalism, or even racism. On these see Rourke, Carter, and Boyer, *Making American Foreign Policy*, p. 102, and Michael H. Hunt, *Ideology and U.S. Foreign Policy* (New Haven, Conn.: Yale University Press, 1987), esp. ch. 3.

9  Crabb, *The Doctrines of American Foreign Policy*, pp. 1–2.

10  Rourke, Carter, and Boyer, *Making American Foreign Policy*, pp. 111–113. *Unilateralism/multilateralism* may also be impulses.

11  Quoted in Kegley and Wittkopf, *American Foreign Policy*, p. 37.

12  Kegley and Wittkopf, *American Foreign Policy*, p. 46.

13  Quoted in Kegley and Wittkopf, *American Foreign Policy*, pp. 40, 48.

14  Rourke, Carter, and Boyer, *Making American Foreign Policy*, pp. 113–114. These orientations may be as sequential (the United States was first isolationist, but

shifted to an internationalist approach) cyclical (the United States has cycled through "moods" of isolationism and internationalism), or simultaneous (the United States embraces both). The sequential interpretation is illustrated by Spanier and Hook, *American Foreign Policy*, and the cyclical interpretation by Frank Klingberg, *Cyclical Trends in American Foreign Policy Moods: The Unfolding of America's World Role* (Lanham, Md.: University Press of America, 1983).

15 See Louis Fisher, *Constitutional Conflicts between Congress and the President* (Lawrence: University of Kansas Press, 1991); Louis Henkin, *Constitutionalism, Democracy, and Foreign Affairs* (New York: Columbia University Press, 1990); Harold Koh, *The National Security Constitution* (New Haven, Conn.: Yale University Press, 1990); and Jean Edward Smith, *The Constitution and American Foreign Policy* (New York: West Publishing, 1989).

16 Edward S. Corwin, *The President: Office and Powers, 1787-1957*, rev. ed. (New York: New York University Press, 1957), p. 171.

17 Philip Zelikow, "Foreign Policy Engineering: From Theory to Practice and Back Again." *International Security* 18:4 (Spring 1994): 156.

18 This discussion draws on James M. Scott's *Deciding to Intervene: The Reagan Doctrine and American Foreign Policy* (Durham, N.C.: Duke University Press, 1996); "In the Loop: Congressional Influence in American Foreign Policy," *Journal of Political and Military Sociology* 25, no. 1 (Summer 1997): 47–75; and "Branch Rivals: The Reagan Doctrine, Nicaragua, and American Foreign Policy-Making," *Political Science Quarterly* 112, no. 2 (Summer 1997): 237–260.

19 For example, see Peter J. Schraeder, *United States Foreign Policy toward Africa: Incrementalism, Crisis, and Change* (Cambridge: Cambridge University Press, 1994); and Jerel A. Rosati, "Developing a Systematic Decision-Making Framework: Bureaucratic Politics in Perspective," *World Politics* 33, no. 1 (January 1981): 234–252.

20 Bruce W. Jentleson, "American Diplomacy around the World and along Pennsylvania Avenue," in Thomas E. Mann, ed., *A Question of Balance: The President, the Congress, and Foreign Policy* (Washington: Brookings Institution, 1990), pp. 146–200.

21 See, for example, Scott, *Deciding to Intervene*; Robert A. Pastor, *Whirlpool: U.S. Foreign Policy toward Latin America and the Caribbean* (Princeton, N.J.: Princeton University Press, 1992); as well as James M. Lindsay, *Congress and the Politics of U.S. Foreign Policy* (Baltimore, Md.: Johns Hopkins University Press, 1994); and Randall Ripley and James Lindsay, eds., *Congress Resurgent: Foreign and Defense Policy on Capitol Hill* (Ann Arbor: University of Michigan Press, 1993).

22 See Gordon Adams, *The Politics of Defense Contracting: The Iron Triangle* (New Brunswick, N.J.: Transaction Books, 1982); Randall B. Ripley and Grace A. Franklin, *Congress, the Bureaucracy, and Public Policy*, 5th ed. (Pacific Grove, Calif.: Brooks/Cole, 1991); and Nick Kotz, *Wild Blue Yonder: Money, Politics, and the B-1 Bomber* (Princeton, N.J.: Princeton University Press, 1988).

23 See Pauline Baker, *The United States and South Africa: The Reagan Years* (New York: Ford Foundation/Foreign Policy Association, 1989); and Scott, *Deciding to Intervene*, esp. ch. 6.

24 The idea of rival alliances is developed in Scott, *Deciding to Intervene*, and "In the Loop."

25 McCormick, *American Foreign Policy and Process*, p. 78.

26 See Richard Melanson, *American Foreign Policy since the Vietnam War*, 2d ed. (Armonk, N.Y.: M. E. Sharpe, 1996); I. M. Destler et al., *Our Own Worst Enemy: The Unmaking of American Foreign Policy* (New York: Simon and Schuster, 1984); Ole Holsti and James Rosenau, *American Leadership in World Affairs: Vietnam and the Breakdown of Consensus* (Boston: Allen and Unwin, 1984).

27 Not all "post–cold war characteristics" are due to the end of the cold war. Some have been developing over several decades (e.g., globalization and interdependence), at the least. On the post–cold war world, see Seyom Brown, *New Force, Old Forces, and the Future of World Politics*, Post-Cold War Edition (New York: HarperCollins, 1995); John Gerard Ruggie, *Winning the Peace: America and World Order in the New Era* (New York: Columbia University Press, 1996); Saskia Sassen, *Losing Control? Sovereignty in an Age of Globalization* (New York: Columbia University Press, 1996); Donald Snow, *The Shape of the Future*, 2d ed. (Armonk, N.Y.: M. E. Sharpe, 1996).

28 Joseph S. Nye Jr., "What New World Order?" *Foreign Affairs* 71, no. 2 (March/April 1992): 88.

29 Joseph S. Nye Jr., "The Changing Nature of World Power," *Political Science Quarterly* 105, no. 2 (Summer 1990): 177–192.

30 Francis Fukuyama, "The End of History?" *National Interest* 16 (Summer 1989): 4.

31 Robert Keohane and Joseph S. Nye Jr., *Power and Interdependence*, 2d ed. (Glenview, Ill.: Scott, Foresman, 1989), p. 27. On the "democratic peace," see Michael Doyle, "Liberalism and World Politics," *American Political Science Review* 80, no. 4 (December 1986): 1151–1169; Bruce Russett, *Grasping the Democratic Peace* (Princeton, N.J.: Princeton University Press, 1993); and Michael Brown et al., eds., *Debating the Democratic Peace* (Cambridge, Mass.: MIT Press, 1996).

32 Donald Snow and Eugene Brown, *The Contours of Power* (New York: St. Martin's, 1996), p. 34.

33 Benjamin Barber, "Jihad vs. McWorld," *Atlantic Monthly* 269 (March 1992): 53; Hans Henrik Holm and George Sørenson, quoted in Kegley and Wittkopf, *World Politics*, p. 249.

34 Max Singer and Aaron Wildavsky, *The Real World Order*, rev. ed. (Chatham, N.J.: Chatham House, 1996), p. 3.

35 See Snow and Brown, *The Contours of Power*. The distinction is also made by Fukuyama, "The End of History?" pp. 3–18 (distinguishing between countries that are at the end of history and those countries still in history); Barry Buzan, "New Patterns in Global Security," *International Affairs* 67, no. 3 (July 1991): 431–51 (discussing the center and the periphery); and Singer and Wildavsky, *The Real World Order* (discussing a "Zone of Peace" and a "Zone of Turmoil").

36 On the rise of nonstate actors, see, for example, Jessica T. Mathews, "Power Shift," *Foreign Affairs* 76, no. 1 (January/February 1997): 50–66. See also David F. Walsh, "The International System in Transition: The New Environment of Foreign Policy," in Kul B. Rai, David F. Walsh, and Paul J. Best, eds., *American in*

the *21st Century: Challenges and Opportunities in Foreign Policy* (Upper Saddle, N.J.: Prentice Hall, 1997), p. 23.

37 Of course, foreign pressures on domestic policy have also increased.

38 Samuel Huntington, "The Clash of Civilizations," *Foreign Affairs* 72, no. 3 (May/June 1993): 22–49.

39 According to Bert A. Rockman, this reduces the role of the president as the preeminent foreign policy maker, triggers a greater fragmentation of responsibility and control, and increases the competition for influence. See "Presidents, Opinion, and Institutional Leadership," in David Deese, ed., *The New Politics of American Foreign Policy* (New York: St. Martin's Press, 1994), p. 73.

40 Robert J. Lieber, "Eagle without a Cause: Making Foreign Policy without the Soviet Threat," in Robert J. Lieber, ed., *Eagle Adrift: American Foreign Policy at the End of the Century* (New York: Longman's, 1997), p. 5.

41 Kegley and Wittkopf, *American Foreign Policy*, p. 3.

42 Lieber, "Eagle without a Cause," p. 14.

# I. ACTORS AND INFLUENCE

·

# 2.

# The Presidency and U.S. Foreign Policy

# after the Cold War

*Jerel Rosati and Stephen Twing*

Most Americans begin to equate the president with the government of the United States at a very young age, and develop an image of the president as a kind of father figure who controls the government and represents the American people. As Stanley Hoffman observed thirty years ago, "The American system of government seems unable to prevent a kind of hand-wringing, starry-eyed, and slightly embarrassing deification of the man in the White House, a doleful celebration of his solitude and his burdens. (When things go badly, there is, of course, a tendency to besmirch the fallen idol.)"[1] In this chapter, we examine the extent to which this popular image of a near omnipotent president is accurate in the realm of post–cold war foreign policy making. As we will see, it is very difficult for a president to govern successfully and lead the country in foreign policy, especially since the Vietnam and Watergate years. The end of the cold war has created new opportunities for U.S. foreign policy, but it has also exacerbated the difficulties that a president faces in exercising power. Ultimately, the ability that a president demonstrates in leading the country and managing the executive branch is consequential in affecting the future conduct of U.S. foreign policy.

## The Paradox of Presidential Power

The president is the most powerful political actor in the United States. He occupies many constitutional roles and has many capabilities that contribute to his power. Among his most important roles are commander in chief, chief diplomat, chief administrator, chief of state, chief legislator, voice of the people, and chief judicial officer. However, the president also faces many constraints and uncertainties that limit his power. In the constant struggle to exercise power, the president is lim-

ited by time (too little) and information (too much and too little). The
president also faces institutional constraints such as an entrenched bureaucracy, an independent Congress, state and local governments, political parties, and interest groups and social movements. Not only must
the president contend with these particular constraints upon his power,
but he also faces uncertain elements that at times may enhance his
power and, at other times, may act to constrain it. These elements include the courts, public opinion, the media, and the larger global environment. These constraints and uncertainties mean that often the president finds that he has great difficulty in successfully getting his way.

When all is said and done, presidents face a "paradox of power": on
the one hand, the president is an extremely powerful actor; on the other
hand, relative to the rest of government, the society, and the larger environment, he faces many constraints in successfully exercising power.[2]
As President John F. Kennedy understood, the president "is rightly described as a man of extraordinary powers. Yet it is also true that he must
wield those powers under extraordinary limitations."[3] In this respect,
it is also important to remember that presidents usually experience a
"life cycle": they are strongest when they enter office and their power
tends to decline over time. Presidents are simply not powerful enough,
nor do they serve long enough, to fulfill the promises and high expectations that get created around them. To what extent, does the paradox of
presidential power and the presidential life cycle affect the president's
ability to govern U.S. foreign policy? What have been the implications
of the rise and collapse of the cold war on presidential power? To these
questions we now turn.

### Presidential Power in the Conduct of Foreign Policy

Although not nearly as powerful as the popular stereotype held by
many, the president has greater strengths and fewer weaknesses in the
exercise of power in foreign than he does in domestic policy. In fact,
it was during the cold war years that presidential power in the making
of foreign policy reached its height. Three of the constitutional roles
contributing to presidential power really involve only foreign affairs:
commander in chief, chief diplomat, and chief of state. These roles allowed the president to exercise considerable power in foreign policy
during the cold war, especially during crises. Since the Vietnam War,
however, the president's ability to govern and lead foreign policy has
declined and become much more complex. Such a state of presidential

power has intensified with the collapse of the cold war as the United States approaches the twenty-first century.

### Some Historical Context

The president has not dominated the foreign policy process throughout American history. The Constitution of the United States produced a central government with "separate institutions sharing powers," resulting in an "invitation to struggle" between the executive and legislative branches.[4] In fact, executive-legislative relations in foreign policy have been fluid and dynamic, and have fluctuated with changes in the political environment.

As described by Arthur Schlesinger Jr. in *The Imperial Presidency*, executive-legislative relations have been characterized by a kind of "pendulum or cyclical effect."[5] In times of national emergency, particularly war, power tends to flow toward the president and the executive branch. During times of peace—that is, when conflict has subsided—power tends to flow back to Congress. Yet, while Congress tends to reassert its constitutional authority and power following war, increases in presidential power during periods of conflict tend to be so extensive that it seldom returns to prewar levels. Thus, the cyclical ebb and flow in executive-legislative relations in foreign policy has enabled a president to accumulate greater power over time.

### Presidential Dominance during the Cold War Years

As a result of World War II and with the rise of the cold war, the president became dominant in the making of foreign policy. Aaron Wildavsky wrote over three decades ago in favor of the "two presidencies thesis," describing a powerful presidency in foreign policy and a weak presidency in domestic policy.[6] Examining the legislative-executive relationship during the fifties and sixties, he found that presidents were much more successful in influencing foreign policy legislation than they were in affecting the outcome of domestic legislation. According to the two presidencies thesis, the paradox and life cycle of presidential power were operative only in the realm of domestic policy; the president was able to govern and lead the country when it came to foreign policy.

In the fifties and sixties—the high cold war era—presidents were extremely powerful political actors in the making of U.S. foreign policy. Constraints were relatively weak and the uncertain elements tended to be supportive of presidential efforts to contain the threat of communism. The foreign policy bureaucracy, for example, expanded and became an important tool for implementing the president's containment policies. Congress largely was acquiescent and supportive of most presidential initiatives during the cold war years of globalism in U.S. foreign policy. A strong anticommunist consensus developed among the American citizenry and foreign policy elite, resulting in strong public, media, and interest group support of a policy of containment and presidential actions abroad. This was also a period in which political party differences were minimal and state and local governments and the courts were inactive in foreign policy. This supportive domestic climate also existed at a time when the United States was the most preeminent power in the world.[7]

It is important to recall that before World War II few institutions within the government were oriented toward foreign affairs and national security. The policy-making elite was extremely small and centered within the State Department. World War II changed this dramatically. Overnight, the U.S. government was redirected to devote itself to fighting a global war: the military expanded enormously, and civilian agencies grew to assist the president in fighting the war. The governmental war effort, in turn, put the economy and society on a war footing to provide the necessary personnel, equipment, and services to achieve U.S. victory. However, unlike previous wars in American history, the United States demobilized only for a short time following victory. With the rise of anticommunism, the United States quickly remobilized and expanded its resources in order to fight a global cold war. The power of the presidency and the foreign policy bureaucracy thus continued to grow during the cold war years, becoming a permanent part of the American landscape.

The 1950s and 1960s were perceived to be a time when communism directly threatened the security of the United States. During such times of perceived national emergency, the president could exert considerable powers as commander in chief, head of state, chief diplomat, and chief administrator, with Congress increasingly acquiescent to presidential initiatives. In fact, by the mid-fifties a bipartisan consensus developed between Democrats and Republicans in support of the president and U.S. foreign policy. Congressional passage of the National Security Act of 1947 resulted in the rise of a large foreign policy bureaucracy. The act created the National Security Council (NSC), reorganized the military into the Department of Defense (DOD), and developed an intelligence community under the Central Intelligence Agency (CIA). These and other bureaucratic agencies grew dramatically in size and scope during the cold war, giving the administration the capacity to implement, and to institutionalize, its national security and foreign economic policies abroad.

The cold war years of American globalism were, thus, a time of extraordinary presidential power in foreign affairs. This is not to say that the president faced no opposition or that he controlled all foreign policy issues. Nonetheless, the president was clearly the dominant political figure and exercised a disproportionate amount of influence over U.S. foreign policy. Presidents had the ability to formulate and implement policies in accordance with their cold war beliefs.[8]

*The Decline of Presidential Power since Vietnam*
*and the End of the Cold War*
The tragedies of Vietnam and Watergate symbolized the end of the dominance of global containment as the basis of U.S. foreign policy and signified the end of the extraordinary power that presidents enjoyed in making foreign policy. The president retained the ability to exercise considerable power in foreign affairs; however, the constraints and uncertainties facing him have increased during the post-Vietnam years, making it much more difficult for the president to successfully dominate foreign policy. With the end of the cold war, the constraints and uncertainties facing presidents in the making of foreign policy have continued to multiply.

The anticommunist consensus that existed throughout government and society could not survive the Vietnam War. Its collapse produced a reassertive Congress, new and varied interest groups and social movements, a more critical media, and a cynical public. The post-Vietnam years also symbolized and accelerated the weakening of American power relative to other world actors in the international political economy. Foreign economics, and other so-called "low policy" and "intermestic" issues, likewise, rose in significance and increasingly became a part of the foreign policy agenda.[9] Therefore, a president entered office facing constraints and uncertainties that hampered his ability to utilize the sources of presidential power described above. In fact, all presidents since Vietnam have experienced considerable problems in governing and leading the country in foreign policy.[10]

In the past, given the rise of anticommunism and the national security state, the president could lead the country, but only in the direction of fervent anticommunism, containment, and interventionism. Since Vietnam, with the collapse of the anticommunist consensus and the rise of pluralist politics, the president—and in reality, the political system—has a difficult time generating leadership in any direction for a sustained period of time. As Ole Holsti and James Rosenau have argued, "Perhaps the only constancy in American foreign policy since Vietnam has been the conspicuous lack of constancy in its conduct."[11] Every post-Vietnam president has failed to generate a new consensus or sustain sufficient support behind their policies for any length of time.

Presidents Richard Nixon and Gerald Ford attempted to promote a more stable global order through a realpolitik policy based on detente with the Soviet Union. Yet, both the liberal Left and the conservative Right attacked their détente policies. Ultimately, Nixon experienced a crisis of legitimacy over Watergate and was forced to resign, while Ford's lack of leadership resulted in his inability to win election to the presidency. President Jimmy Carter tried to promote human rights and a global community in response to a complex world by emphasizing preventive diplomacy across a variety of issues. Yet Carter's stewardship was called into question by the conservative Right over the Iran hostage crisis and the Soviet invasion of Afghanistan, contributing to his failed reelection effort in 1980. President Ronald Reagan, given his view of communist expansionism, attempted to resurrect the containment policy of the past in order to deter Soviet power abroad. Reagan's leadership, the most politically successful in the post-Vietnam era, was nonetheless challenged in foreign policy, first by the liberal Left who opposed his hardline policies against the Soviet "evil empire" and subsequently by the conservative Right who opposed Reagan's arms control efforts with Soviet leader Mikhail Gorbachev. Reagan also became embroiled in the Iran-contra affair, which weakened his presidential power considerably.[12]

George Bush became president at a time when the world would soon witness the collapse of the Soviet Union and communism throughout Eastern Europe. These momentous events have, if anything, intensified the rise of diversity and pluralist politics in the making of U.S. foreign policy that began with the Vietnam War, complicating the president's ability to govern. Bush, who was widely considered to be a strong president in the realm of foreign policy, was unable to take advantage of the post–cold war environment and a tremendously successful and popular war in the Persian Gulf to win reelection in 1992. He was undone predominantly by domestic economic difficulties that he could not control and to which he was publicly viewed as not paying sufficient attention.

Bill Clinton is the first president to serve an entire term in the post–cold war era. Thus far, he has managed to escape the presidential life cycle, won reelection against a weak Republican candidate, and has begun his second term of office with more popularity than he enjoyed when he started his first term. Nevertheless, President Clinton has experienced considerable difficulty in governing throughout his tenure, as will be discussed shortly, both at home and abroad.

In sum, during the cold war years the paradox and life cycle of presidential power did not seem to affect presidents much in the area of foreign policy. However, in the wake of Vietnam and Watergate, and now in the post–cold war era, presidents have had to contend with these patterns. The era of two presidencies and extraordinary presidential power in foreign policy is over.[13] Although the paradox and life cycle of presidential power primarily contribute to weak presidents in the area of domestic policy, they are responsible for much of the frustration experienced by presidents in foreign policy as well. Presidents are still the most powerful individual actors, but the rise of pluralist politics has weakened their ability to govern and dominate the making of U.S. foreign policy. All of these domestic patterns are likely to continue into the twenty-first century.

### Post–Cold War Opportunities and Risks

Due to changes in the domestic environment since Vietnam and the end of the cold war, a crisis of leadership for the presidency and the country now exists. The president, the only person capable of providing sustained national leadership, has a very difficult time leading the country. The fragmented nature of American beliefs, as well as competing domestic interests and institutions, has constrained presidential action. Regardless of what the president promises in either domestic or foreign policy, he has been unable to fulfill expectations for long. The complexity of the domestic environment, reinforced by the complexity of the global system, simply no longer allows much latitude for presidential success.

Presidents find it very difficult to lead and manage foreign policy for a sustained period of time, whether in an interventionist direction or not. The net result of this crisis of leadership has been that with each new administration, as well as over the course of the same administration, U.S. foreign policy has tended to become increasingly "reactive"—as opposed to "proactive"—and, hence, incoherent and inconsistent over time. This is likely to continue into the twenty-first century, making it very difficult for the United States to exercise the kind of sustained global leadership that so many seem to hope for, or fear.[14]

The collapse of the cold war gives a president great opportunities but also creates great risks. Unlike the 1950s, presidents are no longer driven to pursue only an anticommunist containment policy. Presidents now have more flexibility to pursue a wider range of foreign policy options abroad. Yet, at the same time, it is unclear how far a president may go in pursuing any policy before losing public and governmental support.

As Destler, Gelb, and Lake argue, "The making of American foreign policy has been growing far more political—or more precisely, far more partisan and ideological."[15] Hence, according to Alexander George, "the necessity for ad hoc day-to-day building of consensus under these circumstances makes it virtually impossible for the president to conduct long-range foreign policy in a coherent, effective manner."[16] This has meant that each administration since the end of Vietnam has been forced to modify its initial policies abroad, usually toward the ideological center, in response to domestic political challenges. This helps to account for why U.S. foreign policy often appears to lack coherence and consistency since Vietnam, and why this is likely to continue in the post–cold war era.

The Bush administration's foreign policy has been commonly characterized as a "mixture of competence and drift, of tactical mastery set in a larger pattern of strategic indirection."[17] For those issues that were beyond the cold war, such as profound change engulfing Europe and Russia, the Bush administration was usually quite tentative and cautious, allowing others to take the foreign policy initiative. Yet for those issues more reminiscent of the cold war past, such as the conflict in the Persian Gulf, the Bush administration was quick to operate from a power politics perspective reliant on the threat and use of force. It was almost as if the Bush administration's foreign policy was caught between the strong legacy of the cold war past and the great uncertainty of a post–cold war future.

President Clinton has been accused of considerable vacillation and hesitancy in the conduct of U.S. foreign policy. Efforts to promote a more "multilateral-oriented" foreign policy faced early setbacks, especially in Somalia. At the same time, President Clinton did manage to initiate several significant foreign policy actions in Haiti, Mexico, and Bosnia in spite of public and congressional opposition. Nevertheless, the conventional wisdom has been that President Clinton has not taken a strong leadership role or exercised considerable power over U.S. foreign policy. Clearly, not only must a post–cold war president contend with a more complex and turbulent global environment, but the political constraints and uncertainties facing a president at home are quite considerable. Two mutually reinforcing factors in particular stand out:

an increasingly complex and volatile domestic climate, and a Congress which remains quite assertive.

### An Increasingly Complex and Volatile Domestic Climate

Presidents no longer come to office with automatic or long-lasting majorities behind their policies as they did during the cold war era. No matter what the president and his advisers believe, a substantial number of Americans—in the mass public and especially the elite public—disagree, or are open to disagreement, with presidential policy.[18] Such differences in the ideological and foreign policy beliefs among the elite public, coupled with a pragmatic but volatile mass public, have provided a broader set of domestic boundaries, entailing greater opportunity as well as risk, for presidential leadership in the making of U.S. foreign policy into the future.

Isolationist sentiment, in fact, seems to have increased among both the elite and, in particular, mass public with the collapse of the anti-communist consensus and the cold war. On the one hand, this may mean that more people are paying less attention to what goes on abroad, giving the president more leeway in the making of U.S. foreign policy. On the other hand, the rise of isolationist sentiment also suggests that more and more people are likely to oppose efforts by the president to take strong leadership roles abroad. It is important to point out that isolationist sentiment historically has been strong among the American public and may grow in popularity in a post–cold war world.[19] Ultimately, public support is a function of the level of success or failure perceived among a public that tends to be quite pragmatic and impatient.

Since the collapse of the Soviet Union, public opinion polls have shown that the mass public is much more preoccupied with domestic economic concerns than with foreign policy problems. Correct reading of this trend in public opinion in the 1992 presidential campaign allowed Bill Clinton to attack George Bush effectively for devoting too much attention to foreign affairs and not enough time to the domestic economy. A majority of the public appears to favor a more self-interested approach to foreign policy, with more emphasis on national economic competitiveness and other so-called intermestic issues, such as illegal immigration and international drug trafficking. With regard to attitudes toward the use of military force, more public support exists for instances when force is used to alter the aggressive behavior of another state than for instances when force is used to impose internal political change.[20]

It is unclear what effect these post–cold war trends in public opinion will ultimately have on presidential power. During Bill Clinton's first term in office, his administration embarked on several foreign policy initiatives that were opposed by substantial majorities in public opinion polls—such as sending U.S. troops to Haiti and Bosnia, and initiating the 1995 Mexican bailout. None of these unpopular initiatives seemed to do any damage to the Clinton presidency and in the cases of Bosnia and the Mexican bailout he seemed to have gotten a boost in his public approval ratings.[21]

Much of the volatility within the domestic climate stems from the ability of modern news organizations (primarily via TV) to deliver, almost instantly, emotionally charged stories and images from abroad right into Americans' living rooms. U.S. news organizations first achieved this type of impact during the Vietnam War. Such stories and images can have a profound impact not only on public opinion but also directly on policy makers.

Significant post–cold war examples of this include the extensive coverage of the plight of the Kurds in Northern Iraq in 1991, of the starvation in Somalia in December 1992, and the aftermath of the failed U.S. attempts to capture Somali warlord Mohammed Aidid in 1993. In each of these cases the emotionally charged images brought back by television networks like CNN had a substantial impact on not only the viewing public, but also on policy makers who were watching. In the first two cases it helped convince policy makers like President Bush that U.S. military action must be taken to help remedy the situation, and in the third case it led to a major Clinton administration reevaluation of the U.S. military mission in Somalia. While it is important to note that this new type of media effect is not directly a product of the end of the cold war, it does seem to be occurring more frequently and with greater impact on presidents' handling of specific policies in the post–cold war era.

Clearly, the movement from cold war consensus to post–cold war diversity has widened the boundaries of domestic politics and intensified political discourse in the making of U.S. foreign policy. Such changes in ideological and foreign policy beliefs cannot be understated for the collapse of the cold war consensus has produced an era in which not only is public opinion more volatile, but participation has become more active and diverse in electoral and group politics while the media is more likely to act swiftly, independently, and critically of the administration. The rise of such pluralist politics clearly complicates the president's ability to dominate foreign policy.

*Continued Congressional Engagement*
The end of Vietnam and the Watergate affair released a flood of congressional involvement in foreign policy. Members of Congress not only demanded a greater role in the policy-making process, but became increasingly involved in the details of foreign policy making in a wide variety of areas. Congressional reassertion is best symbolized by the passage of the War Powers Act of 1973. Ever since, presidents have had to face a more powerful Congress and have had greater difficulty in governing foreign policy. In fact, virtually every president has faced major foreign policy setbacks as a result of congressional reassertion, contributing to the general perception of "failed" presidents since the Johnson presidency: Nixon experienced Watergate; the Nixon-Ford détente policies toward the Soviet Union were thwarted by congressional concern about Jewish immigration from the Soviet Union and a covert war in Angola; Carter could not get Senate approval of SALT II; and Reagan suffered from Iran-contra.[22]

Congressional engagement in the making of foreign policy has continued with the collapse of the cold war. Despite the triumph of the Persian Gulf War, it is important to remember that President George Bush faced a considerable challenge to his policies within Congress before he took the country to war with Iraq. Following extremely politicized congressional hearings, a vote authorizing presidential use of force was taken and the outcome was very close: 52 to 47 in favor in the Senate; 250 to 183 in favor in the House of Representatives. The rapidity with which the Congress, and the country, became divided over the Persian Gulf policy indicates that presidents no longer automatically dominate crises and war making as they once did during the cold war years. Watergate, Iran-contra, and the Persian Gulf War are testaments to the reassertion of congressional power and the greater uncertainty that presidents face since Vietnam in attempting to govern foreign policy.

With the 1994 Republican takeover of Congress producing a divided government once again—this time with a Democratic president—legislative-executive relations have often become partisan, complicating President Clinton's ability to govern the country in general as well as conduct foreign policy. Under the control of Republican leaders, Congress has significantly cut the foreign affairs budget and foreign aid programs of agencies like the State Department and the Agency for International Development.[23]

Congress also has opposed many of Clinton's foreign policy initiatives. In the case of the deployment of U.S. troops to Haiti, the administration never had the support of Congress, but avoided a major conflict over this issue with a deal negotiated by presidential envoys Sam Nunn and Colin Powell to allow for the peaceful insertion of the troops and the voluntary exit of the military government. In the case of the 1995 Mexican bailout, Congress overwhelmingly opposed the loans, and the administration had to bypass Congress and unilaterally go ahead with the loan. In the case of deploying U.S. troops to Bosnia as part of the NATO Implementation Force, President Clinton again faced significant congressional opposition. It was only by presenting Congress with the *fait accompli* of the Dayton Accords and an American commitment to NATO allies that Clinton was able to obtain grudging approval for the troop deployment. In all three of these cases Clinton took these initiatives in spite of congressional disapproval. Therefore, although constrained, presidents continue to have considerable power over foreign policy but must exercise it in a domestic political world of considerable uncertainty and risk—where much depends on the perception of relative success or failure of these policies over time.

In sum, the domestic political landscape that presidents must operate in has become incredibly complex since Vietnam and the collapse of the cold war. On the one hand, the collapse of the cold war consensus has given presidents the opportunity to take U.S. foreign policy in new directions. On the other hand, the fragmentation of beliefs and the rise of pluralist politics poses great risks that presidents will lose political support quickly. The constraints and political uncertainty faced by presidents in today's domestic political environment does not bode well for a strong proactive foreign policy in the future.

### The Importance of Presidential Leadership

How can presidents maximize their power and success? How can they overcome or minimize the crisis of governance embedded in American politics? How can they increase their ability to govern foreign policy? The key is "leadership"—presidential leadership. Strong leaders are able to maximize their strengths and capabilities, minimize the constraints they face, and force the uncertain elements to work better and longer in their favor. Strong presidents are more able to exercise power and govern. Weak leaders, on the other hand, have great difficulty exercising power and governing for they operate in a world of insurmountable obstacles and constraints. Although this is particularly the case in domestic policy, presidential leadership is also quite important for presidential power and governance in foreign policy.

The classic statement on presidential leadership is *Presidential Power: The Politics of Leadership* by Richard Neustadt.[24] His basic argument is that the key to presidential power is the "power to persuade," which is a function of political leadership. Presidents who enter office and expect to "command" are quickly disappointed and frustrated. Because of the paradox of presidential power and the existence of the presidential life cycle, presidents cannot command. In fact, as Neustadt points out, efforts at exerting presidential power through command are an indication of presidential weakness, for presidents should rely on their legal and formal authority only as a last resort. The command model of governing may be consistent with the way many think about presidential power, but the key for presidential governance is to persuade others that it is in their best interest to do what the president prefers.

Neustadt identified three crucial elements of political leadership and presidential power: professional reputation, public prestige, and presidential choices. "Professional reputation" refers to how other political actors in Washington, D.C., and beyond judge the president's ability to get things accomplished. Presidents with a reputation for being very skillful in exercising power, for having to be reckoned with when opposed, are most persuasive. "Public prestige" refers to how other political actors, whether in the bureaucracy, Congress, interest groups, or the media, perceive the level of public support for the president. Presidents with a positive public image are more powerful, for high credibility and popular support throughout the country are important political assets in Washington. Strong presidents who are able to persuade successfully are those with high levels of professional reputation and public prestige. According to Hedrick Smith in *The Power Game,* "Presidents—past, present, and future—have less power than the country imagines, but the successful ones convey the impression of power and get reputations as strong presidents by playing down their problems and trumpeting their few clear victories."[25] Perceptions and images have always been important in politics, but with the rise of the electronic and instantaneous media, the importance of symbolism and symbolic politics have grown.

The relationship between a president's public prestige and his ability to exercise power may be illustrated in the cases of George Bush and Bill Clinton. During his first two years when his job approval ratings were climbing, President Bush generally faced less opposition in Congress to his domestic legislative agenda. During his last two years when his job approval ratings were dropping, he faced substantial and public opposition from the Democratic-controlled Congress. In the case of Bill

Clinton, with his declining ratings during his first two years he wasn't even able to get major parts of his legislative program (for instance, his first budget or the health care reform program) through a Congress controlled by his own party. When his job approval ratings began to climb in 1995 and 1996, however, he became strong enough to win a major showdown over the budget—which included two government shutdowns— with a Republican-led Congress.

Presidents who are able to govern successfully are those who can promote high levels of professional reputation and public prestige. In foreign policy, this is likely to be especially important for those intermestic issues that have become increasingly salient since the end of the cold war. When the government deals with issues that intersect domestic and foreign policy—such as over economics, immigration, drugs, and the environment—more interest groups and constituencies gain access to the increasingly complex policy-making process. Only a president with high levels of professional reputation and public prestige is going to be able to break through the logjams created by all of the competing constituencies and bureaucratic missions.

The third important element of presidential leadership is "presidential choices." A president's ability to lead and persuade is a function of the choices and the decisions that he makes, for which only he is responsible. The choices that are made by a president affect his professional reputation and public prestige. Presidential choices may allow a president to take advantage of opportunities as they arise, exercising power when little opportunity seems available given existing constraints. Ultimately, this requires that the president, and his staff, be skillful (1) in managing the executive branch and the decision-making process, (2) in building coalitions and politically interacting with other players in Washington, D.C., and beyond, and (3) in symbolically communicating his priorities and preferences throughout society and the world. These are political requirements involving important choices for successful presidential leadership.

Richard Pious, in *The American Presidency*, has added important insights concerning the impact of presidential choice and activism on presidential leadership. He argues that the paradox of presidential power has become so constraining that a president must exercise "prerogative government"—that is, push the Constitution to its limits—if he wants to govern and lead the country, especially in foreign affairs. "The President justifies his decisions on constitutional grounds, on powers enumerated, or on those claimed. . . . When his expansive interpretation is challenged, he appeals to the public for support by defining his actions in terms of 'national security' or 'the national interest.'"[26]

Those presidents who have a more expansive view of presidential power tend to be the most successful in governing. However, activist presidents who exercise prerogative government also run the political risk of abusing their power, which can damage or destroy them. This is because the Constitution is an ambiguous document: it is often unclear whether a president is exercising power legitimately or abusing his authority. Presidents have the greatest opportunity to exercise prerogative government during times of crises and national emergencies. However, the final determinant of the legitimate exercise of presidential power is the political environment.

*Leadership and the Conduct of Foreign Policy*
The concepts of professional reputation, public prestige, and presidential choice, such as exercising prerogative government, are helpful for understanding the president's ability to lead and govern the country. These three elements of presidential leadership explain why Franklin Roosevelt was the most successful president in modern times. Not only did he enjoy high professional reputation and public prestige, but he operated during times of domestic and international emergency allowing him to exercise prerogative government. These concepts also help to explain why Presidents Harry Truman, Dwight Eisenhower, and John Kennedy were able to dominate foreign policy during the cold war years — another time of national emergency in the minds of most Americans, giving presidents extraordinary power over national security and foreign affairs.

The Vietnam War, ironically, represented both the apex of presidential power, as well as the decline of the exercise of prerogative and presidential power in foreign affairs. Lyndon Johnson was the first president to find that what had been accepted as a legitimate exercise of presidential power at the height of the cold war became increasingly viewed as presidential abuse of power—of an "imperial presidency"—in the political climate of the Vietnam era.[27]

Presidents must realize that they can no longer exercise power and prerogative government in the name of national security without risking considerable political backlash and possible overshoot and collapse. Such was the experience of Richard Nixon with Watergate, despite his foreign policy initiatives and successes. As the Iran-contra affair demonstrated, not even Ronald Reagan, with his formidable rhetorical skill and high public prestige, was able to rise above the paradox of presidential power.

Since Vietnam, strong and judicious presidential leadership has become increasingly important for the conduct of U.S. foreign policy. To be able to govern foreign policy, not only must presidents exercise prerogative government while avoiding being perceived as abusing power, they must also make the kind of presidential choices that maximize political support behind their policies and results in electoral success. Unfortunately, most individuals elected as president of the United States since Vietnam have not been viewed as particularly strong and successful leaders—such leadership skills may be quite uncommon. There is no doubt that George Bush was shocked to discover that, despite his great victory in the Persian Gulf War and public approval ratings approaching 90 percent, he was soon voted out of office, largely due to perceptions that he did little to address the domestic ills of the United States. President Bush clearly made the crucial mistake of underestimating the "softness" of presidential support and the volatility of the domestic political environment since Vietnam.

Several of President Clinton's foreign policy initiatives—Haiti, Mexico, and Bosnia—may be considered an exercise of prerogative government. In each case the administration was faced with considerable public and congressional opposition to the initiative in question, and proceeded nonetheless. In each case there were many in Congress who argued that the president did not have the authority to act alone, and yet he acted alone. Furthermore, each of these instances of prerogative government occurred in the absence of any semblance of national emergency. And yet in none of the cases did the Clinton administration suffer from "backlash" or "overshoot and collapse." Perhaps political backlash was avoided in each case because the policies, thus far, were successful—or at least they weren't seen as failures—and seemed distant from the vital concerns of most Americans. The political risks taken by the Clinton administration for each of these initiatives seem to have paid off to the extent that Haiti, Bosnia, and Mexico all ceased being potentially damaging foreign policy problems for Clinton. Hence, the continued importance of prerogative government to presidential leadership and power, although Clinton's second term may help clarify if the risks associated with prerogative government have somehow changed in the post–cold war era.

Now that the cold war is over, the quality of presidential leadership may be more consequential than ever, especially as the United States approaches the twenty-first century at a time of extreme complexity abroad and at home. In addition to professional reputation, public prestige, and prerogative government, the choices a president makes in managing the executive branch and the foreign policy bureaucracy is another significant source affecting his ability to exercise leadership and power, to which we now turn.

## Presidential Management of the Bureaucracy

In order to exercise their power successfully, presidents must be strong managers as well as strong political leaders. Especially given the decline of presidential power following Vietnam and Watergate, the president has to be able to manage the foreign policy bureaucracy if he is to successfully govern in the area of foreign policy. The more successful he is in this management task the more he will be able to exercise presidential power in accordance with his roles as commander in chief, chief diplomat, chief administrator, and chief legislator. Unfortunately, the bureaucracy, because of its huge size and complexity, is both a source of presidential power and a constraint on presidential power. This double-edged bureaucratic sword has become even more complex with the end of the cold war.

### Bureaucratic Constraints and Legacy

It is important to point out that presidents are increasingly constrained by the existence of a huge bureaucracy that remains oriented more to the past than to the future. Currently, the president presides over five million personnel, located in thirteen major departments and hundreds of other organizations and agencies, who spend well over one trillion dollars a year on thousands of programs and policies throughout the United States and the world. Not surprisingly, presidential policies are heavily affected by what the bureaucracy is able and willing to do.

Therefore, the president's ability to successfully manage the bureaucracy will be a crucial determinant of his ability to govern effectively in foreign policy. This remains a very difficult—if not impossible—task, because the foreign policy bureaucracy has become so large, complex, and entrenched over the years. Despite all the talk about the collapse of Soviet communism and the need for reform, the huge national security bureaucracy which developed following World War II to fight the cold war remains largely intact, clearly constraining the president's ability to govern foreign policy into the future.[28]

The end of the cold war has also seen a rise in the perceived importance among both the public and policy makers of intermestic issues such as foreign economic policy, immigration policy, and international drug trafficking. These issues are intermestic in the sense that they do not fit neatly into, and can be seen to blur, the classic dichotomy of foreign and domestic policy. As these intermestic issues become more prominent, they pull more and more traditionally domestic policy-oriented agencies into the foreign policy–making process. These formerly domestic agencies tend to have powerful extragovernmental constituencies and bureaucratic missions that are often at odds with the bureaucratic missions of the traditional national security agencies.

This proliferation of agencies with multiple and competing constituencies and missions leads to a much more intense policy debate and a much more complex policy-making process. To the extent that this makes the president's job of managing the foreign policy bureaucracy much more difficult it constitutes a significant post–cold war constraint on presidential power. This means that successful management of the foreign policy bureaucracy has become much more complex and vital for the ability of the president to successfully govern in the area of foreign policy.

### Organizing the Policy-Making Process

The more successful a president is in managing the bureaucracy, the fewer the bureaucratic constraints and the greater his ability to exercise power. A president's success in managing the bureaucracy is very much a function of his "choices" concerning his personal agenda and level of involvement, the personnel that will staff his administration, and how he organizes the foreign policy–making process. These decisions must be made early if a president wants to enter office ready to exercise power and govern.

The president cannot assume when he takes office that the policy-making system in place will automatically be responsive, allowing him to manage the bureaucracy. On the contrary, if a president wants to manage the bureaucracy, as opposed to responding to bureaucratic momentum, he must initiate a policy process that responds to his demands. Therefore, the president must decide who he will appoint to staff his administration and how they will interact so that he is kept informed, able to arrive at decisions, and have decisions implemented in accordance with his wishes.

Regardless of how decentralized and open a policy process that presidents may initially prefer, the historical record since World War II suggests that within a short time presidents quickly come to rely on a small number of advisers who tend to be part of the White House staff and agencies within the executive office of the executive branch, such as the National Security Council. This occurs because of time constraints, increasing familiarity between the president and his advisers, and questions of trust and loyalty. Therefore, it is not surprising that presidential management of foreign policy tends to revolve around a White House–centered system that becomes more centralized and closed over time, for it is most responsive to presidents, and their policy agendas and personal styles.[29]

*Reliance on the National Security Adviser and the NSC/NSC Staff.* In managing the foreign policy bureaucracy, presidents since World War II have increasingly relied on the National Security Council (NSC) and the special assistant to the president for national security affairs (more commonly known as the national security adviser). Unlike much of the established and entrenched bureaucracy, such as the Department of State and the Department of Defense, members of the White House Office and the National Security Council are most responsive to the president. They lack an independent base of power, working only for him and under his complete authority. Therefore, the national security adviser usually is the single most important appointment the president makes. He is often the most important policy adviser to the president and is responsible for coordinating the foreign policy–making process for the president within the executive branch through the NSC.

The National Security Council came into existence in 1947 with the passage of the National Security Act. It consists of a council—a formal decision-making body composed of high-level foreign policy officials—and a small support staff to advise the president and coordinate the national security process. Although the purpose of the NSC was to rationalize the national security process and force the president to be more responsive to the formal lines of authority throughout the foreign policy bureaucracy, especially within the military, the president has used the NSC as it has suited him. Very simply, presidents will interact with those policy makers they trust the most and will avoid officials with whom they have policy disagreements or personality conflicts. Over time, this has led to a foreign policy process that has become increasingly White House–centered: the council's significance as a "formal decision-making body" has declined while the president has come to increasingly rely on the national security adviser and the NSC staff to manage the process and provide him with an independent source of information and advice.[30] Clearly, the president is the key figure in the dynamics of the policy process, at least at the presidential level, and will manage the bureaucracy in ways that are consistent with his operating style.

Presidential management styles, in fact, have differed with each president and have evolved over time. According to I. M. Destler, Leslie H. Gelb, and Anthony Lake, in *Our Own Worst Enemy: The Unmaking of American Foreign Policy*, there have been three major stages in the evolution of the National Security Council and the foreign policy process at the presidential level. First, Presidents Truman and Eisenhower used the NSC as an advisory body with a staff to support their reliance on their cabinet secretaries and departments. Second, under Presidents Kennedy and Johnson, the NSC was eclipsed, and the traditional role of the cabinet, especially the State Department, was challenged by the rise of the national security adviser and NSC staff. Third, beginning with President Nixon, the national security adviser and the NSC staff became ascendant in the policy-making process.

Clearly, as presidents have come to rely more on their national security advisers, the position has gained in prominence and power. The national security adviser and the NSC staff have become ascendant over the cabinet officers and departments for information, advice, and management of the policy process for the president. The national security adviser often acts as a spokesperson for the president. He is often the first among equals relative to other key foreign policy officials. Consequently, to assist the national security adviser, the NSC staff has grown in size and influence as well.

Many contemporary observers of the governmental process continue to believe that the National Security Council itself serves as a major forum for presidential decisions in foreign policy. Sometimes a new president, especially if he espouses a preference for cabinet government, has attempted to revitalize the council as a deliberating body early in his administration. However, the president quickly learns that the formal council does not serve his needs well. Instead, the policy-making process at the presidential level has tended to involve an informal process among the president's closest advisers, and a formal NSC interagency process through use of the national security adviser and the NSC staff.

The informal process usually involves the president meeting with his closest advisers in person or speaking with them over the phone. The formal process usually involves the national security adviser, along with the use of his staff, coordinating the flow of information and meetings involving a variety of policymakers located throughout the foreign policy bureaucracy. Together, the workings of both the informal and formal policy-making processes are responsible for providing the information and advice that leads to presidential foreign policy decisions.

*The Bush and Clinton Management Styles.* Both post–cold war administrations have continued to rely on an informal advisory process and a formal NSC interagency process. In this respect, not much has changed with the end of the cold war. President Bush developed a formal interagency process dependent on the NSC staff and the coordination of National Security Adviser Brent Scowcroft, a position he held under President Ford earlier. Information and policy recommendations were generated through interagency groups operating at different levels: the interaction of senior governmental officials for more significant and general issues and, for lesser issues, the involvement of groups of lower level officials representing the foreign policy bureaucracy organized along more specific geographical and functional lines.[31]

Specifically, Scowcroft and his deputy national security adviser served as chairs of the two key NSC committees coordinating the foreign policy machinery of the Bush administration—the NSC Principals Committee (NSC/PC—a Cabinet-level group) and the NSC Deputies Committee (NSC/DC—a deputy secretary–level group). Below these committees, the Bush White House established a series of NSC policy coordinating committees (NSC/PCC), which were interagency groups established by the NSC or the two lead NSC committees. In the Bush administration's system, these NSC/PCCs did most of the work to formulate policy options for higher level consideration, and also to supervise and coordinate the implementation of policy choices. Organized into various regional (e.g., Europe, Soviet Union, Latin America) and functional units (e.g., arms control, defense, intelligence), these working groups were chaired by assistant secretaries of state for the regional units, and assistant secretaries (or equivalents) from Defense, Treasury, the CIA, and elsewhere for functional units. However, an NSC staff member served as executive secretary for each NSC/PCC to increase White House control and policy coordination.

The NSC/DC and NSC/PC process helped to further centralize policy control by the White House, the national security adviser, and NSC staff. The NSC/DC, through the deputy national security adviser and the NSC staff, reviewed all work from the coordinating committees and made recommendations to the NSC/PC and the NSC itself. The NSC/PC was a kind of executive committee of the NSC, under the leadership of the national security adviser. Effectively, the NSC/PC served as a White House–led center for considering all national security questions. In this way, the Bush administration attempted to coordinate foreign policy across bureaucratic agencies and place the White House at the center of foreign policy making.

Bush personally relied most on a small inner circle of advisers for most presidential decisions that usually included National Security Adviser Scowcroft, the White House chief of staff (initially John Sununu, then Samuel Skinner), Secretary of State James Baker, Secretary of Defense Richard Cheney, and Chairman of the Joint Chiefs of Staff Colin Powell. These officials made up the NSC/PC and, for instance, were the individuals President Bush turned to for information and advice in formulating policy following Iraq's August 2, 1990, invasion of Kuwait. In effect, the Bush administration cultivated a White House team to manage the foreign policy bureaucracy.

Like his predecessor, President Clinton supplemented a formal NSC interagency process with a heavy reliance upon informal meetings among his principal foreign policy advisers. In his first term Clinton showed a strong preference for informal meetings with his closest advisers like Secretary of State Warren Christopher, National Security Adviser Anthony Lake, and Defense Secretary Les Aspin and, later, Aspin's successor, William Perry. In fact, early on in the administration Clinton's apparent unwillingness to establish more frequent formal meetings on foreign policy created concern among advisers like Secretary of State Christopher.[32]

Clinton's formal NSC interagency process was actually closely modeled on the Bush NSC system. At the top was the Principals Committee (PC), which serves as the senior interagency committee and is chaired by the national security adviser. One new development under President Clinton was that he broadened the circle of principal members to include the secretary of the treasury, the U.S. ambassador to the United Nations, the special assistant to the president for economic policy, and the White House chief of staff. Below the Principals Committee was the Deputies Committee (DC), which is chaired by the deputy national security adviser and which carries out much of the work of the interagency process, supervising policy implementation, and reviewing issue papers to be used by the NSC principals. The Deputies Committee was also charged with setting up and supervising a series of interagency working groups (IWGs) to help prepare policy studies and to help facilitate implementation of decisions within bureaucratic agencies. The Clinton administration also reorganized the NSC staff, dividing up the European Affairs office into an office for Western Europe and an office for Russia, Ukraine, and Eurasian Affairs, and creating offices for nonproliferation policy, environmental affairs, and democracy affairs to reflect new post–cold war policy concerns.[33]

President Clinton's first national security adviser, Anthony Lake, very much like National Security Adviser Brent Scowcroft under President Bush, entered office determined to keep a lower public profile. Lake believed that keeping a lower profile would not only enhance his role as coordinator of the policy process, but would also prevent much of the bitter infighting that occurred between national security advisers and secretaries of state in past administrations. Indeed, observers of the Clinton White House have reported a high degree of collegiality among the principal members of the foreign policy team.[34]

During the first two years of the administration, however, both Lake and his deputy Sandy Berger were criticized by observers for putting too much emphasis on presenting consensus positions to the president, which both slowed the advisory process and watered down the final product. Lake and Berger were also criticized for not being proactive enough in the important tasks of managing the NSC staff and interagency process. Observers of the administration generally agree that the above-mentioned shortcomings were largely worked out during the second half of the president's term with the result being a much more efficient and effective process. With a now experienced Berger being promoted to national security adviser for the second term, the process will likely continue to improve in efficiency and effectiveness.

Although the policy-making process for national security issues has not changed that much with the end of the cold war, President Clinton has instituted a major change in an effort to coordinate and centralize U.S. economic policy, both domestic and foreign, with the creation of the National Economic Council (NEC). It has been recognized for some time that the NSC process has not been all that helpful to the president for intermestic issues, such as foreign economics, that have grown in importance for American society and U.S. foreign policy with time. The national security adviser and the NSC staff tend to lack interest and expertise in these "nonsecurity" areas. It was not, after all, designed with this intent. Nevertheless, efforts to coordinate and centralize foreign economic policy making, which have been made since the seventies, have generally failed—that is, until President Clinton came into office.

The creation of the National Economic Council, under the direction of the special assistant to the president for economic policy (known as the national economic adviser) and a small staff modeled on the NSC, represents a serious step toward strengthening the president's ability to manage the foreign policy bureaucracy (see chapter 3 in this volume) and the foreign economic bureaucracy (see chapter 4 in this volume). Only time will tell whether it will become institutionalized like the NSC and serve as a significant means for dealing with future foreign policy issues now that the cold war is over.

### The Challenges of the Post–Cold War World

The collapse of communism and the Soviet Union provide unique opportunities for more foreign policy change in a direction away from cold war policies of the past, but it has also further weakened the president's ability to govern foreign policy into the future. It was the sense of national emergency associated with the cold war during the fifties and sixties, after all, that was the ultimate source of presidential power and American global leadership following World War II. Clearly, such a sense of national emergency no longer exists in the post–cold war era—the perception of a "cold war" has been replaced with the perception of a time of "relative peace" abroad in the minds of most Americans. This means that the fragmented and pluralist political environment that has prevailed since Vietnam will likely continue in the post–cold war future, posing greater foreign policy opportunities and political risks for presidents and American leadership abroad.

There is no doubt that the United States will continue to have a powerful international presence given its relative power and its legacy of global leadership since World War II. There is also little doubt that the future leadership role of the United States in the world will be influenced by who becomes president. Presidents can affect the general direction of U.S. foreign policy, within the parameters of legitimate foreign policy orientations that prevail throughout American politics. But much will depend on the image that Americans have of a president's policies and of their relative success, at home and abroad—a function of the fate of events and the strength of presidential leadership. And much will depend on the president's ability to manage and harness the huge bureaucracy that has developed over the years.

Clearly, the post–cold war era will present U.S. presidents with new types of constraints on their power, but also with new types of opportunities. As the American public focuses its concern more and more on intermestic—especially economic—issues, both at home and abroad, presidents who are perceived as dealing successfully with those issues are likely to enjoy an increase in their popularity and ability to govern in foreign policy and in general. Such seems to have been the case for both Presidents Bush and Clinton thus far, although only time will tell whether or not this will be a larger post–cold war trend.

Ultimately, the president's ability to govern into the future is clearly impacted by the dynamic interaction between global developments and the domestic environment that determines the politics of United States foreign policy. This makes it difficult to envision a strong, proactive global leadership role for the United States across different administrations navigating the challenges of the twenty-first century over a sustained period of time. It may simply be that the cold war era has been superceded by an increasingly complex global and domestic environment where the days of presidential supremacy and grand design in foreign policy have given way to a time when U.S. foreign policy is more likely to be reactive—a time of muddling through. This may not be what most people mean by American leadership in the world. But this appears to be the case thus far under George Bush and Bill Clinton—the first two post–cold war presidents.

## Notes

1 Stanley Hoffman, *Gulliver's Troubles, or the Setting of American Foreign Policy* (New York: McGraw-Hill, 1968), p. 289.

2 For a general discussion of the paradox of presidential power, see Godfrey Hodgson, *All Things to All Men: The False Promise of the Modern American Presidency* (New York: Touchtone, 1980); Richard E. Neustadt, *Presidential Power: The Politics of Leadership* (New York: John Wiley, 1960); Richard Pious, *The American Presidency* (New York: Basic Books, 1979); and Hedrick Smith, *The Power Game* (New York: Ballantine, 1988).

3 John F. Kennedy, in Theodore C. Sorensen, *Decision-Making in the White House: The Olive Branch or the Arrows* (New York: Columbia University Press, 1963), p. xii (in foreword).

4 The classic statement on this is Edward S. Corwin, *The President: Office and Powers, 1787–1957* (New York: New York University Press, 1957). See also Cecil V. Crabb Jr. and Pat M. Holt, *Invitation to Struggle: Congress, the President, and Foreign Policy* (Washington, D.C.: Congressional Quarterly Press, 1992).

5 Arthur Schlesinger Jr., *The Imperial Presidency* (New York: Houghton Mifflin, 1989).

6 Aaron Wildavsky, "The Two Presidencies Thesis," *Transaction* 4 (1966), 7–14. For a general assessment see, Steven A. Shull, ed., *The Two Presidencies: A Quarter Century Assessment* (Chicago: Nelson-Hall, 1991).

7 See, for example, Jerel A. Rosati, *The Politics of United States Foreign Policy* (Dallas, Tex.: Harcourt Brace, 1993).

8  For a superb discussion of the impediments on presidential power in foreign policy during the cold war years, see Roger Hilsman, *To Move a Nation: The Politics of Foreign Policy in the Administration of John F. Kennedy* (New York: Delta, 1964); and Hoffman, *Gulliver's Troubles.*

9  See Bayless Manning, "The Congress, The Executive, and Intermestic Affairs: Three Proposals," *Foreign Affairs* 55 (1977): 306–332.

10  See I. M. Destler, Leslie H. Gelb, and Anthony Lake, *Our Own Worst Enemy: The Unmaking of American Foreign Policy* (New York: Simon and Schuster, 1984); Hodgson, *America in Our Time;* Thomas E. Mann, "Making Foreign Policy: President and Congress," in Thomas E. Mann, ed., *A Question of Balance: The President, The Congress and Foreign Policy* (Washington, D.C.: Brookings Institution, 1990), pp. 1–34; and Rosati, *The Politics of United States Foreign Policy.*

11  Ole R. Holsti and James N. Rosenau, *American Leadership in World Affairs: Vietnam and the Breakdown of Consensus* (Boston: Allen & Unwin, 1984), p. 1.

12  See Seyom Brown, *The Faces of Power: Constancy and Change in Foreign Policy from Truman to Clinton* (New York: Columbia University Press, 1994); Walter LaFeber, *America, Russia, and the Cold War 1948-1990* (New York: McGraw-Hill, 1991); Richard A. Melanson, *Reconstructing Consensus: American Foreign Policy since the Vietnam War* (New York: St. Martin's Press, 1991); and Jerel A. Rosati, "Jimmy Carter, a Man before His Time? The Emergence and Collapse of the First Post–Cold War Presidency," *Presidential Studies Quarterly* 23 (Summer 1993): 459–76.

13  See Duane M. Oldfield and Aaron Wildavsky, "Reconsidering the Two Presidencies," *Society* 26 (July/August): 54–59. Reprinted in Shull, *The Two Presidencies.*

14  See Jerel A. Rosati, "The Domestic Environment," in Peter A. Schraeder, ed., *Intervention into the 1990s: United States Foreign Policy in the Third World* (Boulder, Colo.: Lynne Rienner Publishers, 1992), pp. 175–191.

15  Destler, Lake, and Gelb, *Our Own Worst Enemy,* p. 13.

16  Alexander L. George, "Domestic Constraints on Regime Change in U.S. Foreign Policy: The Need for Policy Legitimacy," in Ole R. Holsti, Randolph Siverson, and Alexander L. George, eds., *Change in the International System* (Boulder, Colo.: Westview Press, 1980), p. 236.

17  Terry L. Deibel, "Bush's Foreign Policy: Mastery and Inaction," *Foreign Policy* 84 (Fall 1991): 3.

18  See Holsti and Rosenau, *American Leadership in World Affairs;* Miroslav Nincic, "The United States, The Soviet Union, and the Politics of Opposites," *World Politics* 40 (July 1988): 452–475; Jerel Rosati and John Creed, "Extending the Three-Headed and Four-Headed Eagles: The Foreign Policy Orientations of American Elites During the Eighties and Nineties," *Political Psychology* 18 (September 1997): 583–623; and Daniel Yankelovich, "Farewell to 'President Knows Best,'" *Foreign Affairs,* America and the World issue (1978): 670–693.

19  See Gabriel A. Almond, *The American People and Foreign Policy* (New York: Praeger, 1960); Richard J. Barnet, *Roots of War* (New York: Penguin, 1971), pt. 3; and Sidney Blumenthal, "The Return of the Repressed: Anti-Internationalism and the American Right," *World Policy Journal* 12 (Fall 1995): 1–13.

20 See Bruce Jentleson, "Who, What, and How: Debates over Post–Cold War Military Intervention"; and William Schneider, "The New Isolationism" in Robert J. Lieber, ed., *Eagle Adrift: American Foreign Policy at the End of the Century* (New York: Longman, 1997).

21 Schneider, "The New Isolationism," pp. 33–37.

22 See Thomas M. Franck and Edward Weisband, *Foreign Policy by Congress* (New York: Oxford University Press, 1979); Mann, "Making Foreign Policy"; and Jerel A. Rosati, "Congressional Influence in American Foreign Policy: Addressing the Controversy," *Journal of Political and Military Sociology* 12 (Fall 1984): 311–333.

23 See, for example, Steven W. Hook, "Congress vs. Clinton over U.S. Foreign Policy," *Foreign Policy Analysis Notes* (Winter 1996/97); electronic version at http://csf.colorado.edu/isa/sections/fp/22-2w96.htm, pp. 4–11.

24 Neustadt, *Presidential Power*. Since its first year of publication, it has been periodically revised with additional reflections on more current presidents. On the importance of presidential leadership, see also James MacGregor Burns, *Presidential Government: The Crucible of Leadership* (New York: Avon, 1965); Theodore J. Lowi, *The Personal President: Power Invested, Promise Unfulfilled* (Ithaca, N.Y.: Cornell University Press, 1985), and footnote 1.

25 Smith, *The Power Game*, p. 56.

26 Pious, *The American Presidency*, p. 47.

27 See Schlesinger, *Imperial Presidency*.

28 See, for example, Morton H. Halperin and Jeanne M. Woods, "Ending the Cold War at Home," *Foreign Policy* 81 (Winter 1990–91): 128–43; Rosati, *The Politics of United States Foreign Policy*, chs. 3–7; and Wilson, *Bureaucracy*.

29 See, for example, Rosati, *The Politics of United States Foreign Policy*, ch. 3.

30 See, for example, Bert A. Rockman, "America's Departments of State: Irregular and Regular Syndromes of Policy Making," *American Political Science Review* 75 (December 1981): 911–927.

31 See David Hoffman, "President Scales Back National Security Council," *Washington Post*, February 3, 1989, p. A8; Andrew Rosenthal, "Scowcroft and Gates: A Team Rivals Baker, *New York Times*, February 21, 1991, p. A6; Charlotte Saikowski, "Brent Scowcroft: Quiet Adviser," *Christian Science Monitor*, February 14, 1989, p. 8; and Bernard Weinraub, "Bush Backs Plan to Enhance Role of Security Staff," *New York Times*, February 2, 1989, pp. A1, A7.

32 See Terry Atlas, "Clinton Foreign Policy Team Charts Collegial Path," *Chicago Tribune*, July 25, 1993, p. 1; Thomas Friedman and Elaine Sciolino, "Clinton and Foreign Issues: Spasms of Attention," *New York Times*, March 22, 1993, p. A1; Gwen Ifill, "Security Official Guides U.S. Aims at Conference," *New York Times*, July 5, 1993, p. A5; and Elaine Sciolino, "Three Players Seek a Director for Foreign Policy Story," *New York Times*, November 8, 1993, p. A1.

33 See also Vincent Auger, "The National Security Council System after the Cold War," in Randall B. Ripley and James M. Lindsay, eds., *U.S. Foreign Policy after the Cold War* (Pittsburgh: University of Pittsburgh Press, 1997), pp. 42–73.

34 See Atlas, "Clinton Foreign Policy Team Charts Collegial Path"; Thomas L. Fried-

man, "Clinton's Foreign Policy: Top Advisor Speaks Up," *New York Times*, October 31, 1993, p. 8; Jacob Heilibrunn, "Lake Inferior," *New Republic* (September 20 & 27, 1993): 29–35; Elaine Sciolino, "Christopher and Lake Vying for Control of Foreign Policy," *New York Times*, September 23, 1994, pp. A1, A5.

# 3.

## The Foreign Policy Bureaucracy in a New Era

*Christopher M. Jones*

In a 1993 article entitled "Cold War Without End," Thomas L. Friedman observed that many government agencies had not adjusted to the post-Soviet era.[1] At the time, such a finding was not only persuasive; it was accurate. The foreign policy bureaucracy—Department of State, Central Intelligence Agency, and Department of Defense—was having considerable difficulty redefining itself. Friedman's assessment, however, may have been premature in light of bureaucratic inertia and the cold war's recent conclusion. President Bill Clinton's second term offers a more appropriate juncture to examine whether the actors responsible for America's war against communism have been transformed or remain essentially unchanged in a new era. Besides providing analytical distance, the years 1993 through 1997 encompass the first presidency to fall entirely within the post–cold war period.

In certain respects, the foreign policy bureaucracy has not changed. Basic missions remain the same: the State Department conducts foreign relations; the Central Intelligence Agency (CIA) collects, produces, and disseminates intelligence; and the Defense Department provides the military forces needed to deter war and protect national security. Moreover, these organizations continue to shape the direction of foreign policy through technical expertise, control of information, advice to decision makers, and implementation. Last, the institutions continue to behave as classical bureaucratic organizations. Consistent with Max Weber's well-known administrative theory, the agencies under study operate by a set of principles designed to promote efficiency: a clear division of labor, hierarchical authority, hiring based on technical qualifications, a system of written rules and procedures, and merit-based compensation and promotion.[2]

Beyond basic roles and organization, however, State, CIA, and Defense have experienced changes related to mission interpretation, budget, structure, and personnel. While adjustments in these areas have varied in degree over the last several years, even small shifts in behavior are important, since these institutions have traditionally been among the most rigid and resistant of the Washington bureaucracies.

What explains the organizational change experienced by these agencies? Two well-known models of policy making suggest different answers. On one hand, the principal-agent model assumes that elected institutions (principals) shape the behavior of bureaucracies (agents) through rewards and sanctions (e.g., budgets, legislation, political appointments, procedural changes).[3] From this perspective, recent change within the foreign policy bureaucracy has been directed mainly by the White House and Congress. On the other hand, the governmental or bureaucratic politics model claims bureaucracies are more independent and survival-oriented. They protect their jurisdictions, compete with other agencies for influence, and attempt to expand their roles and capabilities.[4] According to this view, organizational change has emanated largely from the agencies themselves. Responding to a host of domestic and international developments, foreign policy institutions have adapted to illustrate their continued relevance, maintain resources, and prevent bureaucratic competitors from eroding their power.

In reality, both models account correctly for why the CIA and the Departments of Defense and State have changed in the post–cold war era. Neither model, however, provides a complete explanation. Since the "shifting constellations image" introduced in chapter 1 encompasses the interactions depicted by both models, it better captures the complex reality of bureaucratic adaptation in the post–cold war era. That is, recent change within the foreign policy bureaucracy has been a product of the international environment, societal factors, the White House and Congress, and the agencies themselves. For instance, organizations have responded to global circumstances (e.g., Soviet disintegration, the demise of communism, new global threats, greater interdependence, and the rising importance of economic power). Institutions also have reacted to societal developments (e.g., less interest in foreign policy, diminished support for U.S. commitments abroad, negative images of some agencies, concern for balancing the budget, and heightened attention to domestic priorities). In addition, agencies have been affected by the Clinton administration's policy agenda (e.g., economic revitalization, improvement of the global environment, humanitarian intervention, greater government efficiency, and a diverse federal workforce). Furthermore, the foreign policy bureaucracy has been changed by Capitol Hill's increasingly conservative agenda (e.g., reduction of government size and perceived waste, elimination of the federal deficit through spending cuts, diminished foreign policy allocations, reservations concerning international peacekeeping, and greater attention to domestic issues at the expense of international affairs). Last, each institution under study has adapted, partly out of a recognition that the competition over roles and budgets has intensified as other agencies encounter the same domestic and global environments.

## The State Department

Even with the end of the cold war, the Department of State continues to perform its long-standing mission: formulating, executing, and articulating U.S. foreign policy. Similarly, a consensus still exists among members of the organization, namely Foreign Service officers (FSOs), that this role can be performed largely through the traditional diplomatic functions of representation, negotiation, and reporting. The significant change that has unfolded recently concerns the issues to which the State Department directs its attention and resources. Instead of conducting U.S. diplomacy with Soviet containment as its central premise, the agency has become focused on a more diverse set of foreign policy challenges after the cold war.

Since 1993, the Department of State has been officially committed to "building democracy; promoting and maintaining peace; promoting economic growth and sustainable development; addressing global problems; and providing humanitarian assistance."[5] In particular, four developments illustrate how the organization has reinterpreted its mission, focusing on less political, more domestically oriented concerns. First, diplomats have assisted domestic and foreign law enforcement agencies with information regarding intellectual property rights violations, terrorist and anti-American groups, and unidentified criminals. For instance, State Department media campaigns in Pakistan were critical to the apprehension of two criminals, the man convicted of killing two CIA employees outside the agency's headquarters in January 1993 and the mastermind of the World Trade Center bombing one month later. A key strategy in both campaigns was the mass distribution of matchbooks containing the suspects' images.[6] Second, the U.S. Agency for International Development (USAID), a State Department–related organization that administers foreign assistance programs, has advised American inner cities on how to improve literacy, immunization, population control, and economic development.[7] Third, the State Department has placed environmental issues at the center of its agenda and duties. Besides devising strategies to respond to the world's major ecological problems, the department has established "regional environmental hubs" in selected embassies to promote sustainable development, natural resource issues, and the sale of U.S. environmental technologies. In the department's inaugural report on environmental diplomacy, released in April 1997, embassies in Costa Rica, Ethiopia, Jordan, Nepal, Uzbekistan, Thailand, and six other states were designated as the first posts responsible for conducting "greener" foreign policy.[8]

Last and perhaps most important, economics have received dramatically expanded attention as the Department of State reorients its mission. While the State Department has stationed economic officers in its embassies for decades, a new commitment to trade promotion within its Washington headquarters and overseas has emerged. In fact, the goal to serve as an "American desk" for U.S. companies wishing to expand their international trade has led diplomats to advocate American exports to foreign officials; seek policy changes in countries designed to open markets; advise companies concerning foreign regulations, policies and markets; and consult with American business on U.S. foreign policy. This new interest in trade promotion has allowed the State Department to retain some foreign posts in an era of shrinking budgets. While the secretary of state has stressed the importance of coordinating its activities with the economic bureaucracy,[9] the organization's foray into this arena may set up a potential conflict with the Commerce Department, which is responsible for U.S. trade promotion and the Foreign Commercial Service (FCS). Nevertheless, State's global reach and its larger presence abroad[10] will be strong assets as it continues to expand its role in this area.

*Budget*
The end of the cold war has not changed certain realities about the financial resources available for the conduct of foreign policy. The total international affairs budget remains a minute portion of the federal budget, constituting 1.2 percent of all government spending.[11] In addition, the State Department's operating budget is still small in comparison to other federal bureaucracies. In FY 1993, for instance, the Pentagon was authorized to spend $278 billion more than State.[12] The United States also continues to devote less than 1 percent of its national wealth to foreign aid, ranking it below Ireland, Spain, and eighteen other industrialized states.[13] Yet public misperception persists over U.S. foreign assistance with the average citizen believing the amount is equivalent to 15 percent of the federal budget.[14] Relatedly, the Foreign Assistance Act of 1961 remains in effect, preserving expensive earmarks within the

foreign aid budget. Israel and Egypt, for example, receive $5.1 billion annually or nearly 40 percent of all assistance.[15]

With these continuities noted, there have been significant changes related to foreign policy spending. Most notably, the overall international affairs budget has declined 50 percent in real terms since 1985.[16] The major effect of this reduction has been inadequate or modest funding for two categories of post–cold war initiatives: (1) new foreign aid recipients (e.g., Russia and the former Soviet republics, Eastern Europe, the Palestinian Authority) and (2) new global challenges (e.g., peacekeeping efforts, family planning, environmental programs, trade promotion). The limited money allocated to these two areas has come at the expense of traditional security and development assistance. In FY 1994, for instance, several longtime foreign aid recipients lost all or most of their American support (e.g., Morocco, Nicaragua, Guatemala, Philippines, Honduras).[17]

This fiscal environment has been largely a creation of a Congress devoted to a balanced budget and seemingly less interested in foreign affairs. Yet it is exacerbated by the large amount of bilateral aid that remains politically sacrosanct. Much of the financial support received by Israel, Egypt, Cyprus, Greece, Turkey, and Ireland is strongly supported by domestic interest groups. The Clinton administration's attempt in 1993 and 1994 to replace aid to individual countries with broad goals like promoting democracy and peace failed, not only due to special interests, but because Congress feared giving executive agencies like USAID too much discretion. One observer has suggested, however, the real problem with shortages in foreign policy spending is the public's unwillingness to tolerate higher taxes or cuts in entitlement programs.[18] Whatever the reason, there were signs that Congress was prepared to halt the negative trend with a marginal increase in FY 1998.

*Structure*
Despite its global responsibilities, the Department of State remains small in comparison to other agencies. Its total workforce of 24,800 employees is less than nine other executive departments and slightly more than one-half of 1 percent of all federal personnel. The roughly 4,300 Foreign Service generalists, who run hundreds of overseas posts, continue to account for only a small portion of the department's overall employment.[19] These individuals are still assigned to geographic bureaus (e.g., Africa, the Near East, South Asia) or to subunits responsible for particular functions or policy areas (e.g., legislative affairs, diplomatic security, and democracy, human rights and labor).

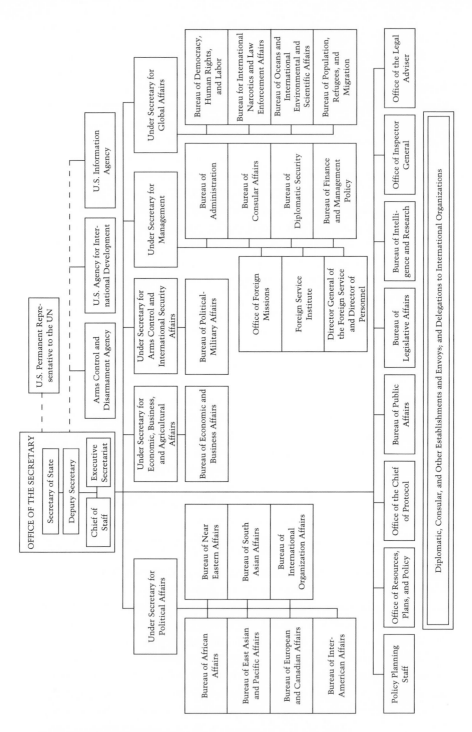

Figure 3.1. The U.S. Department of State: Organization at a Glance
*Source:* U.S. Department of State

Beyond these consistencies, the State Department's internal structure has changed significantly in recent years. Drawing on the recommendations of a department task force and a bipartisan commission,[20] then-Secretary of State Warren Christopher introduced a 1993 directive for reorganization designed to address post–cold war priorities, eliminate duplication and waste, improve internal communication, and facilitate better decision making. Six major adjustments, some of which required congressional approval, were undertaken. First, the Office of Secretary of State, encompassing the secretary, deputy secretary, chief of staff, and executive secretary, was created to improve high-level management and agenda-setting. Second, the department's policy-making echelon was changed from the assistant to under secretary level, thereby reducing the number of people who report directly to the secretary of state. Each under secretary now serves as a principal adviser to the secretary and oversees between one and seven bureaus headed by assistant secretaries (see figure 3.1). Third, a position was established for a new under secretary for global affairs to direct the bureaus concerned with transnational issues (e.g., human rights, democratization, the environment, refugees, narcotics); and a number of these bureaus were renamed or created through the consolidation of former offices and bureaus. Fourth, "business" was incorporated into the title and responsibilities of the under secretary for economic and agricultural affairs. This addition, the establishment of an office and senior coordinator for business affairs, and the assignment of commercial coordinators to geographic bureaus reinforced the State Department's commitment to U.S. trade promotion. Fifth, an ambassador-at-large and special adviser for the former Soviet republics was instituted to reflect the realization that policy toward that region demands high-level attention and coordination. This precedent was followed by Secretary Madeleine Albright in 1997 when she created an ambassador-at-large for war crimes. Sixth, the 1993 reorganization reduced the number of deputy assistant positions (the rank below assistant secretary) by roughly 40 percent.[21]

While elements of Christopher's reorganization were intended to simplify and economize department operations, related actions were taken in response to meager congressional appropriations and the National Performance Review, Vice President Al Gore's reinventing government initiative. From FY 1993 through FY 1996, thirty-two diplomatic and consular posts were closed to generate funds for the establishment of more than twenty embassies in newly independent states and elsewhere (see table 3.1).[22] During the same period, the number of State Department employees was reduced by nearly 2,500. Cuts in personnel

Table 3.1    Closings of U.S. Diplomatic Posts (FY 1993–1996)

| Location | Type of Post |
|---|---|
| *FY 1993* | |
| 1. Alexandria, Egypt | Consulate General |
| 2. Douala, Cameroon | Consulate |
| 3. Geneva, Switzerland | Branch Office |
| 4. Genoa, Italy | Consulate General |
| 5. Honiara, Solomon Islands | Embassy |
| 6. Izmir, Turkey | Consulate General |
| 7. Martinique, FCD | Consulate General |
| 8. Mazatlan, Mexico | Consulate |
| 9. Mombasa, Kenya | Consulate |
| 10. Moroni, Comoros | Embassy |
| 11. Oran, Algeria | Consulate |
| 12. Salzburg, Austria | Consulate General |
| 13. Songkhla, Thailand | Consulate |
| *FY 1994* | |
| 14. Kaduna, Nigeria | Consulate General |
| 15. Maracaibo, Venezuela | Consulate |
| 16. Mogadishu, Somalia | Liaison Office |
| 17. Palermo, Italy | Consulate General |
| 18. St. John's, Antigua | Embassy |
| *FY 1995* | |
| No post closings | |
| *FY 1996* | |
| 19. Barranquilla, Colombia | Consulate |
| 20. Bilbao, Spain | Consulate |
| 21. Bordeaux, France | Consulate General |
| 22. Brisbane, Australia | Consulate |
| 23. Cebu, Philippines | Consulate |
| 24. Lubumbashi, Zaire | Consulate |
| 25. Malabo, Equatorial Guinea | Embassy |
| 26. Medan, Indonesia | Consulate |
| 27. Porto Alegre, Brazil | Consulate |
| 28. Poznan, Poland | Consulate General |
| 29. Udorn, Thailand | Consulate |
| 30. Stuttgart, Germany | Consulate General |
| 31. Victoria, Seychelles | Embassy |
| 32. Zurich, Switzerland | Consulate General |

*Source:* U.S. Department of State.

and overseas missions were even more severe at USAID and the U.S. Information Agency (USIA).[23] Another development was the sale of State Department buildings, vacant lots, and other assets abroad as a means to save money or gain revenue for the construction of new facilities.

Last, the Clinton administration decided in April 1997 to merge the Arms Control and Disarmament Agency (ACDA), USIA, and *some* USAID functions into the State Department. The reorganization plan also placed the USAID director under the authority of the secretary of state. Traditionally, the three agencies have been independent and only required to report to the secretary of state. While many Republican legislators and particularly Senator Jesse Helms (R-N.C.), chairman of the Foreign Relations Committee, advocated a complete absorption of USAID by State, they nonetheless welcomed the Clinton initiative as a means to reduce costs, eliminate bureaucratic redundancies, and increase accountability. The final arrangement, however, will require congressional legislation.

*Personnel*
The Foreign Service subculture remains intact. Diplomats tend to be cautious, elitist, resistant to specialization, and distrustful of outsiders. But like other aspects of their department, FSOs have not been immune to change. The cutbacks (discussed above) and a biennial examination process have made entry into the Foreign Service a more competitive endeavor. For example, 230 new junior officers entered the service in 1991. Five years later, the number of new recruits had declined to 90 (including 35 USAID transfers).[24] The shortage of openings, however, has enhanced the quality of recruits. More new officers hold advanced degrees than at any other time in department history.[25] Another change has involved Foreign Service training, which now extends beyond traditional diplomacy, political issues, and foreign languages to encompass export promotion, trade negotiation, technology, and a variety of new global issues.

Last, the image of the Foreign Service as a bastion of white males from privileged families and Ivy League schools is outdated. Not only do FSOs come from a variety of undergraduate institutions, including public universities, they are now about 24 percent female and 7 percent African American.[26] These figures reflect a long-term process of change, including a rewritten entrance examination and new steps to rank applicants and grant promotions. Greater diversity, however, has not eliminated court action by women and minorities who claim promotion and assignment decisions remain biased against them. Instead, it has prompted reverse discrimination lawsuits from white males who allege they have been passed over for deserved promotions and assignments. This situation has been compounded by the limited opportunities for advancement all career diplomats face regardless of gender or race. Not only has the number of more senior positions been reduced in recent years, but the number of ambassadorial posts awarded to outside political appointees has increased from 23 percent in the Bush administration to 33 percent in the Clinton administration.[27] This trend has led the State Department to lose some of its top experts as senior FSOs have become disenchanted by dead-end assignments or have been forced to leave by an "up-or-out" personnel system.

## The Central Intelligence Agency

In the aftermath of the cold war, the Central Intelligence Agency (CIA) remains the core of the U.S. intelligence community, which encompasses no fewer than thirteen executive branch organizations (see figure 3.2). As charged by the National Security Act of 1947, the CIA is an independent agency designed to collect, analyze, and disseminate national security information for the president and the National Security Council (NSC). The data the CIA presents to policy makers emanates from its own personnel and from a variety of other bureaucracies. In the second case, the CIA is responsible for evaluating and integrating intelligence from these different sources. Additionally, the CIA develops and operates technical collection instruments (such as satellites and spy planes); uses human agents to obtain information clandestinely; and conducts covert political and paramilitary action.

Despite these continuing tasks, the CIA has acquired and lost other responsibilities. For instance, the National Security Act of 1947 was amended in 1992 to compel the CIA to provide substantive analysis to the Congress as it does the White House. The legislation also granted the agency explicit authority to gather foreign intelligence from human sources, even though it has done so for decades. In fact, the clandestine collection of intelligence abroad has been the one function that has traditionally distinguished the CIA from other U.S. intelligence agencies. This monopoly, however, has been challenged by the Pentagon's new Defense Humint Service (DHS). Since its establishment in 1996 through a consolidation of several human intelligence units within the armed services, DHS has collected foreign intelligence clandestinely and used commercial activities as cover.[28] To respond to this incursion and illustrate its relevance after the cold war, the CIA has sought to engage in more spying and covert actions. Recent developments have included funding requests to support large-scale covert operations abroad and efforts to retain the right to recruit journalists and clerics as spies in extraordinary circumstances or to use these occupations to mask CIA operatives. The expansion of clandestine intelligence activities by both the CIA and the Defense Department has been supported by many elected officials who see human agents and intervention as the only effective means available to counter global threats like drug trafficking, nuclear proliferation, and terrorism.

In addition to the challenge it faces in human intelligence, the CIA has lost some of its counterintelligence authority. The National Security Act of 1947 gave the CIA control over foreign counterintelligence and left the Federal Bureau of Investigation (FBI) with responsibility for catching spies within the United States. Without assuming security or law enforcement powers, the CIA was also allowed to conduct counterintelligence activities domestically if it coordinated its efforts with the FBI. The FBI, in turn, was granted similar privileges abroad. This division of labor, however, never operated well. Instead of sharing information and coordinating activities, the two agencies were more inclined to engage in a bitter bureaucratic rivalry rooted in jealousy, suspicion, and different priorities (e.g., law enforcement versus the protection of sources). Consequently, each organization blamed the other for counterintelligence debacles.[29]

This persistent institutional conflict was a major reason why Aldrich Ames, a former CIA officer imprisoned in 1994, was able to sell secrets to the Soviet Union over a nine-year period. Even though both agencies were responsible for the failure to apprehend Ames, a presidential decision directive and congressional legislation in 1994 removed counterintelligence authority from the CIA.[30] Specifically, these actions required the CIA to inform the FBI immediately when it has belief or knowledge that an unauthorized foreign source has obtained classified information. Also, the FBI was granted the capacity to conduct foreign counterintelligence investigations with access to the financial and travel records of CIA employees suspected of spying. Furthermore, FBI personnel were placed in the CIA's own counterintelligence center where they have access to case files and foreign data. Last, senior FBI executives were given the permanent authority to head the CIA's Counterespionage Group and a new National Counterintelligence Center designed to add uniformity to federal counterintelligence procedures and policies. These developments and two interagency boards instituted in 1994 may explain why CIA-FBI cooperation led to the 1996 arrest of

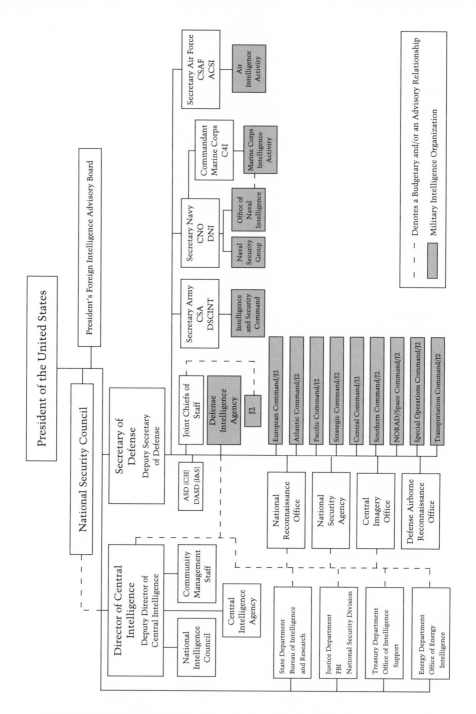

Figure 3.2. The Intelligence Community
*Source:* Commission on the Roles and Capabilities of the United States
Intelligence Community

Harold J. Nicholson, a high-ranking CIA employee who spied for Russia for over two years.[31]

In recent years, the most significant development related to the CIA's mission has been the redefinition and expansion of intelligence targets. During the cold war, the agency's primary focus was gathering information on the Soviet Union, particularly its military capabilities. While the CIA still monitors Russian military power, this task has been accompanied by several post–cold war priorities. After some initial reluctance, the CIA has responded to a statement often made by the former director of central intelligence (DCI), R. James Woolsey: "We have slain a large dragon. But we live in a jungle filled with a variety of poisonous snakes." The behavioral change has been a product of the CIA's desire to justify its existence to outside observers, especially congressional budget cutters, and a reaction to a classified 1995 presidential order setting formal intelligence goals for the first time.[32]

Since 1993, several new intelligence targets have been identified. First, the CIA has devoted more attention and resources to the activities of China and several "rogue states" (e.g., Iran, Iraq, Libya, North Korea, Syria) whose activities may threaten U.S. national security. Second, the agency has combated the drug cartels of Colombia and Peru, an endeavor it had little interest in a few years ago. Also, it has assisted law enforcement officials with foreign violations of U.S. laws by individuals, companies, or organized crime syndicates. Third, there has been greater institutional concern for monitoring arms control treaties and the proliferation of nuclear, chemical, and biological weapons. Fourth, the CIA has expanded its counterterrorist efforts by recruiting new foreign informants, establishing a unit to warn against potential attacks, and using teams of undercover agents to expose plots against U.S. citizens and soldiers abroad.[33] Last, the CIA has stepped up its economic intelligence activities by supplying more foreign economic data to trade negotiators and policy makers, tracking overseas technological breakthroughs, and exposing other countries' industrial espionage within the United States. However, the CIA's practice of not sharing foreign business secrets with domestic companies has continued despite discussions to change it.

*Budget*
The absence of the Soviet Union, the main preoccupation of the CIA for more than forty years, has changed little about intelligence funding. The overall size of the U.S. intelligence budget and the CIA's portion of it have remained officially classified, although the top-line figure for the entire intelligence community ($26.6 billion) was released by the CIA in

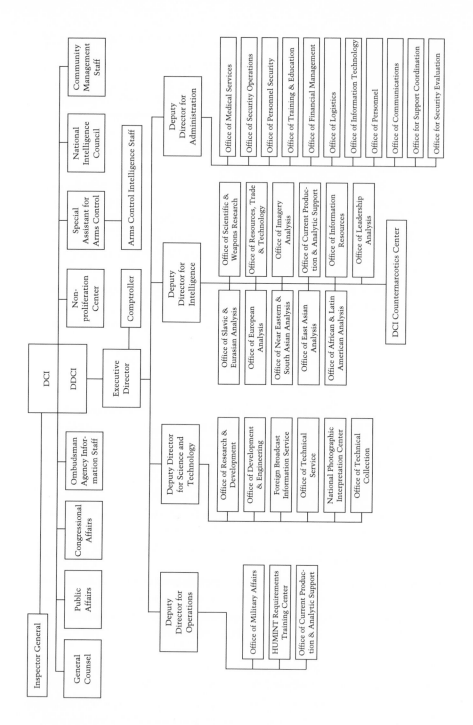

Figure 3.3. The Central Intelligence Agency
*Source:* Central Intelligence Agency

October 1997 in response to a lawsuit filed by the Federation of American Scientists.[34] President Clinton, the Senate, and the bipartisan Brown Commission, appointed by Congress in 1994 to assess the intelligence community and recommend reforms, have all favored such a disclosure annually as a way to create a new sense of openness and democratic responsibility within the intelligence bureaucracy. The House, nevertheless, has opposed the change. This divergence is fairly inconsequential, because the overall level of intelligence funding has always been one of the worst kept secrets in Washington. For years, the annual budgets for the intelligence community and the CIA were widely reported to be $29 billion and $3 billion respectively. Then in 1994, the House Defense Appropriations subcommittee mistakenly published the actual figures, revealing the CIA share was $3.1 billion.[35]

Last, funding levels have not changed significantly. During the 1992 presidential campaign, Bill Clinton pledged to cut the intelligence budget by $7.5 billion over five years (FY 1993–FY 1997).[36] Once in office, however, the new administration attempted to secure a $1 billion increase. Congress denied the request and kept funding constant in FY 1994, FY 1995, and FY 1996.[37] While this pattern reduced spending power slightly because it did not account for inflation, it failed to produce the smaller budgets many observers expected after the cold war. In fact, Congress raised the FY 1998 intelligence budget by 1.4 percent to nearly $27 billion.[38]

*Structure*
Beneath its senior management positions (e.g., director, deputy director, and executive director), the CIA continues to be divided into four subunits (see figure 3.3). The Directorate of Administration (DA) runs the daily operations of the agency; the Directorate of Intelligence (DI) performs research and analysis; the Directorate of Operations (DO) gathers human intelligence and conducts covert actions; and the Directorate of Science and Technology (DS&T) provides technical collection and support for the agency. Each directorate is headed by a deputy director and comprises several smaller offices based on geographic regions, policy issues, or functions.

Today, there are far fewer people working within this enduring structure than during the cold war. According to an experienced CIA observer, the staff, which grew to an estimated 21,000 employees during the Reagan years, is in the process of being downsized to 16,000 employees.[39] This 23 percent reduction is affecting all aspects of the organization—analysts, operatives, and support personnel. While the CIA continues to use college recruiters and may hire a few hundred people each year, it closed its thirteen regional recruitment centers in 1993.[40] Also, one-third of all foreign agents have been eliminated. This dismissal of roughly 1,000 foreign nationals will save the CIA money, but the main motive was to cut ties to individuals who were known criminals or simply incompetent agents.[41]

Reacting to negative internal and external reviews in the aftermath of Aldrich Ames's betrayal, the CIA took steps to restructure its Directorate of Operations (DO). In an effort to reduce the insularity of the clandestine service, the agency instituted a "DO–DI partnership" whereby the two divisions' corresponding geographic subunits interact, coordinate activities, and at times have their personnel work together. Analysts and operatives were placed together in special CIA centers and at stations abroad. Other changes were introduced to assert greater managerial control over the DO, including: new guidelines for hiring foreign agents; accountability boards to assess the suitability of personnel for assignments or continued employment; new evaluation reports by subordinates on their superiors; performance standard teams; and promotions based not on the number of agents recruited but on the quality of intelligence supplied. Last, a new office of personnel security was established to monitor employee performance throughout the entire agency.[42]

### Personnel

Despite the "DO–DI partnership," the CIA continues to have two competing subcultures. On one hand, the Directorate of Intelligence is inhabited by well-educated professionals who value academic knowledge and believe the agency's primary role should be to warn, monitor, and forecast through careful research and analysis. On the other hand, the secretive and patriotic members of the Directorate of Operations see risky endeavors like spying and covert action as the CIA's real contribution to national security. This second subculture is so exclusive, however, it has been characterized as a "fraternity of old boys" that is often too accepting of its own members and too intolerant of oversight. Changing this culture, which has contributed to some troubling episodes (discussed below), has been a priority of recent CIA directors.

One of the most significant developments related to CIA personnel after the cold war has been the decline in morale across all directorates. Employees have had to contend with the loss of their primary intelligence target, staff cuts and, until recently, a no-growth budget. These circumstances, moreover, have been accompanied by several troubling episodes that have created internal embarrassment and a poor public image of the agency. In recent years, it has been reported:

- The CIA passed information from double agents to presidents and policy makers without informing them of the sources.
- Aldrich Ames's betrayal led to the deaths of ten Western agents and the exposure of dozens of CIA operations.
- The agency associated with a Guatemalan colonel implicated in the murder of a U.S. citizen.
- France caught five CIA agents engaged in economic espionage in Paris.
- Female employees, charging sexual harassment and discrimination, won large legal settlements.
- The House Permanent Select Committee concluded the CIA lacks "the analytic depth, breadth and expertise to monitor political, military and economic developments worldwide."[43]

Despite these serious problems and the end of the cold war, there have been no sweeping changes within the CIA. In fact, the Brown Commission disappointed many observers when its final report failed to suggest major organizational reforms.[44]

## The Department of Defense

The disintegration of the Soviet Union, the demise of the Warsaw Pact, and the spread of democracy throughout Eastern Europe have not changed the basic role of the Defense Department. It continues to provide the military forces needed to deter war and protect the security of the United States and its allies. The end of the cold war, however, has altered the department's mission in two ways. On one hand, it has caused the Pentagon to focus on a range of security threats that extend beyond the military capability of the former Soviet Union. The 1997 Quadrennial Defense Review (QDR) initiated by Secretary of Defense William Cohen identified five dangers the U.S. military must guard against: (1) regional dangers—attacks on friendly nations, ethnic conflict, religious wars, and state-sponsored terrorism; (2) weapons of mass destruction including Russian nuclear arms and the global proliferation of biological, chemical, and nuclear weapons; (3) transnational dangers—terrorism, the drug trade, organized crime, and uncontrolled migration; (4) asymmetric attacks—terrorism, information warfare, the use of unconventional weapons, and environmental sabotage; and (5) "wild card" scenarios, such as a new technological threat or the takeover of friendly governments by anti-American factions.[45]

On the other hand, the Pentagon has expanded its mission to include a host of noncombat duties. These endeavors have been undertaken to address issues that have emerged after the cold war, to prevent the rise of future national security problems, and to maintain public support for the department. For instance, the Defense Department has assisted with drug interdiction, a task it initially was reluctant to adopt, using Air Force radar planes, Navy cruisers, and Marine patrols to detect drug-smuggling activities. Additionally, the U.S. military through the Cooperative Threat Reduction Program established by Senators Sam Nunn (D-Ga.) and Richard Lugar (R-Ind.) has helped the former Soviet Union safely dismantle elements of its nuclear arsenal. Another new Pentagon task has involved a major effort to remove toxic and hazardous materials from its military installations. For instance, the Navy has spent $400 million to clear unexploded bombs and artillery shells from the Hawaiian island of Kahoolawe.[46] Last, the Pentagon has implemented defense conversion projects where it assists workers, weapons contractors, and local communities making the transition from a defense-related economy. The Technology Reinvestment Project (TRP), for example, has provided small to medium-size defense contractors with funding to develop technologies with military applications and civilian market potential (e.g., flat-panel screens, computerized shipbuilding, and electric-powered vehicles). Since late 1994, however, Republicans in Congress have resisted devoting large amounts of defense spending to these nontraditional initiatives. They have argued such programs drain funding from critical military needs and, therefore, should be reduced significantly or paid for by other departments.

Republican lawmakers have included other activities in this discussion, such as international peacekeeping, peace enforcement, humanitarian assistance, and disaster relief. These duties, which the Pentagon has always performed, have expanded rapidly in the post–cold war era. No longer considered occasional or peripheral tasks, peacekeeping and humanitarian intervention have been added to the "national military strategy," a document prepared by the Joint Chiefs of Staff.[47] In recent years, U.S. military personnel have served in noncombat roles in places like Bosnia-Herzegovina, Haiti, Rwanda, and Somalia. The Defense Department, however, has been wary about accepting these assignments, because it sees large amounts of its resources (e.g., funding, personnel, equipment, and training time) being diverted from combat readiness.[48]

Responding to this concern and the deaths of eighteen U.S. soldiers in Somalia, the Clinton administration outlined a more selective approach to multilateral peacekeeping operations in Presidential Decision Directive (PDD) 25. The document drafted in May 1994 stated American participation in such interventions was to be contingent upon the evaluation of mission objectives, threats to international peace and security, available resources, and American interests.[49] Whether PDD 25 has actually alleviated the Pentagon's concern over resource constraints is doubtful. Shortly after his confirmation as secretary of defense, William Cohen estimated U.S. military involvement in Bosnia would total $6 billion at a time when the armed forces have pressing readiness and modernization needs.[50]

## Budget

The end of the cold war has not altered two facts about the Defense Department's annual budget. It remains a considerable portion of the total federal budget, roughly 15 percent in FY 1997;[51] and it continues to be far larger than the allocations of the other bureaucracies discussed in this chapter. Whereas the CIA and State Department receive about $3 billion and $2 billion respectively, Congress appropriated $247.7 billion for the Pentagon in FY 1998.[52] Despite these consistencies, the defense budget has changed significantly since the end of the cold war. First, military spending as a percentage of the overall federal budget has declined from a cold war high of 28 percent to 15 percent in FY 1997.[53] Second, defense budget levels have shrunk. In actual dollars, FY 1994 defense appropriations were $240.5 billion or about $10 billion less than in FY 1984.[54] In inflation-adjusted dollars, the average cold war budget (1946–1989) was $304 billion, or $24 billion higher than the average post–cold war budget (1990–2001).[55] Third, weapons procurement funding has fallen more than 70 percent in inflation-adjusted dollars since 1985.[56]

Yet a noted observer of the U.S. defense budget contends such figures have not produced a weaker, less-prepared military. Instead, he writes: "The United States spend[s] . . . three times what any other country on the face of the earth spends, and more than all its prospective enemies and neutral nations combined."[57] Members of Congress, however, appear not to have drawn the same conclusion. In recent years (FY 1996–FY 1998), defense authorization and appropriation acts have exceeded presidential requests by about $4 to $11 billion, with much of the additional funding targeted for weapons procurement. Nevertheless, President Clinton has reluctantly signed these bills, because there is a general consensus among the White House, Congress, and Pentagon that the armed services need to modernize their aging equipment, which was largely acquired during the 1980s defense buildup.

*Structure*

Here, "structure" is interpreted broadly to include employment, organizational divisions, strategic posture, and military installations. In each of these categories, the Defense Department has experienced significant change and continuity in the post–cold war era. With regard to the number of employees, the Pentagon remains the largest federal agency. Recall that the CIA and State Department each employ less than 25,000 people. In contrast, 1.45 million men and women currently serve on active duty in the armed services; another 900,000 individuals participate in the National Guard and Reserves; and roughly 800,000 civilians work throughout the Pentagon. These figures, however, have declined significantly since FY 1989, when there were 2.1 million active duty personnel, 1.2 million members of the National Guard and Reserves, and 1.1 million civilian employees.[58] The active duty reductions, which are expected to continue, have been distributed unevenly across the armed services with the Army suffering the greatest losses.

The Defense Department remains a cabinet agency with six basic divisions (see figure 3.4). First, the secretary of defense heads the department and serves as the chief adviser to the president on defense policy. Second, the Office of Secretary of Defense (OSD) is a large collection of offices responsible for carrying out the tasks of the secretary of defense. Each office is managed by an undersecretary or assistant secretary and performs a different function (e.g., acquisition, operational testing and evaluation, personnel) or oversees a special issue (e.g., regional security, low intensity conflict, NATO affairs). Third, each military service— Army, Navy, and Air Force—is administered and represented by its own department. These separate bureaucracies are led by a civilian service secretary and a military chief of staff. Fourth, the Joint Chiefs of Staff (JCS)—composed of the heads of the three services, the Marine Corps chief of staff, a chairman, and a vice chairman—are supposed to provide strategic planning and promote cooperation and coordination between the services. In addition, the chairman of the JCS is the president's principal military adviser and is supported by a joint staff of military officers. Fifth, the unified combatant commands, which comprise forces from the different services and are led by commanders in chief, are responsible for military missions centered on particular functions or geographic regions. Last, there are a myriad of field activities and Defense-related agencies under the direction of the secretary. Examples include the Defense Intelligence Agency, the Defense Investigative Service, and the National Security Agency.

As a means of simplifying Pentagon management and meeting post–cold war challenges, OSD was completely reorganized in 1993. Former secretary of defense Les Aspin's restructuring initiative, however, was subsequently watered down by his successors, William Perry and William Cohen. Aspin's enduring contributions have been the reduction in the number of administrators reporting directly to the secretary of defense from over twenty to about ten and the creation of department-wide "personnel" and "acquisition" units, which have enhanced the power of the secretary of defense at the expense of the armed services. William Perry continued to limit the number of people with access to the secretary, but he reversed significant organizational changes introduced by his predecessor. For instance, Perry dismantled offices Aspin had established to challenge State Department influence in interagency policy debates (e.g., economic security, democracy and peacekeeping, nuclear security and counterproliferation, and environmental security). He also resurrected the assistant secretaries for international security policy and international security affairs, which Aspin had abolished as cold war relics.[59] Once in office, William Cohen retained the more traditional OSD structure established by Perry. He signaled, however, a commitment to organizational reform when he announced in November 1997 several initiatives to further streamline and economize the Pentagon bureaucracy, including a paper-free electronic procurement system, the acceptance of bids from private contractors to deliver certain services, and the elimination of 30,000 military and civilian administrative positions.[60]

Another area exhibiting both continuity and change is force structure. What is not significantly different from the cold war period or the Bush years is the strategy upon which today's force structure is based. Before 1989, American military posture was designed to fight two and one-half wars simultaneously in Europe and Asia. As the cold war came to a close during the Bush administration, this strategy was altered marginally to a two-war doctrine, where the United States was to have the capacity to fight concurrently two major regional wars in the Middle East and Asia. The logic behind this approach was to deter any potential adversary from starting a conflict while the United States was engaged in another war. When the Clinton administration began, indications were that this strategy would be reformulated to correspond with the defense cuts the new president planned. One proposal considered, for example, was a "win-hold-win strategy" where the United States would

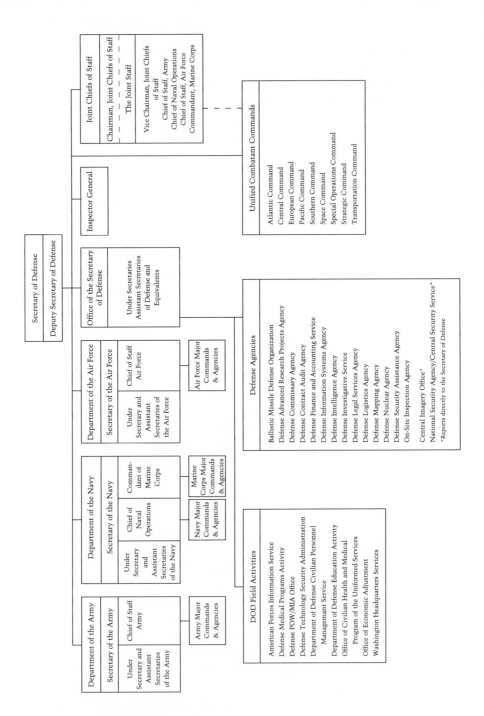

Figure 3.4. The Department of Defense
*Source: U.S. Government Manual 1996/97*

attempt to win a major regional war, hold the line in another, and then fight the second war to win. But to the dismay of many observers, the Pentagon's 1993 "Bottom-Up" and 1997 Quadrennial Defense Reviews ultimately retained the two-war strategy, which, when it was first adopted, was not a significant departure from the cold war approach.

While the two-war strategy has not changed in recent years, the corresponding force structure has shrunk. Before the fall of the Soviet Union, there were 18 active Army divisions, 15 aircraft carrier groups, 546 ships, and 24 active Air Force fighter wings. By FY 1997, active Army divisions stood at 10, aircraft carrier groups declined to 12, Navy ships fell to 128, and active Air Force wings had been cut to 11.[61] This state of affairs has pleased few people. Some observers maintain the current strategy is prudent, but that prevailing budget and force levels are inadequate to sustain it. Others contend the two-war strategy is outdated and in desperate need of revision. The latter viewpoint was embraced by the National Defense Panel, a committee of civilian experts and retired military officers charged by Congress to evaluate how military strategy and forces should be configured in the future. The panel concluded in 1997 that the two-war strategy, instead of corresponding to the real U.S. security environment, is obsolete and little more than "a means of justifying the current force structure—especially for those searching for the certainties of the cold war era."[62]

Finally, the Pentagon has experienced structural change through infrastructure cuts, namely the closing and consolidation of hundreds of military installations in the United States. The Base Realignment and Closure (BRAC) process, initiated in the late 1980s to reflect the post–cold war realities of fewer troops and smaller defense budgets, continued in the first term of the Clinton administration with two significant rounds of base closings. In 1993, thirty-five major and ninety-five minor military facilities were ordered shut while forty-five others received cutbacks.[63] In 1995, seventy-nine closures and twenty-six realignments were recommended by the independent base-closing commission and accepted by the White House and Congress.[64] The underlying logic behind these closings and the earlier rounds of cuts in 1988 and 1991 has remained constant. It was believed the expenditure of hundreds of millions of dollars to close bases, remove environmental hazards, and transfer functions elsewhere would be offset by billions of dollars in long-term savings. Another common feature of the BRAC process has been that a different armed service has suffered each time. The Army was a major target in 1991; the Navy suffered the brunt of the cuts in 1993; and the Air Force was a central focus in 1995. Last, the actual closing of military bases, whether targeted before or during the Clinton administration, has been slower than anticipated. A key reason for delays has been the considerable cost and difficulty of toxic waste removal at many installations.[65]

Despite similarities across the four rounds of base closings, there have been notable differences in the Clinton era. For instance, decisions have been more difficult and painful to arrive at since the easiest choices were made in 1988 and 1991. Also, the number of affected facilities has risen over time, with there being more than twice as many closings in 1995 as there were in 1991.[66] Moreover, the independent commission has increasingly diverged from executive branch proposals. Whereas in 1991 it made no additions to the Defense Department's list and offered reprieves to four facilities, the base-closing commission identified installations in 1993 and 1995 that the Pentagon and President Clinton had preferred to keep operational.[67] In the 1997 Quadrennial Defense Review, the Clinton administration proposed two additional rounds of base closures as a way to free up money for weapons procurement. But Congress resisted the plan, fearing the effect it would have on local economies and political fortunes.

*Personnel*
Regardless of which armed service is under discussion, military personnel continue to share some common attributes that contribute to a Defense Department subculture. In particular, career officers tend to have a deep sense of duty and patriotism, a strong desire to avoid another Vietnam-type war, and fairly conservative political and social values. Of these qualities, conservatism has shaped the status of two personnel issues related to diversity in the armed forces. Instead of initiating significant changes related to homosexuals in the military and women in combat, the Pentagon has been forced by elected officials to tolerate shifts in long-standing practices.

For the last few years, the Defense Department has carried out a new "don't ask, don't tell policy," where personnel can no longer be questioned about their sexual orientation but can be dismissed if they openly acknowledge their homosexuality or an investigation by a commander reveals evidence of a homosexual act. This policy was forged by the White House and Congress in July 1993 after there was strong military opposition to President Clinton's plan to lift the ban on gays in the armed forces. In opposing the president's initiative, military leaders argued publicly that the service of openly gay men and women would damage units' cohesiveness and effectiveness. It is likely, however, this stance was motivated partly by the Pentagon's conservative subculture. That is, most conservative individuals are simply less tolerant of homosexuality.

Such a subculture would also be less supportive of women performing traditionally male-dominated tasks, particularly if those duties carry the risk of death. This sentiment may explain why some military officials were displeased by two changes instituted by the late Les Aspin. In 1993, the former secretary of defense issued an order allowing women for the first time to serve on combat aircraft crews and surface warships. The decision proved particularly challenging for the Navy. Ships needed to be reconfigured to accommodate living quarters and bathrooms for women; and the concerns of fleet personnel and their spouses had to be addressed in seminars. A year later, Aspin instituted another significant change related to women in the armed forces. He opened thousands of combat support jobs in the Army and Marine Corps to U.S. servicewomen by stating they could not be excluded on the basis of risk. As a result, women were only technically barred from military units involved in direct ground combat.[68]

With more women serving in the military and in closer environments, the armed forces will be under increasing pressure to rid its ranks of sexual harassment and abuse. As of late 1997, the Navy was still attempting to repair its image in the aftermath of the 1991 Tailhook scandal where women were assaulted by male aviators at a naval convention; and several Army commissioned and noncommissioned officers (including the Army's highest-ranking enlisted soldier) faced allegations or convictions related to sexual misconduct, including the rape, assault, and maltreatment of female subordinates. The central focus of the Army's difficulties began in November 1996 when male drill instructors were accused of assaulting female recruits at training centers. While Pentagon leaders have moved swiftly to address the problem with structural changes in living quarters and calls for more female drill instructors, they have resisted proposals to separate men and women for much of basic training.

### Conclusion

This chapter illustrates the difficulty of summarizing or drawing conclusions about the foreign policy bureaucracy in the post–cold war era. To say, for instance, that the end of the cold war has led to organizational change within the agencies under discussion would be correct. It also would be a simplification, since domestic factors unrelated to the disintegration of the Soviet Union and the demise of communism have prompted bureaucratic adaptation. Examples of such factors have been an increasingly conservative agenda on Capitol Hill, the revelation of Aldrich Ames's betrayal, and efforts by the Clinton administration to diversify the federal workforce. Furthermore, institutional changes have not emanated solely from the bureaucracies, but have been directed by the White House and Congress, which are particularly sensitive to societal attitudes about the diminishing importance of foreign affairs and the need to address economic priorities and domestic problems. Also, it is important to recognize that organizational change has varied across the bureaucracies. Besides the CIA being less willing than the Pentagon and State Department to adjust to new realities, each agency has been affected differently in terms of its role, budget, structure, and personnel. Last, the developments discussed in this chapter are the beginning of a process of adaptation that will continue for several years.

Despite obstacles to conclusive findings, common patterns regarding the impact of the post–cold war era on the foreign policy bureaucracy have emerged. First, the responsibilities of each agency have become more diverse and complex. Instead of the former Soviet Union and containment policy as the primary focus, the State Department, the CIA, and the Pentagon have shifted their attention to a wide array of transnational issues with domestic implications. Second, the three organizations have been forced to operate in an environment marked by serious fiscal constraints. Each institution has faced (albeit in varying degrees) a shrinking budget, the loss of personnel, and infrastructure cuts. The commitment of both political parties to balance the federal budget will make resource limitations a permanent reality for the foreign policy bureaucracy. Third, the institutions under study have increasingly struggled with diversity issues as their employee bases have become more representative of the general population. The gender-equity lawsuits in the State Department, the charges of sexual harassment in the CIA and Pentagon, and the higher number of military discharges since the adoption of the "don't ask, don't tell" policy[69] illustrate that the foreign policy bureaucracy has not been successful at integrating its ranks. This fact is troubling, since the trends toward greater diversity within the United States and the federal workforce will increase considerably in the next century. Last, the many references in this chapter to budgets, directives, laws, and policy changes indicate that the foreign policy bureaucracy has experienced increased attempts by the White House and the Congress to shape and control it in the post–cold war era. State, CIA, and Defense will continue to be responsive to such efforts as these agencies scramble to demonstrate continued relevance and maintain dwindling resources.

What might these developments mean for policy making? One possibility is that it will become more difficult for the bureaucracy to conduct effective foreign policy as the international environment creates more challenges and the domestic arena presents more constraints. There is no guarantee that elected officials will be able to strike a sound balance between fiscal responsibility and meeting the demands of an increasingly complex and interdependent world. For example, Secretary of Defense William Cohen has expressed concern over the lack of funding available for force modernization and weapons procurement; and Secretary of State Madeleine Albright heads a department where key officials have complained that the United States is endangering its international interests by conducting "foreign policy on the cheap."[70] Another possible implication for future policy making is heightened bureaucratic rivalry. Besides competing for finite budgetary resources, the State Department, the CIA, and the Pentagon have sought new responsibilities in many of the same areas. The potential for conflict over these issues may be exacerbated by differences in the agencies' roles, conceptions of national security, and policy views, as well as the ambiguity surrounding jurisdictions. Also, bureaucratic politics may arise as State, CIA, and Defense become more active and assertive in policy areas traditionally controlled by domestic agencies, and as departments, such as Justice, Treasury, Transportation, and Health and Human Services, become increasingly active overseas. Relatedly, it is important to raise questions about the foreign policy bureaucracy's capacity to offer expertise in areas like law enforcement, trade, and the environment, where until recently it has had little or no involvement.

Finally, a few words are in order about the future influence of specific actors. The State Department would appear to be well positioned to expand its influence. Yet its adaptability, global presence, and control over diplomacy, a critical soft power resource in the post–cold war era, will be overshadowed by its traditional deficiencies: limited financial resources, a small domestic constituency, a cautious Foreign Service culture, and presidential contempt. While the White House and Congress have protected the CIA from major budget cuts and reforms, its capacity to behave as an influential actor is less than certain. A number of troubling episodes have left Director of Central Intelligence George Tenet to preside over an agency devastated by low employee morale and a worsening public image. These difficulties have been compounded by the high rate of turnover among recent CIA directors, who have not enjoyed close working relationships with the president. Last, the Defense Department's recent decline in resources will not diminish its perennial power. It remains a large, politically adept bureaucracy with strong public backing. Whereas most Americans do not care about the State Department or comprehend the CIA, they have a clear understanding of the Pentagon's critical role and its capacity to bring tangible benefits to local communities. Thus, the relative influence of the State Department, Central Intelligence Agency, and Defense Department will remain largely the same in a new era marked by important changes in bureaucratic roles, budgets, structures, and personnel.

## Notes

1 Thomas Friedman, "Cold War Without End," *New York Times Magazine,* August 22, 1993, pp. 28–30, 45.

2 See Max Weber, *The Theory of Social and Economic Organization* (New York: Oxford University Press, 1947).

3 See Terry M. Moe, "The New Economics of Organization," *American Journal of Political Science* 20 (November 1984): 734–749; B. Dan Wood, "Principals, Agents, and Responsiveness in Clean Air Enforcements," *American Political Science Review* 82 (March 1988): 213–234; B. Dan Wood and Richard W. Waterman, "The Dynamics of Political Control of the Bureaucracy," *American Political Science Review* 85 (September 1991): 801–828; and James M. Lindsay, "Congress, Foreign Policy, and the New Institutionalism," *International Studies Quarterly* 38 (June 1994): 281–304.

4 See Graham T. Allison, *Essence of Decision: Explaining the Cuban Missile Crisis* (Boston, Mass.: Little, Brown, 1971); Graham T. Allison and Morton H. Halperin, "Bureaucratic Politics: A Paradigm and Some Policy Implications," *World Politics* 24 (Spring Supplement 1972): 40–80; and Morton H. Halperin, *Bureaucratic Politics and Foreign Policy* (Washington, D.C.: Brookings Institution, 1974).

5 U.S. Department of State, "FY 1994 International Affairs Budget: Promoting Peace, Prosperity, and Democracy," *U.S. Department of State Dispatch Supplement* 4 (April 1993): 2.

6 See Richard M. Moose, "Foreign Policy Challenges in a Changing World," *U.S. Department of State Dispatch* 7 (June 1996): 309; and Tim Weiner, "U.S. Seizes Suspect in Killing of 2 C.I.A. Officers," *New York Times,* June 18, 1997, pp. A1, A6.

7 Thomas L. Friedman, "Foreign-Aid Agency Shifts to Problems Back Home," *New York Times,* June 26, 1994, pp. 1, 18.

8 See Jeff Johnson, "A New 'Green' Direction for U.S. State Department," *Environmental Science and Technology* 30 (1996): 246A; Madeleine K. Albright, "Earth Day 1997," *U.S. Department of State Dispatch* 8 (March/April 1997): 35–36; and Reuters, "Gore Introduces a 'Greener' Foreign Policy," *New York Times,* April 23, 1997, p. A3.

9 See Warren Christopher, "Budget Priorities for Shaping a New Foreign Policy

(Statement before the Subcommittee on Commerce, Justice, State and Judiciary of the House Appropriations Committee)," *U.S. Department of State Dispatch* 4 (March 1993): 138.

10 The Commerce Department has its FCS officers at sixty-seven posts abroad, leaving the State Department effectively in charge of trade promotion at more than two hundred other posts. See Joan E. Spero, "The International Economic Agenda and the State Department's Role," *U.S. Department of State Dispatch* 5 (March 1994): 124.

11 Craig Johnstone, "Foreign Policy on the Cheap: You Get What You Pay For," *U.S. Department of State Dispatch* 7 (March 1996): 146.

12 Monteagle Stearns, *Talking to Strangers: Improving American Diplomacy at Home and Abroad* (Princeton, N.J.: Princeton University Press, 1996), p. 92.

13 This statement is based on foreign assistance as a percentage of the Gross National Product (GNP). U.S. Department of State Bureau of Public Affairs, "An International Affairs Budget—A Sound Investment in Global Leadership: Questions and Answers," *U.S. Department of State Dispatch* 6 (October 1995): 748.

14 Joshua Muravchik, "Affording Foreign Policy," *Foreign Affairs* 75 (March/April 1996): 8.

15 See Casimir A. Yost and Mary Locke, *U.S. Foreign Affairs Resources: Budget Cuts and Consequences* (Washington, D.C.: Institute for the Study of Diplomacy, Georgetown University, 1996), p. 6.

16 Warren Christopher, "Investing in American Leadership," *U.S. Department of State Dispatch* 8 (January 1997): 3.

17 See Carroll J. Doherty, "New Drive to Overhaul Aid Faces Perennial Obstacle," *Congressional Quarterly Weekly Report* 52 (January 1994): 75.

18 See Muravchik, "Affording Foreign Policy," 8–10.

19 As of December 1996, there were 4,353 Foreign Service "generalists" (e.g., political, economic, or administrative officers) and 3,620 "specialists" (e.g., doctors, security personnel, information officers). The remainder of the department's employees were support personnel, many of whom were foreign nationals serving in U.S. embassies abroad. Bureau of Personnel, U.S. Department of State, telephone conversation with author, September 3, 1997.

20 See U.S. Department of State, Office of Management Task Force, "State 2000: A New Model for Managing Foreign Affairs," *Report of the U.S. Department of State Management Task Force* (December 1992), U.S. State Department Publication 10029; and "Special Report: Policymaking for a New Era," *Foreign Affairs* 72 (Winter 1992/93): 175–189. The second report was cosponsored by the Carnegie Endowment for International Peace and the Institute for International Economics.

21 See Warren Christopher, "Department of State Reorganization," *U.S. Department of State Dispatch* (February 1993): 69–73; and Bureau of Public Affairs, "The U.S. Department of State: Structure and Organization," *U.S. Department of State Dispatch Supplement* 6 (May 1995): 1–9.

22 Bill Duffy, Management Policy and Planning, U.S. Department of State, "Post Openings, Closings, and Status Changes," personal correspondence, February 7, 1997, p. 3.

23  U.S. Department of State, "An International Affairs Budget," 747; and Madeleine K. Albright, "Maintaining America's Strategic Interests," *U.S. Department of State Dispatch* 8 (March/April 1997): 12.

24  Yost and Locke, "U.S. Affairs Resources," p. 14.

25  Anne Stevenson-Yang, "Anatomy of an Officer Corps: The Foreign Service in the 1990s," *Foreign Service Journal* 70 (March 1993): 26, 31.

26  Stevenson Yang 1993, 31 and Thomas W. Lippman, "State Dept. Settles Bias Suit," *Washington Post,* April 5, 1996, p. A20.

27  Steven Greenhouse, "Clinton Is Faulted on Political Choices for Envoy Posts," *New York Times,* April 13, 1994, A15; and Yvonne Jackson, presidential appointments staff, U.S. Department of State, "List of Chiefs of Mission," personal correspondence, February 7, 1997, p. 21.

28  See Joseph Finder, "Spy vs. Spy," *New Republic,* April 8, 1996, pp. 18–21.

29  For a detailed overview of the historical antagonism and conflict between the CIA and FBI, see Mark Riebling, *Wedge: The Secret War between the FBI and CIA* (New York: Alfred A. Knopf, 1994).

30  Office of the Press Secretary, the White House, *Statement by the Press Secretary on U.S. Counterintelligence Effectiveness,* May 3, 1994; and U.S. Congress, *Counterintelligence and Security Enhancement Act of 1994,* 103d Cong., 2d Sess., S. 2056.

31  See David Johnston, "U.S. Case Sets Out 2-Year Betrayal by C.I.A. Official," *New York Times,* November 11, 1996, pp. A1, A12.

32  For a discussion of this White House document, see Walter Pincus, "Control Tightened on Spy Agencies," *Washington Post,* March 10, 1995, pp. A1, A24.

33  Tim Weiner, "The C.I.A. Seeks Out Informers on Terrorism, and Finds Them," *New York Times,* September 6, 1996, p. A2.

34  Tim Weiner, "For First Time, U.S. Discloses Budget on Spying: $26.6 Billion," *New York Times,* October 16, 1997, p. A7.

35  Tim Weiner, "$28 Billion Spying Budget Is Made Public by Mistake," *New York Times,* November 5, 1994, p. 54.

36  See R. James Woolsey, "To the Editor: Cuts in Intelligence Budget Stay on Schedule," *New York Times,* March 25, 1993, p. A22; and Gregory J. Bowens, "Clinton Accepts Budget Freeze, Vows to Fight Deeper Cuts," *Congressional Quarterly Weekly Report* 51 (July 1993): 2077.

37  See Gregory J. Bowens, "Budget Freeze Approved; Security Oath Dropped," *Congressional Quarterly Weekly Report* 51 (November 1993): 3280; Bob Benenson, "Committee Spares Budget Knife Despite Anger over Spy Case," *Congressional Quarterly Weekly Report* 52 (April 1994): 1082; and Donna Cassata, "Spy Budget Cleared for Clinton; Plan for New Agency Curbed," *Congressional Quarterly Weekly Report* 53 (December 1995): 3894.

38  See Juliana Gruenwald, "Bill to Fund Spy Agencies Wins Final Passage," *Congressional Quarterly Weekly Report* 55 (November 1997): 2782.

39  Jeffrey T. Richelson quoted in Donna Cassata, "Congress Jumps to CIA's Aid in Its Quest for Identity," *Congressional Quarterly Weekly Report* 53 (January 1995): 43.

40  See Tim Weiner, "It's Back to the Campuses for the C.I.A.'s Recruiters," *New York Times,* May 14, 1996, p. A18.

41 See "The C.I.A. Cleanses Itself," *New York Times,* March 4, 1997, p. A14; and Tim Weiner, "Easy Going for Nominee to the C.I.A.," *New York Times,* May 7, 1997, p. A17.

42 Ronald J. Ostrow, "CIA Chief Tells of Efforts to Reshape Clandestine Service," *Los Angeles Times,* October 7, 1994, p. A22; Richard A. Serrano, "Woolsey Walks Away after Turning CIA down Road to Change," *Los Angeles Times,* December 29, 1994, pp. A12–13; and James Risen, "CIA to Issue Guidelines on Hiring Foreign Operatives," *Los Angeles Times,* June 20, 1995, p. A4.

43 See Tim Weiner, "House Panel Says C.I.A. Lacks Expertise to Carry Out Its Duties," *New York Times,* June 19, 1997, p. A13.

44 The commission, led by former Secretary of Defense Harold Brown of the Carter administration, issued its review and a conservative set of recommendations in early 1996. See Report of the Commission on the Roles and Capabilities of the United States Intelligence Community, *Preparing for the 21st Century: An Appraisal of U.S. Intelligence,* Washington, D.C.: U.S. Government Printing Office, March 1, 1996.

45 See William S. Cohen, *Report of the Quadrennial Defense Review* (Washington, D.C.: U.S. Department of Defense, May 1997), sec. 2.

46 Pat Towell, "Aloha, Bombs," *Congressional Quarterly Weekly Report* 51 (November 1993): 3137.

47 Bradley Graham, "Responsibilities of U.S. Military Expanded," *New York Times,* March 9, 1995, p. A36.

48 See Art Pine, "Pentagon Says 5 Army Divisions Not at the Ready," *Los Angeles Times,* November 16, 1994, pp. A18–19; and Bradley Graham, "Pentagon Seeks $2.6 Billion Emergency Funding to Preserve Force Readiness," *Washington Post,* January 20, 1995, p. A12.

49 See Madeleine K. Albright, "The Clinton Administration's Policy on Reforming Multilateral Peace Operations," *U.S. Department of State Dispatch* 5 (May 1994): 315–321.

50 See Clifford Krauss, "Pentagon Chief Faces Critics in Arguing the Military's Budget," *New York Times,* February 13, 1996, p. A12; and Clifford Krauss, "Pentagon Priority Remains Readiness over New Arms," *New York Times,* January 28, 1997, p. A8.

51 See Cohen, *Report of Quadrennial Defense Review,* "The Secretary's Message."

52 "Special Report: With Tone, Tenor of First Session, It Seemed Like Old Times," *Congressional Quarterly Weekly Report* 55 (December 1997): 2979.

53 See Cohen, *Report of Quadrennial Defense Review,* "Secretary's Message."

54 Pat Towell, "Congress OKs Most Funding for Reagan Defense Buildup," *Congressional Quarterly Weekly Report* 41 (November 1983): 2513; and Pat Towell, "Military Gets 2.2% Pay Raise; R&D Funding Is Trimmed," *Congressional Quarterly Weekly Report* 51 (November 1993): 3135.

55 These figures from the Defense Budget Project are based on 1996 dollars. The post–cold war average includes projections for 1996–2001. Mark Thompson, "Why the Pentagon Gets a Free Ride," *Time,* June 5, 1995, p. 26.

56 Pat Towell, "Perry Cites Readiness as Top Priority . . . And Modernization as Long-Term Goal," *Congressional Quarterly Weekly Report* 54 (March 1996): 628.

57 Lawrence J. Korb, "Our Overstuffed Armed Forces," *Foreign Affairs* 74 (November/December 1995): 23.

58 Cohen, *Report of the Quadrennial Defense Review*, sec. 5.

59 For a complete overview of OSD's structure, see Directorate for Organizational and Management Planning, Office of Secretary of Defense, "Department of Defense Key Personnel Locator," September 1996, distributed to the author by OSD Public Affairs.

60 Pat Towell, "Cohen Unveils Cost-Cutting Plan to Raise Money for Weapons," *Congressional Quarterly Weekly Report* 55 (November 1997): 2864.

61 Cohen, *Report of the Quadrennial Defense Review*, sec. 5.

62 Quoted in Tim Weiner, "Two-War Strategy Is Obsolete, Panel of Experts Says," *New York Times*, December 2, 1997, p. A16; also see Pat Towell, "Commission Urges Pentagon to Think Futuristically," *Congressional Quarterly Weekly Report* 55 (December 1997): 3036–3037.

63 See Elizabeth A. Palmer, "Megaports to Keep Navy Afloat as Other Facilities Close," *Congressional Quarterly Weekly Report* 51 (July 1993): 1755; and Elizabeth A. Palmer, "Senate Declines to Block List, Dooming Military Facilities," *Congressional Quarterly Weekly Report* 51 (September 1993): 2574.

64 Donna Cassata, "Angry Clinton Accepts List, Seeks to Privatize Jobs," *Congressional Quarterly Weekly Report* 53 (July 1995): 2086; and "House Votes to Accept Base-Closing List," *Congressional Quarterly Weekly Report* 53 (September 1995): 2734.

65 See Elizabeth A. Palmer, "Pollution Clogs the Transfer of Land to Civilian Uses," *Congressional Quarterly Weekly Report* 51 (March 1993): 770–771; and Art Pine, "Pentagon Faces a Sharp New Cutback in Bases," *Los Angeles Times*, December 5, 1994, p. A14.

66 There were thirty-four base closings ordered in 1991. Eric Schmitt, "Aspin Is Preparing List for New Set of Base Closings," *New York Times*, March 7, 1993, p. 22.

67 See Elizabeth A. Palmer, "Aspin's Passes Along Unpopular Task as Panel Begins Base Hearings," *Congressional Quarterly Weekly Report* 51 (March 1993): 679; Elizabeth A. Palmer, "Commission Delivers on Promise Not to Be 'Rubber Stamp,'" *Congressional Quarterly Weekly Report* 51 (June 1993): 1674–1675; and Donna Cassata, "Commission Expands List of Facilities to Be Cut," *Congressional Quarterly Weekly Report* 53 (May 1995): 1339–1341.

68 John Lancaster, "Aspin Eases Combat Policy," *Washington Post*, January 13, 1994, pp. A1, A7.

69 See Philip Shenon, "New Study Faults Pentagon's Gay Policy," *New York Times*, February 26, 1997, p. A8.

70 See Johnstone, "Foreign Policy on the Cheap"; and Warren Christopher, "Foreign Affairs Budget: Our Foreign Policy Cannot Be Supported on the Cheap," *U.S. Department of State Dispatch* 6 (April 1996): 285–296.

# 4.

## Foreign Economic Policy Making under Bill Clinton

*I. M. Destler*

The year 1991 witnessed the definitive end to the cold war through the demise of the Soviet Union.[1] The following year brought economic issues to the center of the American foreign policy stage. In January 1992, President George Bush visited Japan, on a trip first postponed and then recast from a standard geopolitical journey to a sales mission for U.S. exports. But this and subsequent Bush efforts failed to recapture the initiative on the economic issues, which were now central to U.S. politics. Instead, that initiative fell to Arkansas governor Bill Clinton, whose presidential campaign symbol became the famous sign at its Little Rock, Arkansas, headquarters, "It's the economy, stupid," and to independent candidate Ross Perot, who shone his spotlight on the federal budget deficit.

During his campaign, Clinton expressed a determination to "elevate economics in foreign policy." Once it was over, Clinton moved "to focus like a laser beam on the economy," as he expressed it on ABC's *Nightline* one day after the election, noting on that same program that he had taken a day to return congratulatory phone calls from foreign leaders. He named his team of senior economic officials in early December, before his foreign policy team. And once inaugurated, he showed far more interest in economic issues than in the strategic diplomacy that had so engaged his predecessor.

### Pre-1992: The Rise of the Economic Complex

In the manner of previous administrations, Clinton and his associates tended to treat his particular priority as a radical departure in Washington governance. In fact, it was the culmination and reinforcement of a trend more than two decades old: toward greater priority to economic issues in U.S. international dealings, and greater autonomy for economic goals vis-à-vis traditional foreign policy concerns. This was reflected in a stronger international role for those executive branch agencies which comprised the "economic complex."[2]

In the early postwar years, U.S. foreign economic policy was largely subservient to national security goals, above all the buttressing of the "free world" coalition to contain the Soviet Union. This priority was reflected in the locus of institutional power. Under Secretary of State Douglas Dillon directed U.S. foreign economic policy in the second Eisenhower administration, and the National Security Council coordinated international economic issues through the 1960s.

Even in this era of overriding U.S. economic primacy, this priority did not go unchallenged. Congressional leaders complained that the State Department neither understood nor represented U.S. economic interests. In 1962, they forced President John F. Kennedy to establish a trade-coordinating office in the White House as a precondition for launching a major new round of trade negotiations. A bigger change came in 1971, however, when President Richard M. Nixon abandoned support of the dollar in international markets rather than take steps that would have depressed the U.S. economy. His secretary of the treasury, John Connally, shook up long-standing allies by demanding painful foreign concessions to U.S. economic interests.

From that time onward, the connections grew between domestic and international economic policy. The White House trade office was transformed: from a special trade representative (STR) with modest staff and limited jurisdiction, to the much larger office of the U.S. trade representative (USTR) with a broad mandate to lead and coordinate all U.S. trade negotiations.[3] The office grew progressively more responsive to Congress, and to domestic economic interests. It was led by a series of talented policy/political professionals: Robert Strauss under President Jimmy Carter; William Brock and Clayton Yeutter under Ronald Reagan; and Carla Hills under George Bush. By 1992, there were also three deputy USTRs with ambassadorial rank, and a staff of about 160 in Washington and Geneva. The office possessed a particularly strong congressional mandate, reflected in successive trade statutes and in the strong informal ties its staff maintained with the key trade committees. And from 1985 onward, the Office of the USTR was aggressive in demanding that trading partners open their markets to U.S. products, notwithstanding the strain this frequently caused in bilateral relationships—particularly in East Asia.

Also increasing its international activity over this period was a much older federal agency, the Department of Commerce (DOC). Its leaders had failed in repeated efforts to win primary jurisdiction over U.S. trade policy. But the trade policy reorganization of 1980 had declared Commerce "the focus of nonagricultural operational trade responsibilities."[4] Transferred to Commerce from Treasury was the authority to administer antidumping and countervailing duty laws, and from state official jurisdiction over commercial attachés. And the Bush administration saw an enlargement in the budget and effectiveness of the Commerce Department's U.S. and Foreign Commercial Service, the agency charged with linking domestic businesses with export opportunities.

The agency that best reflected the rise of the economic complex, however, was the Department of the Treasury. It had long been considered one of the most prestigious Cabinet departments, and its international authority grew during the 1970s and 1980s. Exchange rate policy was important under the new regime of floating currencies, and Treasury (in collaboration with the Federal Reserve Board) monopolized this sphere within the executive branch. Development finance was increasingly provided through the international financial institutions, and Treasury was the executive branch agent dealing with them. So it was also when Third World nations faced debt crises, or the more general need to strengthen their financial and macroeconomic policies. Secretaries like John Connally and George Shultz under Nixon and James Baker under Reagan had dominated international economic policy in prior administrations.

Treasury's international role was strengthened by its domestic policy base—it had authority over tax policy. Its head, moreover, was by convention chair of the troika, the three officials most responsible for advising presidents on U.S. macroeconomic policy. The second of these was the Office of Management and Budget (OMB), responsible for overseeing federal spending. With a staff numbering around six hundred, OMB was by far the largest unit in the Executive Office of the President, and strong directors like Reagan's David Stockman and Bush's Richard Darman had wielded enormous influence over U.S. economic policy. Last and least among the troika agencies was the Council of Economic Advisers (CEA), established by the Employment Act of 1946 to provide the best economic advice to the president (and help avert a repeat of the Great Depression of the 1930s). The CEA had traditionally attracted some of the nation's best policy economists, and council chairs like Walter Heller under John F. Kennedy and Charles Schultze under Carter had exercised influence substantially exceeding their agency's modest power base.

The impact of this economic complex on U.S. international economic policy had been growing long before the end of the cold war. It was buttressed by the advocacy of business groups, concern over the erosion of America's global economic position, and insistence by key members of Congress that U.S. trade interests not be sacrificed on the altar of national security policy. The main institutional loser with the Department of State, which continued to be involved across a range of economic issues, but whose primary jurisdiction had been trimmed to a small number of issues—commercial aviation being perhaps the most important. The National Security Council (NSC) had also lost influence in this sphere.

As long as the cold war persisted, however, the influence of the economic complex was a function of whether economic issues could be *insulated* from security concerns. With a strong Treasury Department, with an increasingly assertive Office of the USTR, and with assertive external constituencies, this was often possible. But national security concerns retained primacy—they engaged presidents the most. As William Hyland wrote, with only modest exaggeration, "in almost every instance where there was a clash in priorities between economic policy and national security, the latter prevailed."[5]

But the fall of the Berlin Wall in 1989 and the disintegration of the Soviet Union in 1991 led to questioning of this primacy at its core. George Bush was slow to recognize this fundamental shift in the policy terrain. Indeed, with his bent toward national security action and economic *in*action, he had come to symbolize the failure to recognize the new urgency of U.S. economic interests. So the door was open for Clinton to make his mark and claim ample credit for doing so.

### Taking Charge: Establishing the National Economic Council

Clinton's declared means for shifting priorities was a new White House staff institution: the National Economic Council (NEC). Prominent among his December economic appointees was the Wall Street impresario, Robert E. Rubin, who was named to direct it. His January 25, 1993, executive order creating the NEC called for it "to coordinate the economic policy-making process with respect to domestic and international economic issues." Before that year was out, the NEC would play an important role in global and regional trade negotiations, and in the new administration's vocal campaign to open markets in Japan.

The institutional idea was not quite as new as Clinton implied. Every president from Nixon onward had established some sort of Cabinet-level economic council with a mandate to lead on international economic policy and to link it to the domestic economy. Some were relatively effective: Nixon's Council on Economic Policy led by then Secretary of the Treasury Shultz; Gerald Ford's Economic Policy Board; and the Economic Policy Council led by then Treasury Secretary Baker in the second administration of Ronald Reagan. All reflected the growing interdependence between national and global economies, and the resulting policy and political need for Washington decision making to connect the two.

Still, as I have written elsewhere, "No newly elected president had launched a broad-purpose, policy-staff operation in his area of highest substantive priority since Nixon had mandated transformation of the NSC under Henry Kissinger in 1969."[6] And few had explicitly drawn a parallel with the long-established National *Security* Council (NSC), which had carved out a strong role on overall U.S. foreign policy making in successive administrations.

The National Economic Council followed the standard form of such entities—a formal, Cabinet-level membership representing the executive departments and agencies engaged in issues within its jurisdiction; a staff, headed by a senior White House aide (Rubin in this case) responsible for making policy coordination a reality. And the council's formal membership reflected the enormous number of agencies with economic policy interests: ten Cabinet secretaries and administrators of operating agencies; six heads of presidential staffs. Some of them were just marginal players—departments like Transportation and Housing and Urban Development come to mind. But at least half represented the core agencies of the economic complex, and some had overlapping policy coordination roles. Clinton had, in general, appointed strong personalities to head these agencies also. The initial problem for Rubin and the NEC, therefore, was how to establish a clear and effective role within this crowded institutional terrain.

Most important was the Department of the Treasury, with key authority over international finance and tax policy. Treasury was accustomed to leading, not following, on economic issues. Clinton's first treasury secretary, Lloyd Bentsen, brought economic experience and prestige unequaled in the administration from his six years as chairman of the Senate Committee on Finance. Another challenge for the NEC was the Office of the USTR. The president's designee as U.S. trade representative, Mickey Kantor, was a longtime "f.o.b." (friend of Bill) who would strengthen that relationship through his service in the trade post.

Three long-standing presidential staff agencies also had roles that overlapped that of their new White House neighbor. The NSC, established in 1947, had long been the president's primary coordinator of international issues. It had not been central to foreign economic matters since the 1960s, but it had played a role, one that deputy national security assistant Samuel (Sandy) Berger, a Washington trade lawyer and another longstanding f.o.b., was determined to maintain. There was also the Council of Economic Advisers, whose new chair, Laura Tyson, could not fail to be concerned about creation of a second "economic council" whose head would inevitably compete as conveyer of economic issues and ideas to the president. And the new director of the Office of Management and Budget, former House Budget Committee chair Leon Panetta, saw himself as playing the leading role in the central economic issue for his agency *and* the administration — trimming the huge federal budget deficit.

Beyond the five agencies with credible claims to policy leadership were others who might well resist being led. In particular, the Departments of Commerce and Labor looked to be stronger than usual with Ron Brown and Robert Reich at their helms. In fact, Ron Brown assumed the leadership of the Cabinet-level Trade Promotion Coordinating Committee. Through the TPCC, the Commerce Department played the principal role in the development of a National Export Strategy in 1993, part of which involved a focus on a number of "big emerging markets" for U.S. market access and export promotion. This base clearly provided Commerce with a claim to international economic policy leadership in this sphere, and the department (especially its International Trade Administration) implemented most of the actions set forth in the National Export Strategy.

Last but certainly not least, there was the president himself. Clinton seemed to want a strong NEC, but he also valued a free-wheeling personal role, probing issues in depth and revisiting them with advisers outside the NEC and its agencies: Vice President Al Gore and senior political aide George Stephanopolous, to name just two. And though his style thus invited advisers to go around the system and get to him personally, he made it clear early on that he wanted harmony, not conflict, within his senior team.

How then could the new NEC carve out a strong role for itself, without clashing with Clinton's *modus operandi* and without picking fights that he didn't want with every other economic agency of consequence? For unlike Kissinger's NSC in 1969, the NEC had no presidential mandate to dominate and direct policy, or to shut out other agencies from key decisions.

Faced with these circumstances, Rubin decided early on that his NEC would not present itself as policy "czar" or competitor to other agencies, but rather as *facilitator*. It would see to it that they got to play their proper roles in the policy process. The NEC would operate as a service agency—to the president first and foremost, of course, but to many others as well. This role concept reflected Clinton's preference, but also NEC leaders' prior experience. Rubin had excelled as low-key manager of Goldman Sachs. Deputy Assistant Bowman (Bo) Cutter, who assumed primary responsibility for running the staff and the interagency deputies process, had been a senior official with Cooper and Lybrand. Sylvia Mathews, who quickly became Rubin's de facto chief of staff, joined the NEC from a position with McKinsey and Company. Mathews had also served as number two to campaign economic policy director Gene Sperling, who himself became the other deputy NEC assistant.

In particular, the emphasis on facilitation and service meant deference to Treasury's Bentsen, and Rubin courted him assiduously, aided by their long-standing professional and personal relationship—among other things, Rubin had managed Bentsen's blind trust at Goldman Sachs. Vis-à-vis the USTR Office, the NEC did become deeply involved in trade and did take over most of the policy coordination role, but typically deferred to Kantor and his deputies on the management of specific negotiations. To minimize conflict with the NSC, Rubin and Cutter negotiated an arrangement with Berger and his boss, national security assistant Anthony Lake, under which the two organizations would share one joint international economic policy staff.[7] Rubin also assuaged the concerns of Tyson at CEA by promising he would keep his staff relatively small, compared to the one-hundred-plus NSC, that he would recruit mainly noneconomists, and that he would employ the facilitation role to improve CEA access to actual decision making.

The NEC approach was first made manifest on budget policy, the issue that dominated the first half of 1993. Rubin took on responsibility for organizing the development of the administration's deficit-reduction plan, allocating responsibilities among Clinton's designees in December and orchestrating a six-hour Little Rock meeting with the president and the vice president in early January. He worked intensively with members of the senior economic team in advance of that meeting to assure that each would present clear proposals and stay on her/his agreed topic. But he distributed responsibilities widely among these future Cabinet and sub-Cabinet and White House aides. And he gave himself no specific substantive role other than moving the meeting along and clarifying points of agreement and disagreement. When it went well, Rubin had established two things: his role as central process manager for economic policy, and his readiness to reinforce others in their areas of responsibility.[8] (The NEC staff never sought to duplicate the budgetary expertise of OMB, for example.) Rubin's role carried on into daily White House meetings in January and February 1993 to put the economic program in final shape, and in fact throughout Rubin's tenure in the NEC position.

### Clinton Foreign Economic Policy Making in Practice, 1993–1994

The budget was generally viewed as a "domestic" issue, though reducing the deficit had international implications.[9] But the early NEC was front and center on international matters as well. Deputy Assistant Cutter and international macroeconomic aide Robert Fauver were instrumental in getting Clinton to convene the first meeting of heads of government for the Asia Pacific Economic Cooperation forum (APEC), which took place in Seattle in November 1993. The NEC took the lead in development of early administration strategy vis-à-vis Japan. And it was the focal point for administration-wide coordination of policy on two key trade matters inherited from Bush—the North American Free Trade Agreement (NAFTA), and the Uruguay Round of multilateral trade negotiations.

Clinton had endorsed NAFTA late in the campaign, after a heated debate among his advisers, but with the requirement that side agreements be negotiated on labor and the environment before he would send the implementing legislation to Congress. The NEC convened and chaired a series of meetings where the large NAFTA issues were debated and (sometimes) decided; USTR Mickey Kantor led the talks with Mexico and Canada on the side agreements. And the divisions of the campaign carried over into the administration, with labor-oriented political advisers wanting the agreement shelved to avert a fierce fight with that important Democratic constituency. The economic agencies were generally supportive, though Kantor did reportedly tell Clinton as late as mid-summer 1993 that he would "blow up" the side agreement negotiations if the president preferred not to do so.[10] And Clinton did, of course, end up giving NAFTA first priority and winning a memorable, come-from-behind victory with Congress. But through the spring and summer, the administration's divisions were visible. For the NEC, this meant overlarge meetings with White House aides crowding into the room, with the inevitable leaks to the press. There was not the same controversy over the other inherited trade negotiation—the Uruguay Round of the General Agreement of Tariffs and Trade.

On these and other administration economic issues, major decisions were debated in "principals meetings" at the Cabinet level. Once the budget was disposed of, "the principals" met an average of once every other week in Clinton's first two years, and these sessions were key to maintaining the NEC role and the visibility of its presidential connection. But the prime interagency work on international issues was done in meetings of the Deputies Committee—composed of the number-two officials in agencies like the Office of the USTR and NSC and the chief international officials in departments like Treasury and State. Participation varied by subject matter, but there emerged a core group. The key players were Cutter, who generally chaired the meetings;[11] Lawrence Summers and Jeffrey Shafer, respectively under secretary and assistant secretary of the Treasury for international affairs;[12] Joan Spero and Daniel Tarullo, the State Department under secretary and assistant secretary for economic issues; Rufus Yerxa or Charlene Barshefsky, deputy U.S. trade representatives; Laura Tyson and/or a CEA colleague, initially Alan Blinder; and sometimes Jeffrey Garten or William Reinsch, under secretaries for trade at Commerce. (An important focal point for coordination was NEC/NSC senior director, Robert Kyle.)

The deputies developed an exceptional degree of collegiality. They typically met twice or thrice weekly, particularly in 1993 and early 1994, and several noted in retrospect how they had "bonded" during these frequent sessions.[13] Discussion was often free-wheeling, as Cutter encouraged exploration of issues and intellectual brainstorming. Participants were not equal, of course: Garten of Commerce found it difficult to influence issues where other agencies had primary responsibility, and difficult also to get the deputies interested in Secretary Brown's aggressive campaign to increase export consciousness and win major contracts for U.S. firms. Hence, that department's "National Export Strategy" and "Big Emerging Markets" (BEMs) program went largely uncoordinated by the NEC, though it was certainly consistent with the overall Clinton emphasis on international competitiveness. (The campaign also avoided the sort of personal conflict between the commerce secretary and the U.S. trade representative that had bedeviled past administrations, by giving the former a high-profile role that did not impinge on the latter's turf.) But in general, the deputies shared information and felt, to some degree, shared responsibility for achieving Clinton international economic goals.

The deputies process worked particularly well for the Uruguay Round. A "rump group" of deputies was set up, limited to six or eight people to avoid the leaks that had plagued NAFTA. Deputy USTR Rufus Yerxa, who had day-to-day responsibility for the negotiations, took the substantive lead in the meetings, which Cutter chaired. Yerxa found he could shape the group's consensus, adjusting the USTR position when necessary, strengthening his position when matters went to the full deputies committee or, on important items, to the principals' level. And unlike in earlier administrations where the Office of the USTR was responsible for doing the coordination with other agencies, the NEC now had this burden, so the office could drive its own position a bit harder. So Yerxa—and his boss, Mickey Kantor—allowed the atrophy of the Trade Policy Review Group, a USTR-chaired body that had managed the interagency trade policy process in previous administrations. This division of labor—NEC coordinating, the Office of the USTR taking a strong negotiating lead—continued through the conclusion of the Uruguay Round in December 1993 and the enactment of its implementing legislation a year later.

The issue that really seized the deputies, however, was economic relations with Japan. Here the administration's economic players were united in believing that a tougher approach was needed to open Japan's markets, and that their own approach was responding to that need. Not for them was the split that had marked prior administrations—between trade "hawks" in the Office of the USTR and Commerce and "doves" at Treasury, State, and the CEA. Nor, with the cold war ended, was there an active NSC-State-Defense coalition in favor of downplaying economic issues so as to protect the bilateral security alliance. Prior personal experiences reinforced people's inclination to take the rather hard line they knew the president favored: Rubin and Spero, for example, had experienced frustration with the Japanese market in their private business dealings. So when Clinton pressed, in his first joint press conference with a Japanese prime minister, for "the rebalancing of our relationship" through "an elevated attention to our economic relations," his subordinates were more than ready to proceed.[14] And many of them—the president included—expressed interest in concluding agreements that contained specific import targets for specific sectors of the economy, as had a prominent, controversial 1986 bilateral deal on semiconductors.

Preparations for the April 1993 Miyazawa visit had engaged the deputies in the specifics of Japan policy. In its aftermath, they needed to help Clinton deliver on a commitment made during that visit: to reaching an agreement with Japan to structure their market-opening negotiations by the time of the president's July 1993 trip to Tokyo for the annual summit meeting of the Group of Seven advanced industrial nations. The question immediately arose as to who should lead the U.S. negotiating team. Neither Treasury nor the Office of the USTR wanted the other to head the overall effort, so Cutter of the NEC was designated. And he and his colleagues succeeded in working out a "framework agreement" with the Japanese, working late into the morning of the president's last day in Tokyo.

The negotiating role was unique for the NEC. It also proved counterproductive. In the months after the "framework" was concluded, talks on specific sectors were farmed out to responsible agencies—the Office of the USTR, Treasury, Commerce, and their Japanese counterparts. But the NEC and Cutter retained an ill-defined overall leadership mandate. Meanwhile, the Japanese were scoring propaganda points by denouncing the U.S. interest in quantitative targets as a new form of managed trade, with Europeans and Asians joining in the attack. The deputies continued to be seized with the talks; as one of them put it, "They traveled and negotiated together." They also held endless meetings in Washington. The NEC structure "clearly facilitated agreement on a more aggressive trade policy [toward Japan],"[15] and it made it hard for Japanese officials to find daylight between U.S. agency positions—as they typically could in prior administrations.[16]

But months went by without progress. Finally, as Tokyo's new reform prime minister prepared to visit Washington in early 1994, Cutter took a chance and conveyed some compromise ideas to Tokyo that went beyond the existing administration consensus. He had apparently checked them out with at least one of the deputies, but when Kantor learned of the effort he intervened. When the Japanese arrived in Washington, they found the Americans holding to the established, harder line. Thereafter, the lead on Japan trade policy moved effectively from NEC to the Office of the USTR, where it remained through the threat of major sanctions on auto imports in May 1995 and the settlement in June.

The NEC continued to be involved in Japan policy, of course, as well as other major trade issues. Relations were now frayed with Kantor, but they remained generally good at the deputies level. The NEC staff was centrally involved in Clinton's May 1994 decision to delink human rights and trade with China. And its reach extended also the management of international economic summits. NEC Senior Director Robert Fauver's staff was designated the U.S. sherpa for planning the G-7 meetings in 1993 and 1994, and he played a particularly important role in the pioneering APEC summit in Seattle, serving as sole note-taker in the "chiefs only" meeting that Clinton hosted. In 1995 and 1996, the sherpa role was assumed by Assistant Secretary of State Tarullo, who retained it when he succeeded Cutter as NEC deputy in February 1996.

On international macroeconomic issues outside the summit context, however, the NEC role was limited. Despite Rubin's strong financial credentials, Treasury dominance prevailed on the exchange rate even during his NEC tenure; one key participant declared, "We don't have an interagency process on international monetary issues." This was true even on the question of the shaky Mexican peso, notwithstanding the strong presidential interest that NAFTA had established. By the time that issue crashed into prominence, however, the NEC was in transition—as was broader Clinton international economic policy.

### From Offense to Defense: Standstill in International Economic Policy, 1995–1996

The administration concluded its second year with triumph after triumph in international economic policy. In late November, the APEC nations made an unprecedented commitment to free trade among themselves by the year 2010 (2020 for the least developed among them). Shortly after that, Congress approved the Uruguay Round implementing legislation by overwhelming bipartisan majorities: two to one in the House, three to one in the Senate. Shortly after that, the Miami Hemispheric Summit hosted by Clinton endorsed negotiation of a Free Trade Agreement for the Americas (FTAA) by the year 2005. When one adds the enactment of NAFTA, the administration had built a trade record matched by few if any predecessors. And it contrasted sharply with the visible failure in health care policy, an issue where the NEC had largely been shut out.

With the APEC and FTAA agreements requiring implementation through new multilateral negotiations, further trade progress seemed likely. Instead, the administration shifted to a holding pattern on trade and broad international economic policy, one that it maintained through the 1996 election. One factor was a disruptive transition at the National Economic Council. In December 1994, Clinton accepted Treasury Secretary Bentsen's long anticipated resignation, and made the almost equally anticipated designation of Rubin as his successor. But he named no one to succeed Rubin at the NEC until almost three months later, and it was almost a month after that before Laura Tyson moved fully into the job from her post at the CEA.

With the NEC early in its transition, before Rubin was confirmed in the Treasury post, the Mexican peso crisis hit. A poorly managed devaluation triggered an unexpectedly ferocious market reaction, putting in doubt Mexico's hard-won economic gains and driving the bilateral trade balance from a modest U.S. surplus to a sizeable deficit. Rank-and-file members of Congress resisted Clinton's proposal that they legislate a financial rescue package, notwithstanding support from the leaders of the new Republican House and Senate majorities. Clinton ended up going ahead on his own authority, ordering a more modest set of guarantees put together by a Treasury-led interagency effort. And the Mexican debacle took the shine off his NAFTA achievement, reducing the appeal of follow-on efforts like the FTAA.

Most important, however, was Clinton's savage election defeat in 1994, with Republicans sweeping into control of both the Senate and the House of Representatives. In the short run, the White House was demoralized, but within months this was replaced by preoccupation with political recovery and the upcoming reelection fight. Clinton had no closer ally in that fight than USTR Mickey Kantor.[17] The longtime loyalist had been exceptionally effective in closing major trade deals and winning congressional approval during Clinton's first two years. Now he would prove equally adept at stalling on some, and tilting others for maximum electoral advantage.

Standing in most dramatic contrast with the successes of 1993–94 was the administration's failure to move aggressively to win new negotiating authority from Congress. At the center was the procedural mechanism known as "fast-track."[18] Since the Trade Act of 1974, congressional authorizations of major new trade negotiations had typically included a commitment to an expedited, up-or-down vote on their results as submitted in the president's implementing bill.

The most recent extension of this authority had been to allow the administration time to complete the Uruguay Round. This it did in December 1993. The administration wanted its 1994 implementing legislation to contain a seven-year extension of fast-track, covering negotiations concluded up to the end of 2001. But it included, in draft language submitted for congressional comment, specific sections calling for talks on trade-related labor and environmental issues. This raised hackles among Republicans and business interests, undercutting the bipartisan consensus that had carried prior fast-track legislation. Kantor made some progress in negotiating compromise language with House Republicans, but the Senate Finance Committee proved resistant. In the end, the bill submitted by President Clinton, and passed overwhelmingly by Congress, included no authorization for follow-on negotiations.

Such authority was necessary if the administration was to begin delivering on its APEC and hemispheric free-trade commitments — including a long-standing promise to negotiate Chilean accession to NAFTA. And the House Committee on Ways and Means, under its new Republican leadership, got the ball rolling in spring 1995 by holding hearings and marking up draft legislation. But Kantor was wary of any action that might be taken as abandoning pledges to labor and environmental constituencies.[19] Administration relations with these key, normally Democratic groups had been damaged by the trade pacts, particularly NAFTA. In electoral terms, it was time to heal the wounds, not create new ones. The president and vice president apparently felt similarly. Both were free-traders by conviction, and Clinton in particular believed that the U.S. future required engaging in the international economy, "making change our friend." But this line was not seen as a clear political winner, so the administration's record in trade liberalization was deemphasized.

Kantor was quite active, on the other hand, on trade matters that offered promise of political dividends. He led the move to threaten sanctions in the U.S.-Japan auto dispute in the spring of 1995, and in tough actions vis-à-vis Mexico involving cross-border trucking and tomato trade. These were seen by Kantor and Clinton political adviser Dick Morris as playing well with labor and the public at large.

The National Economic Council presented alternative views to the president, and convened Cabinet-level meetings on issues like Japan autos. But now it was often a step behind the curve, with the Office of the USTR having taken steps that were hard to reverse. And the NEC was in a poor position to press for consideration of trade initiatives — like compromise on fast-track — which the primary trade agency did not want. Moreover, its position within the administration had been weakened — by the departure of Rubin, and by the budget fight with Congress, which dominated 1995. NEC leaders were deeply involved in this fight, but they were no longer orchestrating administration policy on budget matters. This was being done by White House Chief of Staff Leon Panetta, who had moved to that position from OMB in the summer of 1994.

By early 1996, the budget battle was largely over, and the NEC regained some of its initiative and authority due to director Laura Tyson's persistent efforts. But international economic policy remained in a holding pattern. The economy was in good shape; Republican candidate Bob Dole was not making trade a primary issue. There was little to gain, politically, from policy actions in advance of November. When U.S. exports to Japan rose 20 percent in 1995 and the bilateral deficit declined, the administration claimed credit — though the results owed more to the 1993–95 appreciation of the yen than to Clintonite trade diplomacy. It was enough that there were results to point to. In any case, the administration initiated no new trade issues with Japan, and it referred the most visible pending dispute (that over sales of photographic film) to the new World Trade Organization in Geneva.

### The Second Clinton Administration—And Beyond

William Jefferson Clinton entered office with a message: international economic policy is important because of its impact on the domestic economy, and aggressive action is necessary to open markets around the world. And his actions supported his words: he established the National Economic Council to link domestic and international policies, appointed a strong leader to head it, and moved forward with a range of international economic negotiations.

Four years later, Clinton's priorities seemed elsewhere. The economy was in remarkable shape, with unemployment low and inflation contained. Four years of Clinton economic recovery stood in sharp contrast to sluggishness in Europe and stagnation in Japan. Taking advantage of the unexpected revenue growth that budget had produced, Clinton succeeded in reaching a balanced-budget agreement with Republican congressional leaders that actually increased spending for programs (like education) that he particularly valued. Indeed, while the agreement targeted 2002, the deficit virtually disappeared in FY 1997, with a significant surplus expected for FY 1998.

On international economic policy, the picture was less rosy. Clinton's appointments, on balance, weakened his administration. On the positive side, Rubin stayed on at Treasury with presidential recognition as the ongoing captain of the economic team. Clinton promoted to the USTR position Charlene Barshefsky, who had been deputy and then acting USTR after Mickey Kantor was made secretary of Commerce in mid-1992, in the wake of Ron Brown's tragic death in a plane crash in Croatia. She was respected for her toughness and honesty. Kantor returned to the private sector, and William Daley of Chicago, who had served as coordinator of the NAFTA congressional campaign in 1993, was appointed secretary of Commerce. Sandy Berger was promoted to national security assistant from the deputy position.

At the NEC, however, Clinton's actions reflected more a desire to reward faithful servants than an interest in strong policy management. When Tyson returned, as expected, to her University of California professorship, he promoted Gene Sperling, his tireless servant on a range of economic issues, from NEC deputy to director. As deputy, he had proved an important connector of the economic and political advisers, but he had been an ad hoc player, not a manager, and his engagement was almost entirely domestic. Recognizing this limitation, Clinton simultaneously appointed the other NEC deputy, Dan Tarullo, to the new position of assistant to the president for international economic policy, with ambiguous status and reporting relationships. The choices reflected a president reluctant to bring in outside people, confident in his ability to make policy, and not particularly concerned about the logic of his personnel and institutional arrangements.

Institutional weakness was evident in what became the most prominent foreign economic issue of 1997, renewal of fast-track trade negotiating authority. The administration was still caught between its labor-environmental constituencies and the Republican congressional majorities. Legislative language that appeased the first, by giving priority to labor and environmental issues, would not pass muster with the second—or with the business community whose support was necessary to fast-track's enactment. The squeeze was exacerbated by the early endorsement of labor's stance by House Minority Leader Richard Gephardt (D-Mo.), Vice President Al Gore's expected rival for the 2000 presidential nomination. So Clinton temporized, delaying his own proposal until September, despite the warning of fast-track supporters that time was not necessarily on his side.

The Sperling-Tarullo NEC did not play its coordinating role; indeed, a special interagency group had to be set up under the chairmanship of the new White House chief of staff, Erskine Bowles. Nor was USTR Barshefsky given authority to negotiate for the administration that spring and summer on the terms of fast track, though supportive members of Congress wanted to move forward. And due mainly to the president's penchant for reopening issues at the eleventh hour, his administration irritated its supporters when it missed, by a week, its long-advertised September 9 target for sending the long-awaited fast-track legislative proposal to Capitol Hill.

This time the president paid dearly for his delay. He bowed to Republican-business pressure to limit negotiations on trade-related labor and environmental issues, the only plausible route to a congressional majority. But organized business, wary of past administration proposals, withheld support until it saw the specific legislative language. Meanwhile, organized labor and its allies spent the spring and summer solidifying opposition among Democrats. By the time of the scheduled vote in early November, the president could only count 43 supporters among the 209 House members of his own party, despite intensive, eleventh-hour, face-to-face lobbying. Even with 160-plus Republicans apparently available, this put him 10–15 votes short of the needed 218, so the vote was never taken. And his pledge to press the matter again in 1998 fell before the need to win congressional funding for the IMF and its efforts to contain the severe East Asian financial crisis of 1997–98.

Clinton's motive in pushing for trade action in 1997 was less overridingly economic than it had been in 1993. That motive was present, but so also was the need to maintain broad policy leadership. This was true for global trade negotiations, and particularly in the Western hemisphere, where Clinton's incapacity to move forward toward the FTAA promised at the 1994 Miami Summit had become an embarrassment. In contrast to 1993, trade policy was now treated as part of broader U.S. policy leadership—and that leadership balanced economic and security issues. In 1996, Clinton administration dealings with Japan had exhibited far greater balancing of security with economic concerns than they had in 1993, and this pattern continued into the second term. By early 1998, attention centered on the need for Japan to take strong fiscal action to end six years of lethargic economic performance and thereby help its East Asian neighbors get *their* economies back on track.

The intertwining of economic with national security concerns was also central in dealings with the country that replaced Japan in 1996–97 as the most important single target of U.S. trade policy: the People's Republic of China. Whether the aim was to encourage constructive response by Beijing to the regional financial crisis, to reform Chinese behavior on matters like protection of intellectual property, or to tackle a bilateral trade deficit that was coming to rival that with Japan, the president could not address these issues without linking them to broader concerns about China's emergence as a world power, and its impact on regional—and ultimately global—security.

Clinton began 1997 determined to built a strong overall relationship with the People's Republic. But this campaign was complicated by the annual congressional ritual on renewing normal (most-favored nation) trading status for Beijing. Clinton had won a two-to-one House victory on the issue in 1996, spurring hopes that the issue would recede, but the religious Right joined the opposition to spotlight persecution of Christians in China, and the 1997 vote was closer (albeit still comfortable for MFN supporters). And lethargic U.S.-China talks continued into 1998 on the terms of Beijing's entry into the World Trade Organization.

Substantively, international economic policy remained important in Clinton's second term, but not dominant the way it sometimes seemed in 1993. National security policy issues claimed at least equal billing: ongoing involvement in Bosnia, a successful campaign for Senate ratification of worldwide Chemical Weapons Convention in spring 1997, and an anticipated Senate vote on NATO expansion in spring 1998. Institutionally, Clinton's NEC had declined to the point that its post-Clinton future was uncertain. It was the victim of questionable appointments, but above all of Clinton's general disdain for organized policy making.

Thus the future balance between security and economic concerns remained uncertain, as did the balance between the institutions through which competing perspectives would be played out. Economic interdependence was clearly here to stay. The cold war was over. And notwithstanding occasional rhetoric from the conservative camp, neither China nor any other nation would replace the former Soviet Union as an across-the-board U.S. adversary in the near future. Yet China and other U.S. security concerns were sufficient to prevent a continuous rise in the economic complex at the expense of traditional national security institutions and priorities.

With the end of the cold war, the security complex (the agencies represented in the NSC process) had lost its automatic primacy in U.S. international dealings. But the economic complex has not won comparable primacy. No single set of goals or institutions was dominant in the late 1990s. And none seems likely to be dominant when Washington enters the twenty-first century.

## Notes

1 This chapter draws on the author's *The National Economic Council: A Work in Progress* (Washington: International Institute for Economics, 1996), and on the broader research conducted in the course of its writing.

2 For a fuller discussion, see my earlier essay: "A Government Divided: The Security Complex and the Economic Complex," in David A. Deese, ed., *The New Politics of American Foreign Policy* (New York: St. Martin's Press, 1994), pp. 132–147.

3 The formal change came in 1980, through a reorganization plan submitted to Congress by President Jimmy Carter. But this was just one step in the growth of the trade office, and its growing responsiveness to domestic economic interests. For a full treatment of this evolution, see Destler, *American Trade Politics*, 3d ed. (Washington: Institute for International Economics; NY: Twentieth-Century Fund), ch. 5.

4 This was a bow, of course, to the long-established role of the Department of Agriculture in promoting international trade within its sphere.

5 "America's New Course," *Foreign Affairs* 69, no. 2 (Spring 1990): 7–8.

6 *The National Economic Council*, p. 2.

7 Hence, trade specialist Robert Kyle and international finance expert Robert Fauver were labeled NEC/NSC senior directors for International Economic Policy.

8 Bob Woodward devotes chapter 11 of his "insider" book to recounting this meet-

ing. See *The Agenda: Inside the Clinton White House* (New York: Pocket Books, 1995).

9  For example, the need to finance large budget deficits had made the United States a net international borrower since the Reagan administration. This contributed to large U.S. trade deficits. So, reducing the budget deficit would tend, other things equal, to reduce the trade imbalance as well.

10  Kantor also argued that if Clinton fought labor successfully on NAFTA, "It would be a big win and a big plus for him." Elizabeth Drew, *On the Edge: The Clinton Presidency* (New York: Simon and Schuster, 1994), pp. 288–289.

11  Reflecting the power-sharing arrangement noted earlier, Berger of the NSC sometimes chaired—or cochaired—particularly on matters perceived as linked to security issues.

12  Each was promoted during Clinton's first term—Summers to deputy secretary, Shafer to under secretary.

13  These and subsequent unattributed quotations come from interviews conducted for Destler, *The National Economic Council.*

14  President Clinton during a joint White House press conference with Kiichi Miyazawa, prime minister of Japan, April 16, 1993.

15  Leonard J. Schoppa, *Bargaining with Japan: What American Pressure Can and Cannot Do* (Columbia University Press, 1997), p. 262.

16  For this reason, the process was later criticized for not giving enough voice within the government to U.S. political-military interests vis-à-vis Japan, which might be threatened by protracted economic conflict.

17  By one oft-repeated Washington story, just after his designation as Clinton's trade representative Mickey Kantor had a conversation with William Brock, USTR in Ronald Reagan's first term. Brock asked Kantor, "What do you see as your primary objective in your new position?" Kantor replied, "To get Clinton reelected." "No, I mean what is your primary *trade* objective?" "To get Clinton reelected." For an extended analysis of Kantor's political efforts and the 1996 campaign, see David E. Sanger, "Standing by His Man in Role after Role," *New York Times,* November 2, 1996, p. 37.

18  For a fuller account of fast track from its origins to summer 1997, see my *Renewing Fast-Track Legislation* (Washington: Institute for International Economics, September 1997).

19  For a more extended treatment of how these constituencies affected trade policy throughout the Clinton administration, see Destler, "American Trade Politics in the Wake of the Uruguay Round," in Jeffrey J. Schott, ed., *The World Trading System: Challenges Ahead* (Washington: Institute for International Economics, 1996), pp. 115–124.

# 5.

## Congress and Post–Cold War U.S. Foreign Policy

*Ralph G. Carter*

In figure 1.2's "shifting constellations" image of U.S. foreign policy making, the circle representing Congress is the same size as that of the White House and the foreign policy bureaucracy. However, whether Congress deserves coequal status to these other two actors is the subject of some debate. No one can doubt the legal basis for a congressional role. The Constitution assigns Congress numerous specific powers. According to one legal scholar, the Constitution "expressly divided foreign affairs powers among the three branches of government, with *Congress*, not the president, being granted the dominant role" (emphasis in original).[1]

Yet the conventional wisdom sees the president and other executive branch actors dominating foreign policy making. While members of Congress normally defer to executive decisions during wartime, this view holds that after World War II they did not reassert their traditional foreign policy–making roles. The Soviet threat seemed to put a priority on the president's access to classified information and his ability to act swiftly. To some, the pattern of presidential preeminence and congressional deference characterized foreign policy making well into the 1990s.[2]

However, this conventional view has been challenged on a number of grounds. First, the above pattern applied best to narrow questions of war making, but foreign policy involved more than that. Appropriating the funds needed for foreign and defense policy has long been shaped by congressional preferences. The same was true for structural policy making, in areas such as trade, foreign aid, and immigration. At times, congressional preferences constrained administrations in strategic, substantive areas as diplomacy and national security policy.[3] In short, Congress was more involved in foreign and defense policy making than a study of narrow war powers alone would suggest.

Second, congressional acquiescence to executive initiative during the cold war was often a result of policy agreement.[4] From the late 1940s until the late 1960s, a "cold war consensus" existed in the United States. Politicians and the public generally agreed that Soviet communism was a threat of global proportions whose spread should be contained. As long as presidential policies successfully contained that spread, there was no need for members of Congress to challenge the president on foreign policy.[5]

Third, much congressional foreign policy influence was less visible to casual observation.[6] By controlling procedures, creating new agencies, and mandating of agency responsibilities, Congress predisposed the policy-making process to produce certain types of policies. The conventional wisdom missed the fact that "even when Congress delegates authority to executive branch officials it may still structure the decision-making process so that its preferred policies are chosen."[7]

Fourth, foreign policy decisions routinely required congressional authorizations or appropriations.[8] The appropriations power guaranteed a significant foreign policy–making role whenever Congress chose to exercise it.[9] With the exceptions of use of discretionary funds and illegal covert operations, *the president cannot do what Congress does not fund.*

Additional cold war illustrations weakened the conventional wisdom. Other than diplomatic recognition, there were few foreign policy issues on which presidents acted unilaterally. Further, legislators lobbied executive branch officials to shape administration proposals before they ever got to Congress.[10] Members used their media access to "frame" the public debate on an issue in ways which worked to their advantage. Both members and administration officials sought to anticipate each other's reactions throughout the policy-making process, thereby building the other's preferences into policy proposals when necessary.[11]

The conventional wisdom, of "two presidencies" with the president dominating Congress in foreign policy but not in domestic policy, held for a limited time—not for the entire cold war period.[12] From 1946 to 1949, Congress gave the administration exactly what it wanted in foreign policy 66 percent of the time and acted on its own initiatives only 8 percent of the time. Most of those cases represent interbranch policy agreement, not presidential dominance.[13] From 1950 to 1982, the president got exactly what he wanted from Congress 29 percent of the time, and Congress initiated its own foreign policy agenda 26 percent of the time.[14] The latter hardly suggested presidential "dominance" of Congress. For the post–cold war world, this pattern raises questions:

Has congressional behavior changed, what types of congressional foreign policy activity are present, and what factors prompt members to become active in foreign policy making?

### Policy Making in the Post–Cold War Era

The Cold War's 1991 end brought another escalation in the level of congressional assertiveness in foreign policy making. First a democratically controlled Congress pressed the Republican Bush administration to react more swiftly and positively to the Soviet Union's demise. Then the Democratic Congress pushed the domestically oriented Clinton administration for greater activism and more coherence in its foreign policy. Beginning in 1995, a Republican Congress disagreed with both the ends and means of Clinton's foreign policy. As a result, the 1992–95 period showed a significant, but underestimated shift in congressional foreign policy behavior.

*Changing Congressional Foreign Policy Behavior*
How did congressional foreign policy behavior change, beginning in 1992? A prior study charted the universe of 668 foreign policy behaviors undertaken by Congress from 1946 to 1982.[15] These cases were divided into those representing *compliant* behaviors (where the administration got exactly what it wanted), *resistant* behaviors (where Congress refused to give the administration *exactly* what it wanted), *rejection* behaviors (where Congress rejected the administration's proposals), and *independent* behaviors (where Congress initiated its own foreign policy agenda). Using comparable sources and mirroring that earlier methodology,[16] the 1992–1995 period reveals 105 instances of congressional foreign policy behavior. The results, categorized in percentage terms, are reported in table 5.1.

Compared to the 1946–82 period, in the early post–cold war period members complied less with administration requests (by 29%), changed those requests more often (by 32%), and more often initiated their own foreign policy agenda (by 21%). In short, they were *more assertive.* Thus it appears post–cold war congressional foreign policy influence is increasing.

*Types of Congressional Activity*
This new assertiveness by Congress continues to rest on an array of means for shaping foreign policy. Among those are legislation, appro-

Table 5.1   Congressional Foreign Policy Behaviors
by Type and Period

| Behavior Type | 1946–1982 | 1992–1995 |
|---------------|-----------|-----------|
| Compliance | 34% | 24% |
| Resistance | 31% | 39% |
| Rejection | 12% | 10% |
| Independence | 24% | 28% |
| Total | 101% | 101% |

*Note:* Rounding error produces the totals of 101 percent.

priations, confirmations and ratifications, oversight and institutional control activities, and other informal activities.

LEGISLATION As the post–cold war era began, congressional assertiveness was seen when Congress passed legislation against the wishes of the president or refused to pass legislation requested by the White House. Bush did not always get what he wanted in foreign and defense policy. In 1992, Congress banned all nuclear weapons tests after September 30, 1996, over his objections, and imposed economic sanctions on the foreign subsidiaries of U.S. firms doing business with Cuba. Bush's long opposition to the toughening of the Cuban sanctions were erased when Congress accepted his position, making the sanctions discretionary rather than automatic and "grandfathering" existing contracts.

President Clinton faced bumps in the congressional road as well. In 1993, the Democratic Congress put language in the Defense Authorization Bill that was tougher on gays than Clinton's carefully crafted "don't ask, don't tell" compromise. That year Congress also refused Clinton's request to overhaul the Foreign Assistance Act of 1961, the basic legislation underwriting the foreign aid program. In 1994, Congress challenged the administration by expanding economic sanctions against countries or companies to include those engaged in the proliferation of nuclear weapons materials, components, or technology. Congress also mandated that the United States vote against multilateral development bank loans to those who had expropriated private properties of U.S. citizens or contributed to the spread of nuclear weapons materials. For its part, the Senate rejected an administration plan to distribute frozen Iraqi assets in the United States.

Clinton faced greater policy differences with the Republican Congress in 1995, but circumstances lessened the impact of some disputes. For example, Congress mandated that the embargo on arming Bosnian Muslim forces be dropped, and Clinton vetoed the measure. Only Bosnian Muslim and Croat victories on the battlefield made the issue moot. Further, Congress refused to approve Clinton's request for a $40 billion loan guarantee program for Mexico, but he put together a $50 billion loan guarantee program by combining $47.8 billion in administrative discretionary funds with contributions by Canada and Latin American states. That year Congress also required the U.S. embassy in Israel be moved from Tel Aviv to Jerusalem, thus imperiling the Mideast peace process. Clinton did not veto the bill, since a provision in the act allowed the president to delay the move indefinitely. Finally, Clinton's veto threat delayed passage of the Helms-Burton Act until 1996. When passed, this bill (allowing lawsuits in U.S. courts against foreign companies or individuals using U.S. properties nationalized by the Castro regime) allowed the president to waive its enforcement for increments of six months. Due to that waiver provision, Clinton allowed the bill to become law.[17]

APPROPRIATIONS Congress has relied on the power of the purse. In 1992, Congress cut Bush's requests for HARM missiles (52%), high-speed cargo ships (49%), U.S. troops stationed in Europe after FY 1996 (33%), C-17 cargo planes (28%), Strategic Defense Initiative (SDI) funding (25%), F/A-18 aircraft (25%), and the development of a new Centurion class nuclear submarine (14%). Bush was also forced to accept a total fleet of twenty B-2 Stealth bombers, rather than the seventy-five he had requested just two years before. Congress increased funding for modernization of M-1 tanks (492%), Bradley fighting vehicles (120%), JSTARS radar aircraft (65%), and a helicopter-borne laser for use as a minesweeper (50%). Members also added $1.2 billion for an unrequested helicopter carrier, continued to fund the V-22 Osprey air transport, and refused to stop the Seawolf submarine program after building only one such submarine.

Despite Democratic control of Congress, Clinton faced similar budgetary battles in his first two years. In 1993, Congress cut his requests for a "National Launch System" for heavy payloads (100%), F-16 fighters (50%), Ballistic Missile Defense (26%), the "Brilliant Eyes" satellite and other missile attack warning systems (24%), and C-17 cargo planes (21%). However, Congress increased funding over his requests for dual-use partnerships between military and commercial applications (108%), the JSTARS radar plane (69%), upgraded F-14 fighters (68%), testing naval-based ground-support weapons (43%), and modernization of M-1 tanks (21%). Congress also equipped National Guard and reserve units with $990 million of equipment not requested by Clinton, authorized $150 million not requested for ten additional Apache attack helicopters, and authorized $45 million not requested for MLRS rockets. Foreign operations funding suffered as well. Cut were International Monetary Fund and World Bank funding requests (21%) and foreign aid (10%). In 1994, Congress approved his request for $670 million for U.N. peace-keeping activities but withheld half until the United Nations created an independent inspector general position.

Facing a Republican Congress in 1995, budget battles intensified. Congress tried to increase antimissile defense funding and gain more control over peacekeeping activities, but it was unable to override Clinton's veto. Clinton also vetoed the Foreign Operations appropriations bill, as it cut his requests for the Arms Control and Disarmament Agency (53%), U.N. peacekeeping costs (49%), U.S. Information Agency (16%), and the Department of State (13%). Congress was more successful in cutting multilateral aid requests by 48 percent, bilateral aid requests by 15 percent, and export assistance requests by 10 percent. Moreover, Speaker Gingrich added $18 million to the intelligence budget for an unsolicited effort to overthrow the Iranian government.[18]

CONFIRMATIONS AND RATIFICATIONS Senate approval of personnel appointments and treaties were contentious in the early post–cold war era. In 1993, the Senate refused to act on Clinton's nomination of Morton Halperin for the post of assistant secretary of defense for peacekeeping and democracy and also refused his request to ratify the START II Treaty with Russia. In 1994, the Foreign Relations Committee refused Clinton's request to approve the chemical weapons convention, and the Senate refused to act on Clinton's nomination of Robert Pastor as ambassador to Panama (due to his linkage to Jimmy Carter's Panama Canal Treaties). In 1997, the Senate refused to approve Anthony Lake's nomination as director of Central Intelligence, due to his association with Clinton's policies regarding the arming of Bosnian Muslim forces.

OVERSIGHT AND INSTITUTIONAL CONTROL Congressional oversight activities and control of procedures are not roles that are "policy neutral."[19] Clinton learned that quickly. In 1993, Congress denied his request to make it easier for him to call National Guard and reserve military units to active duty without first declaring a national emergency, and Congress declared in the defense authorization bill that it was Congress's constitutional authority to determine the conditions of service for gays in the military, not the president's. After the Aldrich Ames spy scandal, Congress gave most of the CIA's counterintelligence functions to the FBI and created an ad hoc panel to review the mission and conduct of the CIA and other components of the intelligence community. The latter was in part a response to the Ames scandal, but also to the controversy surrounding the hoarding of $1 billion by the National Reconnaissance Office and the building of a new NRO headquarters office complex with little congressional oversight. In 1995, Congress ordered CIA and defense inspectors general to conduct performance audits of NRO's operations. That same year, Congress slowed CIA and Defense plans to combine imagery and mapping operations so it could review them. Further, the Senate Armed Services Committee castigated former Defense Secretary Les Aspin for refusing military requests to reinforce peacekeeping troops in Somalia with tanks and armored personnel carriers. The report said the United States must either protect troops or remove them.

INFORMAL POLICY-MAKING ACTIVITIES Members of Congress also engage in a variety of informal activities that help shape foreign policy. Most of these fall into one of two major categories: institutional dissent or policy advocacy.[20] Both of these categories arise from policy differences with the White House, which tend to become pronounced when at least one chamber of Congress is controlled by the president's opposition party.

*Institutional Dissent.* In 1992 Bush came under heavy criticism from congressional Democrats for his policy to return Haitian refugees without hearings on their claims of political persecution. The criticism continued when Clinton adopted similar policies in contradiction to his prior campaign statements. Thus the setting was ripe for the administration's later policy change, which restored President Aristide to power and introduced U.S. peacekeeping troops there.

Another example of the power of dissent came with the nomination of Morton H. Halperin as assistant secretary of defense for peacekeeping and democracy. Criticism from Republicans and other conservatives was directed at Halperin's prior opposition to what he viewed as excessive government secrecy regarding questionable defense and intelligence activities. Rather than buck the growing firestorm on Capitol Hill, Halperin withdrew his nomination.

At times, members of Congress engage in policy dissent when they merely suspect that an administration is considering a controversial initiative. In 1993, Congress passed nonbinding resolutions asking Clinton to seek its approval before placing U.S. forces under command of a foreign officer or sending U.S. forces to either Haiti or Bosnia.

*Policy Advocacy.* Quite often, members of Congress go the additional step to advocate a different policy. In 1992 the Democratic Congress charged Bush with missing a historic opportunity to reach out to Russia and other former Soviet republics with foreign aid. Stung by critics, Bush reacted by proposing an international initiative to provide $24 billion for humanitarian and technical assistance for the former Soviet republics. Bush faced other pressures in the summer of 1992, when Congress passed a nonbinding resolution urging the administration to press the United Nations to provide security guards to safeguard food shipments in famine-wracked Somalia. In December, Bush announced that 28,000 U.S. troops would go to Somalia to perform that humanitarian mission.

Clinton also faced congressional policy advocacy. Throughout 1993, the criticism of his Haiti policy did not diminish, and the Congressional Black Caucus put heavy pressures on Clinton to do something to restore the lawful Aristide regime in Haiti. The Haiti peacekeeping mission came the next year. Also in 1994, the Senate passed a nonbinding amendment urging him to end the trade embargo against Vietnam. Given that this was something he already desired, Clinton ended the embargo by executive order the very next week.

However, congressional-executive relations deteriorated after Republicans gained control of Congress in 1995. Policy advocacy occurred on issues such as defense policy (and spending), support for the United Nations and peacekeeping operations, NATO expansion, restructuring the foreign policy bureaucracy, and others. On many, Senate Democrats were able to block action. On others, including the issue of restructuring the State Department, a compromise was worked out. However, Congress still managed to steer the Clinton administration onto a collision course with China. Congress passed a nonbinding resolution urging the issuance of a visa allowing Taiwanese president Lee Teng-hui to make an unofficial trip to the United States to visit his alma mater, Cornell University, and attend an economic summit in Alaska. Irked, the Chinese government expelled a visiting U.S. military delegation and recalled its ambassador to the United States.

In summary, whether through formal powers like legislation, appropriations, confirmations and ratifications, and oversight and institutional control, or informal activities like institutional dissent or policy advocacy, Congress has used a variety of tools at its disposal to try to shape post–cold war U.S. foreign policy. Short of either the electoral coincidence of a White House and Congress controlled by members of the same ideological wing of the same political party or a major foreign policy threat that overwhelms partisan or particularistic interests, such assertive behavior on the part of Congress seems likely to continue.

*Factors Affecting Congressional Activity*
Like all foreign policy makers, members of Congress exist in a multi-faceted setting and react to a wide variety of stimuli. Moving from a macro to a micro perspective, most recurring stimuli can be found in four major categories: international factors, societal factors, institutional factors, and individual factors. Each of these is addressed in turn.

INTERNATIONAL FACTORS Foreign policy making does not take place in a vacuum, and the international system presents foreign policy makers with a series of both threats and opportunities. Among the most significant potential threats of the post–cold war world are

- new major challengers (these could include security threats such as a more nationalistic Russia or bold and assertive China, as well as economic challengers such as Japan and Germany);
- regional and ethnic disputes (such as those between North and South Korea, China and Taiwan, India and Pakistan, Iran and Iraq, Israel and its neighbors, the Balkans, the former Soviet Republics, and others throughout Africa); and
- systemic policy challenges (i.e., the proliferation of weapons of mass destruction, global terrorism, drug trafficking, and refugees and immigration).

Obviously, these could provide ample opportunities for members of Congress to disagree with an administration regarding how best to respond to such threats.

However, the international system offers not just threats, but also opportunities in the post–cold war era, each of which provides additional opportunities for interbranch disagreement over policy specifics, even while commanding widespread support on the generalities. Among these are

- the expansion of democratic, market economies abroad (in what ways, in what places, and at what costs would such action be taken?);
- a variety of trade expansion opportunities (highly contentious, as

the debates over the North American Free Trade Agreement and the 1994 World Trade agreement indicate);
- – the stabilization of Europe (especially the preservation of good relations with Russia and the expansion of NATO); and
- – United Nations reorganization.

In summary, the threats and opportunities in international environment facing both Congresses and administrations in the post–cold war era can be expected to generate interbranch disputes over whether and how to react. Barring the emergence of a new superpower threat or the creation of a new post–cold war consensus, legislators will probably not automatically follow the lead of future presidents. Part of their relative independence may be reinforced by multiple societal factors.

SOCIETAL FACTORS Just as foreign policy making is affected by factors in the external setting, neither can societal factors be ignored. Important among such factors are public opinion, the roles played by interest groups, occasional mass movements, and the activities of the media.

*Public Opinion.* In facing any policy issue, each legislator is subject to a wide array of inputs arising from the domestic political environment.[21] One such domestic input is the impact of public opinion. Once discredited as a meaningful factor in foreign policy making, recent scholarship has documented an important role for public opinion on U.S. foreign policy makers.[22] Recent studies have found the public's opinions and attitudes about foreign policy topics to be influential, as well as sensible, well-structured, prudent, and stable over time, while still being responsive to major changes in the international environment.[23]

Moreover, members of Congress have two related reasons to serve as the conduit of such public opinion on foreign policy issues. The first is the norm of representation in a democracy.[24] From a rational choice perspective, the public plays the role of the "principals," and members of Congress are the "agents" who seek to represent their interests. This agent role is not likely to change as long as there are principals to represent. Without a new foreign policy consensus in society, those principals will disagree more often with future presidential foreign policy initiatives than they did during the cold war era. Second, legislators generally desire reelection, and the public will rely on retrospective judgments to determine how well each incumbent represented their interests in the past.[25] So by doing what their constituents (or principals) want in the foreign policy arena now, savvy legislators will be earning credits with the folks back home that should help in the effort to secure future reelection. So, powerful incentives exist for legislators to represent the public's opinions in foreign policy.

Further, legislators use a variety of opportunities to both create and lead public opinion supportive of their substantive policy desires. Members "use legislative debate, oversight hearings, and media appearances to influence the terms of public debate and, in turn, administration policy."[26] For example, congressional broadsides directed at the foreign aid program, characterizing it as "wasteful" and depicting it in "giveaway" terms, effectively make it harder to make full use of a diplomatic tool seen as highly valuable by every post–World War II administration. This opportunity to "frame" public opinion can be an important tool in congressional attempts to shape the substance of U.S. foreign policy.[27]

*Interest Groups.* The activities of interest groups provide members another opportunity to receive public inputs and to try to help frame the debate on public policy issues. Anyone doubting that interest groups play as important a role in foreign as in domestic policy making has not been paying attention. President Clinton's shift in Haiti policy can largely be attributed to pressures brought on by TransAfrica and the Congressional Black Caucus. Cuban American groups have pressured Congress to impose a secondary boycott on Castro's Cuba, so now other countries that trade with Havana face sanctions in their trade with the United States. Pro-Israeli groups have helped ensure Israel's place as the number-one recipient of foreign aid dollars (on both an absolute and a per capita basis), and with the help of Armenian American groups, Armenia ranks as the second largest per capita recipient of U.S. foreign aid. In short, "Congress is pervasively open to virtually any organized interest that wishes to present its views."[28]

Often, policy debates become contests between interest groups and their congressional allies. For example, both the 1994 population and development conference in Cairo and the 1995 women's conference in Beijing pitted women's groups against conservative religious groups for control of U.S. policy stances on issues like abortion, family planning, and women's rights. Domestically, decisions about the next generation of a major weapons system can become battles between such heavyweights as General Dynamics, Lockheed-Martin, McDonnell Douglas, Boeing, and so on. Finally, recent battles over extensions of most-favored-nation status for China have pitted an alliance of human rights organizations (wanting to punish China for its abuse of political prisoners and use of prison labor) and businesses interested in protecting themselves against Chinese piracy of copyrighted and trademarked products (particularly movie videos, video games, and computer software) against the Big Three auto makers seeking to protect their existing contracts to sell hundreds of thousands of autos to China for use as taxi cabs. What's good for Detroit must be good for the United States, because the Chinese retained their MFN status and escaped any significantly harsh punitive measures; the cabs will roll.[29]

*Mass Movements.* Less common and more transitory than the organized interest groups above, occasional mass movements engulf members of Congress in a wave of public sentiment on a foreign policy issue, thus providing powerful electoral incentives for members to act. While there have been no such movements yet in the post–cold war era, there were two examples in the 1980s—the South African economic sanctions movement[30] and the nuclear freeze movement.[31] These examples suggest that when the administration's stance on a specific, visible foreign policy issue contravenes the preferences of a wide array of domestic constituencies and motivates those constituencies to act, members of Congress will respond to what they hear from Main Street and not what emanates from 1600 Pennsylvania Avenue. Mass movements may never be commonplace, but they may be more likely in the post–cold war era, when no uniting consensus binds both the public and foreign policy makers, than in cold war years.

*Media.* A final societal influence on members of Congress is the media. Like both public opinion and interest groups, the media can both impact and be used by legislators. What the news media choose to cover, how they report stories, and the visibility of the coverage combine to help set the foreign policy agenda and frame the context in which the issues are interpreted, thus making the media a potentially important factor in the foreign policy-making process. While some disagree over whether sensational television coverage of breaking events actually *drives* U.S. foreign policy (the so-called CNN factor), there is no doubt that legislators are aware of news coverage of foreign events, try to anticipate how their constituents will respond to such coverage, and then try to position themselves accordingly.[32] Legislators with foreign policy agendas have access to the media. As James Lindsay notes, "[M]embers increasingly turn to framing opinion in order to push foreign policy closer to their preferences . . . [and] efforts to frame opinion are crucial to advancing any policy, foreign or domestic."[33] For example, usage of the media by members of the Congressional Black Caucus and Minority Leader Dole helped produce tougher responses by the Clinton administration to the policy challenges presented in Haiti and Bosnia, respectively.

INSTITUTIONAL FACTORS One part of the "new institutionalism" literature is the renewed appreciation of the context in which policy making occurs.[34] The president and other bureaucratic actors in the executive branch and the party leadership, standing committees, and caucuses in Congress provide a variety of institutionally based inputs to the policy making process. These policy-making cue-givers are addressed next.

*Presidential Preferences.* Despite the increases in congressional assertiveness noted earlier, presidential preferences are still an important policy-making factor. The fact that 28 percent of the cases from 1992 to 1995 represent independent behaviors on the part of legislators means that, for almost three-fourths of the cases, the president's requests still shape the foreign policy agenda to which legislators respond. They comply with the requests (24%), make changes in the requests (39%), or flatly reject the requests (10%).[35] Thus the stances taken and the cues given by the president help form the context within which congressional foreign policy making is conducted,[36] and members of Congress find it difficult to resist complying with the president's requests if his reading of the international system seems accurate.[37] For example, despite long-standing congressional concerns about both Russia and foreign aid, members agreed with Clinton's stance that Russian democracy had to be supported, and they approved almost the full dollar amounts of his requests for Russian aid in both 1993 and 1994. More dramatically, a Republican-controlled Congress was forced to make significant concessions to President Clinton's 1995 positions on defense spending and support for peacekeeping missions. Unable to convince Democrats that Clinton's reading of the international environment was wrong, congressional Republicans could not override his veto of the FY 1996 defense authorization bill. Thus even in the post–cold war era, strong presidential preferences will be important factors in congressional foreign policy making. The president's role is unlikely to be as strong as it was during the cold war era, but it cannot be ignored.

*Bureaucratic Preferences.* Members of Congress react to the policy stances taken by top bureaucratic officials. As James Lindsay notes, "policies that don't have champions in the bureaucracy are doomed."[38] Further, the degree of influence depends on the officials' political standing with legislators. Secretary of State Warren Christopher was not particularly popular with many in Congress, perhaps due to his reserved personal style. It is hard not to assume that congressional attacks on the State Department and its programs in the first Clinton term would have been made more difficult if Christopher had been a more forceful figure. As his successor, Madeleine Albright's more forceful and forthright manner has already won her the support of Foreign Relations Committee chairman Jessie Helms and many others in Congress.[39] Over at defense, Les Aspin's standing on Capitol Hill could not survive his decisions in the Somalia operation, nor did those decisions allow him to keep his job. His successor, William Perry, garnered more respect as an experienced administrator and defense professional. In turn his successor, William Cohen, can be expected to be an effective advocate for defense policy as the Cabinet's only Republican member. Finally, senatorial concerns about Anthony Lake's advocacy of the Bosnian and Haitian military interventions, his prior academic writings questioning covert operations, and issues concerning his personal finances combined to force him to withdraw his nomination as director of central intelligence. In short, those in Congress will react to bureaucratic cues, whether positively or negatively, depending on the messenger as well as the message.

*Party Leaders.* Since the 1950s, congressional party leaders have been an underappreciated set of foreign policy makers. As Steven Smith notes, "In the foreign policy arena, leaders show increasingly partisan patterns in their support for presidential positions, increasing activity as party spokesman, increasingly partisan patterns of consultation with presidents, and increasing activity as policy leaders."[40] As he goes on to show, these patterns hold more for the House than the Senate.

The rise of Newt Gingrich to the House speakership provides good examples of this leadership role. In 1995, he got House passage of the National Security Revitalization Act. Although this bill arising out of the Republican Party's "Contract with America" did not get through the Senate, it still put powerful pressures on the Clinton administration in the areas of U.N. funding and both funding and U.S. participation in peacekeeping activities. Gingrich also forced that $18 million appropriation, mentioned earlier, to pay for a covert operation to destabilize the government of Iran.

Although perhaps not as active as its House counterparts, the Senate leadership is not immune to such activity. In his role as minority leader of the Senate prior to 1995, Bob Dole was able to put heavy pressure on the Clinton administration to allow arms to be supplied to Bosnian Muslims. Only Bosnian Muslim and Croat victories on the battlefield prevented this issue from generating a larger political battle between Congress and the president. So party leaders, particularly those of the

Table 5.2 House Standing Committees and Subcommittees with Direct or Indirect Foreign or Defense Policy Impacts, 104th Congress

| Standing Committees | Subcommittees |
| --- | --- |
| Agriculture | Department Operations, Nutrition, and Foreign Agriculture |
| | General Farm Commodities |
| | Livestock, Dairy, and Poultry |
| | Resource Conservation, Research, and Forestry |
| | Risk Management and Specialty Crops |
| Appropriations | Agriculture, Rural Development, FDA, and Related Agencies |
| | Commerce, Justice, State, and Judiciary |
| | Foreign Operations, Export Financing, and Related Programs |
| | Military Construction |
| | National Security |
| | Transportation |
| Banking and Financial Services | Domestic and International Monetary Policy |
| Budget | |
| Commerce | Commerce, Trade, and Hazardous Materials |
| | Health and Environment |
| | Telecommunications and Finance |
| Government Reform and Oversight | National Security, International Affairs, and Criminal Justice |
| International Relations | Africa |
| | Asia and the Pacific |
| | International Economic Policy and Trade |
| | International Operations and Human Rights |
| | Western Hemisphere |
| Judiciary | Immigration and Claims |
| National Security | Military Installations |
| | Military Personnel |
| | Military Procurement |
| | Military Readiness |
| | Military Research and Development |
| Resources | Fisheries, Wildlife, and Oceans |
| Science | Basic Research |
| | Energy and Environment |
| | Space and Aeronautics |
| | Technology |

Table 5.2   Continued

| Standing Committees | Subcommittees |
| --- | --- |
| Select Intelligence | Human Intelligence, Analysis, and Counterintelligence |
| | Technical and Tactical Intelligence |
| Small Business | Procurement, Exports, and Business Opportunities |
| Transportation and Infrastructure | Coast Guard and Maritime Transportation |
| Ways and Means | Trade |

*Source: Congressional Quarterly Almanac*, vol. 51, *1995*. Washington, D.C.: Congressional Quarterly Inc., 1996.

opposition party, must be counted as important institutional cue-givers in Congress, and there seems little reason to think that role will lessen in the post–cold war era. Moreover, if divided government becomes the rule rather than the exception, the impact of such leaders will grow even more.

*Standing Committees and Subcommittees.* In Congress, most details of policy are determined by the standing committees; the foreign and defense policy arèna is no exception. Decisions by members on how extensively to participate in the foreign policy–making process is determined by their membership on committees with foreign and defense policy responsibilities,[41] and many committees offer that chance. When the 104th Congress convened in 1995, most of its standing committees could claim direct or indirect foreign policy responsibilities. As illustrated in table 5.2, fifteen of twenty standing committees in the House (sixteen if one counts the Rules Committee) and thirty-seven subcommittees had direct or indirect, identifiable foreign or defense policy impacts. As table 5.3 shows, eleven of twenty Senate standing committees could say the same, as could thirty-four subcommittees.

The post–cold war period has seen some significant shifts in the influence of standing committees dealing with foreign and defense policy. To some degree, all standing committees have lost some influence to other institutional structures like ad hoc task forces or select committees, both of which serve to increase the policy-making influence of the party leaders making the appointments to these bodies. More pointedly, the traditional committee bastions of foreign policy responsibilities (the Senate Foreign Relations and House International Relations Commit-

Table 5.3 Senate Standing Committees and Subcommittees with Direct or Indirect Foreign or Defense Policy Impacts, 104th Congress

| Standing Committees | Subcommittees |
|---|---|
| Agriculture, Nutrition, and Forestry | Forestry, Conservation, and Rural Revitalization |
| | Marketing, Inspection, and Product Promotion |
| | Production and Price Competitiveness |
| Appropriations | Agriculture, Rural Development, and Related Agencies |
| | Commerce, Justice, State, and Judiciary |
| | Defense |
| | Foreign Operations |
| | Military Construction |
| | Transportation |
| Armed Services | Acquisition and Technology |
| | Airland Forces |
| | Personnel |
| | Readiness |
| | Seapower |
| | Strategic Forces |
| Banking, Housing, and Urban Affairs | International Finance |
| Budget | |
| Commerce, Science, and Transportation | Aviation |
| | Communications |
| | Consumer Affairs, Foreign Commerce, and Tourism |
| | Oceans and Fisheries |
| | Science, Technology, and Space |
| | Surface Transportation and Merchant Marine |
| Environment and Public Works | Clean Air, Wetlands, Private Property, and Nuclear Safety |
| Finance | International Trade |
| | Long-Term Growth, Debt and Deficit Reduction |
| Foreign Relations | African Affairs |
| | East Asian and Pacific Affairs |
| | European Affairs |
| | International Economic Policy, Export and Trade Promotion |
| | International Operations |
| | Near Eastern and South Asian Affairs |
| | Western Hemisphere and Peace Corps Affairs |

Table 5.3   Continued

| Standing Committees | Subcommittees |
| --- | --- |
| Judiciary | Immigration<br>Terrorism, Technology, and Government Information |
| Select Intelligence | |

*Source: Congressional Quarterly Almanac,* vol. 51, *1995.* Washington, D.C.: Congressional Quarterly Inc., 1996.

tees) have seen some of their roles usurped by other, more aggressive committees.[42] On the rise are the Senate Armed Services and House National Security (formerly Armed Services) Committees. These committees "frequently challenge the administration on particular weapon systems, security strategies, and administrative procedures," and they have helped initiate the transition of U.S. armed forces to a post–cold war environment.[43] Each chamber's relevant appropriations subcommittees—Defense and Foreign Operations in the Senate, and National Security and Foreign Operations, Export Financing, and Related Programs in the House—are also increasingly influential. These "appropriators can delay presidential initiatives, kill (or at least starve) the occasional 'turkey,' shape the managerial or distributive aspects of structural policy, and significantly influence a vast array of middle-range decisions . . . not subject to broad partisan dispute."[44] In short, sooner or later most foreign and defense policy matters require authorization or funding, and those needs open the door for congressional influence through these committees and subcommittees.

*Congressional Bureaucracies.* Members of Congress have other bureaucratic assets as well that may be applied to foreign and defense policy making. As I. M. Destler has noted regarding congressional foreign and defense policy making, "[T]he Congressional Research Service has been upgraded, the General Accounting Office has moved from a relatively narrow auditing focus to program evaluation, the Congressional Budget Office conducts macroeconomic and budget analyses, and the Office of Technology Assessment studies subjects with important science and technology content."[45] Despite some GAO budget cuts and the abolition of OTA by the Republican-controlled 104th Congress,[46] the net impact of these changes is that members still have considerable assistance in scrutinizing the ends and means of U.S. foreign and defense policy. Consider for example the Pentagon's discomfort when a GAO report indicated that only eight of 14 B-2 stealth bombers are in flying condition. High humidity, precipitation, or extreme temperatures can ground these $2 billion aircraft, as they damage the special coatings that makes these planes "stealthy."[47]

*Congressional Caucuses.* Caucuses have become a final institutional factor to consider in foreign as well as domestic policy making. These voluntary associations of legislators, also referred to as legislative service organizations, not only supplement but at times also compete with the standing committees for influence over lawmaking, oversight, and the representation of constituents.[48] Being informal, their numbers are fluid, but as some disappear, more are formed. There were only three prior to 1969, but by 1987, 120 were active and 40 had become inactive.[49] Thus the post–cold war era may see less activity by the Congressional Coalition for Soviet Jews or the Congressional Task Force on Afghanistan but more by the Senate Caucus on International Narcotics Control.

Various types of caucuses may square off on certain foreign policy issues. As noted earlier, the Congressional Black Caucus had important effects in pushing for changes in U.S. policy toward both South Africa and Haiti. Members of the Congressional Caucus for Women's Issues had concerns about U.S. policy stances at the Beijing Women's Conference, and, given the contracts to produce taxi cabs for China, the Automotive Caucus had a stake in China's recent MFN status debates. The future consideration of Chile's inclusion in NAFTA could mobilize the Border Caucuses of both congressional chambers, the Senate Copper Caucus, the Congressional Hispanic Caucus, the Congressional Human Rights Caucus, and the Export Task Force. Such an issue might break along regional lines, once again pitting the interests of the northeast-midwest caucuses of each chamber and the Conference of Great Lakes Congressmen against those of the Congressional Sunbelt Caucus or the Western State Coalition. Defense issues may mobilize the Conservative Democratic Forum, the Arms Control and Foreign Policy Caucus, the Senate Arms Control Observer Group, the Military Reform Caucus, the Vietnam Veterans Caucus, the Congressional Caucus for Science and Technology, or the Congressional Space Caucus. Depending on their nature, future trade issues could involve members of the Coal, Steel, Textile, or even Wine Caucuses.[50] Thus by linking the efforts of like-minded members of Congress or those with similar needs on the part of their constituencies, caucuses can be significant agents for congressional input in foreign and defense policy issues. Moreover, caucuses offer members another institutional channel to complement, compete with, or avoid standing committees and subcommittees in the policy-making process.

As long as members of Congress share policy interests, there will be a place for caucuses as potential factors in the policy-making process. However, in 1995 the new Republican majority in the House stopped providing caucuses with both public funding and office space. While this has led some caucuses to curtail formerly free publications and lay off staff, informal associations of like-minded or like-interested members of Congress are not likely to end. Consequently, this change might limit the scope of activities of caucuses in the future, but not necessarily their policy influence.

INDIVIDUAL FACTORS After considering the international, societal, and institutional factors above, we cannot forget that Congress is composed of 535 individuals. Their beliefs and perceptions form the "bottom line" on which all these other factors impact. Thus individual factors like ideology, partisanship, the increasing interaction of ideology and partisanship, and anticipated reaction must be addressed as well.

*Ideology.* When discussing congressional action, the first individual factor is what each of the 535 members thinks. Studies have consistently stressed the important role political ideology plays in determining the voting behavior of legislators on foreign and defense policy issues.[51] According to James McCormick, "the liberal/conservative continuum—so long prevalent in American domestic politics—is now also a good predictor of the foreign policy positions of Senators and Representatives."[52] While prior studies of congressional decision making across all policy arenas have long recognized ideology to be an important factor in a member's "field of forces"[53] or general policy position on an issue,[54] the common conclusion of the studies above is that ideology is usually the single, most important factor in members' decision making on foreign and defense issues.

*Partisanship.* These same studies generally indicate that in the few cases when ideology is overridden in importance by another variable, that variable is usually partisanship. According to Steven Smith, "Partisanship has been a common feature of congressional voting alignments in the foreign and defense policy arena since the 1960s,"[55] which is not surprising, since partisanship is a major component of a member's reaction to the internal political environment in which that legislator works. Both chambers of Congress are organized along partisan lines, and members tend to interact and socialize with their chamber colleagues along partisan lines. Moreover, party organizations control access to both committee and subcommittee assignments and to personal and committee staff resources. Party leaders control the legislative schedule and service the needs of their respective party members. In addition, there may be costs to resisting party leaders' requests and rewards for "doing the right thing" in party leaders' eyes. Thus partisanship affects just about every aspect of the human setting within Congress, and so it impacts the foreign policy–making process as well.

Further, partisanship interacts with the institutional factor represented by the president. Members react to the administration's foreign policy initiatives based, in part, on whether they share the president's party identification. All other things being equal, members of the president's party will look for reasons to support his foreign policy requests and members of the opposition party will look for reasons to oppose them.[56]

*Increasingly Ideological Partisanship.* Since the Vietnam War, no consensus regarding the preferred ends and means of U.S. foreign and defense policy has existed to dampen the effects of ideology and partisanship. These factors have increasingly reinforced each other, making the parties more ideological.[57] As David Rohde concludes, "[O]ver the last two decades Congress has grown increasingly assertive in foreign and defense policy and . . . conflict over these issues has grown increasingly partisan. The main domestic cause of these developments was electoral change: alterations in the patterns of political participation and voter loyalty, particularly in the South, resulted in increased homogeneity of preferences on policy among members of Congress in both parties and in greater differences between the parties."[58] Thus policy battles between Senate Foreign Relations Committee chairman Helms and President Clinton over the funding and structure of the State Department and its related agencies or between Speaker Gingrich and President Clinton over the status of U.S. leadership in the international system illustrate how ideological and partisan foreign policy making has become.

The phenomenon of divided government further escalates the impact of an increasingly partisan and ideological policy making process. As table 5.1 shows, the 1992–95 period was marked by 24 percent compliance behaviors, 39 percent resistance behaviors, 10 percent rejection behaviors, and 28 percent independent behaviors on the part of Congress. However the two years of divided government in that four-year period reveal some distinct differences. During 1992, the Democratic Congress resisted the foreign policy requests of the Republican administration 58 percent of the time. During 1995, independent behaviors on the part of the Republican Congress rose to 33 percent, presenting a more difficult challenge to the Democratic president. Unless a new consensus arises on foreign and defense issues, divided government can be expected to exacerbate the impacts of partisanship and ideology on these issues.[59]

*Anticipated Reaction.* Regardless of whether a new consensus arises, anticipated reactions by members of Congress are another constant individual factor related to the dynamics above.[60] First, members will try to anticipate the reactions of the president and other top administration actors. Presidential party members in Congress will often try to shift congressional foreign policy actions in the direction they anticipate the president will support or endorse. Opposition party members may try to push for initiatives that undercut or offset anticipated reactions coming from the White House. When Congress as a whole disagrees with the president, bipartisan leaders will try to anticipate how far congressional action may go before eliciting a presidential veto. Neither branch operates without some regard for the likely reactions of the other.[61]

Second, members will try to anticipate public reactions to the issues on the political agenda.[62] While it is easy to note that "[P]olicymakers in liberal democracies do not decide against an overwhelming public consensus,"[63] the more common practice is for legislators to watch opinion polls carefully for shifts in the mix of public preferences.[64] Most congressional effort is put into trying to anticipate how key constituencies or core supporters will react to new or changed issues, and that seems very unlikely to change in the post–cold war era.[65]

### Conclusions

The cold war's end brought another escalation in the level of congressional assertiveness in foreign policy making. Whether measured by the 29 percent drop in compliant behaviors compared to the 1950–82 period or by the illustrations from recent congressional legislation, appropriations, confirmations and ratifications, oversight and institutional control, or other informal policy-making activities, the 1992–95 period has seen an increased willingness on the part of legislators to challenge both the administration's foreign policy agenda and its preferred means of accomplishing that agenda. This change has not been lost on the president. "Gosh, I miss the Cold War," exclaimed President Clinton in 1993.[66] In late 1995 Clinton mused, "The more I stay here and the more time I spend on foreign policy . . . the more I become convinced that there is no longer a clear distinction between what is foreign and do-mestic."[67]

With no new foreign policy consensus, there is no reason to expect this increased level of congressional assertiveness in foreign policy making to end anytime soon; it seems highly likely to become the new reality post–cold war presidents must accommodate. In the past, one could assume that Congress would involve itself in intermestic issues but not in international issues. Members would delegate low-prominence, international issues to the bureaucracy while allowing presidents to assume the political risks of high-prominence, international issues.[68] However, in the post–cold war era, an ever changing mix of international, societal, institutional, and individual factors will cause members of Congress to define more issues as intermestic, thus demanding congressional involvement.

To put this in terms used earlier in this volume, members are thus more likely to insist that more policy making be done via the processes of congressional leadership (constellation 5) or by interbranch leadership (constellation 3). Congressional support of White House leadership (constellation 1) seems most likely only for high prominence, international issues which carry some notable degree of risk for the country as a whole but *which do not produce significant domestic winners and losers.* Compared to the cold war period, the post–cold war era should have a smaller proportion of such cases. As soon as an issue is defined in Congress as producing domestic winners and losers (thus intermestic), legislators will insist on congressional or interbranch leadership (constellations 5 or 3). That expectation is heightened if the opposition party controls Congress.

In lower risk cases, congressional acceptance of foreign policy bureaucracy leadership (constellation 2) or subgovernment leadership (constellation 4) can be expected only for those issues for which policy agreement exists between the branches and the relevant bureaucratic officials or actors are respected on Capitol Hill. Barring policy agreement between the branches (and that seems less likely in the post–cold war era than before), legislators can be generally expected to oppose White House leadership (constellation 1), foreign policy bureaucracy leadership (constellation 2), or subgovernment leadership (constellation 4).

In terms of types of activities, members can always use the various informal means at their disposal to try to shape U.S. foreign policy. As congressional majorities strengthen, either in terms of numbers or ideological consistency, members can be expected to rely more on the formal means open to them—legislation, appropriations, confirmations and ratifications, and oversight and institutional control. This expectation is further enhanced if it is the opposition party that controls Congress. If the ideological gulf between the president and the opposition majority in Congress widens, the stridency of congressional challenges to the administration should be expected to increase. The reverse of this has been seen in the second Clinton term. Early on, the opposition majority has not become more strident, because Clinton has reduced the ideological gulf by moving back to the political center and because the Republican hold on Congress weakened in the 1996 elections.

In summary, regardless of which party controls Congress, its members have a variety of institutional tools at their disposal. They can tell presidents what to do via legislation, and they can direct executive branch actions by what they choose to fund or not to fund. The Senate can reject or delay top personnel appointments and the confirmation of treaties. Congress can shackle executive branch actors with a myriad of reporting requirements to ensure that congressional intent is followed or create new organizational structures more responsive to legislative control. Finally, informal methods of signaling let presidents know what Congress is willing to support, and wise presidents craft their foreign policy requests based on their anticipation of congressional reaction.

Immediate trends strongly suggest that members will increasingly choose to use such instruments in the post–cold war period. Growing interdependence in international politics means more intermestic policies here at home. Presidents will call them foreign policy issues, but members of Congress will react to them based on their domestic consequences. Further, the lack of a foreign policy consensus in society, the phenomenon of divided government, the increasingly ideological and partisan nature of foreign and defense policy debates on Capitol Hill, the decreasing influence of standing committees and the increasing influence of party leaders on both sides of the aisle combine to present a formidable challenge to presidents. Post–cold war presidents should fasten their seat belts securely; foreign and defense policy making is likely to be an increasingly bumpy ride.

## Notes

I wish to thank James McCormick, James Scott, and an anonymous reviewer for their valuable critiques of earlier versions of this paper. Additionally, my thanks go to Fred Thompson for his citation assistance. I appreciate the assistance of all these scholars and friends, but any mistakes in this analysis are mine alone.

1 Harold H. Koh, *The National Security Constitution: Sharing Power after the Iran-Contra Affair* (New Haven, Conn.: Yale University Press, 1990), p. 75. Such powers include the powers to declare war; raise, maintain, and regulate an army and navy; call forth state militias to repel invasions; regulate foreign commerce; make rules regarding naturalization; and make and implement international law. Congress also has the powers to make the laws necessary to do the above and to appropriate all governmentally expended funds. Finally, the Senate is assigned the powers to approve treaties by a two-thirds majority vote and to confirm top executive appointments by a majority vote.

2 For example, see Stephen R. Weissman, *A Culture of Deference: Congress's Failure of Leadership in Foreign Policy* (New York: Basic Books, 1995); and Paul E. Peterson, "The International System and Foreign Policy," in Paul E. Peterson, ed., *The President, the Congress, and the Making of Foreign Policy* (Norman: University of Oklahoma Press, 1994), pp. 3–22.

3 On these issues and policy types, see, Ralph G. Carter, "Budgeting for Defense," in Peterson, ed., *The President, the Congress, and the Making of Foreign Policy*, 161–178; Ralph G. Carter, "Congressional Trade Politics in the Post–Cold War Era," paper delivered at the Annual Meeting of the International Studies Association, San Diego, April 1996; Barry M. Blechman, *The Politics of National Security: Congress and U.S. Defense Policy* (New York: Oxford University Press, 1990); Sharyn O'Halloran, "Congress and Foreign Trade Policy," in Randall B. Ripley and James M. Lindsay, eds., *Congress Resurgent: Foreign and Defense Policy on Capitol Hill* (Ann Arbor: University of Michigan Press, 1993), pp. 283–303; Pietro S. Nivola, "Trade Policy: Refereeing the Playing Field," in Thomas E. Mann, ed., *A Question of Balance: The President, Congress, and Foreign Policy* (Washington, D.C.: Brookings Institution, 1990), pp. 201–253; John T. Tierney, "Congressional Activism in Foreign Policy: Its Varied Forms and Stimuli," in David A. Deese, ed., *The New Politics of American Foreign Policy* (New York: St. Martin's, 1994), pp. 102–129; Bruce W. Jentleson, "American Diplomacy: around the World and along Pennsylvania Avenue," in Mann, ed., *A Question of Balance*, pp. 146–200; Roberto Suro, *Watching America's Door: The Immigration Backlash and the New Policy Debate* (Washington, D.C.: Brookings Institution, 1996); David A. Deese, "The Hazards of Interdependence: World Politics in the American Foreign Policy Process," in Deese, ed., *The New Politics of American Foreign Policy*, pp. 2–34; James M. Lindsay, "Congress and Diplomacy," in Ripley and Lindsay, eds., *Congress Resurgent*, pp. 261–281; James M. Scott, *Deciding to Intervene: The Reagan Doctrine and American Foreign Policy* (Durham, N.C.: Duke University Press, 1996), Jeremy D. Rosner, *The New Tug-of-War: Congress, the Executive Branch, and National Security* (Washington, D.C.: Carnegie Endowment for International Peace, 1995).

4 Thomas E. Mann, "Making Foreign Policy: President and Congress," in Mann, ed., *A Question of Balance*, pp. 1–34.

5 Richard A. Melanson, *American Foreign Policy since the Vietnam War: The Search for Consensus from Nixon to Clinton*, 2d ed. (Armonk, N.Y.: M. E. Sharpe, 1996).

6 James M. Lindsay, "Congress, Foreign Policy, and the New Institutionalism," *International Studies Quarterly* 38 (1994): 281–304.

7 Lindsay, "Congress, Foreign Policy," 282.

8 See Ralph G. Carter, "Presidential Effectiveness in Congressional Foreign Policy-making: A Reconsideration," in David C. Kozak and Kenneth N. Ciboski, eds., *The American Presidency: A Policy Perspective from Readings and Documents* (Chicago: Nelson-Hall, 1985), pp. 311–325.

9 See Carter, in Peterson, ed., *The President, the Congress, and the Making of Foreign Policy*; and Holbert N. Carroll, *The House of Representatives in Foreign Affairs*, rev. ed. (Boston: Little, Brown, 1966).

10 See Jim Wright, *A Balance of Power: Presidents and Congress from the End of McCarthy to the Age of Gingrich* (Atlanta: Turner Publishing, 1996), and *Worth It All: My War for Peace* (Washington, D.C.: Brassey's, 1993).

11 James M. Lindsay and Randall B. Ripley, "How Congress Influences Foreign and Defense Policy," in Ripley and Lindsay, eds., *Congress Resurgent*, pp. 17–35.

12 Duane Oldfield and Aaron Wildavsky, "Reconsidering the Two Presidencies," *Society* 26 (1989): 54–59.

13 Mann, in Mann, ed., *A Question of Balance.*

14 Ralph G. Carter, "Congressional Foreign Policy Behavior: Persistent Patterns of the Postwar Period," *Presidential Studies Quarterly* 16 (1986): 329–359. These figures are calculated from those found in table 2.

15 Carter, "Congressional Foreign Policy Behavior."

16 The sources used are *Congress and the Nation*, vol. 8, *1989-1992* (Washington, D.C.: Congressional Quarterly Inc., 1993); *Congressional Quarterly Almanac*, vol. 49, *1993* (Washington, D.C.: Congressional Quarterly Inc., 1994); *Congressional Quarterly Almanac*, vol. 50, *1994* (Washington, D.C.: Congressional Quarterly Inc., 1995); and *Congressional Quarterly Almanac*, vol. 51, *1995* (Washington, D.C.: Congressional Quarterly Inc., 1996).

17 *Dallas Morning News*, March 7, 1996, p. 11A; September 5, 1996, p. 15A.

18 *Dallas Morning News*, December 10, 1995, p. 18A.

19 See Lindsay, "Congress, Foreign Policy, and the New Institutionalism," and *Congress and the Politics of U.S. Foreign Policy* (Baltimore, Md.: Johns Hopkins University Press, 1994); and O'Halloran, "Congress and Foreign Trade Policy."

20 See John T. Rourke, Ralph G. Carter, and Mark A. Boyer, *Making American Foreign Policy*, 2d ed. (Guilford, Conn.: Brown & Benchmark, 1996), pp. 234–235.

21 See Burdette Loomis, *The Contemporary Congress* (New York: St. Martin's, 1996); Eileen Burgin, "The Influence of Constituents: Congressional Decision Making on Issues of Foreign and Defense Policy," in Ripley and Lindsay, eds., *Congress Resurgent*, pp. 67–88, and "Representatives' Decisions on Participation in Foreign Policy Issues," *Legislative Studies Quarterly* 16 (1991): 521–546; Mann, in

Mann, ed., *A Question of Balance*; and John W. Kingdon, *Congressmen's Voting Decisions*, 3d ed. (Ann Arbor: University of Michigan Press, 1989).

22  See Bernard C. Cohen, *The Public's Impact on Foreign Policy* (Boston: Little, Brown, 1973); Gabriel A. Almond, *The American People and Foreign Policy*, rev. ed. (New York: Praeger, 1960); Walter Lippmann, *The Phantom Public* (New York: Harcourt Brace, 1925); Arthur I. Cyr, *After the Cold War: American Foreign Policy, Europe, and Asia* (New York: New York University Press, 1997); Ole R. Holsti, *Public Opinion and American Foreign Policy* (Ann Arbor: University of Michigan Press, 1996), and "Public Opinion and Foreign Policy: Challenges to the Almond-Lippmann Consensus," *International Studies Quarterly* 36 (1992): 439–466; Jon Krosnick and Shibley Tehlami, "Public Attitudes toward Israel: A Study of Attentive and Issue Publics," *International Studies Quarterly* 39 (1995): 535–554; and Mark Peffley and Jon Hurwitz, "International Events and Foreign Policy Beliefs: Public Response to Changing Soviet–U.S. Relations," *American Journal of Political Science* 36 (1992): 421–461.

23  See Steven Kull, "What the Public Knows That Washington Doesn't," *Foreign Policy* 101 (1996): 102–115; Kurt Taylor Gaubatz, "Intervention and Intransitivity: Public Opinion, Social Choice, and the Use of Military Force Abroad," *World Politics* 47 (1995): 534–554; Thomas W. Graham, "Public Opinion and U.S. Foreign Policy Decision Making," in Deese, ed., *The New Politics of American Foreign Policy*, pp. 190–215; Ronald H. Hinckley, *People, Polls, and Policymakers: American Public Opinion and National Security* (New York: Lexington, 1992); Bruce W. Jentleson, "The Pretty Prudent Public: Post-Vietnam American Opinion on the Use of Military Force," *International Studies Quarterly* 36 (1992): 49–73; Miroslav Nincic, "A Sensible Public: New Perspective on Popular Opinion and Foreign Policy," *Journal of Conflict Resolution* 26 (1992): 772–789; Benjamin I. Page and Robert Y. Shapiro, *The Rational Public: Fifty Years of Trends in Americans' Policy Preferences* (Chicago: University of Chicago Press, 1992); and James A. Stimson, *Public Opinion in America: Moods, Cycles, and Swings* (Boulder, Colo.: Westview, 1991).

24  See Tierney, in Deese, ed., *The New Politics of American Foreign Policy*; and Daniel Yankelovich, *Coming to Judgment: Making Democracy Work in a Complex World* (Syracuse, N.Y.: Syracuse University Press, 1991).

25  See John Aldrich, "Rational Choice Theory and the Study of American Politics," in Lawrence C. Dodd and Calvin Jillson, eds., *The Dynamics of American Politics* (Boulder, Colo.: Westview, 1994), pp. 208–233; and John Ferejohn, "Incumbent Performance and Electoral Control," *Public Choice* 50 (1986): 5–25.

26  Lindsay, *Congress and the Politics of U.S. Foreign Policy*, p. 6.

27  Lindsay, *Congress and the Politics of U.S. Foreign Policy*, p. 132.

28  John T. Tierney, "Interest Group Involvement in Congressional Foreign and Defense Policy," in Ripley and Lindsay, eds., *Congress Resurgent*, p. 126.

29  See Rourke, Carter, and Boyer, *Making American Foreign Policy*, ch. 11.

30  See Kevin A. Hill, "The Domestic Sources of Foreign Policymaking: Congressional Voting and Mass Attitudes toward South Africa," *International Studies Quarterly* 37 (1993): 195–214; and Frederic I. Solop, "Public Protest and Public

Policy: The Anti-Apartheid Movement and Political Innovation," *Policy Studies Review* 9 (1990): 307–326.

31 See Heidi H. Hobbs, *City Hall Goes Abroad: The Foreign Policy of Local Politics* (Beverly Hills, Calif.: Sage, 1994); David S. Meyer, *A Winter of Discontent: The Nuclear Freeze and American Politics* (Westport, Conn.: Praeger, 1990); and James M. McCormick, "Congressional Voting on the Nuclear Freeze Resolutions," *American Politics Quarterly* 13 (1985): 122–136.

32 See Paula Dobriansky and Diana A. McCaffery, "Do the Media Make Foreign Policy?" in Annual Editions series, *American Foreign Policy* 1995/96 (Guilford, Conn.: Brown and Benchmark, 1995), pp. 102–105; Leon Hadar, "Covering the New World Disorder: The Press Rushes in Where Clinton Fears to Tread," *Columbia Journalism Review* 33 (1994): 26–30; James F. Hoge, "Media Pervasiveness," *Foreign Affairs* 73 (1994): 136–144; and Richard Davis, "The Foreign Policy Making Role of Congress in the 1990s: Remote Sensing Technology and the Future of Congressional Power," *Congress and the Presidency* 19 (1992): 175–192.

33 Lindsay, *Congress and the Politics of U.S. Foreign Policy,* p. 139.

34 See Lindsay, "Congress, Foreign Policy, and the New Institutionalism."

35 Rounding error produces the total of 101 percent.

36 James Meernik, "Presidential Support in Congress: Conflict and Consensus on Foreign and Defense Policy," *Journal of Politics* 55 (1993): 569–587; Jon R. Bond and Richard Fleisher, *The President in the Legislative Arena* (Chicago: University of Chicago Press, 1990); Mark A. Peterson, *Legislating Together: The White House and Capitol Hill from Eisenhower to Reagan* (Cambridge, Mass.: Harvard University Press, 1990); Kingdon, *Congressmen's Voting Decisions;* and Aage R. Clausen, *How Congressmen Decide* (New York: St. Martin's, 1973).

37 Peterson, "The International System and Foreign Policy."

38 Lindsay, *Congress and the Politics of U.S. Foreign Policy,* p. 102.

39 *Newsweek,* February 10, 1997, pp. 22–29.

40 Steven S. Smith, "Congressional Party Leaders," in Peterson, ed., *The President, the Congress, and the Making of Foreign Policy,* pp. 154–155.

41 Burgin, "Representatives' Decisions on Participation in Foreign Policy Issues."

42 James M. McCormick, "Decision Making in the Foreign Affairs and Foreign Relations Committees," in Ripley and Lindsay, eds., *Congress Resurgent,* pp. 115–153.

43 Christopher J. Deering, "Decision-Making in the Armed Services Committees," in Ripley and Lindsay, eds., *Congress Resurgent,* p. 181.

44 White, in Ripley and Lindsay, eds., *Congress Resurgent,* p. 205.

45 I. M. Destler, "Executive-Congressional Conflict in Foreign Policy: Explaining It, Coping with It," in Lawrence C. Dodd and Bruce I. Oppenheimer, eds., *Congress Reconsidered,* 3d ed. (Washington, D.C.: CQ Press, 1985), p. 359.

46 Bruce I. Oppenheimer, "Abdicating Congressional Power: The Paradox of Republican Control," in Lawrence C. Dodd and Bruce I. Oppenheimer, eds., *Congress Reconsidered,* 6th ed. (Washington, D.C.: CQ Press, 1997), pp. 371–389.

47 *Dallas Morning News,* August 23, 1997, p. 6A.

48 Leroy N. Rieselbach, *Congressional Politics: The Evolving Legislative System,* 2d ed. (Boulder, Colo.: Westview, 1995).

49  Susan Webb Hammond, "Congressional Caucuses in the Policy Process," in Lawrence C. Dodd and Bruce I. Oppenheimer, eds., *Congress Reconsidered*, 4th ed. (Washington, D.C.: CQ Press, 1989), pp. 351–371.

50  See Rieselbach, *Congressional Politics*; Ann L. Brownson, ed., *1990 Congressional Staff Directory* (Mount Vernon, Va.: Staff Directories, 1990); and Hammond, "Congressional Caucuses."

51  See William M. Leogrande and Philip Brenner, "The House Divided: Ideological Polarization over Aid to the Nicaraguan 'Contras,'" *Legislative Studies Quarterly* 18 (1993): 105–136; James M. McCormick and Eugene R. Wittkopf, "At the Water's Edge: The Effects of Party, Ideology, and Issues on Congressional Foreign Policy Voting, 1947–1988," *American Politics Quarterly* 20 (1992): 26–53; Bond and Fleisher, *The President in the Legislative Arena*; Ralph G. Carter, "Senate Defense Budgeting, 1981–1988: The Impacts of Ideology, Party, and Constituency Benefit on the Decision to Support the President," *American Politics Quarterly* 17 (1989): 332–347; Richard Fleisher, "Economic Benefit, Ideology, and Senate Voting on the B-1 Bomber," *American Politics Quarterly* 13 (1985): 200–211; Bruce A. Ray, "Defense Department Spending and Hawkish Voting in the House of Representatives," *Western Political Quarterly* 34 (1981): 439–446; Stephen Cobb, "Defense Spending and Defense Voting in the House: An Empirical Study of an Aspect of the Military Industrial Complex," *American Journal of Sociology* 82 (1976): 163–182; and Robert A. Bernstein and William W. Anthony, "The ABM Issue in the Senate, 1968–1970: The Importance of Ideology," *American Political Science Review* 68 (1974): 1198–1206.

52  McCormick, "Congressional Voting on the Nuclear Freeze Resolutions," p. 123.

53  Kingdon, *Congressmen's Voting Decisions*.

54  Clausen, *How Congressmen Decide*.

55  Smith, "Congressional Party Leaders," p. 129.

56  See Bond and Fleisher, *The President in the Legislative Arena*; and Peterson, *Legislating Together*.

57  See James M. Lindsay and Randall B. Ripley, "Foreign and Defense Policy in Congress: A Research Agenda for the 1990s," *Legislative Studies Quarterly* 17 (1992): 417–449: and David W. Rohde, "Partisanship, Leadership, and Congressional Assertiveness in Foreign and Defense Policy," in Deese, ed., *The New Politics of American Foreign Policy*, pp. 76–101.

58  Rohde, "Partisanship, Leadership, and Congressional Assertiveness," p. 98.

59  See James M. McCormick, Eugene R. Wittkopf, and David Danna, "Bipartisanship, Partisanship, and Ideology in Congressional-Executive Relations: The Bush and Clinton Years," paper presented at the Annual Meeting of the International Studies Association, San Diego, April 1996; and David W. Rohde, "Presidential Support in the House of Representatives," in Peterson, ed., *The President, the Congress, and the Making of Foreign Policy*, pp. 101–128.

60  For more on anticipated reactions, see Mary Parker Follett, "The Psychology of Control," in H. C. Metcalf, ed., *Psychological Foundations of Business Administration* (New York: McGraw-Hill, 1927), pp. 148–174 and Carl J. Friedrich, *Constitutional Government and Democracy*, rev. ed. (Boston: Ginn, 1950).

61  See Wright, *Balance of Power*; and James M. Lindsay, "Congress and Foreign

Policy: Avenues of Influence," in Eugene R. Wittkopf, ed., *The Domestic Sources of Foreign Policy*, 2d ed. (New York: St. Martin's, 1994), pp. 191–207.

62 See Stimson, *Public Opinion in America*; and Thomas Risse-Kappan, "Public Opinion, Domestic Structure, and Foreign Policy in Liberal Democracies," *World Politics* 43 (1991): 479–512.

63 Risse-Kappan, "Public Opinion, Domestic Structure, and Foreign Policy," p. 510.

64 Hinckley, *People, Polls, and Policymakers*.

65 See Cheryl Lynn Herrera, Richard Herrera, and Eric R. A. N. Smith, "Public Opinion and Congressional Representation," *Public Opinion Quarterly* 56 (1992): 185–205; Burgin, "The Influence of Constituents"; and Catherine R. Shapiro, David W. Brady, Richard A. Brody, and John A. Ferejohn, "Linking Constituency Opinion and Senate Voting Scores: A Hybrid Explanation," *Legislative Studies Quarterly* 15 (1990): 597–620.

66 Quoted in Bruce W. Jentleson, "Who, Why, What, and How: Debates over Post–Cold War Military Intervention," in Lieber, ed., *Eagle Adrift*, p. 65.

67 Quoted in Steven L. Spiegel, "Eagle in the Middle East," in Lieber, ed., *Eagle Adrift*, p. 296.

68 This logic is developed in Rourke, Carter, and Boyer, *Making American Foreign Policy*, ch. 6.

# 6.

## Public Opinion and U.S. Foreign Policy

## after the Cold War

*Ole R. Holsti*

In one of several public addresses on the appropriate prerequisites for deployment of American combat forces abroad, Secretary of Defense Casper Weinberger in 1984 specified six conditions that must be met prior to any such intervention. According to Weinberger, one of those preconditions was that "there must be some reasonable assurance that we will have the support of the American people."[1] His Cabinet colleague, Secretary of State George Shultz, publicly disagreed with the "Weinberger Doctrine," characterizing it then and later in his memoirs as an unreasonably stringent set of preconditions that would rarely, if ever, be met. Consequently, Shultz argued, these restrictions effectively would serve as an excuse for inaction, even when vital American interests abroad were potentially threatened.[2] During the intervening years, others have weighed in on one side or the other of the debate. The differences between Weinberger and Shultz are part of a venerable debate among philosophers and statesmen as well as historians and political scientists about a central issue regarding the theory and practice of democratic government: namely, what is the proper role of public opinion in the conduct of foreign affairs?

Two competing perspectives—liberalism and realism—address the relationship between foreign affairs and public opinion. Liberalism, whose long tradition dates back at least to Immanuel Kant and Jeremy Bentham, holds that public opinion can and does play a constructive role in constraining policy makers. Realism, on the other hand, is much more skeptical about whether the public does matter, and about whether it should matter to policy makers. The period encompassing World War II featured two developments that weighed heavily on this debate. First, scientific public opinion polling made survey data available. Second, the assumption of a leadership role in world affairs by the United States made the question of foreign policy more important. Together, these developments stimulated a growth industry in analyses of public opinion. In the two decades following World War II, these analyses produced a basic consensus that centered on three major propositions: (1) public opinion is highly volatile and thus provides very dubious foundations for a sound foreign policy; (2) public attitudes on foreign affairs are so lacking in structure and coherence that they might best be described as "nonattitudes"; (3) in the end, public opinion has a very limited impact on the conduct of foreign policy. Because these propositions featured prominently in the analyses and observations of Walter Lippmann and Gabriel Almond, they can be described as the "Almond-Lippmann consensus."[3]

Other studies buttressed this consensus, providing evidence that the public did not influence foreign policy and arguing that, given its volatility and lack of structure and coherence, public opinion should not guide policy makers.[4] Consequently, by the 1960s the consensus mirrored the comment of one State Department official: "To hell with public opinion. We should lead, and not follow." Overall, State Department officials viewed the public as an entity to be "educated" rather than a lodestar by which to be guided.[5] The consensus was that the U.S. government, and especially the president, did and should have "almost a free hand" in the conduct of foreign affairs.

The Vietnam War stimulated a reexamination of this consensus. Most broadly, the Vietnam experience led many observers to question whether foreign policy should be divorced from public opinion; the belief in a strong executive, free from public pressure, came under particularly harsh scrutiny. At a narrower level, some analysts became increasingly persuaded that existing surveys distorted public attitudes by posing excessively restrictive and simplistic questions. The conflict in Southeast Asia thus stimulated independent surveys designed specifically to assess foreign policy attitudes in greater depth and breadth.

The results of these surveys subsequently led to a challenge to each of the propositions of the Almond-Lippmann consensus. For example, John Mueller's study of public opinion during the Korean and Vietnam wars challenged the characterization of the public's views as mindlessly volatile. Mueller found that, while the public's support for both military ventures declined over time, it did so in explicable ways; opposition to the conflicts coincided with rising battle deaths, suggesting the use of understandable, if simple, guidelines.[6] Later, in a comprehensive analysis of more than fifty years and six thousand public opinion questions that have been posed at least twice since the 1930s, Benjamin Page and Robert Shapiro challenged the proposition that public opinion is unstructured and incoherent, finding that, in the aggregate, public opinion on foreign policy is characterized by considerable stability, and that shifts in attitudes are "reasonable, event-driven" reactions to the real world in spite of only marginally adequate information.[7]

Finally, the premise of public impotence has come under challenge as well. Although policy makers clearly attempt to shape opinion, with varying degrees of success, some recent evidence indicates that the public is both capable and willing to express views on foreign affairs that do not necessarily follow those of policy makers or opinion leaders.[8] Moreover, additional evidence suggests that such views matter to foreign policy. A study of presidential campaigns between 1952 and 1984 reveals that foreign policy issues had "large effects" in five of the nine elections,[9] and two major studies have identified substantial congruence between changes in public preferences and policy changes over extended periods. Alan Monroe found consistency between policy outcomes and public preferences in two-thirds of his cases spanning the years 1960–74, with especially high consistency on foreign policy issues.[10] Similarly, Page and Shapiro examined 357 significant changes of public preferences between 1935 and 1979. Of the 231 instances in which domestic and foreign policy also changed, 153 (66%) were congruent with the changes in public preferences.[11]

Although such studies have yet to produce a consensus to replace the Lippmann-Almond thesis, growing evidence suggests that public opinion is more structured, coherent, and influential than suggested by the earlier consensus. However, most of the evidence on these issues was derived from the cold war era. Can we assume that findings drawn from a period dominated by the confrontation between Washington and Moscow remain valid? This question makes careful analysis of the nature and impact of public attitudes on foreign affairs during the 1990s a vital one for the post–cold war U.S. foreign policy setting. The remainder of this chapter addresses the nature of public attitudes for both the general public and opinion leaders in the wake of the cold war. Utilizing survey data from the years before and since the end of the cold war, it lays out the general trends, elements of continuity, and aspects of change in public views toward U.S. foreign policy. The final section of the chapter explores some of the likely effects on the substance and formulation of post–cold war U.S. foreign policy.

## Aspects of Public Opinion in the Post–Cold War Era

The dawn of the "age of polling" coincided with bitter debates during the second Roosevelt administration on the proper American policy toward expansionist dictatorships in Europe and Asia. Surveys revealed strong isolationist sentiments that contributed to Roosevelt's caution in confronting a Congress intent upon passing various forms of "neutrality legislation" to ensure that the United States would not be drawn into a world war, as it had been in 1917.

### Internationalism or Isolationism

After Pearl Harbor brought the country into the conflict, Roosevelt and others who pointed to American isolationism during the interwar period as one of the causes of World War II took an active interest in what public attitudes might be toward active international engagement after the war. Since 1943, Gallup, the National Opinion Research Center (NORC) and other polling organizations have asked the public whether the United States should "play an active role in world affairs, or should it stay out." The first survey found that 76 percent favored the internationalist option, whereas only 14 percent preferred withdrawal from world affairs. The subsequent half-century of responses to nearly fifty surveys, summarized in figure 6.1, encompassed the end of World War II; the onset of the cold war; two long costly wars in Asia and a short victorious one in the Persian Gulf region; crises in the Caribbean, the Taiwan Straits, Berlin, and the Middle East; several periods of warming relations between Moscow and Washington; and, finally, the end of the cold war and disintegration of the USSR.

Despite this period of almost unprecedented international turbulence and some variations in the precise wording used in the surveys, responses to these questions about the appropriate international stance of the United States have remained relatively stable. Notwithstanding fears of a public reversion to isolationism expressed periodically by an array of distinguished analysts—including Handley Cantrill, Roosevelt's private pollster; Gabriel Almond; Walter Lippmann; and George Kennan—not a single survey during that period has shown a ratio of less than three to two in favor of internationalism. By the late 1980s, a period marked by dramatically improving relations between Washington and Moscow, that margin had increased to more than two to one.

Just as many critics of the public expressed deep concerns about an American return to isolationism after 1945, some recent commentators have charged that post–cold war America appears ready to return

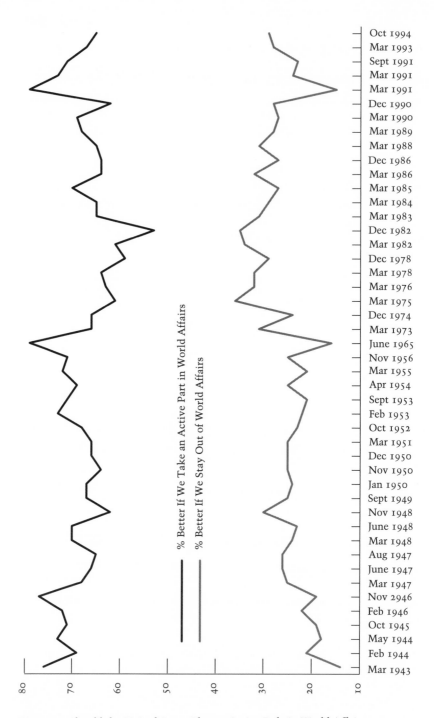

Figure 6.1. Should the United States Play an Active Role in World Affairs, or Should It Stay Out?

*Source:* Gallup Poll, National Opinion Research Center, Chicago Council on Foreign Relations, *Fortune, Washington Post.* The exact wording of the questions and response options varied somewhat from survey to survey.

"back to the womb."[12] However, the end of the cold war did not bring about a dramatic reorientation of public attitudes toward internationalism. A 1991 NORC survey revealed that almost three-fourths of the public favored an active American role in the world, a figure that is quite comparable to peaks of internationalist sentiments during the cold war. Two years later, when it had become clear that the disintegration of the Soviet Union did not necessarily mean an end to troubling conflicts abroad, support for an internationalist American role remained quite high; 67 percent favored that position as against only 28 percent who preferred to "stay out of world affairs." Even continuing controversies over the appropriate American role in peacekeeping operations, such as those in Somalia, Haiti, Bosnia, and elsewhere, had little impact on the strong majority (65 to 27 percent) favoring "an active part in world affairs" during the weeks leading up to the 1994 congressional elections.[13] Thus, at the most general level, the end of the cold war has not triggered a dramatic change in public sentiments toward engagement in world affairs.

Although comparable evidence about leaders' preferences is less extensive and it is heavily concentrated in the post-Vietnam era, most of it indicates that elites outstrip the general public in their support for active involvement in international affairs. The Chicago Council on Foreign Relations (CCFR) surveys, conducted every four years since 1974, have posed the question directly to the general public and to a smaller sample of elites starting in 1978. These six surveys reveal strong and consistent differences between leaders and the general public. During the twenty-year period, the general public preferred an active American international role rather than withdrawal from world affairs by margins ranging from 66 to 24 percent (1974) to a low of 53 to 35 percent (1982). In contrast, leaders taking part in the CCFR studies have been virtually unanimous in judging that it is better for the United States to "take an active part in world affairs"; that option never failed to gain the support of fewer than 97 percent of them.

The data in figure 6.1 would seem to raise some questions about charges that the public is leading a post–cold war stampede back to isolationism, but it is important not to read too much into them. Because "an active part in world affairs" can encompass a wide array of international commitments and undertakings, the data certainly should not be counted as decisive evidence of a broad foreign policy consensus or of sustained support for all manner of international activities. Nor do they reveal how the public might react when confronted with trade-offs or with the costs of active international involvement, especially when the price is measured in terms of casualties. Thus, we need to turn to preferences of both the general public and opinion leaders on more specific issues.

*Foreign Policy Goals*

The CCFR surveys have asked respondents to assess the importance of various U.S. foreign policy goals. The results for the six surveys reveal that in 1994 the general public tended to give top priority to goals that promote and defend the country's economic interests (table 6.1). This does not, however, constitute a sudden post–cold war change of priorities. Protecting the jobs of American workers ranked as the number-one goal in all but two of the surveys; in the most recent study (1994) it ranked second to stopping the flow of illegal drugs into the United States. Energy security also has consistently been accorded a high ranking, and the two most recent surveys saw an increase in the number of respondents who rated "protecting the interests of American business abroad" as a "very important" foreign policy goal.

In contrast, such goals as "containing communism" and "matching Soviet military power" have ranked at the top of the foreign policy agenda in none of the CCFR surveys, not even in those conducted during the cold war. A more general military/security goal—"maintaining superior military power worldwide"—ranked only tenth among respondents to the 1994 CCFR survey; moreover, another cold war goal, "defending our allies' security," did not appear among the top three until the cold war had ended. No doubt its high ranking in 1990 reflected events surrounding the invasion of Kuwait by Iraq and, perhaps, the fact that the United States and Soviet Union were on the same side rather than adversaries in that conflict, thereby eliminating the risks of a confrontation between the superpowers. Four years later, the goal of protecting allies received its lowest rating since 1978 as fewer than half of the respondents rated it as very important. In this instance, the collapse of the Soviet Union, the declining effectiveness of the Russian army, and a general sense that the country's most important alliance— NATO—does not face a serious external security threat probably contributed to the reduced importance attributed to protecting allies.

For several issues it is not possible to measure opinion changes because there are no cold war baselines against which to assess judgments expressed in 1994; for example, stopping the flow of illegal drugs and controlling illegal immigration ranked among the top three foreign policy goals in 1994, but the questions had not been included in previous surveys. The public also rated efforts to prevent nuclear prolif-

Table 6.1   The Importance of American Foreign Policy Goals: Assessments in
Chicago Council on Foreign Relations Surveys, 1974–1994

| | PERCENT "VERY IMPORTANT" RATINGS | | | | | |
|---|---|---|---|---|---|---|
| | 1974 | 1978 | 1982 | 1986 | 1990 | 1994 |
| *World order security issues* | | | | | | |
| a. Preventing the spread of nuclear weapons | — | — | — | — | 59 | 82 |
| b. Worldwide arms control | 64 | 64 | 64 | 69 | 53 | — |
| c. Strengthening the United Nations | 46 | 47 | 48 | 46 | 44 | 51 |
| d. Protecting weaker nations against aggression | 28 | 34 | 34 | 32 | 57 | 24 |
| *World order economic and environmental issues* | | | | | | |
| e. Improving the global environment | — | — | — | — | 58 | 58 |
| f. Combatting world hunger | 61 | 59 | 58 | 63 | — | 41 |
| g. Helping to improve the standard of living in less developed countries | 39 | 35 | 35 | 37 | 41 | 22 |
| *U.S. economic interest issues* | | | | | | |
| h. Stopping the flow of illegal drugs into the U.S. | — | — | — | — | — | 85 |
| i. Controlling and reducing illegal immigration | — | — | — | — | — | 72 |
| j. Securing adequate supplies of energy | 75 | 78 | 70 | 69 | 61 | 62 |
| k. Reducing the U.S. trade deficit with foreign countries | — | — | — | 62 | 56 | 59 |
| l. Protecting the jobs of American workers | 74 | 78 | 77 | 78 | 65 | 83 |
| m. Protecting the interests of American business abroad | 39 | 45 | 44 | 43 | 63 | 52 |
| *U.S. values and institutions issues* | | | | | | |
| n. Promoting and defending human rights in other countries | — | 39 | 43 | 42 | 58 | 34 |
| o. Helping to bring a democratic form of government to other nations | 28 | 26 | 29 | 30 | 28 | 25 |
| *Cold War/security issues* | | | | | | |
| p. Maintaining superior military power worldwide | — | — | — | — | — | 50 |
| q. Defending our allies' security | 33 | 50 | 50 | 56 | 61 | 41 |
| r. Matching Soviet military power | — | — | 49 | 53 | 56 | — |
| s. Containing Communism | 54 | 60 | 59 | 57 | 56 | — |

*Note:* Respondents were asked the question: "For each [foreign policy goal], please say whether you think that it should be a very important foreign policy goal of the United States, a somewhat important foreign policy goal, or not an important goal at all."

*Source:* John E. Rielly, ed., *American Public Opinion and U.S. Foreign Policy 1975* (Chicago: Chicago Council on Foreign Relations, 1975). Also, similar monographs edited by Rielly in 1979, 1983, 1987, 1991, and 1995.

eration as a very important goal; this represents continuity rather than change as all of the previous CCFR surveys also revealed a high priority to arms control. Finally, the public has rarely expressed a great deal of enthusiasm for promoting American values and institutions abroad. With a single exception, the goals of promoting human rights or democratic forms of government generally ranked among the least important foreign policy goals.

The "goals" questions also were posed to leaders in the six CCFR studies (with some variation in the specific items) and in six Foreign Policy Leadership Project (FPLP) questionnaires as well. These two studies thus provide assessments of a wide range of possible foreign policy goals in twelve surveys of leaders conducted over the 1974–96 period. Aside from a shared judgment that energy security is "very important," other goals accorded the highest rating by leaders revealed a somewhat different and broader set of priorities than those of the general public. The differences are generally consistent with the proposition that leaders are more internationally oriented. Thus, their most highly ranked goals usually included such world order issues as arms control, "fostering international cooperation to solve common problems, such as food, inflation and energy," "improving the global environment," and "combatting world hunger." The latter goal also was accorded a high priority by the general public in surveys prior to 1990, when the question was dropped. By 1994 it ranked only eighth among the sixteen foreign policy goals in the judgment of the general public. In contrast to the views of the general public, "Defending our allies' security" was accorded a high priority by leaders in three of the CCFR surveys (1978, 1982, 1986); after declining in importance in 1990, it rebounded in the judgment of leaders to rank as the third most important goal (behind only preventing nuclear proliferation and energy) in 1994.

On the other hand, compared to leaders, the CCFR surveys found that the general public gave higher priority to "strengthening the United Nations." What might at first appear to be an anomaly is perhaps consistent with the rest of the data. Although the evidence does not permit the proposition to be tested, it is possible that many among the general public view a stronger United Nations as an *alternative* to American interventions and other international undertakings, or at least a way of sharing the burdens of such activities. This hypothesis suggests that a pro–United Nations attitude may in fact be consistent with public yearning for a somewhat less active international role for the United States. It might be noted that support for the United Nations among leaders increased sharply in the 1990 CCFR and 1992 FPLP surveys, probably as a result of Security Council activities in the wake of Iraq's invasion of Kuwait in August 1990, before dropping in 1994, when only one third of the leaders taking part in the CCFR survey rated "strengthening the United Nations" as a "very important" foreign policy goal. A similar decline in the importance attributed to strengthening the United Nations—from 44 percent in 1992 to 26 percent in 1996—was recorded in the FPLP survey.

There are, finally, some broad similarities in the less highly rated goal priorities of the general public and leaders. Such cold war goals as containment or "matching Soviet military power" dominated the rankings of neither group. Nor did either leaders or the general public exhibit a great deal of fervor for promoting U.S. values and institutions abroad, although the end of the cold war has opened up greater opportunities for supporting human rights and expanding democracy, while reducing the risks of triggering a great power confrontation—with the possible exception of relations with China—by doing so. "Promoting and defending human rights in other countries" as a foreign policy goal only once received a "very important" rating from even one half of either group; the exception was the public appraisal of that goal in 1990. Even in the wake of the collapse of many communist and other authoritarian regimes in the late 1980s and early 1990s, few respondents, whether among the opinion leaders or the general public, expressed much interest in "helping to bring a democratic form of government to other nations." The difficulties of achieving success in such undertakings, especially in countries lacking any tradition of democratic institutions, probably contributed to these ratings. Perhaps abuse of the term "democracy" by American officials when referring to friendly tyrants—for example, when President Reagan compared the Nicaraguan contras to the American founding fathers, or when other presidents toasted the Shah of Iran or Ferdinand Marcos of the Philippines in glowing terms as friends of democracy—has also made both opinion leaders and the general public somewhat cynical about America's ability to export democracy. The lack of public support for exporting democracy notwithstanding, both the Bush and Clinton administrations have declared that expanding the "zone of democracy" is an important foreign policy goal.

*Trade and Protectionism*
The Vietnam era coincided with a fading U.S. hegemony in international economic matters; the most visible symptoms included worsening trade balances and eroding confidence in the dollar. The "Nixon economic shock" of August 1971, effectively ending the Bretton Woods

monetary regime established at the end of World War II, symbolized the declining U.S. economic position. During the preceding quarter century, polling organizations only infrequently posed questions about trade and protectionism. Among those who knew of such issues during this time, proponents of reducing tariffs outnumbered the protectionists by substantial margins.

As international economic issues became more contentious, survey evidence about public and elite attitudes toward them became more plentiful. The five most recent CCFR surveys have asked both the general public and leaders whether they "sympathize more with those who want to eliminate tariffs or those who think such tariffs are necessary" (table 6.2). The results indicate a wide gap between the two groups, with a steady majority of the general public supporting tariffs through 1990. Four years later, in the midst of energetic efforts by the White House and many congressional leaders in both political parties to gain approval of the treaty incorporating the Uruguay Round of the GATT agreement and the establishment of the World Trade Organization, support for tariffs had fallen below 50 percent; however, proponents of such trade barriers still outnumbered those who would eliminate them by a margin of 48 percent to 32 percent. Contrary to the widespread belief that protectionism is largely confined to union members and blue-collar workers, retention of tariffs actually received higher than average approval from the college-educated (51%) and those with annual incomes above $50,000 (53%).[14]

In contrast, although there had been some increase in support for protectionism among leaders during the dozen years ending in 1990, that position was espoused by no more than one-third of those polled in any of the CCFR surveys. By 1994 only one leader in five wanted to retain tariffs, whereas more than three-fourths of them favored their elimination. Leadership opposition to protectionism also emerges from a question posed three times between 1984 and 1996 to larger samples of leaders in the FPLP surveys. Even though the question was phrased in a manner that explicitly incorporates the most widely used argument for protectionism—"erecting trade barriers against foreign goods to protect American industries and jobs"—fewer than one-fourth of the leaders expressed either strong or moderate agreement with such a policy in any of the four surveys.

Finally, assessments of the North American Free Trade Agreement (NAFTA, see chapter 14), provide a further evidence of attitudes on trade. Leaders were overwhelmingly in favor of NAFTA, whereas the public

Table 6.2   Opinions on Trade, Protectionism, and the North American Free Trade
Agreement (NAFTA): The General Public, and Leaders, 1978–1996

| | Date | Survey | General Public | Leaders |
|---|---|---|---|---|
| | | | *% Tariffs Are Necessary* | |
| Generally, would you say you sympathize more with those who want to *eliminate* tariffs or those who think such tariffs are *necessary?* | 1978 | CCFR | 57 | 23 |
| | 1982 | CCFR | 57 | 28 |
| | 1986 | CCFR | 53 | 29 |
| | 1990 | CCFR | 54 | 33 |
| | 1994 | CCFR | 48 | 20 |
| | | | *% Agree Strongly or Agree Somewhat* | |
| Please indicate how strongly you agree or disagree with | | | | |
| Erecting trade barriers against foreign goods to protect American industries and jobs | 1984 | FPLP | — | 24 |
| | 1988 | FPLP | — | 16 |
| | 1992 | FPLP | — | 21 |
| | 1996 | FPLP | — | 22 |
| Opening negotiations for a free-trade zone with Mexico | 1992 | FPLP | — | 84 |
| Creating a free-trade zone with Canada | 1992 | FPLP | — | 95 |
| | | | *% Favor NAFTA* | |
| Do you favor or oppose the North American Free Trade Agreement? | 1993 | T-M | 46 | 89 |
| | 1993 | Gallup* | 38 | — |
| | 1994 | CCFR** | 50 | 86 |
| | 1996 | FPLP | — | 80 |

*Average of "favor" NAFTA responses in four surveys conducted in August, September, early November and mid-November. The average "oppose" and "no opinion" responses in these surveys were 43 percent and 19 percent, respectively.

** Respondents who rated NAFTA as "mostly good" for the U.S. economy.

*Key:* CCFR: Chicago Council on Foreign Relations surveys; FPLP: Foreign Policy Leadership Project Surveys; T-M: Times-Mirror survey, "America's Place in the World."

was much more evenly divided on the agreement, with the opponents slightly outnumbering the supporters until 1994; the CCFR poll in that year found that NAFTA was judged as "mostly a good thing for the U.S. economy," but that survey was undertaken just before the financial crisis triggered by devaluation of the Mexican peso. Thus, the wide gap between the general public and leaders on trade issues encompasses both general attitudes toward protectionism and support for such specific undertakings as NAFTA.

*Economic and Technical Aid*

Strong majorities among the general public favored such early post–World War II foreign aid undertakings as the European Recovery Program; a November 1948 Gallup survey found that the public supported the Marshall Plan, as the ERP was widely known, by a margin of 65 percent to 13 percent. During the past two decades, however, international economic and technical assistance programs have fallen into public disfavor. They often rank as the most popular candidates for reduced budget allocations, although there is also evidence that this negative view of foreign aid is grounded in widespread misconceptions about the actual level of U.S. spending for assistance abroad. According to the results emerging from a 1995 survey, "A strong majority says that the United States is spending too much on foreign aid. But this attitude is based on the assumption that the U.S. is spending vastly more than it is in fact. Asked what an 'appropriate' amount would be, the median level proposed is five times the present spending level."[15]

The six CCFR surveys again provide directly comparable evidence about support for such programs among leaders and the general public. When asked, "on the whole, do you favor or oppose our giving economic aid to other nations for purposes of economic development and technical assistance," the general public was generally quite evenly divided on the question, with support for such programs ranging between 45 percent (1990, and 1994) and 53 percent (1986). These figures actually reveal a surprisingly high degree of support for foreign assistance as most other surveys have shown considerably less enthusiasm. Respondents favored reduction of assistance to all major recipients, most notably Israel and Egypt, the countries receiving the largest amounts of U.S. aid. College graduates, liberals, travelers abroad, and those with higher incomes were strongest supporters of foreign aid. The contrast with elite opinions is quite dramatic, as leaders have consistently stated their strong approval of economic and technical assistance. In none of the CCFR surveys through 1990 did fewer than 90 percent of the leaders express support for foreign assistance; in 1994, the comparable figure—86 percent support for foreign aid—was still double that of the general public. Leaders expressing the strongest opposition were those in business (24%) and the Congress (19%).[16] A related question asked opinion leaders taking part in the six FPLP surveys whether they would support economic aid to poorer countries "even if it means higher prices at home." After an equal division between supporters and opponents on the question in 1976, moderate majorities of respondents in the subsequent four surveys have favored such assistance. In 1996, however, support for aid fell to 44 percent.

### U.S. Troops Abroad

The deployment of troops abroad has been among the most controversial aspects of American foreign policy. During the War of 1812, militia units refused to invade Canada on the grounds that fighting for "the common defense" could only be done on American soil. Before World War II there were also numerous deployments of U.S. troops abroad without declarations of war—for example, to quell the Philippine insurrection after the Spanish-American War and to pursue Pancho Villa in Mexico in 1916. The issue became even more visible with the expanded American international role after 1945. During World War II, Franklin Roosevelt told Winston Churchill that the public would force him to withdraw all troops from Europe within two years after the end of the conflict. Roosevelt's prognosis, which did not take into account the deterioration of East-West relations over such issues as the fate of Poland and other Eastern European countries, the status of Berlin, and the other events that contributed to the cold war, proved to be wrong. Nevertheless, the overseas deployment of troops rarely has been free of controversy. Contentious debates centered on the obligations entailed in the NATO Treaty and the constitutionality and wisdom of the War Powers Resolution of 1973, a congressional effort to restrict the president's ability unilaterally to send troops into combat or into situations that might entail combat.

Each of the CCFR surveys asked leaders and the general public to indicate whether they favored or opposed the use of U.S. troops in various hypothetical situations, including four that involved an enemy invasion of American friends or allies: Western Europe, South Korea, Israel, and Saudi Arabia. A very similar question was included in a 1993 Times-Mirror survey on "America's Place in the World" and in the 1996 FPLP study of opinion leaders.[17] At the time of these surveys (table 6.3), U.S. troops were already stationed in Western Europe and South Korea. The only case in which majorities among the general public consistently approved of such action by Washington concerned a hypothetical Soviet or Russian invasion of Western Europe. Presumably much of the public was aware that U.S. troops were already stationed in Germany and thus would almost surely be involved if Western Europe were attacked.

Table 6.3  Opinions on Use and Stationing of U.S. Troops Abroad: The General
Public and Leaders, 1976–1996

| | Date | Survey | General Public | Leaders |
|---|---|---|---|---|
| | | | *% Favor* | |
| Would you favor or oppose the use of U.S. troops if | | | | |
| Soviet troops invaded Western Europe | 1978 | CCFR | 54 | 92 |
| | 1982 | CCFR | 65 | 92 |
| | 1986 | CCFR | 68 | 93 |
| | 1990 | CCFR | 58 | 87 |
| Russia invaded Western Europe | 1994 | CCFR | 54 | 91 |
| | 1996 | FPLP | — | 88 |
| North Korea invaded South Korea | 1978 | CCFR | 21 | 45 |
| | 1982 | CCFR | 22 | 50 |
| | 1986 | CCFR | 24 | 64 |
| | 1990 | CCFR | 44 | 57 |
| | 1993 | T-M | 31 | 69 |
| | 1994 | CCFR | 39 | 82 |
| | 1996 | FPLP | — | 63 |
| Arab forces invaded Israel | 1978 | CCFR | 22 | 31 |
| | 1982 | CCFR | 30 | 47 |
| | 1986 | CCFR | 33 | 57 |
| | 1990 | CCFR | 43 | 70 |
| | 1993 | T-M | 45 | 67 |
| | 1994 | CCFR | 42 | 72 |
| | 1996 | FPLP | — | 62 |
| Iran invaded Saudi Arabia | 1982 | CCFR | 25 | 54 |
| | 1986 | CCFR | 26 | — |
| Iraq invaded Saudi Arabia | 1990 | CCFR | 52 | 89 |
| | 1993 | T-M | 53 | 74 |
| | 1994 | CCFR | 52 | 84 |
| | 1996 | FPLP | — | 78 |
| People in Cuba attempted to overthrow the Castro dictatorship | 1994 | CCFR | 44 | 18 |
| | 1996 | FPLP | — | 15 |
| | | | *% Agree Strongly or Agree Somewhat* | |
| Please indicate how strongly you agree or disagree with the statement | | | | |
| Stationing American troops abroad encourages other countries to let us do their fighting for them | 1976 | FPLP | — | 60 |
| | 1980 | FPLP | — | 54 |
| | 1984 | FPLP | — | 63 |

Table 6.3  Continued

|  | Date | Survey | General Public | Leaders |
|---|---|---|---|---|
|  |  |  | *% Agree Strongly or Agree Somewhat* | |
|  | 1988 | FPLP | — | 66 |
|  | 1992 | FPLP | — | 65 |
|  | 1996 | FPLP | — | 58 |

*Key:* CCFR: Chicago Council on Foreign Relations surveys; FPLP: Foreign Policy Leadership Project surveys; T-M Times-Mirror survey.

In 1990, while American forces were being deployed in the Persian Gulf area after Iraq's invasion of Kuwait, a slight majority also approved using U.S. troops if Iraq invaded Saudi Arabia; this attitude remained little changed through 1996, long after the troops that had been engaged in Operations Desert Storm and Desert Shield had been withdrawn. In contrast, questions in 1982 and 1986 about protecting Saudi Arabia from a revolutionary Islamic regime in Iran yielded minimal support, even though few Americans had a great deal of affection for the Teheran government. Although Israel has never asked for aid in the form of American manpower, Saddam Hussein's frequent threats, combined with Scud missile attacks against that country during the Persian Gulf crisis, also appear to have resulted in a sharp increase among those favoring assistance to Israel. In short, the evidence in table 6.3 does not indicate that, with the end of the cold war, the public is less willing to come to the aid of specific important allies should they become victims of aggression.

Compared to the general public, leaders have consistently been more willing to use American troops in the hypothetical situations described above, with one notable exception; whereas only 18 percent of leaders would send American troops to Cuba if people on that island attempted to overthrow the Castro dictatorship, more than twice as many among the general public would approve a deployment of U.S. forces in such circumstances. Differences between the two groups on the uses of troops abroad were typically quite large, ranging from 9 percent to more than 40 percent. An FPLP survey item posed the issue of troops abroad in a somewhat different and more general way. It asked leaders to appraise the general critique that "[s]tationing American troops abroad encourages other countries to let us do their fighting for them." Consistent majorities in these six leadership surveys expressed agreement with this proposition. Thus, it appears that while leaders are generally predisposed to come to the aid of key friends and allies under siege, they are also wary of more general commitments, especially to countries that may be willing to turn the conflict over to the United States because they are unable or unwilling to make a full commitment to self defense. No doubt these views are in part a lingering residue of the war in Vietnam.

The expansion of United Nations peacekeeping activities during the past decade has added new and controversial dimensions to the issue: Under what circumstances should U.S. forces be included in such international forces, and under whose command should they be permitted to serve? Former senator Robert Dole's proposed "Peace Powers Resolution" would restrict the president's ability to deploy American forces in the context of international peacekeeping efforts.[18] In this political climate, proposals to send troops to Bosnia stimulated vigorous debates about the feasibility and desirability of American intervention, the proper role of public opinion in policy making, and the meaning of survey data on the Bosnia issues.[19]

Proponents of intervention acknowledged the lack of public enthusiasm for deploying U.S. troops but asserted that it was imperative for the United States to assume a leadership role in maintaining a tolerable world order.[20] Emphasizing that American interests rather than values should govern foreign policy decisions, opponents of intervention attacked President Clinton for "applying the standards of Mother Teresa to U.S. foreign policy."[21] Survey data revealed stable opinions on several points: A solid majority believed that solution of the Bosnia issue was a "very important" or "somewhat important" foreign policy goal; an equally large proportion of the public asserted that Congress must approve any military involvement; and, although few Americans believed that unilateral intervention in Bosnia was either a moral obligation or in the national interest, there was moderately strong support for deploying U.S. troops as part of a United Nations peacekeeping force. These opinions remained relatively stable after President Clinton's decisions to send American forces into Bosnia as part of a multinational effort to enforce the 1995 Dayton Accords. Whether public support for the Bosnia peacekeeping undertaking would collapse if it were to result in even moderate casualties—a proposition that, fortunately, had not been put to a test by early 1998—is not clear. Survey evidence on this point depends on the manner in which the question is posed.[22]

The data summarized here reveal a consistent pattern of substantially higher support by leaders for various aspects of internationalism, not only in the form of stronger approval for an "active part in world affairs," but also in greater support for liberal trade policy, economic assistance, and deployment of American troops abroad. The evidence also indicates that leaders and the general public make distinctions between various types of international policies and undertakings; these distinctions appear to reflect developments in the international arena.

*Partisanship: Persistence or Abatement?*
During the middle 1980s, three perceptive analysts of American foreign policy, one of whom served as national security adviser during President Clinton's first term, asserted: "For two decades, the making of American foreign policy has been growing far more political—or more precisely, far more partisan and ideological."[23] Although their observation was not specifically focused on or limited to public opinion, it brings up an interesting question: Has the end of the cold war served to bridge partisan differences on foreign policy? Alternatively, have those cleavages persisted into the post–cold war era? Even if Destler, Gelb, and Lake were correct in identifying partisanship and ideology as the primary sources of cleavages of foreign policy during the early years of the Reagan administration, is it possible that their diagnosis is no longer valid? After all, Ronald Reagan, a highly partisan and ideological president, underwent an almost complete reversal in attitudes about the USSR during the period of his presidency, as did the general public. Could these changes have also brought about a significant erosion of partisan and ideological stances on foreign affairs?

"Politics stops at the water's edge" has been a favorite political slogan, especially among leaders debating critics of their foreign policies. Whether it is also a broadly accurate depiction of the foreign policy process is more questionable. Partisan differences colored debates on issues as diverse as responses to the wars arising from the French Revolution, the tariff issue at various times during the nineteenth and early twentieth centuries, and the question of American participation in the League of Nations. On the other hand, deliberate efforts by the Roosevelt administration to develop a bipartisan coalition in support of American membership in the United Nations were highly successful, and the Hull-Dulles agreement assured that the United Nations would not become a partisan issue in the 1944 presidential election. During the early post–World War II years, bipartisan cooperation between the White House and Congress on many issues related to Europe made possible such initiatives as aid to Greece and Turkey [the Truman Doctrine], the Marshall Plan, and the North Atlantic Treaty Organization. Each of these striking departures from traditional American foreign policies had rather solid public support. Agreement among prominent leaders of the two major parties no doubt contributed to the fact that, among the general public, Democrats and Republicans differed little with respect to these and other major internationalist foreign policy undertakings. For example, a 1946 Gallup survey revealed that 72 percent of respondents in both political parties favored an "active" international role for the United States, and the 1947 program of aid to Greece and Turkey also received identical levels of approval from Democrats and Republicans. Issues relating to the Far East tended to be more contentious and placed greater strains on bipartisan cooperation, especially after the Truman-MacArthur confrontation during the first year of the Korean War. But even on most issues related to Asia, survey data revealed limited partisan differences. The absence of strong partisan cleavages extended into the early years of the Vietnam War, as majorities within both parties expressed strong support for the policies of the Johnson administration.

For two decades spanning the Truman, Eisenhower, Kennedy, and early Johnson administrations, then, whatever differences divided the American public on foreign policy issues rarely fell along a cleavage defined by partisan loyalties. Writing in the 1970s, Barry Hughes concluded that the "evidence points overwhelmingly to insignificant party differences in the general population" on most foreign policy issues.[24] Indeed, during the pre-Vietnam period the distribution of attitudes among supporters of the two major parties was sufficiently similar that the self-identified "independents" usually stood on one side or another of the Democrats and Republicans, rather than in between them.

The period since the end of the Vietnam War has witnessed the emergence of striking partisan differences on a broad range of issues relating to foreign and defense policy. The very concept of bipartisanship came under increased attacks from several quarters. At the same time, efforts by several administrations to create a foreign policy consensus fell short of enduring success. The Nixon-Kissinger campaign to create a post-Vietnam foreign policy consensus grounded in détente with the Soviet Union ultimately failed. Attempts by the Carter administration to achieve the same goal through an emphasis on human rights, and by the first Reagan administration to create a consensus around a more assertive and confrontational stance toward the Soviet Union, were equally unavailing in the longer run. Surveys during the 1980s revealed sharp partisan differences on foreign and defense issues as varied as the intervention in Lebanon (25%), the appropriate size of the defense budget (31%), the trade embargo on Nicaragua (39%), aid to the contras in Nicaragua (15%), and the Strategic Defense Initiative (29%). Gallup polls since the end of the cold war have shown little change in this respect, as most foreign policy issues continue to generate wide partisan gaps; these include the decision to lift economic sanctions against South Africa (21%), the North American Free Trade Agreement (12%), cuts in defense spending (14%), and deployment of U.S. peacekeeping forces in Bosnia prior to (20%) and after (27%) the Dayton agreement. The bifurcation along partisan lines was sufficiently great that, unlike during the pre-Vietnam period, responses of political independents typically fell between those of Democrats and Republicans.

The end of the cold war has been marked by diminution of partisan differences on questions such as the perception of a diminished threat from Moscow, as well as on a few nonstrategic issues such as immigration. Recall that in the 1994 CCFR survey almost three-fourths of the general public rated "Controlling and reducing illegal immigration" as a "very important" foreign policy goal (table 6.3). Members of both parties also favor reducing limits on legal immigration. Despite these areas of converging opinions, there is little evidence of a broad post–cold war foreign policy consensus. Even the Persian Gulf War—a short, successful conflict against an adversary that almost everyone could "love to hate," and that resulted in relatively light American casualties—revealed partisan differences before, during, and after the war. The fruits of the Persian Gulf conflict have not included a bipartisan post–cold war foreign policy consensus on such questions as when, how, against what adversaries, and for what purposes force should be used.

Surveys of opinion leaders also reveal that many partisan differences have persisted through the end of the cold war. Although there is evidence of a bipartisan consensus on such general questions as the structure of the post–cold war international system—both Republicans and Democrats regard it as multipolar rather than bipolar or unipolar—agreement does not necessarily extend to more specific policy-oriented areas, including the appropriate post–cold war roles for the United States and the priorities that should be attached to various international goals. Substantial majorities among both Republicans and Democrats may oppose an undiscriminating retreat into post–cold war isolationism, but there is considerable disagreement on *what kind of international role* is most appropriate, as well as on strategies and means for pursuing U.S. interests abroad. More generally, Republicans tend to favor a leadership role consistent with American superpower status, whereas Democrats are more supportive of a U.S. role as a "normal nation" that pursues its interests in conjunction with others, including through United Nations. Stated somewhat differently, members of the GOP appear more inclined to favor unilateral action in the pursuit of national interests, whereas multilateralism finds stronger support among Democrats.

We can gain some further clues about the prospects for persistence or abatement of partisan cleavages by examining factors that may buttress or cut across divisions created by party preferences. The obvious starting point is ideology. For two decades or more each of the two major parties has become ideologically less diverse as the GOP has moved sharply toward the right and the Democrats to the left. For example, some prominent conservative Democrats have defected to the Republican party, and, despite rhetorical espousal of the "broad tent" concept of parties, such "litmus test" issues as positions on taxes and abortion have increasingly been applied to candidates. Can ideological cleavages also be found in public attitudes toward foreign policy issues? In the views of opinion leaders?

Wittkopf's analyses of the Chicago Council on Foreign Relations surveys examined the relative potency of party and ideology on foreign policy attitudes. His conclusion was that the latter tends to dominate the former: "Compared with ideology as a source of the divisions that so often seem to have plagued recent American foreign policy, partisanship is again shown to be the less important factor."[25] More specifically, he found that liberals tend to have an *accommodationist* orientation toward foreign affairs, supporting cooperative internationalism while opposing militant internationalism. In contrast, conservatives typically take precisely the opposite positions, and thus are *hard-liners*. He further found that political moderates are likely to be *internationalists* owing to their support for both varieties of internationalism.[26] The potency of ideology remained fairly stable through the 1974–86 period covered by the first four CCFR surveys. Similar findings about the powerful impact of ideology on public attitudes emerge from the "Americans Talk Security" and "Americans Talk Issues" surveys initiated prior to the 1988 presidential campaign and continuing into the mid-1990s.[27] Finally, an analysis of the 1994 CCFR survey confirms again that party and ideology remain powerful correlates of foreign policy beliefs, with the sharpest polarization between liberal Democrats and conservative Republicans. However, a somewhat more complex pattern also may be emerging; when partisanship was held constant, the most liberal and conservative respondents were the only political groups with strong *isolationist* tendencies.[28]

Compared to the general public, opinion leaders are more likely to think about public affairs in coherent ideological terms. During the post-Vietnam era, for example, there is evidence of consistently strong correlations between attitudes on domestic and foreign policy issues, suggesting the existence of ideological belief systems. Moreover, these are strongly correlated with party identification.[29] When party preferences of opinion leaders are cross-tabulated against ideological self-placement, a strong relationship between the two attributes clearly emerges. Members of the GOP are overwhelmingly conservatives, and a vast majority of Democrats identify themselves as liberals. Indeed, conservative Democrats and liberal Republicans appear to represent endangered species. Moreover, the relationship between party and ideology, as measured by the correlation between them, has steadily strengthened. The end of the cold war has witnessed no erosion of the trend toward increasing confluence of party and ideology among opinion leaders.[30]

The correlation between party and ideology is not by itself sufficient to ascertain whether ideological cleavages buttress partisan ones specifically on foreign affairs issues. An initial answer may be obtained by examining how leaders of all combinations of party identification and ideological preference are distributed across four foreign policy orientations—*hard-liners*, *internationalists*, *isolationists*, and *accommodationists*. As was true of the general public, ideological preferences sustained rather than cut across party identification among leaders taking part in the four FPLP surveys during the cold war (1976–88). As revealed in table 6.4, the strong ideological underpinnings of foreign policy orientations have not been dissolved by the end of the cold war. Irrespective of party loyalties, liberals are overwhelmingly in the two groups that support cooperative internationalism—*accommodationists* and *internationalists*. Conservatives, on the other hand, are almost equally likely to be found among the two groups—*hard-liners* and *internationalists*—that support militant internationalism. Although there are relatively few cross-pressured leaders (liberal Republicans and conservative Democrats) their foreign policy orientations are revealing; they tend to resemble those of their ideological brethren far more than of those with whom they share a party identification.

The Persian Gulf War in 1991 provides a further opportunity to determine the extent to which partisan and ideological foreign policy differences may have persisted or dissolved in the post–cold war period. Because it was a *victorious* undertaking that took place over a *short* period and resulted in relatively *light U.S. casualties*, the Gulf War avoided at least three of the characteristics that ultimately ignited widespread public opposition to the conflict in Vietnam. These reasons, combined with

Table 6.4   Party, Ideology, and Foreign Policy Orientation of Opinion Leaders in the 1996 FPLP Survey

| Party | Ideology | N | Hard-Liners | Inter-nationalists | Isola-tionists | Accommo-dationists |
|-------|----------|---|-------------|--------------------|----------------|--------------------|
| Republican | Very liberal | 5 | 0% | 0% | 0% | 100% |
| | Somewhat liberal | 22 | 0 | 18 | 0 | 82 |
| | Moderate | 135 | 11 | 35 | 16 | 38 |
| | Somewhat conservative | 416 | 26 | 42 | 11 | 21 |
| | Very conservative | 160 | 45 | 28 | 18 | 10 |
| Independent | Very liberal | 10 | 0 | 0 | 0 | 100 |
| | Somewhat liberal | 93 | 3 | 22 | 5 | 70 |
| | Moderate | 199 | 7 | 28 | 10 | 55 |
| | Somewhat conservative | 121 | 16 | 36 | 16 | 33 |
| | Very conservative | 18 | 61 | 22 | 11 | 6 |
| Democrats | Very liberal | 146 | 1 | 15 | 2 | 82 |
| | Somewhat liberal | 396 | 2 | 20 | 6 | 73 |
| | Moderate | 209 | 2 | 36 | 9 | 53 |
| | Somewhat conservative | 40 | 28 | 28 | 10 | 35 |
| | Very conservative | 4 | 50 | 50 | 0 | 0 |

*Phi* = .44
*Key:* FPLP: Foreign Policy Leadership Project.

the nature of Iraq's action and the character of its leaders, suggest that the war against Iraq should be a strong candidate for the "rally round the flag" phenomenon. If in fact vast numbers of Americans, irrespective of party, ideology, and other attributes, rallied behind the administration, the impact of these background characteristics would be suppressed. Conversely, any sociodemographic correlates of foreign policy attitudes that persisted in these circumstances would be especially significant. The 1992 FPLP survey asked opinion leaders about their preferred options for dealing with the Iraqi aggression, both before and after the United States launched military operations against the Baghdad regime. As indicated in table 6.5, the strong partisan and ideological differences that characterized prewar policy preferences were only partially reduced in postwar views.

Space limitations do not permit a full discussion of other background factors—including gender, generation, region, education, and race—that may be associated with foreign policy opinions.[31] Suffice it to say that while these are not necessarily irrelevant for explaining foreign policy views, they do so less consistently and, when they do, they only rarely

Table 6.5  Party, Ideology, and Policy Preferences of Opinion Leaders before and after the Persian Gulf War

| Party | Ideology | N | % Favoring Each Policy Option | | | | | |
|-------|----------|---|---------|----------|------|---------|----------|------|
| | | | BEFORE THE WAR STARTED | | | RETROSPECTIVELY AFTER THE WAR | | |
| | | | Force Now | Economic Sanctions | Stay Out | Force Now | Economic Sanctions | Stay Out |
| Republican | Very liberal | 4 | 0 | 75 | 25 | 33 | 67 | 0 |
| | Somewhat liberal | 17 | 65 | 35 | 0 | 67 | 27 | 7 |
| | Moderate | 129 | 72 | 26 | 2 | 81 | 12 | 3 |
| | Somewhat conservative | 457 | 88 | 10 | 2 | 92 | 6 | 1 |
| | Very conservative | 105 | 88 | 9 | 2 | 88 | 10 | 2 |
| Independent | Very liberal | 18 | 13 | 56 | 25 | 7 | 53 | 40 |
| | Somewhat liberal | 120 | 32 | 61 | 7 | 42 | 44 | 9 |
| | Moderate | 263 | 56 | 37 | 5 | 63 | 22 | 9 |
| | Somewhat conservative | 164 | 75 | 19 | 3 | 85 | 9 | 5 |
| | Very conservative | 14 | 64 | 14 | 21 | 85 | 0 | 15 |
| Democrat | Very liberal | 171 | 14 | 68 | 17 | 19 | 58 | 22 |
| | Somewhat liberal | 444 | 29 | 65 | 5 | 38 | 46 | 10 |
| | Moderate | 202 | 45 | 46 | 7 | 52 | 33 | 8 |
| | Somewhat conservative | 61 | 76 | 22 | 2 | 75 | 17 | 2 |
| | Very conservative | 2 | 100 | 0 | 0 | 100 | 0 | 0 |
| *Phi* | | | .55 | | | .54 | | |

*Notes:* Respondents were asked the following question: "People differed over President Bush's decision to start the war against Iraq. Some felt he was right to use military force right away. Others felt he should have given economic sanctions a longer time to work. Still others opposed getting involved at all. Please indicate which position comes closest to your own feelings—both just before the U.S. launched military operations on January 16, 1991, and retrospectively after the war ended."

Majority positions within any party-ideology group in italics.

Because "Not sure" responses are excluded, some row totals are less than 100%.

serve to bridge the dominant partisan and ideological cleavages. Thus, the Destler, Gelb, and Lake diagnosis, although published more than a decade ago, appears to be as valid in 1998 as it was in 1984. On most foreign policy issues, partisan and ideological differences continue to characterize attitudes of the general public issues and, to an even greater extent, those of opinion leaders.

## Conclusion: Public Opinion in the Post–Cold War Era

The evidence reviewed in the previous section gives rise to several generalizations about how the end of the cold war has affected public opinion on world affairs. First, similarities and continuities across the pre– and post–cold war eras are in greater evidence than are striking differences. To be sure, there have been some specific changes in public views—for example, in appraisals of Moscow's foreign policy goals and threats arising from them—but these are so obvious that they require no further elaboration. Despite the disintegration of the Soviet Union and the Warsaw Pact a substantial majority of the public continues to believe that the United States should continue to play an active role in world affairs (figure 6.1). But continuity is not limited to such general expressions of opinion; it also dominates the appraisal of goals that the country might pursue in its external relations. As during the years prior to disintegration of the Soviet Union, such economic goals as protecting jobs, securing adequate supplies of energy, and reducing the trade deficit remain high on the list of public priorities, whereas promoting American values and institutions abroad lag far behind (table 6.1). Although dominant security concerns have been dramatically altered by the end of the cold war, public willingness to use American troops in support of beleaguered allies has not evaporated. Indeed, in the cases of Israel and South Korea, it has actually increased slightly during the 1990s (table 6.3).

Second, there have also been some changes, most notably reflecting what is sometimes referred to as "compassion fatigue"—declining concerns for and commitments to eradicating economic problems in the Third World (table 6.1). Declining support for foreign assistance programs is a related trend.

Third, the gap between leaders and the general public in support for international undertakings, a consistent feature of the cold war period, has persisted, and it encompasses virtually all aspects of foreign relations, including many foreign policy goals, trade relations (table 6.2), and security commitments to key allies (table 6.3).

Fourth, the period between the Vietnam War and the collapse of the Soviet Union witnessed growing partisan and ideological cleavages on the appropriate American role in the world, the specific goals that the United States should pursue in its foreign relations, and the most effective instruments of statecraft. Although those differences often centered on many aspects of the dominant cold war confrontation with the Soviet Union and its allies, the cleavages have survived the end of the cold war (table 6.4). Even the successful war to drive the hated Saddam Hussein's forces out of Kuwait—the first major military undertaking since the end of the cold war—did not wholly bridge the partisan-ideological gap (table 6.5).

What is this likely to mean for the conduct of American foreign relations? Deep divisions within American society on foreign policy issues are likely to persist and, under some circumstances, they could even become deeper, although the coalitions may well take somewhat different shape than they have in recent years. For example, opponents of trade liberalization may be found in both major political parties, as well as among lesser ones. Given the high priority that the public attaches to international economic issues, would a major recession heighten the electoral prospects of candidates who have expressed a commitment to alter or even withdraw many of the institutions through which the United States has pursued its interests, including the United Nations, NATO, the World Trade Organization, the North American Free Trade Association?

Foreign policy leaders may also be able to find some areas of bipartisan agreement. However, the record of the past few years does not suggest that the quality of policy will automatically improve in such circumstances. The Helms-Burton Act and the crusade to deny Boutros Boutros-Ghali a second term as secretary general of the United Nations, actions that had the support of a Democratic president and Republican Congress, have inflicted a heavy cost on America's reputation and relations with its allies. Bipartisan leadership support for expanding NATO, an undertaking whose risks are at least as significant as the potential gains, also suggests that bipartisan accord is no guarantor of wisdom.

But divided or not, it seems likely that the public will play a more significant role during the post–cold war era. Were this to come to pass, it would be profoundly distressing to many realists. The realist thesis, some features of which were described earlier, is that public opinion can contribute very little to the effective conduct of foreign affairs. In some versions of the realist position, public opinion is depicted as an ill-informed, volatile, and mood-driven force that, if heeded, would sometimes deflect policy makers from the steady pursuit of the long-range interests and goals that constitute the essence of the country's national interests and, at other times, would push the government into ill-considered undertakings that have little, if any, relationship to those interests. Other critiques focus on the alleged rigidity rather than the volatility of public opinion. The public is described as so firmly set in its ways of thinking that serious attention to public preferences would make it impossible for policy makers to act with sufficient flexibility and dexterity to cope effectively with international opportunities and challenges. More specifically, the essence of the case against public opinion is that effective diplomacy requires some important features, none of which is enhanced by a more active public participation: secrecy, speed, flexibility, and the ability to act on the basis of intelligence that cannot be shared with the public. These requirements are deemed by critics, not all of whom are realists, to be essential in order to bargain and negotiate effectively with other countries, to meet challenges and take advantage of opportunities as they arise, to maneuver adroitly in a rapidly changing global system and, most importantly, to avoid war.

The case for the importance of these features in the conduct of foreign affairs is most plausible in times of war, crisis, and confrontation such as the cold war. Without in any way suggesting that traditional security concerns have vanished with the end of the cold war and the disintegration of the Soviet Union, it seems increasingly likely that the top echelons of the U.S. foreign policy agenda during the post–cold war era will include some issues on which it is difficult to make a compelling case for excluding the public and its representatives from involvement in the policy process. This agenda will probably include but not be limited to a number of issues on which the public is likely to have strong views and on which the thesis that "the president knows best" may appear less compelling than, for example, during World War II and the cold war. Among these are such economic and social issues as trade and protectionism, refugees and immigration, drug trafficking, and environmental problems. These are also concerns toward which public attention is likely to be directed. Recall from table 6.1 that coping with these issues has consistently ranked among the public's most important foreign policy goals.

It is also clear, moreover, that post–cold war foreign policy leaders will not have the luxury of focusing all of their energies on international economic, social, and environmental issues, if only because of the persistence of ethnic, racial, religious, nationalist, and tribal conflicts in many regions. For example, the disintegration of the Soviet Union and its withdrawal from Eastern Europe have also opened up opportunities for ancient rivalries and hatreds to resurface as civil wars. At least some of these conflicts, which are not confined to areas within the former Soviet empire, are also likely to stimulate political activity by ethnic and other interest groups in the United States, thereby magnifying the impact of at least parts of the public.

Thus, if we are indeed entering into a period of fewer crises and confrontations among the major powers and greater attention to such post–cold war issues as those listed above—there are ample survey data that much of the American public believed this to be the case even before the end of the cold war[32]—it is also likely to be an era in which public opinion plays a more autonomous role. Even those who do not fully subscribe to the thesis that the public is merely the hapless object of elite manipulations would acknowledge that crises and confrontations abroad provide a setting in which opportunities and temptations for manipulation of the public are far greater than on nonsecurity issues. The latter are typically resolved over a longer time period, thus providing greater opportunities for the public, interest groups, the media, Congress, and other domestic actors to play a significant role. Nonsecurity issues also tend to be more resistant to claims that the needs for secrecy, flexibility, and speed of action, as well as the president's constitutional role as commander in chief of the armed forces, make it both necessary and legitimate for the executive to have a relatively free hand. In short, we may be moving into a period in which the relationship between public opinion and foreign policy takes on added rather than diminished significance.

The hypothesis that public opinion is likely to play a more potent role during the post–cold war era is plausible, but its impact on the White House, Congress, and bureaucracies will be determined not merely by the issues that constitute the foreign policy agenda, but also variables that have probably been unaffected by the end of the cold war, such as the *level of public support or opposition to policies, the decision context,* and *policy makers' beliefs about and attention to public opinion.*[33] The latter point is especially important. Although all administrations since World War II have had access to immense amounts of evidence about public attitudes, it should not be assumed that this information is taken uniformly into account in policy deliberations. Moreover, officials in varying locations within the government may be concerned with public opinion in different degrees. Political appointees are more likely than civil servants to pay attention to it, and elected officials are likely to be even more sensitive to public sentiments.

Although elected officials can never be utterly indifferent to public sentiments, even a cursory reading of memoirs, biographies, and accounts of important foreign policy decisions reveals that top ranking leaders have shown wide variations in their assessments and uses of, sensitivity to, and strategies for dealing with public opinion. They may also have quite different conceptions of what constitute the most valid and politically significant indicators of those attitudes. Policy makers may use public opinion as a guide to policy choices or to rule out certain options that seem destined to arouse powerful and sustained public disapproval; American policies toward China during the 1950s and 1960s and toward Cuba since Castro came to power illustrate the latter point. But information about public opinion may also play other roles in the policy process: for bargaining leverage in negotiations with other nations; to provide a rationale for decisions that have been made for reasons that do not necessarily reflect public sentiments; and for purposes of attempting to manipulate the public. This brief list is by no means a comprehensive survey of the roles that public opinion may play in the foreign policy process. It may, however, illustrate the point that the public opinion–policy relationship is usually complex, variable, and interactive rather than simple, constant, and unidirectional. That was the case prior to 1989, and it is likely to be true in the post–cold war era.

Finally, if a growing agenda of issues that fall at the intersection of domestic and foreign policy gives rise to an enhanced role for public opinion, it is worth contemplating whether the policy makers will gain more by manipulating, misleading, or bypassing the public in order to facilitate their short-term tasks than by frank efforts to engage the public in constructive debates about the proper American role in the world, definitions of national interests, and the appropriate strategies (if not necessarily the tactics) for pursuing them. A highly selective sample of American foreign policy successes (the Marshall Plan, NATO, the Limited Nuclear Test Ban Treaty) and failures (Vietnam, the Iran-contra episode) may offer some clues, but certainly not definitive answers, to this question. The former cases featured extensive debates in which substantial majorities of the public and Congress ultimately came to support innovative foreign policy undertakings. Policy makers in the Vietnam and Iran-contra cases, strong candidates for inclusion on any list of the most disastrous American foreign policy debacles of the cold war era, often made deliberate efforts to mislead the public and its representatives in the Congress. Such a highly selective group of cases does not constitute an adequate discussion of the public's proper role in foreign policy making. Moreover, perhaps the correlations between policy processes and outcomes in these cases are merely spurious, but at least they suggest some caution before we accept as an iron law of politics the realist thesis that public opinion can only damage the quality of foreign policy.

## Notes

1 *New York Times,* November 29, 1984, p. A5, 1.

2 George P. Shultz, *Turmoil and Triumph: My Years As Secretary of State* (New York: Charles Scribner's Sons, 1993), pp. 84, 103, 649–651.

3 See Walter Lippmann, *Public Opinion* (New York: MacMillan, 1922); *The Phantom Public* (New York: Harcourt, Brace, 1925); and Gabriel Almond, *The American People and Foreign Policy* (New York: Harcourt, Brace, 1950). For a fuller analysis of these issues, see Ole R. Holsti, *Public Opinion and American Foreign Policy* (Ann Arbor: University of Michigan Press, 1996).

4 See for example, Philip Converse, "The Nature of Belief Systems in Mass Publics," in David E. Apter, ed., *Ideology and Discontent* (New York: Free Press, 1964), pp. 206–261. Converse concluded that the political beliefs of the mass public lack underlying ideological structure that might provide some coherence to political thinking. Studies such as the one by Warren E. Miller and Donald E. Stokes, "Constituency Influence in Congress," *American Political Science Review* 57 (1963): 45–56, revealed that constituents' attitudes on foreign policy has less impact on members of Congress than did their views on domestic issues.

5 Bernard C. Cohen, *The Public's Impact on Foreign Policy* (Boston, Mass.: Little, Brown, 1973).

6 John Mueller, *War, Presidents and Public Opinion* (New York: John Wiley, 1973).

7 Benjamin I. Page and Robert Shapiro, *The Rational Public: Fifty Years of Trends in Americans' Policy Preferences* (Chicago: University of Chicago Press, 1992).

8 See Michael Clough, "Grass-Roots Policymaking," *Foreign Affairs* 73 (January/February 1994): 191–196; and Maxine Isaacs, *The Independent American Public: The Relationship between Elite and Mass Opinions on American Foreign Policy in the Mass Communication Age,* Ph.D. dissertation, University of Maryland, 1994.

9 John H. Aldrich, John L. Sullivan, and Eugene Borgida, "Foreign Affairs and Issue Voting: Do Presidential Candidates 'Waltz before a Blind Audience?'" *American Political Science Review* 83 (1989): 123–141.

10 Alan D. Monroe, "Consistency between Public Preferences and National Policy Decisions," *American Politics Quarterly* 7 (1979): 3–19.

11 Benjamin I. Page and Robert Y. Shapiro, "The Effects of Public Opinion on Policy," *American Political Science Review* 77 (1983): 175–190.

12 Arthur Schlesinger Jr., "Back to the Womb?" *Foreign Affairs* 74 (July/August 1995): 2–8.

13 John E. Rielly, ed., *American Public Opinion and U.S. Foreign Policy, 1995* (Chicago: Chicago Council on Foreign Relations, 1995), p. 6.

14 John E. Rielly, ed., *American Public Opinion and U.S. Foreign Policy, 1995,* pp. 29–30.

15 Steven Kull, *American and Foreign Aid: A Study of American Public Attitudes* (College Park, Md.: Center for International and Security Studies, 1995).

16 John E. Rielly, ed., *American Public Opinion and U.S. Foreign Policy, 1995,* p. 31.

17 Times-Mirror, *America's Place in the World: An Investigation of the Attitudes of*

*American Opinion Leaders and the American Public about International Affairs* (Los Angeles: Times-Mirror Center for The People and The Press, 1993).

18  Robert Dole, "Peacekeepers and Politics," *New York Times*, January 24, 1994, p. 25.

19  For example, Steven Kull, "What the Public Knows That Washington Doesn't," *Foreign Policy* 101 (1995–96), 102–115; Jeremy D. Rosner, "The Know-Nothings Know Something," *Foreign Policy* 101 (1995–96), 116–129; Frank Newport, "Presidential Address on Bosnia Changed Few Minds" (Princeton, N.J.: Gallup Organization, November 30, 1995); Lydia Saad, "Americans Back Clinton's Plan to Keep the Peace in Bosnia" (Princeton, N.J.: Gallup Organization, October 27, 1995); Lydia Saad and Frank Newport, "Americans Want to Keep at Arm's Length from Bosnian Conflict," *Gallup Monthly* 358 (July 1995): 16–18; Richard Sobel, "What People Really Say about Bosnia," *New York Times*, November 22, 1995, p. A23.

20  Arthur Schlesinger Jr., "Back to the Womb?"

21  For example, Michael Mandelbaum, "Foreign Policy as Social Work," *Foreign Affairs* 75 (January/February 1996): 16–32.

22  Compare Lydia Saad, "Americans Back Clinton's Plan," with Steven Kull, *American Public Attitudes on Sending U.S. Troops to Bosnia* (College Park, Md.: Center for International and Security Studies, 1995).

23  I. M. Destler, Leslie Gelb, and Anthony Lake, *Our Own Worst Enemy* (New York: Simon and Schuster, 1984).

24  Barry B. Hughes, *The Domestic Context of American Foreign Policy* (San Francisco: Freeman, 1978), p. 128.

25  Eugene R. Wittkopf, *Faces of Internationalism: Public Opinion and American Foreign Policy* (Durham, N.C.: Duke University Press, 1990).

26  Wittkopf, *Faces of Internationalism*, p. 46. Using attitudes toward cooperative internationalism (CI) and militant internationalism (MI), Wittkopf defines *internationalists* as those who support both CI and MI, *hard-liners* as those who oppose CI but support MI, *accommodationists* as those who support CI but oppose MI, and *isolationists* as those who oppose both CI and MI. Although constructed with responses to different questions, the FPLP surveys have used the same categories (see table 6.4). For details on construction of the four MI/CI groups, see Ole R. Holsti and James N. Rosenau, "The Structure of Foreign Policy Beliefs among American Opinion Leaders—after the Cold War," *Millennium* 22 (1993): 235–278.

27  Americans Talk Security, fourteen national surveys on national security issues (Winchester, Mass.: Americans Talk Security, October 1987–September 1990); Americans Talk Issues, serial national surveys of Americans on public policy issues (Washington: American Talk Issues Foundation, 1991–95).

28  Eugene R. Wittkopf, "The Faces of Internationalism Revisited," paper presented at the annual meeting of the American Political Science Association, Chicago, 1995, p. 14.

29  Ole R. Holsti and James N. Rosenau, "Liberals, Populists, Libertarians, and Conservatives: The Link between Domestic and International Affairs," *International Political Science Review* 17 (1996): 29–54.

30  The correlation (*phi*) between party and ideology among opinion leaders in the

FPLP surveys has increased steadily since 1976: 1976 (.64), 1980 (.67), 1984, (.70), 1988, (.72), and 1992, (.75).

31 For evidence on the impact of generation and other sociodemographic variables, see Ole R. Holsti, *Public Opinion and American Foreign Policy* (Ann Arbor: University of Michigan Press, 1996).

32 Americans Talk Security, No. 9 of fourteen national surveys on national security issues (1988), pp. 51–54.

33 Thomas W. Graham, *The Politics of Failure: Strategic Nuclear Arms Control, Public Opinion and Domestic Politics in the United States—1945-1980*, Ph.D. dissertation, MIT, 1989; Thomas W. Graham, "Public Opinion and U.S. Foreign Policy Decision Making," in David A. Deese, ed., *The New Politics of American Foreign Policy* (New York: St. Martin's Press, 1994), pp. 190–215; and Douglas Foyle, *The Influence of Public Opinion of American Foreign Policy: Context, Beliefs, and Process*, Ph.D. dissertation, Duke University, 1996.

# 7.

## Interest Groups and the Media in Post–Cold War

## U.S. Foreign Policy

*James M. McCormick*

How successful are interest groups in shaping American foreign policy? How successful are the media in affecting foreign affairs? During the cold war, the usual answer to both questions was "not much." With the exception of some ethnic and economic groups under specific circumstances, most analysts would conclude that interest groups did not fare very well, and the media largely played a supportive role to official policy, at least until the Vietnam War.[1] With the end of the cold war, however, are the answers to these questions likely to be the same?

In this chapter, I discuss the access, involvement, and influence of these two nongovernmental actors in the foreign policy process after the cold war. In particular, I focus upon how and why the role of interest groups and the media in foreign policy have changed in recent years. In doing so, I shall explore several domestic and international factors that have increased interest group and media access to the foreign policy decision-making machinery, discuss how new and differing interest groups and media flourish in this changed environment, and analyze how more and more foreign policy decisions have moved away from the crisis to the structural and strategic varieties, a change that enhances the impact of interest groups and the media on the foreign policy process.[2] Finally, and as others have done before, I take up the more difficult issue of relative influence of these actors in this new environment.

### Factors Limiting the Role of Interest Groups and the Media during the Cold War

The usual reason for arguing that interest groups had limited impact on foreign policy during the cold war turned on several structural and process arguments.[3] First of all, American foreign policy was more likely to be initiated by the president than by Congress. As such, interest groups had much greater difficulty gaining access to the former than to the latter, since Congress had numerous committees and subcommittees that were accessible. Although Bernard Cohen points out that interest groups sought to influence the bureaucracies at the executive level, their efforts yielded limited results and may have aided the interests of the bureaucracies more than the interests of the lobbyists.[4] Second, foreign policy issues and decisions were usually quite remote from the lives of Americans, and rallying support or opposition by interest groups posed a significant challenge.[5] Third, crucial foreign policy decisions were likely to be crisis decisions—characterized by short decision time, high threat, and surprise. For such situations, foreign policy making was more likely to be centered in a small group in the executive branch, allowing little, if any, congressional participation. In short, interest group influence was further curtailed during these important decision-making periods. Fourth, with the number of interest groups operating in the policy arena, opposing groups would likely arise over any divisive issue, weakening the impact of any one interest group or a set of coalitional interest groups. In such a competitive environment, policy makers actually gained more latitude for dealing with competing pressures from one group or another.[6]

During the cold war, the media exercised limited influence because of self-imposed constraints and the nature of the foreign policy process itself. The media tended to be deferential to governmental officials and governmental policies, as one analysis noted: "The press was often a sideline player and occasional cheerleader in the policy process simply because the process, itself, was anything but open to public view."[7] Thus, the members of the media more often seemed to elicit support for official policies from the public than to challenge them. In an environment that offered the prism of the cold war for interpreting global events, the media were less likely to advance new policy options themselves or from others. Put somewhat differently, "The press was often critical but of the execution of policy more than the aims."[8] Finally, and as with interest groups generally, the media operated in a conflict-prone and crisis-prone environment during the cold war, further muting its criticisms of policies and options.

### Factors Facilitating the Role of Interest Groups and the Media after the Cold War

Since the end of the Vietnam War and cold war, however, some analysts have suggested that access by interest groups and the media in the foreign policy process is no longer what it was. Tierney and Uslaner, among others, imply that earlier assessments about foreign policy interest groups may be somewhat timebound, pointing to several new domestic and international factors.[9] Likewise, Bennett dates the rise of greater media access to the process as coming "after the late 1960s (late Vietnam War)"; he also argues that the media's greater role "in the crumbling elite consensus" within the country began about that same time.[10] As issues became more contentious at home among competing elites (e.g., between the White House and the Congress), the media also became more involved and offered more criticism of official policy to the public at large. In short, after the cold war—and with the dramatic changes in global politics that James Scott and A. Lane Crothers discuss in the opening essay of this volume—media access and involvement increased proportionately.

*Global Factors and Increased Interest Group/Media Access*
The end of the cold war—vividly dramatized by the opening of the Berlin Wall, the reunification of Germany, the collapse of communism in Eastern Europe, and the implosion of the Soviet Union—shook the foundation of American foreign policy. With the communist threat no longer serving as such an important unifying force for American foreign policy making, new issues—economic, environmental, and social-cultural—are now on the agenda. More often than not, these issues divide, rather than unite, the American public and policy makers. Trade issues, like the North American Free Trade Agreement (NAFTA) divided the Democrats in Congress from President Clinton in 1993, while environmental issues have fissured both political parties. The trade-offs between trade and human rights considerations, as in the case of most-favored-nation (MFN) status for China, have divided Democrats and Republicans, liberals and conservatives, and even various regions of the country. Furthermore, even as some security issues remain on the agenda (or as some new ones gain a place there), they, too, are more likely to divide than to unify. As the controversy surrounding the expansion of NATO or American action in Bosnia demonstrates, no American position toward these questions is self-evident or widely supported, as might have occurred during the cold war years. Americans of Central European back-

ground may clamor for more rapid expansion of NATO, but political elites worried about the future of Russia may not. Contrast, too, the array of domestic positions toward Russia, the former Soviet republics, or toward Bosnia with the rather singular American response to the Soviet invasion of Hungary during the height of the cold war or toward Castro's Cuba in the 1960s.

This new global policy environment and its issues have important implications for enhancing interest groups and media access to the foreign policy process. Because these issues increasingly tend to be divisive domestically and because no unified American position is readily obvious on many of them, they offer immediate opportunities for interest group involvement in the foreign policy process. Indeed, they invite interest groups to mobilize and to attempt to influence policy in the executive and legislative branches to a much greater degree than was possible during the cold war. The media similarly benefit from this environment, since these policy controversies within official Washington are grist for their reporting. Additionally, as more actors are increasingly involved in the foreign policy process, and as policy making has become a more disjointed and untidy process than during the cold war, the media may seek out various political actors—even as those participants in turn seek out the media to get their message out. In short, the media now can play a more significant role in setting the agenda or in exacerbating the debate over foreign policy issues.

### Domestic Factors and Increased Interest Group/Media Access

In the domestic arena, at least two important changes have occurred that enhance interest group and media access and involvement on foreign policy issues: one has occurred within the congressional constellation of factors; the other within the society at large.

*Congressional Change and Interest Groups.* Due to internal reforms dating back to the end of the Vietnam War (see chapter 5), foreign policy interest groups now have greater access to Congress. First, congressional committees now share more jurisdiction on foreign policy matters. By one estimate, some sixteen committees in the House and the Senate have at least some responsibilities over foreign and defense policy issues.[11] In addition to the increase in jurisdictional decisions made by Congress, multiple referrals on legislation by the congressional leadership also have led to this greater dispersal of responsibilities. More committees and subcommittees now consider aspects of foreign policy legislation. To be sure, with the Republicans in control of the Congress since 1995 and some efforts being made to pare back the size of subcommittees and committees, joint referrals have ended (although not sequential or split referrals), but dispersal of foreign policy responsibilities within Congress remains.[12]

These internal changes are perhaps best manifested in the two principal foreign policy committees in the Congress, the House International Relations (formerly Foreign Affairs) Committee and the Senate Foreign Relations Committee. Both committees have held more and more hearings on both legislative and oversight matters in recent decades. In the 1950s and 1960s, the House International Relations Committee (then Foreign Affairs) held about 300 hearings during a particular Congress. Near the end of the Vietnam War, during the 93rd Congress (1973–74), the committee held 295 committee and subcommittee hearings. By the 97th Congress (1981–82), however, the number of hearings had grown dramatically, totally 702 during those years. During the 104th Congress (1995–96), the number had fallen back to 452, but the intervening Congresses had all been over 600 hearings per year.[13] By contrast, the number of hearings by the Senate Foreign Relations Committee is smaller, but that committee, too, has increased its use of hearings and special committees and subcommittees to investigate particular concerns.[14] This kind of committee activism has important implications for interest groups in that it offers more and more avenues of access to the foreign policy process.

Second, congressional staff dealing with foreign policy have increased. For instance, the staff for the House International Relations Committee in 1971 totaled eleven; in 1991, eighty-five; and in 1996, sixty-five.[15] For the Senate Foreign Relations Committee, the important change was in the decision to provide the subcommittees with some staff of their own (previously the committee staff served the subcommittees as well) and to enlarge the number of aides from twenty-five in 1979 to sixty-seven in 1991 (although the staff size declined to forty-six by 1996).[16] Both of these changes in the House and the Senate have enabled more points of contact for interest groups, especially since efforts to influence the committees are more frequently directed toward staff than toward the members themselves. While the recent cutbacks in congressional staff militate against interest group activity, staff size remains reasonably large by historical standards, facilitating sustained interest group activity.

Third, the operation of the armed services committees have changed. Both the House National Security (formerly the Armed Services) Committee and the Senate Armed Services Committee are now involved not only in authorizing the defense budget, but also in devising strategies for the post–cold war era. As Paul Stockton has noted, "[L]egislators are no longer satisfied to focus on budgetary details and ignore more fundamental issues."[17] To be sure, this judgment does not mean that members of Congress have abandoned efforts at "micromanaging" the defense budget. Instead, it means that now, without an overarching American strategy toward the world, Congress has joined the executive in thinking about the structure of forces *and* strategic goals for the U.S. military. Paul Stockton has nicely summarized this new environment: "[I]ncentives for members to strategize now exist side by side with incentives for micromanagement."[18]

As a result, interest groups have more access and potential impact than before. While micromanagement of the defense budget traditionally meant protecting favorite pork-barrel programs back home— the substance of interest group politics—strategizing also aids interest group activity, inviting even more groups into the process. Because congressional staffs will not likely have the time or inclination to devise wholly new grand strategies, congressional offices and committees will become receptive to the work of think tanks or other outside lobbying groups. Stockton once again goes to the heart of the matter: "Strategy is the province of think tanks and—perhaps—the Pentagon."[19] Furthermore, the use of annual authorizations as opposed to open-ended authorizations facilitate strategizing and micromanagement[20]—ensuring an ongoing role for interest groups.

Finally, and beyond the internal change within the Congress, congressional campaigns and interest groups have been more intertwined in the post–cold war era. Through the use of "soft money" to political parties and through "independent" campaigns by interested groups (e.g., the large number of campaign ads by the AFL-CIO in the 1996 election), interest groups are more and more a fixture of congressional life. While the post–cold war milieu may have accelerated the involvement, interest groups and congressional campaigns have long been intertwined.

*Congressional Change and the Media.* Much as the congressional changes facilitate interest group activity, these changes also enhance the media. Indeed, the process is a synergistic one between the media and Congress. As the congressional process becomes a more open one, the media have greater access to the committee process and enhance their ability to report the partisan and ideological conflicts that may result; as the media become an increasingly standard feature of congressional process, members increasingly seek to use such outlets to shape their message to their colleagues and to the public at large.

The end of the cold war did not begin the process of the media's role; instead, it has expanded considerably from the Vietnam War to the present. Beginning with the televised hearings on the Vietnam War in the Senate Foreign Relations Committee in the mid-1960s, the role of television coverage, for example, has expanded dramatically. First, television coverage of the House and the Senate began. Next, C-Span, the cable network, offered "gavel-to-gavel" coverage of all House and Senate sessions as well as many committee hearings on legislation, nominations, and investigations. In turn, the House and Senate press galleries offered almost instantaneous venues for congressional reactions to foreign events and to White House announcements. As President Clinton was announcing his foreign policy team for his second term in December 1996, for instance, members of the Senate appeared within minutes in the gallery to offer their evaluation of the new personnel. Earlier, after President Clinton announced that Secretary of State Warren Christopher would not continue in a second term, Senator Richard Lugar (R-Ind.) held a press briefing to outline the criteria for a new secretary and the foreign policy issues that the United States needs to address in the years ahead.[21] Added to this television coverage, other electronic (i.e., radio and now the internet) and print media have continued their coverage of both ends of Capitol Hill.

The other side of this synergistic relationship is the effort that members make to use the media for their own ends. Increasingly, members of Congress are "media entrepreneurs," who take advantage of the expanded number of media outlets and the increased coverage of the Congress to influence the public policy debate, including foreign policy.[22] Members may use a variety of techniques to obtain media coverage both inside and outside the institution. Within the institution, and in addition to regular floor and committee debate, House members may use "one-minute" speeches to attract attention to an issue, while Senate members may use the "morning business" period for the same purpose. Similarly, and as suggested above, members may hold news conferences on foreign (and domestic) policy issues. The possible advantages of these institutional measures are that they may be picked up by the national networks and their impact is magnified. As a result, members engage in conscious efforts to produce short, pithy statements that may capture the media's attention.[23]

Members also seek to use the media to influence policy to a wider audience and to enhance their reputation as policy experts. By writing op-ed pieces for national newspapers (e.g., the *Washington Post*, the *New York Times*, or the *Wall Street Journal*), or issuing press releases, members may gain attention and be invited on daily television interview programs, such as the *The NewsHour* with Jim Lehrer, or on the Sunday morning interview programs, such as *Meet the Press, Face the Nation,* or *This Week.* In these ways, the members gain national exposure and begin to influence or even shape the debate. Such actions, as Karen Kedrowski reminds us, go beyond simply reaching their own constituents and are particularly important at the agenda stage in dealing with an issue.[24]

*Societal Change and Interest Groups.* The second significant domestic change to assist interest groups in the foreign policy realm is the change in American society and politics at large. The political process within the United States has perceptibly moved toward greater partisan and ideological divisions. Divisions exist on foreign policy issues (as they probably always have),[25] but they have become more intensified in the current period without the dampening effect of the cold war environment.[26] As a result, as partisan and ideological divisions have become more pronounced, opportunities for interest groups are enhanced—and even magnified—on some foreign policy issues.

Prominent foreign policy controversies from the 1980s to the early 1990s accentuate the new role of interest groups in the foreign policy process over partisan and ideological issues. Aid to the Nicaraguan contras in the 1980s elicited a great deal of controversy along partisan and ideological lines and a great deal of interest group activity. Two observers of interest group activity on this issue reported this new intensity: "What distinguished the groups in the Nicaraguan case . . . was the scale, duration, and intensity of their activity. For a period of more than seven years, between 1982 and 1989 and peaking in 1985–86, over two hundred organizations became involved in efforts to influence congressional votes on U.S. policy toward Nicaragua."[27] Once again, these organizations ranged from groups that were formed to support or oppose this singular issue only to more general conservative and liberal political groups that decided to lobby on this particular policy question.

Interest group activity over a sanctions bill toward Saddam Hussein's Iraq (after the leadership of that country had brutally used chemical weapons on its Kurdish population in March 1988) illustrates this pattern as well. In the words of one congressional aide, the lobbying "was obscene."[28] A principal sponsor of the bill, Senator Claiborne Pell (D-R.I.), apparently agreed with this assessment, albeit in more understated language: "All the special interests got into the act."[29] Despite the fact that a tough, wide-ranging economic sanctions bill was introduced in the U.S. Senate with bipartisan support and was approved by the full Senate only one day after its introduction,[30] opposition quickly

emerged. It came from the Reagan administration and several prominent interest groups. The lobbying effort included those agricultural
interests that saw Iraq as "a large and growing market for U.S. agricultural exports," oil companies that were increasingly importing Iraqi
oil into the United States, and defense contractors and large industrial
countries with trading interests in Iraq. Further, the U.S.-Iraq Business
Forum, a group of American companies with business interests in Iraq
and with informal links to the Iraqi embassy in Washington, pressured
for the defeat of this kind of economic sanctions bill. As a result, alternate bills and watered-down bills were subsequently introduced, and
the original measure failed to become law.

At the end of the cold war, trade issues, such as the NAFTA and
GATT agreements, have accelerated interest group activity as well. The
groups involved on this issue range from the traditional economic interest groups to environmental, consumer, and single-issue or political
organizations, such as Empower America and Americans for Democratic Action. While the total number of interest groups involved in the
NAFTA debate is difficult to estimate with much precision, the array of
groups was quite substantial, probably numbering in the hundreds. By
one set of estimates, too, the total spending by interest groups was extraordinary; U.S. interest groups spent some $10 million while Mexican
interest groups spent $30 to $45 million "on no fewer than twenty-four
lobbying, public relations and law firms."[31]

As more and new kinds of issues arise in the post–cold war era
(e.g., the question of immigration, U.S. intervention abroad, new trade
regimes), and activate many different types of interest groups, their role
becomes an even greater feature of the foreign policy process. Furthermore, as some issues, and particularly issues that require technological
and scientific knowledge to sift through the debate (e.g., global warming
or the handling of fissile materials with the dismantlement of nuclear
weapons), gain a larger place on the agenda, specialized interest groups
will enjoy even more privileged access to the policy process than in
the past.

*Societal Change and the Media.* These societal changes have also had
an impact on the media. As partisan and ideological divisions in American society have intensified, more and more controversies have arisen.
Controversies are the stuff of greater media access and involvement on
issues, including foreign policy. As controversies widen, the purview of
the media spreads as well. No longer is media coverage limited to foreign policy issues at the White House, the Pentagon, and the State Department (or the "Golden Triangle," as Lance Bennett called it).[32] That

is, the media now move beyond official statements and Washington policy makers in covering foreign policy events. Once again, with controversial issues such as immigration, nuclear proliferation, and trade policy crowding the foreign policy agenda, more and more actors have a part to play in shaping the direction of foreign policy. These actors, in turn, enable the media to have greater access.

The movement away from the cold war in American society enhances the media in yet another way: it enables the media to try to add new issues to the foreign policy agenda, sometimes successfully. Consider, for example, the powerful effect of the media in portraying the death and starvation in Ethiopia in the mid-1980s and Somalia in the early 1990s. When NBC television showed a 1984 report on the Ethiopian famine, the effect on American foreign policy was dramatic: "The impact was immediate and overwhelming. The phones started ringing at NBC and at the Connecticut headquarters of Save the Children. . . . The next night, NBC aired another BBC report and, again, the response was staggering. CBS and ABC a week later aired more reports on the famine — with even more response, more reports. The story had exploded."[33] U.S. policy makers took note as well, and they began to shape an American response.

In the immediate aftermath of the cold war, too, the media aided in prodding President Bush to address the starving and suffering in Somalia. Media pictures and accounts of the death and suffering resulted in part in American military aircraft being used to transport food and, eventually, American ground forces being deployed to aid in the distribution of food. In some ways, the media went even further. They met the American forces as they came ashore in Somalia, turning it into a media event: "Among the most vivid scenes from that operation was the look of startled Navy seals in war paint hitting the beaches which had already been secured by television news crews to record the landing."[34]

The ability of the media to place new issues on the agenda and to shape American foreign policy should not be exaggerated, as some recent analysts suggest. The so-called "CNN effect" may not be quite as potent as some imply, even in the Somalia case mentioned above. As one careful analysis of this episode reveals, the media "did not independently drive Somalia to the surface." Rather they reflected the policy goals of those in the Bush administration, the Congress, and the international community who wanted to enlarge American actions in that country.[35] Similarly, despite vivid portrayal of the killings and the suffering in Bosnia, the media hardly propelled that issue to action by foreign policy makers in the early 1990s. It was not until the slaughters of July

1995 that the Clinton administration finally decided to take decisive actions to try to resolve the festering issue. The same proved to be the case for Rwanda. Although the media dramatically catalogued the slaughters in Rwanda in 1994 and the desperation in that country in 1996, American actions were largely delayed by the Clinton administration, in the latter instance, until after the presidential election. In short, as another analyst contends, the media are much less effective in shaping policy and policy makers than a first look might suggest: "The CNN Effect is narrower and far more complex than the conventional wisdom holds."[36]

### New Interest Groups and New Media

A third element in this changed post–cold war environment is the sheer growth of new interest groups and media. Both the new global environment and societal changes directly contribute to the expansion of interest groups and the media.

*The Rise of New Groups.* While one estimate puts the total number of interest groups at about 12,500,[37] those with a foreign policy focus is surely a fraction of that number. Even so, the number of foreign policy interest groups continues to grow. While traditional foreign policy groups often mirrored the key domestic groups (i.e., business, labor, and agricultural groups with their foreign policy concerns), they also included a few prominent ethnic lobbies and some veterans groups. Over the past two or three decades, though, several new groups—foreign lobbies, some religious lobbies, think tanks, and scattered single-issue lobbies—have come along and have increasingly exercised some foreign policy clout.

While the Jewish lobby has been, and remains, the most prominent ethnic lobby, it, too, has been undergoing some change. With increasing, successful efforts to obtain peace in the Middle East, and with some accompanying fissures in Israeli society, some divisions have been detected in the Jewish lobby in the United States, eroding some of its impact and allowing the emergence of other ethnic lobbies to garner significant attention.[38]

Still, ethnic group actions to shape the direction of foreign policy have reached "a historic high water mark," in the estimate of one analyst.[39] One significant change is the lobbying effort by American citizens with origins in the old Soviet empire. In 1993, several different American ethnic associations (e.g., Armenian Americans, Ukrainian Americans, Czech Americans, Slovak Americans, Polish Americans, Hungarian Americans, Latvian Americans, and a host of others) joined together to form the Central and East European Coalition. Among the goals of this coalition are promoting the expansion of NATO, fostering more economic assistance to the countries of Eastern Europe, and reducing the emphasis on Russia in the Clinton administration's policy. While ethnic members with these origins are relatively small in number (about 9 percent of the American population), they are mainly located in some key Midwestern states that could have significant political clout in closely contested elections (at either the presidential or congressional level). As a consequence, President Clinton sought to gain the support of these ethnic voters by his actions and the Republican Congress promoted actions consistent with the wishes of these voters as well.[40] A separate lobbying effort by one of these groups, the Armenian Assembly, has also proved potent. It has been able to direct economic assistance to Armenia and has gained congressional approval for banning aid to Azerbaijan, its rival in the region.[41]

Two other changes in this area are the growth of congressional caucuses to deal with these concerns and the growth of ethnic-based political action committees (PACs). In 1988, six ethnic congressional caucuses existed (e.g., the Hispanic Caucus), while in 1997, fifteen such caucuses exist (e.g., the Portuguese American Caucus). In 1988, twenty ethnic PACs existed, while that number in 1996 was up to fifty-one.[42] Both kinds of organizations are mechanisms for ethnic groups to exert more influence in the political process.

Two increasingly influential ethnic lobbies are the Cuban American lobby and the African American lobby. The Cuban American National Foundation is the most prominent of the Cuban American groups, and it has affected the behavior of both political parties in how they address the issue of Cuba. While Republican administrations have generally been more receptive than Democratic ones, the Clinton administration stopped appointments to the Department of State, opposed cuts in Radio Marti, the U.S. government–run station broadcasting to Cuba, and responded promptly to the Cuban attack on two unarmed planes in international waters off Cuba. One congressional member, commenting on the foundation's power, claimed that the interest group "uses difficult, difficult tactics whenever you disagree with them."[43]

The African American lobby has been quite successful lately as well.[44] Trans-Africa, its most prominent lobby, was largely responsible for initiating a coalition lobbying effort to impose economic sanctions on South Africa in the mid-1980s. Indeed, the Anti-Apartheid Act of 1986 could be traced rather directly to its efforts. Equally so, the actions of Trans-Africa and its head, Randall Robinson, were pivotal in keeping the Haitian issue on the foreign policy agenda during 1993 and 1994 and in pushing for stronger action against the military rulers in 1994. A hunger strike by Randall Robinson seemingly had an important impact on U.S. policy makers at the time. As a consequence, this interest group and the Congressional Black Caucus seemed to have been pivotal in affecting the Clinton administration's decision making over taking action on Haiti in the fall of 1994.

 Another important transformation among new interest groups has been associated with religious lobbies. While religious lobbies were particularly prominent on foreign policy issues during the Vietnam War in the 1960s and 1970s and over El Salvador, Nicaragua, and the nuclear freeze issues in the 1980s, these groups have not declined in activism. Indeed, the end of the cold war, with such difficult issues as Somalia, Haiti, and Bosnia, has actually sparked renewed activity and involvement to infuse a moral and ethical component into American foreign policy. In a reversal of positions from earlier decades, some religious activists now favor and lobby for greater use of America's intervention capabilities to address the underlying social ills. According to Father J. Bryan Hehir, a foreign policy adviser to the American Catholic bishops and a professor at the Harvard Divinity School, "The nuclear question has moved out of the terms of the debate [for religious groups]. What has taken its place are questions about the need for intervention because of human rights violations or civil wars or ethnic conflicts."[45]

Far and away, the most prominent change in lobbying of the American foreign policy process has been growth and pervasiveness of foreign lobbies, interest groups initiated and funded—directly or indirectly—by other countries. Table 7.1 catalogs this growth in countries represented and number of firms or individuals employed by each country over the past two decades. Particular increases have occurred among Eastern European and African countries in their lobbying efforts in Washington, although all regions of the world show growth. Several examples of these newest interest groups will convey a better sense of their prevalence.

In recent years, the Japanese lobby effort has received the most attention and publicity,[46] but that foreign lobby is only one among many foreign lobbies that now occupy the interest group arena in Washington. The foreign lobbies coming from the republics that used to comprise the old Soviet Union are the newest groups in Washington. These new nations are rapidly hiring law and public relations firms to advance their views in both the executive and legislative branches of the American government. Azerbaijan, Belarus, Kazakhstan, Kirghizstan, Latvia, Moldova, Russia, Ukraine, and Uzbekistan are some of the countries

Table 7.1   Number of Foreign Interest Groups by Region, Represented in Washington, 1977, 1986, and 1996

| Region | Year | | |
|---|---|---|---|
| | 1977 | 1986 | 1996 |
| **Africa** | | | |
| Total Countries | 13 | 26 | 33 |
| Total Representatives | 30 | 46 | 72 |
| **Asia** | | | |
| Total Countries | 16 | 18 | 21 |
| Total Representatives | 80 | 256 | 257 |
| **Pacific** | | | |
| Total Countries | 5 | 3 | 7 |
| Total Representatives | 23 | 20 | 26 |
| **Western Europe** | | | |
| Total Countries | 19 | 18 | 21 |
| Total Representatives | 155 | 207 | 254 |
| **Eastern Europe** | | | |
| Total Countries | 10 | 6 | 24 |
| Total Representatives | 44 | 17 | 92 |
| **Middle East** | | | |
| Total Countries | 14 | 10 | 18 |
| Total Representatives | 38 | 57 | 108 |
| **North America** | | | |
| Total Countries | 23 | 20 | 23 |
| Total Representatives | 95 | 176 | 210 |
| **South America** | | | |
| Total Countries | 10 | 7 | 13 |
| Total Representatives | 43 | 58 | 83 |

*Sources:* These totals were calculated from the listings in *Directory of Washington Representatives of American Associations and Industries* (Washington, D.C.: Columbia Books, 1977); *Washington Representatives,* 10th ed. (Washington, D.C.: Columbia Books, 1986); and *Washington Representatives,* 20th ed. (Washington, D.C.: Columbia Books, 1996).

that now have representatives. Russia, too, has joined these lobbying efforts by late 1993; indeed, the government of Russia or Russian firms had signed agreements with nine different law and consulting firms.[47] The People's Republic of China also has established a large contingent of representatives to make their case with the American government, especially for dealing with the sensitive issue of trade relations between the two nations. Top-flight lawyers and former officials of the American government have been employed by U.S. business concerns interested in gaining access to Chinese officials, and other lobbyists are promoting Chinese businesses within the United States.[48] These joint efforts, by officials of American business and by representatives of Chinese business and government, provide for a persuasive effort to maintain most-favored-nation (MFN) status for China and for promoting and expanding American trade and investment with China.

Many less familiar and powerful states have hired their own Washington representatives or sent their own representatives to lobby their particular cases. These officials represent countries from virtually every corner of the world. For many years, Nigeria, Rwanda, Swaziland, and Zaire in Africa have had hired representatives in Washington, while a representative for Mauritania was contracted more recently.[49] Indonesia and India from Asia have similarly sought representation.[50] Haiti, Mexico, and Guatemala from the Caribbean and Central America have hired lobbyists in recent years as well.[51] From the South Pacific, for example, New Zealand has considerable direct lobbying occurring by its key groups. Members of the New Zealand Dairy Board and the New Zealand Meat Producers Board, for example, are visitors to Washington with the Department of Agriculture and the Congress as their important targets.[52] In short, foreign lobbies are now the standard in the Washington interest group community.

Even some unpopular political factions from foreign countries have hired firms to represent them in Washington. Sinn Fein, the political wing of the Irish Republican Army, and the Ulster Unionist Party have joined the parade by hiring representatives in Washington. Likewise, the Russian party of Vladimir V. Zhirinovsky, the Liberal Democratic Party, has sought to bring its nationalist message here as well. The National Council of Resistance in Iran, a party labeled as Marxist by the U.S. State Department, hired a Washington public affairs firm in a $15,000-a-month contract to convey its views to the Congress. These factions join others, such as the Kashmiri American Council, a group committed to Kashmir's independence, as a way to counteract governments in power with representation in the United States.[53]

Finally, the recent revelations of foreign campaign contributors to President Clinton's 1996 election campaign even more vividly dramatize the role of foreign lobbies. Contributions came from, either directly or indirectly, the Lippo Group in Indonesia, supporters in Taiwan, a consultant with ties to a Thai business conglomerate, a South Korean entrepreneur, and perhaps from the Chinese government or its representatives. While some of these funds were returned, and investigations are ongoing over the legality of activities, the flow of foreign money into the political process totaled in the millions of dollars.[54]

*New and Old Media.* Several important media changes have occurred near the end of the cold war and continue apace in the post–cold war period. The growth of the electronic media has been most pronounced to the point that those media are more pervasive than the print media. The "CNN-ization of the world," referring to the power and influence of the Atlanta-based network of the Turner broadcasting system (and now owned by Time-Warner), epitomizes this new electronic explosion. Yet, the growth goes beyond that station to include the expansion of cable stations and cable systems, both nationally and worldwide (e.g., C-Span, Fox Broadcasting, MSNBC, the NBC Station in Europe, and Britain's Sky TV) and the proliferation of radio stations.[55] The literal explosion in the use of the fax machines and the internet, too, has virtually assured instantaneous global communications.[56] Through these media outlets, the impact of the media on foreign policy is more "immediate, sensational, and pervasive."[57]

The first part of table 7.2 provides some sense of the growth in the electronic media over the past two decades and the stability in the circulation of the print media. While the number of radio stations has grown slowly over the past two decades, the number of television stations and cable systems has doubled or even tripled since the early 1970s. By contrast, newspaper circulation has remained markedly stable until about 1990, and it has experienced a slight decline to this day.

The impact of such coverage on the foreign policy process and on American society generally remains unclear, especially when several other different indicators are considered. As the second half of table 7.2 reveals, the amount of interest in news about other countries and about U.S. foreign policy among the American public has remained stable and generally low over the last two decades. The percentage of the public that is "very interested" in information about other nations remains in the mid-30 percent range, and the percentage "very interested" in U.S. relations with other nations averages somewhat higher at 45 to 50 percent.[58] More troubling, although not shown in table 7.2, viewership of nightly broadcasts on the major networks continues to decline to only 42 percent in 1996 compared to about 80 percent in the 1970s. Among those under thirty, the viewership is even lower at only 22 percent.[59] Furthermore, foreign policy coverage by the news media remains markedly small. Estimates of such coverage range from 11 to 16 percent for all print and network coverage.[60] In one study of ten newspapers, more-

Table 7.2  Changes in the Media Outlets and Interest in Foreign News, 1974—1994

|  | Year | | | | | |
|---|---|---|---|---|---|---|
|  | 1974 | 1978 | 1982 | 1986 | 1990 | 1994 |
| Newspaper circulations | 62 mil. | 62 mil. | 62.5 mil. | 62.5 mil. | 62.3 mil. | 60 mil. |
| Number of radio stations | 4361 | 4316 | 4668 | 4863 | 4987 | 4913 |
| Number of television stations | 694 | 720 | 1065 | 1235 | 1442 | 1512 |
| Number of cable systems | 3158 | 3875 | 4825 | 7600 | 9575 | 11,230 |
| Percent of the public "very interested" in news about other countries | 35 | 26 | 28 | 31 | 36 | 33 |
| Percent of the public "very interested" in news about U.S. foreign relations with other countries | 50 | 44 | 45 | 49 | 53 | 50 |

*Sources:* The data for the first four entries in this table were taken from U.S. Bureau of the Census, *Statistical Abstract of the United States,* various years and editions (Washington, D.C.: U.S. Government Printing Office); data and questions for the last two entries are taken from John E. Rielly, ed., *American Public Opinion and U.S. Foreign Policy 1995* (Chicago: Chicago Council on Foreign Relations, 1995), figure 1-1 at p. 9.

over, the foreign policy coverage was even smaller at about 2.6 percent,[61] and the foreign coverage by the major American networks and the number of foreign correspondents continues to decline as well.[62]

Still, and importantly, the media seemingly have enlarged their ability to bring more and more dramatic international events into the homes of Americans. In this sense, by the decisions on what international events the media shall report and how those events are covered, the media can affect the direction of foreign policy debate at home.

*The Locus of Decision Making and Interest Groups*

A final factor that has enhanced interest group and media access to the foreign policy process is the changing locus of decision making. Most foreign policy issues during the cold war were crisis issues—issues that required a quick, immediate response to meet some impending threat. Because those policies and decisions were largely decided within the executive branch, interest groups had limited access (and influence). While such security issues may still confront policy makers in the post–cold war environment, their aggregate number seems to have declined, and the kinds of security issues have changed, as noted earlier. As a result, access for interest groups is likely to increase as decisions move toward those decisions that have been identified as strategic and structural in nature.

Strategic policies are those that "specif[y] the goals and tactics of defense and foreign policy."[63] Within this very broad category, decisions focusing on the policy guidelines for American actions toward a particular region (e.g., Southeast Asia), country (e.g., Russia), or issue (e.g., trade) would qualify as strategic policy. While the president has the advantage of recommending the basic policy direction in a given area, these strategic decisions are increasingly subject to review and evaluation in Congress, especially when they do not require immediate action. As such, the locus of these decisions is shifting to the Congress or to a combined legislative-executive decision. As the time allowed for decision making increases and the locus of decision making moves toward the Congress, interest groups have more opportunities to convey their stances on the outcome. Indeed, as we shall note shortly, the Congress has often passed procedural legislation requiring congressional review of executive actions in a number of strategic areas, further expanding interest group access.

Structural policies are even more ripe for interest group activity.  These policies are directed at the details of actions in the foreign and defense areas. As Lindsay and Ripley note, these policies focus on "procuring, deploying, and organizing military personnel and material . . . [and] which countries will receive aid, what rules will govern immigration."[64] Both by tradition and constitutional requirements, the ultimate locus of such decisions are in the Congress, not in the executive branch. In this policy area, as in the strategic policy area, interest groups have an ever larger role to play, owing to the locus of decisions in the congressional arena and the greater frequencies of these decisions.

Coupled with the changing nature of foreign policy issues is the growth in the procedural requirements placed upon the executive branch by the congressional branch. These procedural requirements, virtually by definition, require congressional involvement—an involvement which allows the time and venue for interest groups to have more access and impact on foreign policy. Over the past two and a half decades, several key areas of executive foreign policy have become subject for congressional review: the war-making area, the commitment-making area, the trade and aid area, and the general oversight of foreign policy.[65]

Several illustrations will demonstrate this more direct involvement of Congress and identify the additional avenues for interest groups to play a part in the process. While the war-making and commitment-making areas are less successful in enabling Congress to play a larger role (despite actions such as the passage of the War Powers Resolution of 1973 or the Case-Zablocki Act of 1972), the trade and aid areas and the oversight activities, by contrast, have seemingly been more conse-quential for a congressional role and for interest group activity as well. These areas, too, epitomize the focus on important strategic and struc-tural policy questions.

First, since the Trade Act of 1974, Congress has actually written into law requirements that private groups advise the administration during any trade negotiations.[66] This process has been accelerated even more in recent years with the use of the so-called fast-track procedures. At the negotiating stage of the process, for example, four types of advi-sory committees from the private sector may participate: (1) a broadly based committee drawn from key sectors of the country; (2) a general advisory committee from industry, agriculture, labor, and other sectors; (3) sector or functional committees composed of those interests directly affected by any prospective agreement; and (4) policy advisory com-mittees from state and local governments and their representatives.[67] Depending upon the particular representatives chosen and industries represented, some of the most important private sector companies and interests can have a direct and tangible impact on the negotiating pro-cess. Once the negotiation process is completed, these committees and advisory panels may then submit their evaluations to the executive branch, the legislative branch, and the United States trade representa-tive (USTR).[68] Here, too, these groups could affect the outcome of the process. Finally, congressional committees must draw up the imple-menting legislation for the negotiated agreement, allowing yet another avenue for interest group influence.

Second, foreign economic and military assistance allows interest group access. Because arms sales legislation passed in the mid-1970s now requires both a report to, and a review by, the Congress of any proposed arms sales, foreign policy interest groups have a ready oppor-tunity to mobilize and weigh in on the final disposition of any sales proposal. This review period lasts for fifty days from the time of the an-nouncement of the arms sales (a thirty-day formal review period and a twenty-day informal review period) and affected interest groups could still have an opportunity to affect the final outcome.

Third, congressional procedural changes have enhanced interest group access in the area of oversight. Because an increasing number of issues are subject to the congressional review process and because these reviews generally involve structural and strategic policy questions, the sheer volume of activity, as noted earlier, advantages interest groups. Both the principal foreign policy committees (House International Relations and Senate Foreign Relations) have expanded the number of oversight hearings, with the House side particularly noted for the increased number of such activities. Similarly, the national security committees (House National Security and Senate Armed Services) have undertaken these kinds of oversight hearings as well, even as they also move into the area of devising strategy. Such ready forums allow outside interested parties to seek to influence the Congress, and, ultimately, policy.

*The Locus of Decision Making and Media Access*
The media also benefit from the change in the locus of foreign policy decision making from crisis to structural/strategic issues and from the executive to the Congress. Structural and strategic issues are more likely to spark controversy, require expert analysis, take more time, and lack a readily identifiable policy consensus. For each of these reasons, media access and involvement will increase.

First, since structural and strategic issues, almost by definition, have a greater prospect of being linked to domestic politics, they are likely to generate controversy—the lifeblood of the media. Issues on base closings, the building of new weaponry systems, the granting of trade concessions, the reduction of tariffs, or the imposing of new environmental standards—all are likely to stimulate partisan and ideological differences at home. Such differences, too, are apt subjects for increased coverage by the media on a regular basis.

Second, structural and strategic issues often require policy "experts" and the exploration of viable policy options, further aiding the media. The appropriate means for disposing of surplus fissile materials from the dismantlement of nuclear weapons, for instance, requires those knowledgeable both technically and politically. The media thus can search out these experts for their reporting. (Interestingly, too, these experts are likely to come from prominent interest groups.) Furthermore, with this kind of issue and with other current ones, such as the uses and abuses of foreign aid, human rights violations in China, or drug trafficking from Latin America, investigative reports on these subjects by the media are appropriate and potentially useful. Furthermore, the media can play a large role with these investigations through ferreting out issues that others may try to conceal (witness the role of the media over foreign campaign contributions in the 1996 presidential campaign). In this way, the media contribute to, and shape, the foreign policy agenda in a way they could not when crisis issues dominated the political landscape.

Third, because structural and strategic issues involve more decision-making time for policy makers, the media are advantaged as well. Much as with interest groups, the media can play a larger role, the more a decision is extended over time. The expanded time allows the media to explore and report on the various aspects of the controversy and assess the impact of the controversy on the domestic arena. As the decision time expands, then, the various "players" on a given issue will be able to seek out the media to try to make their case with the American public.

Fourth, these structural and strategic issues oftentimes do not enjoy a readily identifiable policy position. The question of the expansion of NATO or the wisdom of expanding free trade areas is fraught with controversy. While the media may contribute to the debate over such questions with their investigative work or with the reliance on policy experts, those actions also fuel the debate and indirectly enhance the impact of the media.

Finally, and as with the discussion of interest groups, the locus of decision making of these issues largely remains outside the exclusive purview and control of the executive branch. That is, Congress plays a role in deciding on both strategic and structural issues. In this way, access is more assured for the media, and their involvement enlarged.

### Policy Influence: The Impact of Interest Groups and the Media

With all these points of access, the issue that still remains is over the degree of interest group and media influence on foreign policy. While involvement and access may arguably be necessary conditions for policy influence, they are not sufficient ones. At the same time, with marked domestic and international changes, the prospects look seemingly bright for interest groups and the media to have a significant impact in the years ahead.[69] In this sense, in the post–cold war era, we should likely see an increase in interest groups and media influence across a wider array of foreign policy issues.

While confirmatory data on this assessment remain fragmentary, some selective analyses provide initial support for expanding interest group influence. The effect of foreign policy interest groups in the trade area, most recently over NAFTA and GATT, is well recognized. Indeed, in the case of the former, for example, lobbyists were actually asked to "lend a hand" to get the pact through the Congress, and, in a reversal of the usual roles, an official of the Office of the USTR attended the meetings of a business group supporting the pact.[70] In the foreign aid area (e.g., in the case of Zaire or Israel), the conclusion about interest group influence remains the same. While certain conditions (such as the receptivity of the interest groups' target and the level of campaign funding to individual members of Congress) had to exist in the Zaire case, Congress still kept open the money spigot flowing to that regime, despite a dismal human rights record.[71] Similarly, agricultural credits continued —and economic sanctions were postponed—toward Iraq, owing to the sustained lobbying efforts of selected foreign policy interest groups.[72] More recently, questions have been raised over the impact of foreign campaign contributions to the Clinton administration's Asian policy. While official denials remain, the magnitude of the contributions and the level of sustained activity by foreign groups leave lingering doubts.

Despite these illustrative examples, though, significant barriers still hamper interest groups from working their will on foreign policy makers even as these groups are increasingly involved in the process. First,  interest group effectiveness still probably requires the mobilization of a larger group or the public at large to have an immediate and sustained impact.[73] Only in rare instances do foreign policy issues produce such an effect among the public. Second, the dispersal of more and more interest groups involved in the decision process has the effect of reducing the influence of any one group. What matters as a result is the relative power and capabilities of particular groups in the political arena, not the sheer number of political actors. In this sense, there is hardly a linear relationship between the growth in interest group activity and their policy impact. Indeed, the relationship might actually be curvilinear, with issues generating few interest groups or those generating many interest groups producing limited policy impact in both instances, albeit for differing reasons: A small number of groups does not have sufficient clout, while a large number of competing groups cancel out one another's influence.

Third, the complexity of the American political system, coupled with the continued (albeit weakened) presidential discretion on foreign policy questions, works against interest groups gaining their will in the foreign policy process. The usual judgment that interest groups can be more effective in stopping action than in changing directions remains as accurate in the foreign policy arena as it does in the domestic arena.[74] Yet the ability of these groups to initiate changes in policy likely will remain a problem in the post–cold war era as much as it was in the cold war environment. Despite the magnitude of lobbying on both sides of this issue, Arnson and Brenner still felt compelled to conclude that "interest groups may have had a limited impact on the direction of U.S. policy toward Nicaragua in the 1980s because of the limited scope and opportunities for influence offered to them by the Congress."[75]

Fourth, new lobbyist registration laws and incipient campaign finance reform efforts do not bode well for either domestic or foreign policy interest groups. Under the new lobbying bill passed in late 1995, lobbying by lawyers for foreign interests is not exempt, and lobbying lawyers must now register with the House and the Senate. Lobbyists must now report on the names of their clients, the issues that they are working, and what part of the federal government that they have tried to lobby. In addition, these lobbyists must also provide an estimate of the income derived from each lobbying activity.[76] Furthermore, if campaign reform were to become a reality in the wake of the 1996 presidential campaign scandal, restrictions on campaign contributions, arguably the most important avenues of access and influence for interest groups, would likely be incorporated. In this sense, interest groups, including the foreign lobbyists, will have a difficult time impacting the process.

Confident conclusions about the media's influence, however, are more difficult to make. While the media have expanded their access and involvement, their influence remains hotly debated. While the sheer magnitude of the media coverage appears greater across a host of issues, and conditions exist for greater influence, analysts remain divided. Some analysts still see the media as largely a captive of official administration policy. In this sense, the media never veer too far from the official policy line of the administration in its reporting on foreign policy. When they do, they do so because "the sphere of legitimate controversy" has been expanded by officials themselves. Thus, the notion of an "oppositional media" since the Vietnam War is hard to sustain.[77] In short, the media remain largely supportive of official policy or at least followers of the lead provided by policy makers.[78]

Other analysts see the emergence of an increasingly independent role for the media in influencing policy. The media can work to set the foreign agenda through the stories that they report (e.g., famine in Ethiopia and Somalia) or even engage in what Doris Graber labels "media diplomacy." That is, members of the media become part of the foreign policy event (e.g., the role of CBS newsman Walter Cronkite in bringing Israeli prime minister Menachem Begin and Egyptian president Anwar Sadat together, which resulted in Sadat's visit to Israel).[79] Furthermore, there remains the view among the public that the media possess a liberal bias in their reporting and try to influence the public and policy makers with those views.[80]

Finally, a more recent argument about the influence of the media charts a middle position among these differing views of the media's influence. Patrick O'Heffernan contends that the media and the government have a "mutually exploitative" relationship with one another.[81] As Heffernan argues, "[B]oth [the foreign policy community and the media] are adept at supporting, manipulating, or attacking the other. The relationship is sometimes competitive and sometimes cooperative, but that is only incidental to its central driving force: self-interest."[82] Increasingly, then, policy makers and the media view one another as part of the foreign policy process, and, as a result, each influences the other.[83]

## Conclusion

This chapter has sought to look at a series of factors that seem to challenge the traditional view regarding the influence of interest groups and the media in the foreign policy, especially as we enter the post–cold war era. Although many of the arguments have been raised by others, they have not received the kind of treatment in the American foreign policy literature that they deserve. Perhaps it is best to close this discussion on these concerns with a plea for more systematic work on these two subjects in combination and for greater assessment of how one impacts the other and, in turn, affects the foreign policy process. There has been, for example, a renaissance in the study of American foreign policy and public opinion in the past decade, but it has not been matched by a similar rebirth in the study of interest groups and their effects on foreign policy. By contrast, the efforts to study the role and impact of the media is largely in its embryonic stage. As a result, we remain left with much of the conventional wisdom about interest groups, media, and foreign policy—a wisdom that may not be very conventional for the post–cold war world.

## Notes

1 Throughout this chapter, I draw upon material from my *American Foreign Policy and Process*, 2d ed. (Itasca, Ill.: F. E. Peacock, 1992), and 3d ed. (Itasca, Ill.: F. E. Peacock, 1998), specifically the chapters discussing interest groups and the media; and from my "Congress" entry in Bruce W. Jentleson and Thomas G. Paterson, eds., *Encyclopedia of U.S. Foreign Relations* 1 (New York: Oxford University

Press, 1997), 312–328. For one prominent assessment of the limited role of interest groups during the height of the cold war, see Aaron Wildavsky, "The Two Presidencies," *TRANS-action* 3 (December 1966): 7–14. On the role of the media during this time period, see W. Lance Bennett, "The Media and the Foreign Policy Process," in David A. Deese, ed., *The New Politics of American Foreign Policy* (New York: St. Martin's Press, 1994), p. 170. On how the cold war affected press coverage, see James F. Hoge Jr., "Media Pervasiveness," *Foreign Affairs* 73 (July/August 1994): 137.

2 See James M. Lindsay and Randall B. Ripley, "How Congress Influences Foreign and Defense Policy," in Randall B. Ripley and James M. Lindsay, eds., *Congress Resurgent: Foreign and Defense Policy on Capitol Hill* (Ann Arbor: University of Michigan Press, 1993), pp. 17–35.

3 The most succinct argument for this limited influence of interest groups in foreign policy is in Barry B. Hughes, *The Domestic Context of American Foreign Policy* (San Francisco: Freeman, 1978), pp. 198–202, from which part of this argument is drawn. Also see, however, Bernard Cohen, *The Public's Impact on Foreign Policy* (Boston, Mass.: Little, Brown, 1973); and Robert H. Trice, "Domestic Interest Groups and the Arab-Israeli Conflict: A Behavioral Analysis," in Abdul Aziz Said, ed., *Ethnicity and U.S. Foreign Policy*, pp. 128–129, on the problem of gaining access to the Congress and the executive.

4 See Cohen, *The Public's Impact on Foreign Policy*, pp. 100–103.

5 On this point, see Eric M. Uslaner, "All Politics Are Global: Interest Groups and the Making of Foreign Policy," in Allan J. Cigler and Burdett A. Loomis, eds., *Interest Group Politics*, 4th ed. (Washington, D.C.: CQ Press, 1995), p. 370.

6 Thomas L. Brewer, *American Foreign Policy: A Contemporary Introduction* (Englewood Cliffs, N.J.: Prentice-Hall, 1980), p. 89.

7 W. Lance Bennett, "The Media and the Foreign Policy Process," in David A. Deese, ed., *The New Politics of American Foreign Policy*, p. 170.

8 Hoge Jr., "Media Pervasiveness," p. 137.

9 See John T. Tierney, "Interest Group Involvement in Congressional Foreign and Defense Policy," in Ripley and Lindsay, eds., *Congress Resurgent*, pp. 89–111. Also see Uslaner, "All Politics Are Global," pp. 372–373.

10 Bennett, "The Media and the Foreign Policy Process," p. 170.

11 Roger H. Davidson, and Walter J. Oleszek, *Congress and Its Members*, 4th ed. (Washington, D.C.: CQ Press, 1994), p. 428. They also report that nine other House committees and six other Senate committees deal with issues related to the foreign and defense areas.

12 Steven S. Smith and Eric D. Lawrence, "Party Control of Committees in the Republican Congress," in Lawrence D. Dodd and Bruce I. Oppenheimer, eds., *Congress Reconsidered*, 6th ed. (Washington, D.C.: CQ Press, 1997), p. 172. Note, though, that the Republican majority used the "additional initial referral" to replace the joint referral used previously. See Smith and Lawrence, "Party Control of Committees," p. 190.

13 For data on these hearings on a Congress-by-Congress basis, see Committee on Foreign Affairs, *Survey of Activities*, 97th Cong. (Washington, D.C.: U.S. Gov-

ernment Printing Office, 1983), pp. 263–264; *Survey of Activities*, 99th Cong. (Washington, D.C.: U.S. Government Printing Office, 1987), p. 253; Committee on Foreign Affairs, *Legislative Review Activities of the Committee on Foreign Affairs: One Hundred Third Congress* (Washington, D.C.: U.S. Government Printing Office, 1994), p. 169; and Committee on International Relations, *Legislative Review Activities of the Committee on International Relations: One Hundred Fourth Congress* (Washington, D.C.: U.S. Government Printing Office, 1997), p. 123.

14 See James M. McCormick, "Decision Making in the Foreign Affairs and Foreign Relations Committee," in Ripley and Lindsay, eds., *Congress Resurgent*, 1993, pp. 128–129.

15 These totals for 1971 and 1991 are from McCormick, "Decision Making in the Foreign Affairs and Foreign Relations Committee," p. 128. The figure for 1996 was calculated from *The 1996 Congressional Staff Directory Summer* (Alexander, Va.: CQ Staff Directories, 1996), pp. 754–757.

16 McCormick, "Decision Making in the Foreign Affairs and Foreign Relations Committee," pp. 128–129; and *The 1996 Congressional Staff Directory Summer*, pp. 394–396. The total includes professional staff and support staff.

17 Paul Stockton, "Beyond Micromanagement: Congressional Budgeting for a Post-Cold War Military," *Political Science Quarterly* 110 (Summer 1995), p. 233.

18 Stockton, "Beyond Micromanagement," 244.

19 Stockton, "Beyond Micromanagement," 258. While the telling point here is surely the potential role for think tanks, but also note how lobbying can occur by governmental groups as well (e.g., the Pentagon).

20 On annual authorizations within these committees, see Christopher J. Deering, "Decision Making in the Armed Services Committees," in Ripley and Lindsay, eds., *Congress Resurgent*, pp. 155–182.

21 "Lugar Outlines Rubric for Choosing Next Secretary of State," Media Release, Richard G. Lugar, United States senator for Indiana, November 8, 1996.

22 On the topic of media entrepreneurs, see Karen M. Kedrowski, *Media Entrepreneurs and the Media Enterprise in the U.S. Congress* (Cresskill, N.J.: Hampton Press, 1996).

23 Kedrowski, *Media Entrepreneurs*, 2, on the amount of effort that Congressman Jim Traficant (D-Ohio) spends on his "1-Minute" speeches. Also see pp. 3–7.

24 Kedrowski, *Media Entrepreneurs*, pp. 71–106.

25 On this point, see James M. McCormick and Eugene R. Wittkopf, "Bipartisanship, Partisanship, and Ideology in Congressional-Executive Foreign Policy Relations, 1947–1988," *Journal of Politics* 52 (November 1990), 1077–1100.

26 See Jeremy D. Rosner, *The New Tug-of-War: Congress, the Executive Branch, and National Security* (Washington, D.C.: Carnegie Endowment for International Peace, 1995).

27 Cynthia J. Arnson and Philip Brenner, "The Limits of Lobbying: Interest Groups, Congress, and Aid to the Contras," in Richard Sobel, ed., *Public Opinion in U.S. Foreign Policy* (Lanham, Md.: Rowman and Littlefield, 1993), p. 192.

28 Quoted in Bruce W. Jentleson, *With Friends Like These* (New York: W.W. Norton,

1994), p. 86. The information on interest group activity over Iraq is drawn from pp. 77–86.

29 Jentleson, *With Friends Like These*, p. 86.

30 Jentleson, *With Friends Like These*, p. 78.

31 A wide array of interest groups lobbying for and against NAFTA is summarized in Stephen D. Cohen, Joel R. Paul, and Robert A. Blecker, *Fundamentals of U.S. Foreign Trade Policy: Economics, Politics, Laws, and Issues* (Boulder, Colo.: Westview Press, 1996), pp. 254–255. The spending on lobbying estimates are given at p. 254.

32 Bennett, "The Media and the Foreign Policy Process," p. 178.

33 Quoted in David D. Newsom, *The Public Dimension of Foreign Policy* (Bloomington: Indiana University Press, 1996), pp. 47–48.

34 W. Lance Bennett, "The News about Foreign Policy," in W. Lance Bennett and David L. Paletz, eds., *Taken by Storm: The Media, Public Opinion, and U.S. Foreign Policy in the Gulf War* (Chicago: University of Chicago Press, 1994), p. 12.

35 Steven Livingston and Todd Eachus, "Humanitarian Crises and U.S. Foreign Policy: Somalia and the CNN Effect Reconsidered," *Political Communication* 12 (1995): 413–429. The quote is at p. 427.

36 Warren P. Strobel, "The CNN Effect," *American Journalism Review* (May 1996): 33–37. The quote is at p. 37.

37 McCormick, *American Foreign Policy and Process*, 2d ed., 452.

38 See Uslaner, "All Politics Are Global," pp. 378–380.

39 See Tony Smith in Paul Glastris, "Multicultural Foreign Policy in Washington," *U.S. News and World Report*, July 21, 1997, pp. 31, 34.

40 See Dick Kirschten, "Ethnics Resurging," *National Journal*, February 25, 1995, pp. 484–486 with the quoted passage at p. 486.

41 Glastris, "Multicultural Foreign Policy in Washington," p. 35.

42 Glastris, "Multicultural Foreign Policy in Washington," p. 34.

43 Dick Kirschten, "From the K Street Corridor," *National Journal*, July 17, 1993, p. 1815.

44 For a more extended treatment of this lobbying group and the Arab American lobby, see Yossi Shain, "Multicultural Foreign Policy," *Foreign Policy* 100 (Fall 1995): 69–87.

45 See W. John Moore, "Soldier for the Lord?" *National Journal*, October 2, 1993, pp. 2361–2365. The quoted passage is at p. 2363.

46 See, for example, John B. Judis, "The Japanese Megaphone: Foreign Influences on Foreign Policy making," *New Republic* 202, January 22, 1990, pp. 20–25; and Pat Choate, *Agents of Influence* (New York: Alfred A. Knopf, 1990).

47 See the listing of countries and firms in Dick Kirschten, "Greetings, Comrades!" *National Journal*, October 2, 1993, at p. 2191.

48 Peter H. Stone, "China Connections," *National Journal*, March 26, 1994, pp. 708–712. Representatives include former members of Congress (e.g., Howard Baker and Gary Hart) and former officials in the executive branch officials (e.g., Carla Hills, Lawrence Eagleburger, and Alexander Haig), among others.

49 On Zaire's lobbying, see Stephen R. Weissman, *A Culture of Deference: Con-

*gress's Failure of Leadership in Foreign Policy* (New York: Basic Books, 1995), pp. 70–104; and, on Nigeria's recent efforts, see Dick Kirschten, "From the K Street Corridor," *National Journal*, June 5, 1993, p. 1354. For Rwanda, Swaziland, and Mauritania, see Peter H. Stone, "From the K Street Corridor," *National Journal*, May 8, 1993, p. 1125.

50  Kirk Victor, "From the K Street Corridor," *National Journal*, November 25, 1995, p. 2930.

51  On Haiti, see Dick Kirschten, "From the K Street Corridor," *National Journal*, March 25, 1993, p. 751.

52  Interviews with representatives of these two boards in Wellington, New Zealand, July 1995.

53  Eric Moses, "Casablanca on the Potomac River?" *National Journal*, November 11, 1995, pp. 2810–2811.

54  See "Monkey Business," *Economist*, January 18, 1997, p. 23; Jane Meyer, "Inside the Money Machine," *New Yorker* 72, February 3, 1997, pp. 32–37; Tim Weiner, "F.B.I. Is Investigating Whether China Funneled Money to Democrats through Clinton Friends," *New York Times*, February 14, 1997, p. A12; and Jeff Gerth, Stephen Labaton, and Tim Weiner, "Clinton and Friends: Strong Ties, Few Questions," *New York Times*, February 14, 1997, pp. A1, A12.

55  For some recent data on the explosion of the electronic media and the decline of the print media, see McCormick, *American Foreign Policy and Process*, 3d ed., ch. 12.

56  By contrast, and importantly, the use of foreign correspondents on the ground by the print media and television networks seemingly has eroded. See Stephen Hess, *International News and Foreign Correspondents* (Washington, D.C.: Brookings Institution, 1996).

57  Hoge, "Media Pervasiveness," p. 136.

58  See John E. Rielly, ed., *American Public Opinion and U.S. Foreign Policy 1995* (Chicago: Chicago Council on Foreign Relations, 1995), p. 9.

59  "Old News Ain't Beat Yet," *Economist*, May 18, 1996, p. 32. The subheading for this section draws its title from the ideas in this article.

60  Doris A. Graber, *Mass Media and American Politics*, 3d ed. (Washington, D.C.: CQ Press, 1989), p. 328.

61  Michael Emery, "An Endangered Species: The International Newshole," *Gannett Center Journal* 3 (Fall 1989): 151–164.

62  Garrick Utley, "The Shrinking of Foreign News: From Broadcast to Narrowcast," *Foreign Affairs* 76 (March/April 1997): 2–10. See especially p. 5.

63  Lindsay and Ripley, "How Congress Influences Foreign and Defense Policy," p. 19.

64  Lindsay and Ripley, "How Congress Influences Foreign and Defense Policy," p. 19.

65  McCormick, *American Foreign Policy and Process*, 2d ed., pp. 307–351.

66  James M. Lindsay, "Congress, Foreign Policy, and the New Institutionalism," *International Studies Quarterly*, 38 (June 1974), p. 286.

67  Sharyn O'Halloran, "Congress and Foreign Trade Policy," in Ripley and Lindsay, eds., *Congress Resurgent*, pp. 291–292.

68  O'Halloran, "Congress and Foreign Trade Policy," p. 293.

69 On the problems of disentangling the influence of interest groups in the foreign policy arena, see Tierney, "Interest Group Involvement in Congressional Foreign and Defense Policy," pp. 97–98.

70 See Peter H. Stone, "Lobbyists Lend a Hand on NAFTA," *National Journal*, October 30, 1993, pp. 2595–2596.

71 Weissman, *A Culture of Deference*, pp. 70–104.

72 Jentleson, *With Friends Like These.*

73 Uslaner, "All Politics Are Global," p. 374.

74 See Tierney, "Interest Group Involvement," pp. 98–99.

75 Arnson and Brenner, "The Limits of Lobbying," p. 216.

76 Adam Clymer, "Congress Passes Bill to Disclose Lobbyists' Roles," *New York Times*, November 30, 1995, p. A1; Ronald G. Shaiko, "Changing the Washington Culture: Lobby Disclosure and the Gift Ban," *Extension of Remarks* (July 1996): 1–2.

77 See Daniel C. Hallin, *We Keep America on Top of the World: Television Journalism and the Public Sphere* (London: Routledge, 1994). The quoted phrases are at pp. 54 and 51, respectively.

78 See Livingston and Eachus, "Humanitarian Crises and U.S. Foreign Policy."

79 See Doris A. Graber, *Mass Media and American Politics*, 5th ed. (Washington, D.C.: CQ Press, 1997), p. 349.

80 For evidence on the liberal leanings of members of the media, see S. Robert Lichter, Stanley Rothman, and Linda S. Lichter, *The Media Elite* (Bethesda, Md.: Adler & Adler, 1986); and James K. Glassman, "Obvious Bias . . . ," *Washington Post*, May 7, 1996, p. A19.

81 See Patrick O'Heffernan, "A Mutual Exploitation Model of Media Influence in U.S. Foreign Policy," in Bennett and Paletz, eds., *Taken by Storm*, pp. 231–249.

82 O'Heffernan, "A Mutual Explanation Model," p. 233.

83 O'Heffernan, "A Mutual Explanation Model," pp. 233–234.

# II. CASES

# 8.

## Making U.S. Foreign Policy toward China

## in the Clinton Administration

*John T. Rourke and Richard Clark*

When Bill Clinton sought the presidency in 1992, he assailed President George Bush for his realpolitik approach to relations with China and other autocracies. Clinton charged that Bush, "from the Baltics to Beijing, from Sarajevo to South Africa, has sided with the status quo instead of democratic change, with familiar tyrants rather than those who would overthrow them." Clinton promised that he would "assert a new vision for our role in the world" and would "summon all of our strengths, our economic power, our values and—when necessary—our military might in the service of our new vision."[1]

To the contrary, the policy of the Clinton administration toward China has been, in essence, a continuation of the policy and the rationale of the Bush White House. Bush had defended his pragmatic approach on the grounds that China is important to the "entire world's peace and prosperity," and he had argued that the United States could best promote democracy and human rights in China through "constructive engagement" with the government in Beijing.[2] As Clinton began his second term, he characterized his policy toward China in words that echoed Bush. According to Clinton, "the policy we're following is the right one" because "over the long run being engaged with China . . . helps us on a whole range of security issues that directly bear on the welfare of the American people, . . . [while] continuing to be honest [about U.S. disapproval of Beijing's domestic oppression] has the greatest likelihood of having a positive impact on China."[3]

Even President Clinton has had to admit that "it would be fair to say that my policies with regard to China have been somewhat different from what I talked about in the [1992 presidential] campaign."[4] The purpose of this essay is to explain how the post–cold war international context, the American societal context, and the institutional context of the U.S government interacted to shape China policy during the first Clinton administration. In effect, together these three layers of contexts interacted to cause Clinton's change with regard to China from idealistic candidate to realpolitik president.

The gulf between what candidate Bill Clinton said he would do about China and what President Bill Clinton actually did about China was in part symptomatic of the frequent divergence of political rhetoric and policy reality. But Clinton's shift from idealist to pragmatist and the reasons that he did so also reveal a great deal about new and strengthened realities in U.S. foreign policy making in the post–cold war years. One factor, as Scott and Crothers point out in chapter 1, is that power shifted in important ways as the cold war wound down and the post–cold war era emerged. A second factor, which also reflects the commentary of Scott and Crothers is that the post–cold war period witnessed changing relationships among the shifting constellations of U.S. foreign policy making. These policy-making factors are addressed in detail in the following pages.

### Background

During the last two decades of the cold war, U.S. policy toward China revolved around a shared strategic interest—countering the Soviet Union. Cooperation was further enhanced when Deng Xiaoping assumed the leadership of the People's Republic of China and initiated reforms designed to modernize the Chinese economy. As political and economic ties grew, U.S.-Chinese relations improved. Then, suddenly, the relationship was jolted in June 1989 when the Chinese government brutally crushed protestors in Tiananmen Square, Beijing. As one analyst noted, "the honeymoon was over."[5]

The end of the cold war and the collapse of the Soviet Union also contributed to a steady deterioration of the U.S.-Chinese political relationship, even as the economic relationship continued to expand. As a rising power, China was obviously important, but the strategic equation that had sustained the U.S.-Chinese relationship for two decades had changed dramatically.

On the one hand, the Bush and Clinton administrations recognized the need to cooperate with China in order to achieve U.S. strategic goals. The most significant of these included China's role in nuclear proliferation and, in particular, China's sale of technology applicable to the construction of missiles and nuclear weapons.[6] The United States also sought Chinese cooperation in the renewal of the Non-Proliferation

Treaty (NPT) and the negotiation of a comprehensive test ban treaty (CTBT). These goals meant that the United States needed to avoid alienating China. Similarly, Washington required Beijing's help in defusing an explosive situation that developed in 1993 over North Korea's alleged nuclear weapons program. The U.S.-led demand that North Korea desist and Pyongang's defiance created a crisis, and Beijing was one of the few countries with any influence on North Korea. At the same time, U.S.-Chinese trade and investment grew substantially, creating an important link between the world's largest economy and its fastest growing economy.

On the other hand, China's human rights abuses, its increasingly anti-American line, and its embrace of the "Asian developmental authoritarianism" model raised serious questions for U.S. policy makers and other observers. Moreover, specific trade issues roiled Sino-American relations. The most prominent of these was "piracy," the unauthorized reproduction of copyrighted and patented American intellectual properties, such as movie video tapes, music compact discs, and computer software. Additionally, however, there was growing unease over the rapidly expanding U.S. trade deficit with China. In 1995, China's exports to the United States were $48.5 billion, against a mere $10.0 billion in imports from the United States. This made the U.S trade gap with China the second largest in total dollars after the gap with Japan and the largest in terms of imports as a percentage of exports.

The consequence for the Clinton administration was a complex situation with multiple and often competing goals. Moreover, these diverse interests generated competing interests in the U.S. societal and institutional contexts as well. First, a wide variety of nongovernmental actors became more active and influential on China policy. As two analysts have put it, "As economic and ecological considerations rival in importance military-security considerations, more groups within the United States will legitimately claim to have their interests directly taken into account as policies are formulated and implemented."[7] Some of these actors, such as the human rights activist group Amnesty International, favor using economic sanctions and other measures to press reform on China. Many other and more powerful groups take an opposite view and have worked to minimize or eliminate the impact of American moral impulses on China policy. Economic interest groups have been prominent in the pragmatic camp. Second, there were splits within Congress and the bureaucracy and among interest groups over China policy. The State Department, for one, has subunits on both sides of the issue. At other times, the specific issue meant that a bureaucratic unit was more or less favorable toward China. The Defense Department took a harder line on matters involving China's sale of missile technology and a softer line on human rights. It is in this context that the Clinton administration was required to address foreign policy toward China.

## Making China Policy: Competing Interests and Complex Policy Making

Any examination of U.S. foreign policy toward China in the post–cold war world must begin by assessing the international context within which that policy developed. In reference to this, Secretary of State Warren Christopher summed up the administration's view when he observed that "China can tip the balance in Asia between stability and conflict." Furthermore, the secretary continued, "Its booming economy holds a key to Asia's continued prosperity and, increasingly, to our own."[8] Hence, the Clinton administration's efforts responded to both the political and economic importance of China.

### China as a Rising Political and Economic Power

The Clinton administration repeatedly emphasized China's strategic importance. For example, Clinton had declared while a candidate in 1992 that he "would deny most-favored-nation status [MFN] to China, . . . impose trade sanctions, and encourage the younger [Chinese] generation's democratic aspirations."[9] Once he became president, however, Clinton renewed China's MFN status, and in 1994 formally "delinked" the issues of trade and human rights. The president explained that "China has an atomic arsenal and a veto in the UN Security Council. It is a major factor in Asian and global security. We share important interests, such as in a nuclear-free Korean peninsula and in sustaining the global environment."[10] The president was also mindful of China's potential, commenting: "I believe among the great security questions of the 21st century—and there are, you know, five or six really big questions—one of them is how will China . . . define [its] greatness."[11]

Clinton's rationale reflected several specific areas where he needed China's cooperation. At the time of the MFN decision, Washington was working to convince Beijing to support the U.S. desire to renew and make permanent the NPT and to reach agreement on the CTBT. In the U.N. Security Council, China's veto could have blocked U.S.-supported resolutions on such matters as peacekeeping in Bosnia, the effort to topple the military junta in Haiti, and the continuation of the U.N. sanctions on Iraq. Most immediately, Washington was trying to enlist Beijing to pressure Pyongyang to give up its nuclear weapons program.

The policy of the Clinton administration toward China was also constrained by the importance of trade and investment opportunities to the U.S. economy in an interdependent world. With only some hyperbole, the diplomatic impact of interdependence was captured by the *New York Times*, which wrote that by delinking human rights and trade policy Clinton was "acknowledging publicly the underlying shift evident in all the industrial democracies today: economic concerns have taken center stage in foreign affairs decision-making. This is the age of the Finance Minister. . . . The game of nations is now geo-Monopoly, and it is first and foremost about profits, not principles."[12] With U.S. exports to China in 1994 at over $9.3 billion and with U.S. investments there at over $2 billion and rapidly climbing, Chinese countersanctions could have put at risk tens of thousands of American jobs and vast profits potential. This made Clinton averse to initiating a trade war with what he described as "the world's fastest growing economy."[13]

*Societal Pressures on U.S. Policy Making toward China*
Within the societal context, the Clinton administration's China policy was shaped by political culture, as reflected in American public opinion, and by interest groups. The strength of Americans' sense of moralism and liberalism has been evident in polls indicating that in the abstract the public consistently favors demanding improved human rights policies over stable trade relations.[14] Reflecting this general attitude, a Times/cnn poll in May 1994 found that only 28 percent of Americans favored delinking human rights issues from trade issues, and a resounding 60 percent favored continuing to press China on human rights issues before granting it preferences.

These polls suggest that Clinton's annual decisions to renew China's mfn status ran counter to American public opinion. That is true in one sense, but there were two mitigating factors. First, human rights in China was not a particularly salient issue with the general public. Most Americans will respond that they favor human rights, but there is no evidence that the public has an intense feeling about the issue. Second, in shaping policy toward China, the liberal, moralistic bent in American political culture had to vie with the isolationist and pragmatic tendencies that are also part of American political culture. The public was not willing to pursue the lofty ideals of human rights when acting on them conflicted with economic objectives. For example, when one poll asked Americans the applied question of whether they favored pressing for human rights even if doing so hurt U.S. businesses opportunities in China and cost American jobs, 56 percent of the respondents favored keeping human rights separate from trade relations, while only 36 percent favored linking the two issues.[15] The policy of the Clinton administration accurately reflected these views by continuing its rhetorical championing of human rights while placing a pragmatic emphasis on American jobs.

Various domestic interest groups within the societal context actively tried to influence U.S. policy toward China. These groups can be divided into two types: economic interest groups and human rights groups.

*Economic Interest Groups.* The role of economic interest groups in shaping U.S. policy toward China was substantial. These groups did not, however, form a monolith. Some groups, such as the entertainment production industry, sought sanctions against China. The U.S. aviation and auto industries and most other groups favored normal relations with China, however, and the weight of these pro-China groups was much greater in the foreign policy process.

Companies that export to China and those that benefited from imports from China were part of what might be called the pro-China coalition. This alliance claimed that massive job losses would be brought on by a rupture with China. For instance, the Business Council, an organization of the CEOs of the hundred largest U.S.-based companies, estimated that ending China's MFN status would cost 100,000 U.S. jobs. At another point, Michael Armstrong, CEO of Hughes Aircraft, told Vice President Al Gore that the administration's confrontational strategy with China had already cost Los Angeles 20,000 high-paying jobs. Such forecasts, one analyst pointed out, were "a difficult pill to swallow for a president who [had] made employment expansion job one."[16]

The Business Council also was active during the 1996 confrontation over China's piracy of intellectual property rights (IPRs). It met with Secretary of State Warren Christopher and Secretary of the Treasury Robert E. Rubin in May and, as Edgar S. Woolard Jr., chairman of Dupont, put it, expressed the hope that "if sanctions are invoked, we very much hope that the government will work to keep them from escalating into other areas of industry."[17] Individual industries and companies also lobbied hard against imposing sanctions in 1996 because of the IPR violations or because of China's human rights record. The chairman of General Motors Corporation, John F. Smith Jr., argued that China's MFN status should be made permanent because "most-favored-nation status is the basis for a stable, credible economic policy toward China." Smith went on to hint that failure to maintain amicable relations with China could have dire economic consequences. "It is no secret," he said, "that the days of substantial growth in the U.S. automotive market are over. . . . [G]rowth must come from outside North America, notably in Asia. . . . China is the ideal cornerstone for growth in Asia."[18]

Taking the opposite view of sanctions on China was a smaller, less active, and less coherent coalition of economic interest groups that felt disadvantaged by economic relations with China. The makers of movies, music tapes and compact discs, and computer software pressed Washington to protect their products from the piracy that was annually costing American music businesses about $345 million and the American software industry about $322 million.[19] "We are an intellectual property company. . . . Our business requires a set of laws and culture that protects that," explained William H. Neukom, Microsoft's general counsel.[20] There were some other industries, such as textile manufacturers, that also had been undercut by imports from China and would not have opposed sanctions that raised the tariff on Chinese goods.

Labor was another economic interest group that, in part, lined up with the anti-China coalition. Lane Kirkland, then president of the AFL-CIO, urged termination of MFN in 1994. He argued that China had "not met the most minimum conditions for satisfying the requirements of granting most-favored-nation treatment" and was abusing "our brothers and sisters in China who work for a living." This humanitarian view was buttressed by the belief, as Kirkland put it, that American labor is "losing jobs to [imports from] China."[21]

In the end, the anti-China coalition was no match for its pro-China counterpart. There were several reasons. First, the policies favored by the pro-China coalition reinforced the Clinton administration's estimate of U.S. strategic interests. Second, the simple weight of the two coalitions was one-sided. Boeing, Ford, GM, and others that opposed sanctions had more clout than the businesses that favored them. Third, some of the pro-sanction forces were divided internally. Labor, for example, at first favored revoking China's MFN status, but then top union leaders fell largely silent because they realized that countersanctions by China would cost the jobs of many union workers at Boeing and elsewhere. Fourth, the pro-China economic groups prevailed because even the companies being damaged by China were torn between current losses and the prospect of future gains. This made these companies reluctant to confront China. Microsoft Corporation bemoaned its losses to piracy, but its head, Bill Gates, nevertheless twice traveled to Beijing to woo President Jiang Zemin. "We do Windows, not foreign policy," was how Charles Stevens, Microsoft vice president for the Far

East, characterized his company's view.[22] Many businesses also doubted that measures against China would yield any fundamental change. As a Microsoft representative put it, "Sanctions get you no place." All they do, he said, "is close down a few factories for a few months" to make the United States "shut up and go away."[23]

Last, the pro-China coalition was stronger because during the various confrontations over threatened U.S. sanctions, China played deftly on the fears of American groups that might be harmed by Chinese counter-measures. When, in May 1996, the administration published a $3 billion list of items that would have 100 percent tariffs imposed if China did not agree to end its intellectual property piracy, Beijing announced retaliatory tariffs that carefully targeted several powerful U.S. industries. Vehicles and auto parts were, for example, on this list, precipitating predictable protests from U.S. automakers. "We do not believe that unilateral sanctions by either country are constructive or likely to lead to a solution of the problem," protested W. Wayne Booker, executive vice president of Ford Motor Company.[24] Beijing also dealt painful blows to Boeing Aircraft. The Chinese decided unexpectedly to buy $1.5 billion in aircraft from the European consortium, Airbus Industry, rather than the American manufacture. Ronald B. Woodard, president of Boeing's Commercial Airplane Group, complained that "there's no doubt we are being punished" and related that he had been warned specifically by one of China's vice premiers that "because your government constantly chooses to kick us and harass us, many, many business opportunities that should go to the U.S. [could go] elsewhere."[25] Companies that might lose their ability to export to China were joined in opposition to the sanctions by companies who relied on inexpensive imports from China. The National Retail Federation, whose members include Sears, Kmart, and Toys "R" Us, denounced the threatened sanctions as "clearly illegal."[26]

There can be little doubt that economic groups had a strong impact on policy. One indication was that administration officials occasionally expressed aggravation at the pressure. Referring to the auto industry, for example, one White House official complained that "we save their butts in the auto talks [with Japan] last year, and in China they stiff-arm us."[27] More commonly, the president and other top officials were highly accommodating when they met with industry officials and addressed their gatherings. President Clinton, for example, chose to speak before the Pacific-Basin Economic Council and to tell its members that his trade policy would be "a vote for America's interests," and "not a referendum on all China's policies."[28] In the same vein, Secretary of State Christopher defended the decision not to impose sanctions in China in 1996 as a policy that "will help protect the jobs of American workers" and "open up opportunities for American companies."[29]

The pro-China coalition was also effective in lobbying Congress. "They're all over the Hill schmoozing breakfast, lunch and dinner," said sanction advocate Representative Nancy Pelosi (D-Calif.) of the pro-China lobbyists. "It has been shoe leather," explained Calman Cohen of the Business Coalition for U.S.-China Trade; "we have done everything we could to explain the situation to legislators."[30] The effort paid off. In 1994, for example, 106 members of the House signed a letter urging President Clinton to abandon the use of MFN status to try to reform China's human rights policies. The letter was particularly important because it was bipartisan, including several leaders from both parties. Part of this bipartisan harmony, one journal reported, was based on the fact that "many of the lawmakers who favor breaking the link (between human rights and trade) come from the states that export the most to China, including California and Washington."[31] Such support meant both that Congress would not overturn a Clinton decision to continue China's MFN status and that the president would be safe from partisan attack on the issue. As one lobbyist put it, "The whole game is to convince the president that if he does de-link, he won't be alone."[32]

*Human Rights Groups.* These groups, as might be expected, were solidly in favor of sanctions, especially in 1994. Humanitarian and human rights groups such as Amnesty International, Human Rights Watch, the International Campaign for Tibet, and the U.S. Conference of Catholic Bishops were among these. They lobbied both the government and public opinion. In 1994, for example, they compiled a list of 235 names of "illustrative cases" of people allegedly jailed for political dissent, religious affiliation, or other reasons and presented it to the State Department and the press. A similar list was put together by Human Rights Watch/Asia, which issued a sixty-page report in May 1994 identifying nearly 500 previously unknown cases of political prisoners arrested after Tiananmen Square. A State Department official involved with China responded by saying that "the organization is very good, very professional, and we're reading the report with interest."[33] Human rights groups were also able to play a role in 1995 when the Chinese government launched a crackdown of human rights activists and other political dissidents. Among those arrested was Harry Wu, a visiting Chinese American, whom China charged with espionage and subversion. Beijing finally freed Wu after Washington threatened to cancel the scheduled trip of Hillary Rodham Clinton to China as head of the U.S. delegation to the U.N.'s Fourth World Conference on Women.[34]

In the end, the human rights groups did not prevail on the MFN issue and Ms. Clinton's chastisement proved little more than a momentary embarrassment for Beijing. Still, it would be wrong to dismiss the role of these groups as inconsequential. They represent the liberal idealistic strain in American political culture that puts human rights on the agenda of U.S. diplomacy, and their views found a sympathetic hearing and even support in many places within the formal institutions in government. It is to these institutions that we can now turn our attention, beginning with the foreign policy bureaucracy.

*Forming the Policy: Institutional Interaction*
Whatever the pressures created by the international and societal contexts, the battle of the specifics of U.S. policy making are carried out within the institutional context. There are three institutional actors—the foreign policy bureaucracy, Congress, and the White House—that are the formal, legally established players in the foreign policy process.

THE FOREIGN POLICY BUREAUCRACY Like the economic interest groups, the foreign policy bureaucracy was not monolithic in its attitudes toward China. Indeed, the competing bureaucratic views helped create what one senior Clinton administration official termed "a cacophony, not an orchestra" with "no sense of setting priorities [to signal] the Chinese about what was truly important."[35] In the end, though, and also in parallel to the economic interest groups, those bureaucratic units that wished to shun sanctions on China overpowered those which wanted a confrontational policy. This bolstered the position of the pro-China coalition.

*The State Department.* Initially, the department tended to favor sanctions; later it moved into the antisanction coalition. During the 1994 MFN controversy, much of the State Department leaned in favor of sanctions against China. Those in the department who dealt with human rights formed the core of the bureaucratic forces urging sanction.

The assistant secretary of state for democracy, human rights, and labor, John Shattuck, was the most consistent voice in the department advocating a strong U.S. stance on the issue of human rights. A former director of the American Civil Liberties Union and vice chairman of Amnesty International, Shattuck and his staff compiled an annual report on human rights and took other steps to keep the issue on the political agenda. The report issued in February 1995 said that China's "overall human rights record in 1993 fell far short of internationally accepted norms as it continued to repress domestic critics and failed to control abuses by its own security forces." Making it even more obvious that the department was trying to press Clinton to end China's MFN status, a spokesperson told reporters that "much more significant progress is going to be necessary" for China to avoid cancellation of its MFN status.[36]

The attitude of the department's human rights unit was also evident March 1994 when Shattuck visited Beijing and met with dissident Wei Jingsheng. At this point there still seemed to be some willingness at the highest level of the State Department to confront China. Secretary Christopher publicly defended Shattuck's meeting with Wei as "appropriate," even though it cast a pall on the secretary's approaching visit to China.[37] The prospects for fruitful diplomacy grew even dimmer when, just before Christopher's trip, Beijing ordered the arrest of several dissidents, and the secretary responded by remarking pointedly that "it would be hard to overestimate the strong distaste that we all feel over the recent detentions and hostile measure taken by the Chinese. Certainly these actions will have a negative effect on my trip to China as well as on the subsequent review of the favored nation trade question."[38] With the diplomatic well thus poisoned, Christopher's trip to China "was an in-your-face visit," according to one U.S. official. Premier Li Peng told Christopher that "China will never accept the United States' human rights concept" and that "the United States will lose its share of the big China market" if MFN status were to be withdrawn.[39] Christopher was equally adamant because, he reportedly later told a Cabinet-level meeting at the White House, he was convinced that "the bottom line . . . was that we need to stay steady and to encourage China to make progress" on human rights.[40]

Christopher's views, it turned out, were not as firm as he suggested. Soon thereafter he and much of the rest of the State Department became firm opponents of imposing sanctions on China. Shattuck's office continued to issue annual reports castigating China's human rights policy, but the issue became peripheral to the basic stance of the department. This change resulted from several factors. One was the criticism from many quarters that human rights were being overemphasized. The assistant secretary of state for Asia, Winston Lord, an earlier proponent of a stern stance vis-à-vis China, wrote to Christopher in April 1994 that denying China's MFN status would "risk corroding our positive image [in Asia], giving ammunition to those charging [that] we are an international nanny, if not bully."[41]

A second factor was China's adamant rejection of what it saw as U.S. meddling in its internal affairs. When in May 1994 President Clinton met in Washington with Deputy Prime Minister Zou Jiahua and personally urged that China ease human rights abuses, Zou responded by telling Clinton that the United States should stay out of China's internal affairs. "They sort of talked a little bit past each other" during a meeting that was "stiff and uncomfortable," according to one White House source.[42] These two factors reinforced the organizational culture preference of the State Department to maintain good relations with other countries and seem to have persuaded Christopher that no one issue was worth pushing China to the point of a serious rupture of relations.

Christopher's conversion is illustrated by the issue of whether or not in 1996 to apply sanctions on China in response to its sale of M-11 missiles and ring magnets to Pakistan. Faced with a legal mandate to apply sanctions if China was selling missiles or nuclear weapons–applicable material, the secretary finessed the issue. With regard to the missiles, the department chose to interpret information to suit its bureaucratic disposition. Most agencies agreed that "the evidence . . . is incontrovertible that M-11s have been delivered and are there" in Pakistan.[43] Contrary to these reports, State Department analysts reportedly did not "believe [that] the weight of the evidence" proved conclusively that M-11s had gone to Pakistan.[44] Ergo, no sanctions were necessary.

As for the ring magnets, a senior State Department official told reporters that "we regard it as very serious. The next question is what do we do about it." The answer was nothing. Secretary Christopher accepted Beijing's improbable assurances that "the government of China was unaware of any transfers."[45] Arguing that the sale had been made by a private firm, Christopher reasoned that sanctions were neither required nor appropriate. Department representatives also emphasized that they had wrung from China assurances that it would sell no more such material to Pakistan. This put the department in the odd position of claiming that it had gotten China to agree to stop doing what China argued (and the department agreed) it had not been doing in the first place.

By the end of Clinton's first term, the State Department had virtually abandoned the pretense of seriously pressing China on human rights. The annual human rights report for 1996 spoke dutifully of "China's retreat on human rights" that year, but few paid the report much heed and it did not threaten to disrupt improving relations between the two capitals.[46]

In contrast to earlier sharp U.S. reactions to the arrest of dissidents by China, similar incidents in 1996 had neglible impact on Washington's "business as usual" approach. A State Department spokesperson said the United States was "seriously concerned," but that worry did not affect either Secretary Christopher's trip nor the Clinton-Zemin visit, at which the two agreed in principle to reciprocal visits to each other's capitals in 1997 or 1998.

*The Defense Department.* The Pentagon's approach to China policy generally reflected the military's view of China as a future threat. For example, a 1995 study by the Defense Department concluded that "Chinese military officials believe [that] the present gap in their capabilities is temporary and the long-term goal is to be a global military peer of the U.S."[47] The military also worried about specific matters, such as the sale of missiles and ring magnets to Pakistan. On this issue, for example, Secretary of Defense William Perry took a tough stand that seemed to favor sanctions. "It takes two to tango," Perry told an audience about China. "It takes two to engage. While we are committed to engagement [with China], we are not committed to engagement at any price."[48]

The Pentagon also favored sending strong forces to the Taiwan region in 1996 to serve as a tangible message to warn China about a military move against Taiwan. Washington, among other things, canceled a scheduled visit of China's defense minister to Washington on the grounds, said Secretary of Defense Perry, that "a large-scale official visit is not appropriate in the current climate."[49] More pointedly, the White House warned that "China knows that the use of force will have consequences" and ordered a major naval flotilla centered around two aircraft carriers into the waters off Taiwan.[50] China needed to act with restraint, growled Perry, because "America has the best damned navy in the world."[51]

The concern by the Pentagon about specific Chinese policies in the military realm did not, however, translate into the department advocating sanctions against China on other issues. Instead, Pentagon officials generally favored not pressing China to the point of a sustained, angry reaction.[52] Putting too much pressure on China, Perry reasoned at one point, "could actually undermine [U.S.] security, because a China that feels encircled is quite unlikely to cooperate on vital U.S. security interests."[53]

Such logic led the Defense Department to oppose proposals to apply sanctions in 1994 to imports from factories associated with the People's

Liberation Army (PLA). Pentagon officials maintained that it would be counterproductive to single out China's military. Instead, they contended, the PLA had to be wooed, not alienated, especially given the potential turmoil that Washington worried might follow the death of the aged Deng Xiaoping. Putting the department's perspective into action at a time when the United States was supposed to be pressuring China, a high-level delegation headed by Assistant Secretary of Defense Chas Freeman Jr. visited China in November 1993. It was the first such military contact since 1989 and was justified by Freeman as important to opening channels to PLA. "It's just a matter of logic," explained Freeman, "if you don't have contact and dialogue, it's easy to be unaware of the other side's viewpoint and to misinterpret that viewpoint on occasion. In other words, ignorance can breed suspicion and mistrust."[54]

*Other Departments and Agencies.* There were a number of other bureaucratic units in addition to the State and Defense Departments that played important roles in the debates over China policy. The decline of military security concerns and the rise of economic interdependence in the post–cold war period has enhanced the role of the Commerce and Treasury Departments and other economic-oriented agencies. They gained their greatest voice in formulating U.S. policy on China through a White House coordinating group, the National Economic Council (NEC), which will be discussed in the next section. The views of these economic agencies tended to favor the pro-China position. Predictably, the Commerce Department opposed any move that would harm U.S. trade and investment. Demonstrating this stance, Secretary of Commerce Ron Brown traveled to Beijing in the company of the presidents of Ford and Boeing and declared China to be the center of "commercial diplomacy."[55] Based on a similar urge to protect its domestic client group, the Department of Agriculture opposed sanctions that might cause China to retaliate against American farm exports. The reason, Agriculture Secretary Mike Espy told reporters, was that China is "one of our most important agriculture markets."[56] Other agencies also reacted according to their perspective. For example, the Customs Service supported the Defense Department's opposition to putting sanctions on goods from PLA-run factories on the grounds that many similar products were also made by other factories and it was impossible to tell one from the other and trying to do so would overburden customs officials.

CONGRESS The views of Congress on U.S. policy toward China were based on several factors, including the constituency interests of individual members, their ideological views, their partisan affiliation, and their reflection of American political culture.

Like the American public, Congress could in the abstract take a strong stand in favor of human rights in China. In 1995, for example, the House of Representatives passed a resolution denouncing China's human rights violations by a vote of 416 to 10. House Democratic leader Richard Gephardt said that "China must get one message from this debate, and that is: this country will not stand by forever and have people's human rights violated."[57]

Also like the public, however, Congress was unwilling to spark an economic war with China in order to promote human rights there. This was evident in 1996 when some legislators introduced a measure to revoke China's MFN status. The House blocked the effort by the wide margin of 141 in favor to 286 opposed, with both 72 percent of the Republicans and 61 percent of the Democrats casting their votes against the measure.

This lopsided vote was the result of several factors. First, many of those most likely to worry about human rights in Congress are Democrats, and most of them were unwilling to belabor Clinton in the same way they had assailed Bush. Democrat after Democrat who had once criticized Bush now echoed Clinton's argument that "constructive engagement" with China is more likely to yield positive results than is confrontation. "Yes, things are bad in China," admitted Representative Sam Gibbons (D-Fl.), but "by cutting off normal trade relations, we'd only succeed in isolating China again. We should be building bridges instead of burning bridges."[58]

Other members of Congress calculated the economic harm that sanctions would do their states and districts. It was, for example, Representative Jim McDermott (D-Wash.), whose Seattle district includes Boeing Aircraft, who organized the signing by 106 House members of a letter to Clinton in 1994 urging him to continue China's MFN status. The economic factor also persuaded many Republicans to put aside their ideological antipathy toward communist-governed China and to vote in accord with their normal support of business-oriented trade and investment policy.

Yet other members concurred with the administration's view of the strategic importance of China. Sam Nunn (D-Ga.), chairman of the Senate Armed Services Committee, opposed sanctions on the grounds that "our top priority [in Asia] has to be . . . to prevent proliferation, to prevent the nuclear arms race" and that "a total cutoff of MFN is too heavy a weapon, particularly when we have the other stakes in north-east Asia . . . [such as] North Korea."[59]

On nontrade issues, Congress tended to be less supportive of Clinton and to push him toward policies that angered China. Congress was instrumental in 1995, for example, in causing the administration to allow President Lee of Taiwan to attend his class reunion at Cornell University, where he had received a Ph.D. in agricultural economics in 1968. Lee's seemingly routine request for a visa was politically charged because of the tacit policy that Washington followed since switching its diplomatic recognition from Taipei to Beijing of not allowing Taiwan's leaders into the United States for fear of offending China. Beijing demonstrated its strong opposition to Lee's visit by calling its ambassador home for "consultations" and by warning the U.S. ambassador that "if the United States clings to its erroneous decision, it will inevitably cause severe damage to Sino-U.S. relations."[60] Understandably, then, the first instinct of the Clinton administration was to deny the visa request. An administration official told reporters that granting the visa would have "serious consequences for United States foreign policy" by causing a rift with China.[61]

Congress was of a different mind, though. By votes of 97 to 1 in the Senate and 360 to 0 in the House, legislators called on Clinton to give Lee a visa. "This is unmistakable proof that the U.S. Congress believes it is our nation's best interest to improve relations with Taiwan," said Senator Frank Murkowski (R-Alaska).[62] The administration complained to the press about "Congress's meddling" and wondered aloud, "What will we do when [Lee] requests a visit next, and members of Congress begin inviting Taiwan officials to meet them not in Ithaca but in Washington?"[63] Nevertheless, the White House retreated and admitted Lee rather than face the prospect that Congress might pass legislation giving Lee a visa or even upgrading U.S. relations with Taiwan to official status. "There was a desire by this administration to pre-empt new binding legislation that could hurt our relations with China," a State Department official explained.[64]

Later, during the military maneuvering that preceded Taiwan's presidential election in early 1996, the House Republican Policy Committee urged Clinton to commit the United States "to the defense of Taiwan."[65] Perhaps even more telling, Clinton also came under fire from members of his own party. "It was one thing to normalize [relations] with China when both Beijing and Taiwan had authoritarian regimes," said Democratic House member Nancy Pelosi. "The fact is, Taiwan is now a democracy, and that makes all the difference in the world."[66] Especially in an election year, neither Clinton nor members of Congress wanted to stand accused of abandoning a democratic government for an authoritarian one. Moreover, the administration became concerned that Congress might infuriate China by passing one or more of the various measures that members of Congress had introduced. These included providing more sophisticated weapons to Taiwan, supporting Taiwan's membership in the United Nations, and inviting President Lee and other ranking officials to visit Washington to celebrate his election. Perhaps more than anything, Clinton feared that Congress might try to stiffen the clause in the Taiwan Relations Act of 1979 which said, with studied vagueness, that the United States would consider "any effort to determine the future of Taiwan by other than peaceful means . . . a threat to the peace and security of the Western Pacific area and of grave concern to the United States." Some Republicans were suggesting committing the United States definitively to defend Taiwan, with Senator Dole saying, for instance, that "if necessary, we should protect" Taiwan.[67]

Another characteristic of the treatment of China in the Congress was that ideology made for some strange congressional bedfellows. When, for instance, the administration decided in 1996 not to punish China for selling missiles to Pakistan, it was criticized from both left and right. Liberal representative Nancy Pelosi (D-Calif.) said Clinton had made "the U.S. appear weak" in the face of "a clear, verifiable transfer of nuclear and missile technology to Pakistan."[68] Congressional conservatives made a similar argument. Marc Thiessen, a top staff member for Senate Foreign Relations Committee chairman Jesse Helms (R-N.C.), asked, "What concessions has the administration gotten on any issue of importance to the American people in exchange for this capitulation?" Thiessen then supplied his own answer: "Nothing!"[69]

Ideological stands also sometimes brought liberals and conservatives together on trade issues. For example, two of Clinton's chief congressional allies, House Minority Leader Richard Gephardt (D-Mo.) and House Minority Whip David Bonior (D-Mich.), both of whom are strongly identified with the U.S. labor movement, voted to revoke China's MFN status in 1996. They were joined in that stand by such conservatives as Representative Gerald Solomon (R-N.Y.), who asked, "Whatever happened to U.S. foreign policy that looked out for human decency around the world. Appeasement of tyrants does not work."[70]

THE WHITE HOUSE Although President Clinton came to the White House with a domestic policy orientation, China decisions most frequently wound up on his desk because of the complexity and importance of policy toward China, the disagreements in the bureaucracy, and the involvement of Congress. In the preceding discussion, the various economic, strategic, human rights, and other issues have, to a degree, been discussed in isolation to clarify the considerations involved. They did not happen in a vacuum, though, and it is important to remember that during Clinton's first term there were a range of contentious issues occurring simultaneously with China. There was also a range of issues, such as resolution of the North Korea nuclear crisis and conclusion of the CTBT, on which the United States needed China's cooperation. The importance of the strategic and economic issues involved, combined with the shifting and cross-cutting positions of various societal and institutional actors on the issues, meant that it was difficult to settle on policy without strong White House direction.

The Clinton White House tried initially to deal with China policy by setting up a task force called the Senior Steering Group led by the assistant secretary of state for East Asian and Pacific affairs, Winston Lord, and Deputy National Security Advisor Samuel Berger. The task force tended to lean toward the anti-China coalition for a variety of reasons. One was the individual dispositions of some members, especially Lord, to favor sanctions on China. Even though he compared the looming confrontation with China over human rights to a possible "train wreck," Lord still insisted in late 1993 that China "has got to understand that movement is required [on improving human rights] or we're all going to be in trouble come next spring" on renewal of its MFN status.[71] The prosanction orientation of the task force was also fostered by the tendency of the Congressional Liaison office, with which it worked closely, to overestimate the strength of confrontationalists in Congress by focusing on the most vocal critics of China's human rights policies.[72]

Although it was initially influential, the view of the Senior Steering Group became a minority position in the battle to control China policy in Washington; the Lord-Berger group soon began to lose influence on the issue to the National Economic Council (NEC). Reflecting Clinton's emphasis on improving the domestic economy, the new administration had established the NEC to coordinate economic policy (see chapter 4). The newly formed NEC had little influence in the MFN debate in 1993, but by the following year it had become a major player in the formation of China policy. In March 1994, the Senior Steering Group lost primary responsibility for the coordination of China policy in the White House to a newly formed joint NEC/NSC team led by Berger and Deputy National Economic Advisor Bowman Cutter. The

NEC gave greater voice to the interest of the Treasury and Commerce Departments, which had traditionally been lesser players in foreign policy formation. As one press report noted, "Just as Richard Nixon elevated the National Security Council as a counterweight to the State Department and the Pentagon, Clinton created the National Economic Council, to coordinate domestic and foreign economic policy. In the biggest policy arguments—[such as] confronting China on its piracy of intellectual property . . . the Treasury Department, Commerce Department and Trade Representative have been key players."[73]

As part of this shift, the lead role of the NEC made National Security Adviser Anthony Lake and then-National Economic Adviser Robert Rubin major players in China policy and gave economics more weight in the determination of policy. This brought a set of players to the forefront who were wary of confrontation with China. Rubin and Stanley Roth, the top NSC Asian specialist, were both leery of the negative impact an economic confrontation would have on the U.S. economy. Roth's view was that "the main victim [of sanctions] is U.S. business, and China doesn't suffer."[74] Lake and others on the NSC also focused on China's strategic role. Although Lake often spoke of such liberal goals as promoting democracy early during his four-year tenure as national security adviser, this view seemed to fade to the point where, in a 1996 address, he could observe that "until human nature changes, power and force will remain at the heart of international relations."[75]

The movement of the White House toward a predominantly pragmatic policy toward China resulted from numerous factors. One was Clinton's conclusion, which he drew with the help of powerful economic interest groups and bureaucratic actors, that confrontation with China would cause serious damage to U.S. economic interests. Even when Clinton threatened sanctions, he was careful to structure them in the best economic and political way. For example, the placing of apparel and textiles high on the 1996 list of projected sanctions was calculated to appeal in part to apparel and textile plants and their workers throughout the South, who had been hurt by low-cost imports from China and elsewhere. Toys, which were initially on the list recommended by U.S. Trade Representative Mickey Kantor, were dropped in anticipation of a consumer backlash. "It didn't take a political genius to see that we would be blamed for taking toys out of the hands of little kids," one administration official explained.[76]

President Clinton also grew to appreciate more clearly the strategic importance of China and, additionally, both to focus more on foreign policy and to take firmer control of it. This elevated decision making on China policy to the highest level of government. One illustration of this high-level focus on China is that the decision in May 1996 to place sanctions, albeit briefly, on China was taken in a meeting attended by Secretary of State Christopher, Secretary of Defense Perry, Secretary of Commerce Kantor, Secretary of the Treasury Rubin, chairman of the Joint Chiefs of Staff General John Shalikashvili, and other Cabinet-level officials. This mix of players, each for his own reason, was averse to confrontation with China, and their influence far outweighed the forces that favored confrontation. In combination with the president's own conversion from the confrontationalist to accommodationist position, this balance of international and domestic factors had made U.S. policy toward China one of profound pragmatism.

### Conclusion

This analysis reveals a number of characteristics for the making of U.S. foreign policy in the post–cold war world. One simple observation that emerges is that Washington and Beijing did not deal with issues as separate entities. Instead, issues were, to a degree, linked. For example, whether or not Washington was going to penalize China for missile sales was linked to the status of talks on intellectual property rights.

Second, U.S. policy making resulted from a blend of realpolitik international forces and cross-cutting domestic pressures. To a significant extent, Clinton was an idealist candidate who became a realist president. Yet U.S. strategic interests were not all that shaped Clinton's policy. He experienced considerable pressure from societal forces, including interest groups and the public, from Congress, and from the bureaucracy. In the main, both the dictates of the international system and the U.S. domestic system favored maintaining at least nonhostile relations with China. Therefore, the thrust of Clinton's policy was to press China to meet various U.S. policy objectives without putting so much pressure on Beijing that there would be a serious, long-term breakdown in relations.

Third, international forces, societal pressures, and institutional actors were not monolithic entities. Within all the various international and domestic constellation circles there were yet other smaller circles. Business interest groups, as an example of nongovernmental institutional actors, and the different elements of the bureaucracy were not unanimously in favor or opposed to confronting China. To the contrary, they were split on the question, and specific industries and bureaucratic units sometimes changed sides on differing issues.

This last point leads to a series of broad observations on post–cold war U.S. foreign policy making suggested by this case. Clearly, the case suggests something about priorities in the post–cold war world. As indicated in the preceding pages, economic interests have become much more central to the calculations of U.S. policy makers in the White House and elsewhere. In fact, this case suggests that less tangible concerns, such as human rights, will continue to be traded off against other interests. During the cold war, security interests were the chief victor in the trade-off game. China policy in the post–cold war period suggests that tangible interests in the economic arena first, and the security arena second, will continue to occupy the preferred position in policy debates.

The making of China policy in the Clinton administration also provides some insight into the more complex policy-making environment in which choices are made. Among the many observations that could be gleaned from this analysis, three appear to stand out. First, the "foreign policy bureaucracy" was broadened significantly to include economic agencies, whose perspectives on the issue appear to have provided a substantial counter to those traditional foreign policy agencies who initially took an "anti-China" position. In this regard, the rise of the NEC on China policy merits special note. Second, Congress was heavily engaged in the policy debate, pushing, prodding, and constraining executive branch actions. As might be expected, the economic interests that structured the debate also seem to have structured the positions taken by members of Congress. Finally, as might be expected on an issue with "intermestic" characteristics, congressional involvement, and active bureaucratic actors from economic agencies, the process was considerably more open to interest group activity, particularly economic interest groups, whose tangible claims and appeals appear to have carried special weight in the institutional arena. As might have been expected, those groups attempting to reinforce the status quo rather than change it were more successful, although the tangibility of their appeal to economic concerns was clearly as important.

The overview of the international, societal, and institutional contexts of U.S. policy and the detailed examination of the process by which the first Clinton administration made policy toward China in this essay well illustrate the themes of this book. First, U.S. foreign policy toward China was the result of the impacts of and the interplay among the international context, the societal context, and institutional context. Second, the institutional context was the scene of shifting constellations of alliances between elements of the foreign policy bureaucracy, Congress, and the White House. Third, the policy process has changed in important ways. International economic policy has come to rival national security policy as the primary focus of the country's foreign policy. This change has, among other things, increased the role and influence of domestic economic interest groups, Congress, and such economic agencies as the Departments of Commerce and Treasury.

## Notes

1 *New York Times*, August 14, 1992, p. A15.
2 *Time*, June 10, 1991, p. 35.
3 *New York Times*, January 29, 1997, p. A6.
4 *New York Times*, July 29, 1996, p. A17.
5 Edward Friedman, "The Challenge of a Rising China: Another Germany?" In Robert J. Lieber, ed., *Eagle Adrift: American Foreign Policy at the End of the Century* (New York: Longman, 1997), p. 217.
6 There were recurring reports that China was supplying Pakistan with the technology to build M-11 missiles, which have a range of 185 miles and are capable of delivering both conventional and nuclear warheads. Furthermore, U.S. intelligence concluded in 1996 that China had sold ring magnets. These devices are dual-use technology in that they have civilian application but are also used in centrifuges to produce the enriched uranium for nuclear weapons.
7 Robert J. Art and Seyom Brown, "U.S. Foreign Policy in the Post-Cold War World: Introduction and Overview," in Robert J. Art and Seyom Brown, eds., *U.S. Foreign Policy: The Search for a New Role* (New York: Macmillan, 1993), p. 6.
8 *New York Times*, May 19, 1996, p. A2.
9 *Time*, April 13, 1992, p. 28.
10 *New York Times*, May 27, 1994, p. A8.
11 *New York Times*, July 29, 1996, p. A17.
12 *New York Times*, May 27, 1994, p. A8.
13 *New York Times*, May 27, 1994, p. A8.
14 See, for example a series of NBC News/Wall Street Journal polls between December 1993 and May 1996.
15 See the Los Angeles Times poll of April 29, 1996.
16 David Zweig, "Clinton and China: Creating a Policy Agenda That Works," *Current History* 92, no. 546 (1993): p. 251.
17 *New York Times*, May 11, 1996, p. A5.
18 *New York Times*, May 21, 1996, p. D2.
19 *Business Week*, 20 February 1995, pp. 32–33.
20 *New York Times*, June 9, 1996, p. F1.
21 *Hartford Courant*, April 14, 1994, p. A5.
22 *New York Times*, June 9, 1996, p. F1.
23 *New York Times*, June 9, 1996, p. A11.
24 *New York Times*, May 16, 1996, p. A1.

25  *New York Times*, June 9, 1996, p. F1.

26  *New York Times*, May 16, 1996, p. A1.

27  *New York Times*, June 9, 1991, p. A11.

28  *New York Times*, May 21, 1996, p. A1.

29  *New York Times*, June 18, 1996, p. A1.

30  *Hartford Courant*, May 20, 1994, p. E1.

31  *CQ Weekly Report*, 30 April 1994, p. 1055.

32  *Hartford Courant*, May 20, 1994, p. E1.

33  *New York Times*, May 20, 1994, p. A9.

34  *Time*, September 18, 1995, p. 80.

35  *New York Times*, July 29, 1996, p. A16.

36  The human rights report and the statement of the spokesperson are both quoted in the *New York Times*, February 5, 1994, p. A8.

37  *New York Times*, March 15, 1994, p. A3.

38  *New York Times*, March 9, 1994, p. A11.

39  *Hartford Courant*, March 13, 1994, p. A1.

40  *Hartford Courant*, March 23, 1994, p. A3.

41  *Newsweek*, May 3, 1994, p. 51.

42  *New York Times*, May 3, 1994, p. A6.

43  *Hartford Courant*, July 3, 1995, p. A2.

44  *New York Times*, April 13, 1996, p. A5.

45  *New York Times*, May 11, 1996, p. A1.

46  *New York Times*, January 28, 1997, p. A7.

47  *Time*, March 25, 1996, p. 38.

48  February 21, 1996, p. A9.

49  *New York Times*, March 23, 1996, p. A5.

50  *New York Times*, March 12, 1996, p. A1.

51  *New York Times*, March 22, 1996, p. A10.

52  Joseph Fewsmith, "America and China: Back from the Brink," *Current History* 93, no. 584 (September 1994): 250.

53  *Time*, March 25, 1996, p. 39.

54  *Hartford Courant*, November 3, 1993, p. A8.

55  *New York Times*, July 29, 1996, p. A16.

56  *New York Times*, May 24, 1994, p. A1.

57  *Washington Times*, July 21, 1995, p. A10.

58  *New York Times*, June 28, 1996, p. A10.

59  *Hartford Courant*, January 31, 1994, p. A2.

60  *New York Times*, May 24, 1995, p. A8.

61  *New York Times*, May 24, 1995, p. A8.

62  *New York Times*, May 11, 1994, p. A6.

63  *Time*, June 5, 1996, p. 34.

64  *New York Times*, June 29, 1995, p. A3.

65  *New York Times*, March 7, 1996, p. A1.

66  *New York Times*, March 12, 1996.

67  *New York Times*, March 12, 1996, p. A1.

68 *New York Times*, February 8, 1996, p. A7.

69 Both the Pelosi and Thiessen quotes are from the *Hartford Courant*, May 11, 1996, p. A3.

70 *New York Times*, June 28, 1996, p. A10.

71 *New York Times*, December 12, 1993, p. A7.

72 Charles A. Goldman, "Managing Policy toward China under Clinton: The Changing Role of Economics," RAND Corporation. A paper prepared for the Center for Asia-Pacific Policy, July 1995.

73 *New York Times*, July 29, 1996, N.Y. Times on the Web, HTTP://www.nytimes.com/docsroot/library/politics/0729clinton-foreign-policy.html#1.

74 *New York Times*, February 21, 1996, p. A9.

75 *New York Times*, March 7, 1996, p. A10.

76 *New York Times*, February 5, 1995, p. A1.

# 9.

## American Assistance to the Former

## Soviet States in 1993–1994

*Jeremy D. Rosner*

The collapse of the Soviet empire and Soviet Union was the most significant change in the security environment facing the United States during the last half of the twentieth century. With the toppling of the Berlin Wall in 1989 and the last lowering of the hammer and sickle over the Kremlin on Christmas 1991, the threat of Soviet expansion disappeared, while new challenges arose. In particular, these events confronted the U.S. and the international community with the question of whether and how to assist the Soviet Union's fourteen successor states with their political, economic, and military transitions. Washington's response to that question in the early 1990s reveals a great deal about U.S. foreign policy making after the cold war. The case especially highlights the changing dynamics of executive-legislative relations, and suggests some circumstances that may favor cooperation between the White House and Congress in this new era.

### Background

As the Soviet Union began to dissolve, many U.S. policy makers believed that assistance to its successor republics could advance a range of American interests. It could prevent the collapse of these states into a dangerous chaos in which four—Russia, Ukraine, Belarus, and Kazakhstan—would hold the former Soviet nuclear arsenal, perhaps under loose controls. It could help safeguard or dismantle those weapons themselves. Aid could help lock in the dissolution of the Soviet empire—and with it, reduced U.S. defense budgets—by strengthening the states on Russia's periphery and giving Moscow incentives to withdraw its troops from the Baltics and elsewhere in the "near abroad." Aid could bolster fledgling democracies, which in Russia's case might reduce the likelihood of neoimperialism, and which for all the states might improve internal human rights and external behavior. Assistance also could help prosperous markets rise from stagnant command economies, and thus create new opportunities for Western trade and investment.

Yet as the United States attempted to provide such aid and pursue these interests, it found that the breakup of the Soviet Union had altered the American politics of national security nearly as much as that breakup changed the Eurasian map. Gone was the unitary threat that had provided conceptual coherence for Congress, elites, and the public. Gone was the sense of danger that had justified large foreign aid outlays, even to unsavory regimes. Gone was the urgency of anticommunism that had glued Republican isolationists to an activist agenda abroad. Gone was the public's willingness to defer attention to domestic ills that had festered during the late cold war years, from unbalanced budgets to uninsured patients.

Extending aid to former Soviet states would not only occur in a new political environment; it would also be a fairly novel enterprise for American policy makers. It would require them to change their view of these states—from adversaries to be kept down, to potential partners in need of lifting up. Compared to the U.S. cold war stance, the new policy toward Eurasia implicitly would be less *realpolitik* and somewhat more *idealpolitik.* It would draw less on the military budget and more on the foreign affairs budget.

The end of the cold war also brought changes to America's political institutions that would affect the ability of Washington to provide aid to Russia and the other Newly Independent States (NIS). Just as the end of World War II saw both American and British electorates soon give the boot to governing parties that had led them to victory on the battlefield, the end of the cold war ushered in a reaction against incumbents and a transformation in the profile of federal officeholders. In 1992, Democrats regained the White House for only the second time in twenty-four years. Their candidate became the first president born after World War II, and the first in the modern era not to have served in the military.

The election of 1992 also brought a flood of congressional newcomers —110 in the House and 11 in the Senate. That historically large wave was followed by another in 1994—86 in the House and another 11 in the Senate—and this one swept out the Democratic majorities in both chambers, producing the first Republican-controlled Congress in four decades.

By 1995, over half of the House had been elected since the Berlin Wall had come down. The newer members had been elected on domestic platforms and tended to have less grounding in international security issues. The rate of military service among those elected to the House in 1994 was only about 20 percent, whereas only a decade earlier 56 percent of House members had served in the armed forces.

This political turnover, Congress's reduced concern over foreign affairs, divided government (after 1994), a safer security environment that made it politically safer for Congress to resist presidential initiatives abroad—all these dynamics helped increase friction between the executive branch and Congress on national security issues. During the 104th Congress (1995–96), President Clinton would win only 50 percent of the defense and foreign policy votes in Congress on which the White House had declared a position—the lowest level of presidential success since World War II. There would be acrimonious fights over deployments to Haiti and Bosnia, U.S. development aid, the defense budget, and the organization of the foreign policy bureaucracy. The level of bipartisan support for major national security votes would continue to fall, reaching its lowest level since World War II.

Yet throughout this period, relations between the White House and Congress were relatively amicable when it came to programs to aid the former Soviet states. In 1992, a Democratic Congress worked closely with the Republican Bush administration to craft a $400 million aid package. The Clinton administration in its early months proposed a sixfold increase in this amount and Congress faithfully honored the request, even at a time when its partisan divisions had doomed a domestic stimulus package. Even after U.S.-Russian relations became strained over the Aldrich Ames spy scandal, Moscow's war on Chechnya, Russia's proposed sale of nuclear reactors to Iran, and the rise of Vladimir Zhirinovsky and Gennady Zhuganov, Congress continued to look relatively favorably on these aid efforts. During the mid-1990s, Congress repeatedly zeroed out requests for certain categories of foreign aid, such as those for Africa, yet it provided over 90 percent of what the Clinton administration requested in aid for the former Soviet states.

One of the most important periods in the genesis of these programs was 1993, the first year of the Clinton administration. That year, Washington enacted a substantial expansion of those programs—from $417 million to $2.5 billion—even at a time when competing domestic priorities and instability in Russia posed significant obstacles to such action. Moreover, this policy constitutes a fundamental departure from previous policies: it was both the first big aid package, and the first clear embrace of the new realities of the post–cold war world as they related to U.S.-Russian relations. Accordingly, an examination of that year's efforts by the White House and Capitol Hill to expand the funding for the Russian/NIS aid programs provides a useful window on the politics of U.S. foreign policy after the cold war.

### Aiding a Former Enemy: The 1993 Assistance Package to Russia

American efforts to provide direct support for reform in the Soviet bloc began in earnest in 1989, as cracks began to show in the Soviet bloc. President George Bush proposed an assistance package on April 17, immediately following the signing of the Polish "Roundtable Accord." On June 6, Representative Lee Hamilton (D-Ind.) introduced the Democracy in Eastern Europe Act of 1989, which proposed assistance to Poland and Hungary. In October, House Foreign Affairs Committee Chairman Dante Fascell (D-Fl.) introduced the Support for East European Democracy (SEED) Act of 1989, which proposed over $900 million of assistance over three years. The SEED Act, plus accompanying funding, were passed by Congress with heavy and bipartisan majorities and signed into law in late November.[1]

As the Soviet Union itself began to weaken, proposals surfaced to provide American aid to that country as well. In March 1990, House Majority Leader Richard Gephardt (D-Mo.) sounded the first major call for direct assistance to Moscow; his speech provoked sharp criticism from not only the Bush White House but also a bipartisan array of members of Congress and pundits. Within eighteen months, the case for aid had become stronger and the political environment more receptive. In August 1991, Representative (and later Clinton's secretary of defense) Les Aspin (D-Wisc.), chair of the House Armed Services Committee, proposed to use $1 billion of defense funds to provide humanitarian aid to the Soviet Union. That fall, Aspin joined with his Senate counterpart, Sen. Sam Nunn (D-Ga.), in attempting to add such a provision to the annual defense authorization bill. Their effort died for lack of support from the Bush administration and other members of Congress, but was partially revived in a bill, signed into law in December 1991, which authorized the president to use up to $100 million in defense funds to support humanitarian assistance and up to $400 million for denuclearization (this portion became known as the Nunn-Lugar program).[2]

The first major package of bilateral aid for Russia followed the next year, when the Bush administration proposed and enacted the Freedom Support Act.[3] The Bush administration invested heavily in the bill's passage: Secretary of State James Baker lobbied for it personally, and the administration brought Ambassador Robert Strauss back from Russia so he could contribute his congressional skills. The final legislation, signed October 24, authorized about $400 million for a range of activities, including humanitarian assistance, promotion of democratic reform, economic privatization, and environmental protection.

*Phase I: The Clinton Administration Proposal*
These efforts helped lay the foundations for the 1993 package. Having been enacted by a Republican administration and Democratic Congress, they set precedents for bipartisan cooperation on these issues. Also, the Bush White House, Congress, and many advocacy groups had mounted extensive outreach efforts, including sessions for business leaders and ethnic groups. For example, during consideration of the Freedom Support Act, Representative David Nagle (D-Iowa) convened regular meetings of advocacy groups and ethnic American organizations who could lobby in favor of the bill. Both the bipartisan relationships and the outreach networks became assets in the Clinton administration's efforts to expand the levels of aid.[4]

The 1992 presidential campaign also helped set the stage for the 1993 package of assistance. One of candidate Clinton's main criticisms of President Bush's foreign policy record was that Bush was "overly cautious on the issue of aid to Russia."[5] Following similar criticisms by some prominent Republicans, especially former President Nixon, the Bush administration accelerated development of its aid package (which became the Freedom Support Act).[6] It announced its initiative on April 1, 1992—the same day Governor Clinton delivered a major campaign speech stressing the issue. This race to "own" the issue helped to elevate it and give it a bipartisan face.

Within its first weeks in office, the Clinton administration's foreign policy team began crafting an aid package for Russia/NIS. Starting on February 6, 1993 and through the next three months, a senior team met to decide overall strategy toward Russia and the NIS. That group typically included the president, Vice President Gore, Secretary of State Christopher, National Security Adviser Anthony Lake, his deputy, Samuel "Sandy" Berger, Ambassador-at-Large (and later Deputy Secretary) Strobe Talbott, Vice Presidential National Security Adviser Leon Fuerth, NSC staffers Toby Gati and Nicholas Burns, and presidential adviser George Stephanopoulos.

From the start, the effort to craft a strategy toward Russia/NIS had the benefit of the president's intense interest in the subject. One participant notes: "We never had 'senior adviser' meetings on this; they were all presidential meetings."[7] One of the ways in which the president signaled his interest in the issue had been his selection of Strobe Talbott, a close personal friend, to be the Russia/NIS "czar." The impact of that choice on the internal policy-making process was substantial. As another senior official noted: "There was no other foreign policy issue that could contend with us. Nobody would dare cross Strobe at that point."

This group decided, among other things, to label support for Russia/NIS reform the new president's "number-one priority" in foreign policy; to schedule an early summit, for April 3, with Russian president Boris Yeltsin; to make that summit President Clinton's first trip outside the U.S. (it was held in Vancouver, British Columbia); to increase the proposed Russia/NIS budget request for FY 1994 to $704 million, up from $417 proposed by the Bush administration in 1992;[8] and to seek additional support from other G-7 nations and multilateral financial institutions. All these were intended to signal the importance the president placed on this issue—a signal aimed not only at Russia, but also at Congress. Additionally, the president decided he would announce at the summit a $1.6 billion package of assistance. This package was composed of funds already appropriated, although not all of the funds had been slated to go to Russia. Yet even before he left for the summit, the president had decided to propose an additional package of assistance, composed of new funds.[9]

On March 18, the Russia team met with the president to suggest the shape of such a package. They proposed a total of $1 billion, nearly 50 percent more than the $704 million already locked in by the administration for its FY 1994 budget proposal. The $1 billion figure had been developed, in part, based on judgments by Talbott and career staff at State about what Congress would support. According to participants, the president's reaction was, "Not bold enough." He told the team: "You guys go out and be bold. Tell me what you think substantively needs to be done. Don't worry about how Congress will react to the price tag. I'll worry about Congress. That's my job—to sell it to the Hill." Not all administration officials agreed with the president's instincts. Some top political aides thought a bold foreign aid bill would interfere with attempts to pass the president's budget and other domestic initiatives. One top political adviser to the president said, "I voiced some concerns about how such foreign spending would be perceived" at a time of tight domestic budgets.

Another type of risk was added to the equation on March 21, when President Yeltsin announced an April 15 national referendum and said he was prepared to take extraconstitutional measures in order to settle his disputes with the Russian parliament. President Clinton, however, issued a statement within hours of Yeltsin's announcement, stressing that "as Russia's only democratically elected national leader, he has our support."[10]

Despite such worries, however, the president persisted in demanding a more ambitious aid package. At one point, at an April 6 meeting, he even suggested that a popular program toward Russia and the NIS might help, rather than hurt, his efforts to get Congress to fund domestic programs, such as the stimulus package: "I want some of those guys out there committed to spending billions for Russia so they have to explain why they won't spend anything on the U.S."

The Russia/NIS team and their staff developed several new options, with one totaling $5 billion. Ultimately, the highest option presented to the president was $2.5 billion, and at the April 6 meeting, he adopted this target. The administration's package contained a mix of housing for military officers returning from the Baltics, privatization assistance, assistance to Russia's agricultural, energy and environmental sectors, exchanges, humanitarian assistance and other efforts.

The administration did not intend to unveil the details of the package and the total price tag until later in the spring or even the summer. As a result, the individual elements of the package were never reviewed with members of Congress, nor did the package include any proposal for how to finance the increase in assistance. But many elements reflected congressional preferences that had been heard in earlier consultations and during the effort to pass the Freedom Support Act. For example, administration officials understood the political appeal of programs that could promote U.S. exports and agricultural sales. One member of the Russia/NIS team notes: "We knew certain things were politically easier to get, like wheat, because of interest from people like [Senate Minority Leader Robert] Dole, even when such elements may not have been the best thing to do."

The package also anticipated congressional political sensitivities. For example, during the February 6 meeting of the Russia team at the State Department, Ambassador Talbott stressed the need to address Russia's tattered "social safety net." State Department Counselor (and later Undersecretary) Timothy Wirth, who had just retired from the Senate, injected some legislative wisdom: "Strobe, if you call it that, Congress will eat you alive, because we've got a social safety net crisis here in the U.S." From then on, funds to address the social consequences of Russia's transitions consistently were labeled "privatization."

In mid-April, a week after the president had settled on the $2.5 billion target, Secretary Christopher and Treasury Secretary Lloyd Bentsen flew to Tokyo for a meeting of G-7 ministers. The meeting had been convened by President Clinton to develop multilateral responses to the challenge of Russian/NIS reform. By mistake, Secretary Bentsen divulged the proposed $2.5 billion figure not only to his G-7 counterparts but also to the press, and the administration's new goal became public.

*Phase II: The Administration Takes Its Proposal to Congress*
The job of persuading Congress to provide such a sizable sum began even before the Vancouver Summit. On March 25 and 26, the president hosted two dinners at the White House for the congressional leaders of both parties and the chairmen and ranking Republicans of each of the committees with a stake in decisions on Russia and the NIS. The first was for representatives, the second for senators. The two dinners were among the first major meetings between the new president and Congress on national security policy.

According to those present, the president made a compelling case. He argued that the course of reform in Russia and the other republics was crucial to U.S. national security interests. He stressed that he planned to use U.S. aid to leverage additional assistance from other nations. He noted it would be a hard year to appropriate funds for this purpose and stated that it must be a bipartisan effort to be successful. He then went around the room to hear comments and suggestions from the members. Many of them stressed particular programs areas, such as food aid, assistance to Russia's energy sector, space cooperation, housing for military officers returning from the Baltics, and exchanges for students and businesspeople. At the dinner for House members, Minority Whip (and future Speaker) Newt Gingrich (R-Ga.) said that if the president were willing to commit to the initiative personally and make the case to the public, Republicans in Congress would stand by him. Republicans expressed support at the Senate dinner as well, and made similar requests that the president help make the case to the American public.

The president began making the public case on April 1, just before leaving for the Vancouver summit. In a speech to newspaper editors delivered at the Annapolis Naval Academy, the president called for "a strategic alliance with Russian reform." The president stressed that the highest security interests were at stake: "The danger is clear if Russia's reforms turn sour—if it reverts to authoritarianism or disintegrates into chaos. The world cannot afford the strife of the former Yugoslavia replicated in a nation, as big as Russia, spanning eleven time zones with an armed arsenal of nuclear weapons." He also stressed the domestic benefits of a peaceful, democratic Russia, such as lower defense spending and increased trade: "Our ability to put people first at home requires that we put Russia and its neighbors first on our agenda abroad."[11]

The speech was intended, in large part, to help signal the president's commitment and to build domestic support for the assistance effort. A senior official involved with the speech who has worked for both Democratic and Republican administrations notes: "It's a Washington thing. It's one thing for a president to stand up at a congressional dinner to say that he wants something. It's another thing to say it in a prepared text before the nation. We didn't think the Annapolis speech would reach everyone in Dubuque. It was aimed at Congress and the Russians. In Washington, speeches are important." Comments by a congressional committee staff director suggest the signal was received: "The dinners and speeches sent a message that this is something the White House and the president care about."

Congress's efforts on the SEED Act, the Nunn-Lugar provisions and the Freedom Support Act created a base of congressional expertise and bipartisan familiarity with many elements of the FY 1994 package. Yet all those initiatives had been enacted under a Republican administration. Even with their own party's president leading the charge, House Republicans had split nearly evenly on final adoption of the Freedom Support Act (78 to 77 favoring the conference report, October 3, 1992). It was not clear whether Republican members of Congress would continue to support such initiatives under a Democratic administration.

One of the keys to retaining that support, and to the bill's final passage, was a congressional delegation that traveled to Russia and Ukraine in April 1993. The trip was conceived by Majority Leader Gephardt and cochaired by Minority Leader Robert Michel (R-Ill.). The delegation they assembled read like a Who's Who of the House members needed to pass the bill. According to one Hill staffer: "It was as high profile of a substantive delegation as I've ever seen in my fifteen years here." Representative Gephardt's decision to organize the delegation reflected two factors. The first was the high priority he placed on support for Russian reform. According to a former aide, "Dick decided long ago that Russia was the number one most important national security issue, principally due to their nukes." The second was his judgment that "it was necessary to build a bipartisan foundation for this that would endure."

The Gephardt-Michel delegation was a turning point for Congress. According to one aide who went on the trip: "Members were impressed with the magnitude of what had to be accomplished there. They saw young, friendly faces of the new Russian leadership juxtaposed with old Soviet men who were never going to change." The most frequently mentioned event on the trip was a meeting with Russian vice president Alexandr Rutskoi, in his spacious office, filled with models of military hardware and large wall maps. One of the maps was of the pre-1991 Soviet Union. One of the congressmen asked: "Isn't that map a bit out of date?" Rutskoi responded: "Maybe now; maybe not in the future." According to a senior Republican lawmaker congressman on the trip, "It was a frightening reality check."

The delegation returned committed to support dramatic action. Their trip report to the president—which was signed by every member in the delegation—concluded: "The delegation believes that the United States and its allies should show a strong sense of urgency in addressing and assisting the transformation. . . . American opinion and leadership is very important to the Russian people. If the United States clearly expresses confidence in the Russian reform process and in President Yeltsin, as its current leader, our influence can be felt. . . . The United States cannot afford *not* to help the Russian people. . . . Our national interest is deeply and lastingly affected by what happens in the former Soviet Union."[12]

*Phase III: Congress Acts*

Despite the base of support created by the Gephardt-Michel delegation and the assistance packages from previous years, Clinton's April 1993 aid request for Russia and the NIS got off to a troubled start. Senator Patrick Leahy (D-Vt.), chair of the relevant Appropriations Subcommittee, stated bluntly just days after the president had announced his $2.5 billion request: "[A]ssuming that we do not hit the mega-bucks lotto we have ourselves a problem. The money is not there."[13] A key House staffer says: "We couldn't believe the number at first. The White House got out ahead of itself with a number it had no way of achieving." The *Los Angeles Times*, citing the views of congressional Democrats, called the new budget target "difficult—perhaps impossible."[14] Even parts of the administration did not think Congress would ever provide the full amount; a senior administration official who helped design the aid package says: "It was an opening offer. I didn't think we'd get all the money." Nor was public opinion encouraging: polls suggested that a solid majority of the American public opposed using more of their tax dollars to assist reform in Russia and its neighboring states.[15]

Congress's willingness to fund the $2.5 billion package was further set back by the way it was unveiled. Few things are more infuriating to a member of Congress than being blindsided by an administration proposal—particularly if the member is chair of a committee of jurisdiction. Yet the unveiling of the $2.5 billion figure in Tokyo on April 14 had caught them completely by surprise. Senator Leahy's office first heard about the $2.5 billion proposal when a reporter phoned in from Japan to get the chairman's reaction.[16] Leahy's House counterpart, Representative David Obey (D-Wisc.), had a similar reaction; a staffer says: "Obey is a volatile personality, so of course he was p.o.'d. He was upset about the dollar level and upset about not being talked to."

In the days immediately after the surprise announcement, the congressional environment became even more hostile and prospects for the Russian aid package dimmed further as the president's $16 billion domestic stimulus package succumbed to a Republican filibuster in the Senate. In a heated hearing, Sen. Leahy told the ambassador-at-large for Russia/NIS, Strobe Talbott: "We have a jobs program . . . on the floor for American jobs. That has been voted down. . . . Now, we are going to be asked to vote . . . for a job program for Russians."[17] Moreover, the filibuster had signaled an end to the new president's honeymoon period and hardened partisan lines in Congress; Senator Orrin Hatch (R-Utah) noted: "Bill Clinton has succeeded in doing something George Bush never did; he united the Senate Republicans."[18]

Yet despite these missteps and obstacles, there emerged a clear determination among key members in both parties to make good on the president's commitment. One of the most important signs of that determination was the intensive effort by Representative Obey to assemble the financing for the assistance package. Obey had a long-standing interest in the issue—his master's degree had been in Soviet studies—and, along with others such as Representative Gephardt, he had been one of the early advocates of direct assistance to Russia. Now he became the architect of the financing for the president's proposal. One Hill staffer notes: "Obey felt very strongly about the request. He wanted to deliver for Clinton. First, he believed in the cause, even if he doubted the short-term ability to use the money. Second, he saw this as a new president in office; he'd waited twelve years for a president of his own party. So he wanted to deliver."

Obey utilized his position on the Foreign Operations Subcommittee of the House Appropriations Committee to work on developing the necessary support for the president's proposal. According to those who participated in the effort, Obey and his staff began "by squeezing absolutely everything else" in the international affairs account.[19] Next, they saw that there was unused budget authority remaining in the current fiscal year, FY 1993—about $600 million for the Foreign Operations Appropriations Subcommittee and about $1 billion for the Defense Subcommittee. This $1.6 billion in FY 1993 funds could be used toward the $2.5 billion total as long as the funding bill was enacted by September 30—the end of the fiscal year—after which these "supplemental" funds would no longer be usable.[20]

It would be easy enough for Obey to tap the unused budget authority for aid from his own subcommittee for the new bill, but efforts to use defense money for foreign aid generally, and especially for Russia/NIS, were problematic. In particular, House Defense Subcommittee chair, Representative John Murtha (D-Pa.), had been resistant to the idea of using defense funds for any efforts in Russia/NIS other than demilitarization, and even then with reservations. Another difficulty in using the defense funds was that Murtha saw Obey as a competitor for future leadership of the full Appropriations Committee.

Obey's staff approached Murtha's staff to discuss the Defense Subcommittee's unused budget authority. According to one participant, "their first reaction was, 'Hell, no.' Murtha has not been enthusiastic about [Nunn-Lugar]. He's been more interested in protecting military pay and readiness at a time of military downsizing. Of course, the staff reaction on Defense is 'hell, no' because everyone wants to raid their funds. Murtha had to protect his flank. If someone saw us tapping his money for Russia, then people would start asking what else you could use it for." The only chance to obtain the needed defense funds for the package was a direct appeal by Chairman Obey to Chairman Murtha. The two met in the conference room of the full Appropriations Committee. Obey said, "Look, this is the end of the cold war. You've got to do this." Murtha was more receptive than expected.[21]

Once Representatives Obey and Murtha had worked out a basic agreement and discussed it with members of the leadership and other key members, formal action in the House proceeded quickly. On May 26, Obey's Foreign Operations Appropriations Subcommittee approved by voice vote that included the $2.5 billion for Russia and the NIS. The full House Appropriations Committee took up the bill on June 10. Representative Sonny Callahan (R-Al.) attempted to strip the funds for Russia/NIS. He cited, in particular, the support for housing for Russian troops returning from the Baltics: "We're downsizing 3,000 military people a week in this country and we're not giving them any housing." But the bipartisan support assembled earlier prevailed. Representative Livingston, who had been part of the Gephardt-Michel delegation, countered: "We are talking about the single most important move this country could make for future generations."[22] Callahan's motion was defeated and the bill was adopted by the full committee on a voice vote.

The package was brought to the House floor a week later, on June 17. Prospects for passage generally looked good. Just the day before, the House had managed to pass the Foreign Aid Authorization bill—legislation that had not made it into law since 1985—and had fended off an amendment to delete authorization for much of the funding for Russia/NIS.[23] Even so, there were rumors the Congressional Black Caucus would oppose the Russia/NIS assistance provisions, just as many of its members the previous year had opposed the Freedom Support Act. As a result, the administration worked the vote hard. Secretary Aspin sent a letter to members indicating his support for the use of defense funds in the bill. The president sent a letter to all members urging passage and stressing the administration's bipartisan efforts in developing its aid proposal.[24]

As it turned out, there was some opposition from CBC members. CBC chairman Representative Kweisi Mfume (D-Md.) spoke in favor when Representative Callahan offered an amendment to strike the $1.6 billion in supplemental funds from the bill.[25] "To defeat the domestic stimulus package in April and then somehow mysteriously pass Russian aid in June would create the perception that our priorities are in the wrong place."[26] About half the Black Caucus (17 of 38) agreed. So did a majority of House Republicans (93 to 79). House freshmen voted to cut the funds for Russia and the other NIS by about 7 percentage points more than nonfreshmen—a gap that was reflected in both parties. But the division among the Republicans, combined with a solid Democratic bloc (46 to 210 against the amendment), was enough to save the funds for Russia and the NIS. Callahan's amendment lost by a wide margin, 140 to 289. Ultimately, the entire bill passed easily, 309 to 111, with a solid majority of Republicans—107 to 63—joining most Democrats in voting for final passage.

The administration and some in Congress were eager to gain quick Senate approval as well. But tensions between Congress and the administration on national security were beginning to rise—principally over the U.S. mission in Somalia. And there were problems with the Foreign Operations bill. First, Senator Daniel Inouye (D-Hawaii), Chairman of the Senate Defense Appropriations Subcommittee, was not yet prepared to follow Representative Murtha's lead in allowing nearly $1 billion of defense money to be used for Russia/NIS. While Inouye was generally sympathetic to foreign aid—he had previously been chair of the Foreign Operations Subcommittee—he was concerned about the impact of this expenditure on the Defense Department budget for the coming year.[27]

Second, there was an arcane problem involving loan guarantees for Israel. Under federal budgeting rules, Congress had to appropriate a fraction of the value of the guarantees as a hedge against default on the loans. But setting these funds aside would make it virtually impossible to fund the entire $2.5 billion for Russia/NIS. As the end of the fiscal year drew near, concerns mounted that the full $2.5 billion simply could not be obtained. As in the House, the impasse could only be broken by a direct meeting of the principals. In early September, Senators Inouye and Leahy met with two other key players—Senate Appropriations chair Robert Byrd (D-W.V.) and Budget Committee chair Jim Sasser (D-Tenn.). According to participants, the meeting was "difficult" and at times "acrimonious." Senator Leahy laid out the general case for the Russian aid package. Senator Byrd then spoke firmly in favor of the effort, stressing the need to support "a young president who is willing to make some hard decisions here and take some political risks." Byrd apparently gained Inouye's cooperation simply by asking him for it— direct requests from the Appropriations Committee chair are hard to refuse—and by stressing his own willingness, as part of the solution, to support the Israeli loan guarantee provision. This was an important consideration for Inouye, who is one of the most ardent congressional supporters of aid to Israel, and a major concession from Byrd, who is not.

Finding a way to eliminate the accounting cost of the Israeli loan guarantees was more difficult. Some of those present proposed that Senator Sasser exercise his prerogative as Budget Committee chair and direct the Congressional Budget Office (CBO), in essence, to assume the Israeli loans bore no default risk. Sasser refused to do so, arguing that directing the CBO in this way would weaken the integrity of the congressional budget process. He suggested an alternative: in essence, that the Senate agree not to count this expense against the overall budget caps set in the 1990 budget deal worked out between Congress and President Bush. But as one of the negotiators in 1990, Senator Byrd held a passionate commitment to these caps. He also objected to this approach since it would make the entire bill vulnerable to a budgetary point of order on the Senate floor, which would require sixty votes to overcome. Finally, however, Byrd agreed to exempt the provision from the 1990 budget caps.

Why did the powerful Appropriations chairman embrace such an exceptional package? Part of the answer lay in historical circumstance.

The meeting occurred just as Israel and the PLO were forging their breakthrough declaration. According to one participant in the meeting: "People were saying, 'My God! Can you believe Rabin and Arafat are shaking hands?' And, second, they believed Russia was too important to mess up." Another factor in the support of Senator Byrd—and many other members—was former President Nixon. Some weeks earlier, Byrd and about a dozen Senate colleagues of both parties had met with the former president to hear his reasons for supporting aid to Russia/NIS. The meeting reportedly had a significant impact on Byrd and the others present. Like the Gephardt-Michel delegation, it appears to have been a major factor in firming up bipartisan support for the initiative. Once the deal was struck, things moved quickly. Senator Leahy's Appropriations Subcommittee met September 13 and approved the bill by voice vote. The full Appropriations committee approved the bill unanimously the next day.

History intervened a week later, on September 21, when President Yeltsin disbanded Russia's parliament and called for December elections. There was initial concern within the administration about the impact these events would have on the bill in Congress. The president quickly signaled his support for Yeltsin, calling him the same day and issuing a White House press statement that said, "As the democratically elected leader of Russia, President Yeltsin has chosen to allow the people of Russia themselves to resolve this impasse . . . and I support him fully."

Given the tumultuous backdrop in Russia, Senator Leahy said it would be "a real roll of the dice" to bring his bill to the floor. Yet when the bill was taken up by the Senate the next day, September 22, many senators cited the events in Russia as a reason to vote for—not against—the bill. Senator Mitch McConnell (R-Ky.), the ranking Republican on Leahy's subcommittee, said that "the events in the past few days [make] our support for democracy and economic reform . . . more important than ever."[28] *Congressional Quarterly* noted that "senators followed Clinton's lead in rallying around the Russian president."[29] The bill passed the next day, 88 to 10, with Republicans voting 36 to 7 in favor.

The budgetary point of order that had worried Senator Byrd was never raised on the Senate floor. In part, this was because Senators Byrd, Leahy, Inouye, and Sasser, soon after their meeting, consulted with several key Republicans and secured their support. At that point, other potential opponents abandoned any thought of blocking or cutting the aid package. For example, Senator Jesse Helms (R-N.C.), ranking Republican on the Senate Foreign Relations Committee and one of the strongest critics of the administration, foreign aid, and using defense funds for nondefense purposes (as this bill did), refrained from an attempt to impede the process. A Helms aide says: "We knew about the budget point of order. But Nunn, Strom Thurmond [ranking Republican on the Armed Services Committee], and Lugar were comfortable with the impact on defense; Pete Domenici [ranking Republican on the Budget Committee] was supportive; and Dole thought it was imperative to pass the package."

The House and Senate quickly moved to conference committee, so that the final bill could be crafted before the fiscal year—and the $1.6 billion of supplemental funds in the financing package—expired. The conferees quickly negotiated compromises on the more than a hundred differences between the two chambers' versions of the bill. Although few of the changes affected the Russia/NIS provisions, the conferees agreed to eliminate Senate "earmarks" for Ukraine and Armenia. Instead, they simply urged the administration to allocate $300 million and $18 million, respectively, to these two nations. The House approved the conference report on September 29, 321 to 108. The Senate followed suit, by a margin of 88 to 11, on the next day, September 30. As evening and the end of the fiscal year fell, the bill was rushed across the city to the White House, and in to the president, who was at work in the Oval Office. At 7:15 P.M., less than five hours before the financing package would have been unusable, President Clinton signed the package into law.

### Conclusions: Russian Aid and Post–Cold War U.S. Foreign Policy Making

Through this elaborate maneuvering, the United States enacted broad changes to its policy toward Russia. There are many possible conclusions to draw from this story of the 1993 package of assistance to Russia and the other former Soviet states. In part, the case displays many of the dynamics that have become hallmarks of the post–cold war period. House freshmen voted disproportionately against the measure, as they have tended to do on a range of foreign policy measures. Post–cold war deficit concerns constrained the options for funding the bill: the idea of relying on a deficit-increasing "emergency supplemental" was never seriously entertained on the Hill. The case also demonstrated how—partly due to deficit pressures—power has shifted from authorizing committees, such as the Senate Foreign Relations Committee, to committees concerned with funding, such as the appropriations and budget committees. In the 1993 saga, virtually all of the action centered around the appropriations committees.

It is harder to draw conclusions from this case about the quality of post–cold war decision making and program design in the executive and legislative branches. Some observers, who view many of the programs funded that year as wasteful and ineffective, see this as a case of naive idealism in the White House, and of Congress abandoning its responsibilities to ask probing questions because it was on a honeymoon with both Russian democracy and the new U.S. administration.[30] Others, who saw the need for a much larger aid effort toward Russia and the other states, may view the president's proposal, and Congress's assent to it, as proof that both branches have become cautious and penny-pinching in their post–cold war exercise of leadership abroad. Still others will conclude that President Clinton was bold and wise to propose such a large assistance package at a time when domestic concerns were dominant, and that Congress was bold and wise to fund it.

Such conclusions about the two branches' performance ultimately depend on judgments about the effectiveness of the programs themselves—a matter that is beyond the scope of this chapter. Yet even without attempting to resolve that question, it is still possible to conclude that the behavior between the two branches in this case was exceptional in several regards. First, at a time when many foreign aid accounts were being deeply cut, Congress was willing to fund a significant increase in this one account. Second, at a time when congressional voting on major foreign policy questions was becoming more partisan, the 1993 package of aid for Russia and the NIS succeeded with strong bipartisan support. Third, while Congress would resist other post–cold war initiatives abroad such as the deployments to Haiti and Bosnia partly on the grounds that the public did not support them, Congress backed the increase in aid for Russia and the NIS even though public opinion tilted against such action.

Finally, at a time when Congress was unwilling to use the defense budget to fund other foreign policy efforts—for example, the Clinton administration's effort to pay U.N. peacekeeping dues out of the Pentagon budget failed completely—Congress was willing to do so in this case. Whatever one thinks of the aid programs themselves, it is worth inquiring why the executive-legislative relationship on the 1993 aid bill exhibited these qualities. Four features seem particularly important: (1) a shared perception by the two branches that the issue involved high national security stakes; (2) the promise of domestic economic benefits for the U.S.; (3) an executive branch strategy toward Congress that was high-level and bipartisan; (4) the absence of areas of constitutional dispute. The remainder of this chapter will develop each of these points.

*The Magnitude of National Security Stakes*
The politics of U.S. national security is always partly a reflection of the sense of national danger. As Alexis de Tocqueville once noted, the power of the executive branch in foreign policy relative to Congress would tend to rise and fall with the level of external threat to the country. When President Truman was preparing his speech to a joint session of Congress in March 1947 to call for anticommunist aid to Greece and Turkey, Senator Arthur Vandenberg translated Tocqueville's equation into more practical advice: he advised Truman that in order to get Congress's cooperation, the speech would need "scare the hell out of the country." Similarly, one of the key reasons for the cooperative relations between the White House and Congress in the Russia/NIS aid case was a substantial consensus between the two branches that clear and sizable U.S. security interests were at stake.

For example, asked to explain why Congress was so much more amenable to this initiative than some others in recent years, such as various peacekeeping operations, one senator on a defense panel responds: "People feel more strongly that the survival of Yeltsin and [Russian] democracy are important to our security than the ability of the U.N. to run military operations." Similarly, a key House staffer says: "The key [to passage of the Russia/NIS package] was that there was an overwhelming national interest involved. The most liberal member and the most conservative member could understand how important this was." Members found that the security case on Russia/NIS survived the acid test: politically active constituents seemed willing to support it despite a general aversion to foreign aid. A conservative Republican representative says, "My voters understood the military argument—like the case for the Nunn-Lugar funds—and I could also make the case well when I was asked about why it's worth assisting Russia in other ways. People understood."

One indicator of the way in which executive and legislative officials perceived the security stakes is their use of martial imagery in discussing the initiative. Secretary of State James Baker had advocated for the Freedom Support Act in 1992 by describing it as "defense by other means."[31] During the House debate on the 1993 aid package, then Minority Whip Gingrich concluded: "we have a chance today to do what we can to make the world safer so our sons and daughters do not die in a war and so our cities are not incinerated.[32]

It is worth probing *why* U.S. policy makers shared such a strong sense that there were high U.S. security stakes involved in sending billions of dollars to a former adversary in the midst of chaotic conditions. One reason is that the cold war had left them with a framework for thinking about the issue. Throughout U.S. history, leaders have tried to make the case for addressing the security challenges of a new era by comparing them to the dominant threats of the preceding era. Thus, when President Truman addressed the joint session of Congress in 1947, he sought to cast this first cold war initiative in World War II terms: "One of the primary objectives of the foreign policy of the United States is the creation of conditions in which we and other nations will be able to work out a way of life free from coercion. This was a fundamental issue in the war with Germany and Japan."[33] In recent years, it has been hard to frame such foreign efforts as peacekeeping or global environmental programs in terms that hearken back to preceding security challenges. Not so with aid to Russia and the NIS. One conservative representative describes the bill as a way of "putting some neat wrapping" around the cold war.

The shared perception of high security stakes created for Congress a sense of high political stakes. Former President Nixon had warned President Bush in 1992 that a failure to provide more aid to Russia would leave the latter vulnerable if a debate were to break out over "who lost Russia"—a politically potent formulation. A senior administration official notes that the Clinton administration in 1993 was able to play on this political worry in order to gain congressional cooperation: "We were covering *their* [Congress's] behind. They were buying an insurance policy. If there was a debate over who lost Russia, they couldn't be blamed. You couldn't lose on this vote."

The perception of high security stakes sheds light on many aspects of Congress's action on the $2.5 billion aid package. It helps explain, for example: why Representative Obey was willing to invest so much effort into constructing a financing arrangement; why Obey and Senator Leahy were willing to lead the fight for the bill even after the White House had failed to consult with them before announcing the proposal; why Representative Murtha and other defense hawks were willing to use the Pentagon's money to fund aid for Russia and the NIS; why Senator Byrd and other deficit hawks were willing to bend the most important budget rules in order to accommodate the legislation; and why the proposal continued to retain bipartisan support even at a time when rising partisan tensions were defeating core elements of the president's economic program.

*The Promise of Domestic Economic Benefits*

Major wars are often followed by economic contractions and a public demand for attention to domestic conditions. Foreign policy initiatives are hard pressed to compete with domestic programs unless they can lay claim to domestic economic benefits. So it has been in the U.S. after the cold war, where the collapse of the Soviet bloc was followed by the recession of 1990–91, and anxieties for an even longer period over corporate layoffs, sluggish job growth, and stagnant median incomes. The political implications for foreign programs became clear early in the 1990s. In a closely watched special election in 1991, Democratic Senate candidate Harris Wofford picked up a formerly Republican-held seat with the slogan, "It's time to take care of our own." His focus was on health care reform, but his message implicitly pushed off against foreign programs. During the 1992 presidential race, President Bush was criticized for spending too much time on foreign affairs and lost to a candidate whose campaign mantra was "It's the economy stupid." More recently, Senate Foreign Relations chair Jesse Helms has derided foreign aid as "rathole" spending, and Senate Foreign Operations Appropriations chair Mitch McConnell has bluntly stressed the need to focus America's foreign programs on its domestic economic needs: "We can strengthen popular support for foreign aid by making it more clearly serve American business interests."

The aid package for Russia and the NIS produced close executive-legislative cooperation in part because it was designed and marketed to Congress in a way that emphasized domestic economic benefits. The administration placed heavy emphasis on trade and agricultural assistance. President Clinton's first advocacy of increased aid to Russia/NIS after taking office was in an address about the importance of foreign programs in fueling America's economic renewal. In that speech and others that followed, he stressed two domestic benefits. The first was lower defense budgets: "[T]he reductions in our defense spending that are an important part of our economic program . . . are only tenable as long as Russia and other nuclear republics pose a diminishing threat to our security."[34] The second economic benefit was the long-run potential for increased trade with Russia: "[T]his rebirth of Russia . . . could mean . . . a source of raw materials and manufactured products and a vast market for American goods and services."[35] It soon became clear there were other domestic economic benefits to the package: a *Wall Street Jour-*

*nal* article in 1994 revealed that 50 to 90 percent of many aid contracts funded by the bill were going to U.S. business and media consultants.[36]

As members considered the aid package, many could point to district-level benefits for their constituents, in the form of exchanges or trade opportunities. One administration official notes, "Congress was focused on laying the groundwork for our own private sector; it was a domestic issue for them, too." Members repeatedly stressed such economic benefits during Congress's floor debates on the package. For example, Representative Henry Hyde (R-Ill.) argued: "[The bill offers an opportunity] to turn what have been 300 million enemies into 300 million customers. . . . Access to oil, to natural gas, to rare metals, to minerals, they have a boundless amount of them over there, and when we become trading partners instead of adversaries, the benefits will be incalculable."[37]

The 1993 aid package for Russia and the NIS also succeeded in Congress because its content responded to the economic imperatives of deficit reduction. As noted, there was never any serious prospect that the sudden request for a sixfold increase in aid to these states would be financed with "emergency" supplemental funds that increase the deficit. Rather, the package was financed in an appropriations bill that was smaller than the previous year's bills and within deficit reduction targets previously set for the year. Congress's aversion to new spending on foreign ventures was clear from its floor debates; for example, in the House debate on the Russia/NIS package, Representative Obey stressed to his colleagues: "Not one dime of aid to the Soviet Union is coming out of any program to help people here at home. This program is being funded by reductions in our other foreign aid accounts and by taking almost $1 billion out of the military budget."[38]

*High-Level and Bipartisan Strategy toward Congress*
National security initiatives do not sell themselves in Congress, no matter how high the security stakes and economic benefits. The experiences of Presidents Wilson, Truman and Clinton—as well as many others—suggest that the executive branch's management of its relations with Congress matters. In particular, in proposing a national security initiative to Congress, it matters whether the executive branch reaches out to both parties and sends clear signals from the Oval Office on down that the proposal is a presidential priority. The executive did both to build support for the Russia/NIS aid package. During the post–cold war period, such direct presidential attention and bipartisan effort are likely even more necessary than they were while the Soviet threat loomed.

The lower level of presidential involvement on certain other recent initiatives, from U.N. funding to reorganization of the foreign policy bureaucracy, may help explain the difference in legislative outcomes.

As noted above, key officials in both the executive branch and Congress recognized early on that obtaining expanded assistance for Russia and the other NIS would require bipartisan cooperation. The president began lobbying members of Congress of both parties, at the White House dinners and through other means, long before announcing the package. The White House encouraged and assisted the bipartisan Gephardt-Michel delegation, which ultimately played an important role in building congressional support. Certainly it was helpful that assistance to Russia and the NIS had enjoyed the support of the preceding Republican administration, and that a Republican former president, Richard Nixon, weighed in to push the initiative. Yet without deliberate efforts by both branches and both sides of the aisle, it is not clear that the bipartisan coalition for Russia/NIS aid would have endured. President Yeltsin's March 20 declaration of extraconstitutional powers and the disbanding of Parliament on September 21 both came at crucial times; both could have fueled Republican arguments against the package. A senior Clinton administration official notes the uncertain atmosphere that prevailed in the spring of 1993: "There was potential for partisan differences. Yeltsin hadn't won on the streets. Some urged us to be more cautious." The wide, bipartisan margins by which the legislation passed were not inevitable.

The administration also clearly communicated to Congress and the public the high priority that President Clinton placed on the aid initiative. Within days of his inauguration, the president tagged Russia and the other NIS as his "number-one" foreign policy priority, gave major speeches laying out the case for the aid package, and brought key members of Congress to the White House to ensure they heard the message. Moreover, the administration was unwavering in its commitment to the proposal, even in the face of disruptions at home and in Russia.

The administration reinforced this message of presidential concern by deploying powerful champions in support of the proposal. The president, Secretary of State Christopher, and National Security Adviser Lake all weighed in with Congress early and often. Ambassador Talbott spoke extensively with members of Congress, and they understood he was speaking for his close friend, the president. Secretary of Defense Aspin, who had been an early proponent of using defense funds for assisting Russia, stressed his support for the bill. All of these executive branch signals helped bolster Congress's own long-time champions of assistance to the former Soviet Union, such as Majority Leader Gephardt, Representative Obey, and Senator Nunn.

### Absence of Areas of Constitutional Dispute

A final important reason for the cooperation between the two branches on the Russia/NIS aid package derived from what did *not* happen in this case: the two branches did not run into the kind of constitutional conflicts that have troubled some other post–cold war initiatives. E. S. Corwin long ago noted that the Constitution created "an invitation to struggle for the privilege of directing American foreign policy," but that invitation has always extended to some issues more than others. Most notably, recent peacekeeping operations, policy questions, and funding issues have directly or indirectly raised contentious war powers questions that are deeply rooted in constitutional interpretation. Those issues were part of the reason that Congress ultimately declined to authorize the U.S. troop deployments to Somalia, Haiti, Rwanda, and Bosnia. Those issues also played a role in congressional efforts to place restrictions on the use of American troops in peacekeeping operations, and Congress's refusal to budget Pentagon funds in order to pay for peacekeeping dues or operational costs.

In the case of aid to Russia and the NIS, by contrast, the division of executive-congressional labor was clear and it fit well with each branch's views of its duties and prerogatives. The administration conducted the diplomacy, drew the broad outlines of its program, declared a goal in the form of a dollar figure and made the case to the public. Congress figured out how to fund the package and get it passed. The most contentious issue of executive-congressional prerogatives involved earmarks for Ukraine and Armenia; even on these, the executive branch met or exceeded the amounts that Congress had urged.

These four factors—the level of national security stakes, the domestic economic benefits, the manner of executive outreach to Congress, and the absence of constitutional obstacles—may offer a useful guide to the level of cooperation across the full range of foreign policy challenges after the cold war. At a minimum, they help explain why the 1993 aid package for Russia and the NIS received such strong congressional support, and why these programs have continued to fare relatively well on Capitol Hill in the years that have followed. In the coming years, the politics of relations between the United States and the former Soviet states may change in a variety of ways. There will likely be more differentiation in congressional support among the various programs toward these states as the Hill begins to focus more scrutiny on their relative track records. There will tend to be periodic backlashes against certain of these programs when Russia or one of the other states pursues policies that the U.S. opposes, or when they elect less reform-minded leaders. The likely addition of new Central European states to the North Atlantic Treaty Organization may change the political dynamics on these issues in a number of ways. As in 1993, however, American iniatives toward these states in the post–cold war period will most likely continue to produce higher levels of interbranch attention and, often, cooperation.

## Notes

The author now holds a position in the United States Department of State. This essay was written before he assumed that position and its views are his alone.

1  The Democracy in Eastern Europe Act of 1989 was H.R. 2550. The SEED Act was H.R. 3402, enacted as Pub. L. 101-179.

2  The bill was H.J. Res. 157, enacted as Pub. L. 102-229.

3  The bill was S. 2532, enacted as Pub. L. 102-511.

4  Although Nagle lost his reelection bid in 1992, he helped reassemble the coalition to press for passage of the 1993 bill.

5  Bill Clinton, Speech to the Foreign Policy Association, Washington, D.C., April 1, 1992.

6  See, Marvin Kalb, *The Nixon Memo* (Chicago: University of Chicago Press, 1994).

7  These and other unattributed quotations that follow are from interviews conducted by the author during 1994 and 1995; interview subjects were promised anonymity in order to foster candor.

8  Budget of the United States Government: FY 1994, April 8, 1993, pp. A241–242. The federal fiscal year begins October 1; FY 1994 runs from October 1993 through September 1994.

9  The president suggested this in his remarks in Vancouver, when he said that he would go back and approach Congress about "broader cooperative initiatives" beyond the $1.6 billion package. "The President's News Conference with President Boris Yeltsin of Russia in Vancouver," *Papers of the President*, April 4, 1993.

10  Statement of the president, March 20, 1993.

11  Gwen Ifill, "President Urges American to Back Help for Moscow," *New York Times*, April 2, 1993, A1, 4.

12  "CODEL [congressional delegation] Gephardt-Michel: Trip Report," April 1993.

13  U.S. Senate Appropriations Committee, hearing before the Subcommittee on Foreign Operations, Export Financing, and Related Programs, *Foreign Operations, Export Financing, and Related Programs, Appropriations for Fiscal year 1994*, 104th Cong., April 21, 1993.

14  "U.S. Pledges $1.8 Billion More in Aid to Russia," *Los Angeles Times*, April 15, 1993, p. A12.

15  A Gallup poll conducted in late March 1993 asked, "Do you think the United

States should increase financial aid to Russia, keep it the same as it is now, or decrease aid?" The poll found that 18 percent favored increasing aid, 46 percent favored keeping it at the same level and 35 percent favored decreasing aid. Another Gallup poll conducted in late June, 1993, asked, "Would you favor or oppose the United States increasing economic aid to Russia?" Thirty-four percent favored the idea, while 64 percent opposed it. Polls taken during the 1992 presidential campaign found that by a margin of 50 to 29 percent, voters would be less likely to favor a candidate who favored "increasing U.S. economic aid to the former Soviet Republics (Gallup, January 1992). Interestingly, voters by 77 to 11 percent perceived George Bush as favoring such an idea, but incorrectly perceived (by 32 to 28 percent) Bill Clinton as *opposing* such an idea (Princeton Survey Research Associates/Times-Mirror, May 1992; all polling from the Roper Center for Public Opinion Research. Some polls were somewhat more encouraging. A New York Times/CBS poll in April 1993 reported that "52 percent of those polled said they were willing to support aid to Russia if it means averting civil war there," but that support fell to 41 percent when the economic aid was intended to "help Russia reform its economy." And only 29 percent favor offering such support if its aim is to "keep Mr. Yeltsin . . . in power." Gwen Ifill, "President Urges America to Back Help for Moscow," *New York Times*, April 2, 1993.

16 Leahy had been angry at the Bush administration when he first learned of its proposal to write off $7 billion in Egyptian debt by reading about it in the *Washington Post*. He had warned President Clinton early in the new administration: "Don't surprise me." According to several sources, Leahy was furious to be caught unaware by a president of his own party. According to one source: "This was a seminal event. He went ahead, but it was with anger and bitterness throughout."

17 Senate Appropriations Committee, hearing before the Subcommittee on Foreign Operations, Export Financing, and Related Programs.

18 Adam Clymer, "G.O.P. Senators Prevail, Sinking Clinton's Economic Stimulus Bill, *New York Times*, April 22, 1993.

19 Under the final legislation, many major accounts sustained deep cuts in order to make room for the assistance to Russia/NIS. Funding for multilateral financial institutions was cut about $500 million from the administration's request. The bill funded development assistance at a level more than $100 million under the administration's request. The Economic Support Fund was funded about $300 million less than the preceding year. The administration's request for antinarcotics activities, about $150 million, was cut by about one-third.

20 The $1.6 billion in supplemental FY 1993 funds should not be confused with the initial $1.6 billion package of assistance that President Clinton had extended to President Yeltsin in Vancouver in April, 1993.

21 One reason for Murtha's willingness to cooperate was likely the steady attention that the administration had devoted to him. Both Howard Paster, chief of White House Legislative Affairs, and Leon Panetta, then director of the Office of Management and Budget, had lobbied him on the Russian aid package. In addition, the president had worked on building relations with the powerful chairman during private meetings and golf outings. An administration official describes the first private session between the two this way: "It was a no-agenda meeting. Purely

social. The two of them sat down together on the yellow wing-back chairs in the Oval Office. After a little while, the President calls in the steward for some coffee. When the steward comes in, he turns to Murtha and asks, 'are you hungry?' Murtha says, 'yeah.' So the President asks the steward to bring them a couple of big pieces of pie. Well, after you've got him there in the Oval Office, in those yellow chairs, with both of them sitting with a piece of pie balanced on their knees, then you've got a friend."

22 "$2.5 Billion Approved for Ex-Soviet States," *Congressional Quarterly Almanac, 1993*, p. 606.

23 The amendment, by Rep. John Kyl (R-Ariz.), was defeated by a vote of 118 to 317. As it turned out, the Foreign Aid authorization bill failed to pass this year as well; it never made it to the floor of the Senate.

24 President Clinton, letter to Speaker of the House Tom Foley, June 16, 1993; the letter read in part, "My Administration has worked closely with members of Congress from both parties to develop this bill. This bi-partisan approach is in keeping with the best American tradition of speaking with one voice on foreign policy and national security."

25 That is, the approximately $1 billion in FY 1993 defense budget authority, and about $600 million in FY 1993 foreign operations budget authority.

26 *Congressional Quarterly Almanac, 1993*, p. 607.

27 Congress focuses most on two measures of each account in the federal budget: budget authority and outlays. The first is the up-front grant of authority to spend funds. Outlays are actual expenditures. A bill that approves $1 in budget authority in a given year often results in several years of outlays that add up to this sum. The $1 billion in defense funds in this bill was budget authority; it was estimated at the time that these funds would be spent over several years, with approximately $210 billion to be spent during the first year, FY 1994.

28 *Congressional Record*, 22 September 1993, p. S12221.

29 "$2.5 Billion Approved for Ex-Soviet States," *Congressional Quarterly Almanac, 1993*, p. 609.

30 See, for example, Charles Flickner, "The Russian Aid Mess," *National Interest*, no. 38 (Winter 1994/95): 13–19.

31 James A. Baker, III, *The Politics of Diplomacy: Revolution, War and Peace, 1989–1992* (New York: Putnam: 1995), p. 658.

32 *Congressional Record*, 17 June 1993, p. H3745.

33 Harry S. Truman, "Special Message to the Congress on Greece and Turkey: The Truman Doctrine (March 12, 1947)," *Public Papers of the President: Harry Truman, 1947* (Washington: U.S. Government Printing Office, 1963), p. 178.

34 Remarks by the president at American University Centennial Celebration, February 26, 1993.

35 Remarks of the president to the American Society of Newspaper Editors, United States Naval Academy, Annapolis, Maryland, April 1, 1993.

36 John J. Fialka, "U.S. Aid to Russia Is Quite a Windfall—For U.S. Consultants," *Wall Street Journal*, February 24, 1994, p. A1.

37 *Congressional Record*, June 17, 1993, p. H3743.

38 *Congressional Record*, June 17, 1993, p. H3742.

# 10.

# The Promotion of Democracy at the End

# of the Twentieth Century: A New Polestar

# for American Foreign Policy?

*Rick Travis*

After the cold war, the notion that the historical evolution of political society had approached its final stage became fashionable. Specifically, it has been argued that the end of the cold war served to point out the higher natural order of free-market democracy. This thesis, however presumptuous, has been taken as a key point for reorganizing American foreign policy. During the early years of his first administration, President Clinton and his top foreign policy advisers missed few opportunities to sprinkle general foreign policy speeches with references to the benefits of democracy and the need of the United States to be actively involved in its promotion. Thus, Clinton's national security adviser, Anthony Lake, called for a foreign policy guided by the doctrine of "enlargement of the world's free community of market democracies" as a replacement for the successful and now archaic policy of containment.[1] In fact, along with restoring prosperity and modernizing the military, promoting democracy abroad was identified in early 1993 as one of the three pillars of Clinton foreign policy. Yet, a scant four years later the policy of democratic enlargement appeared to be relegated to a peripheral position, attacked by a truculent Congress under Republican control and cast adrift by a White House more interested in economic security and the stability of allies.[2]

As with the other cases in this book, the birth, maturation, and subsequent diminishing of the enlargement of democracy as a foreign policy goal offers insights into this new era of post–cold war policy making. And, as with other cases, the identification and subsequent pursuit of a policy of democratic enlargement were products of the international and domestic societal setting at the end of the cold war, while the specific policies and strategies were a consequence of institutional actors and arrangements found in a shifting constellation of foreign policy making.

### The Need for a New Polestar: The International and Domestic Contexts

Although feelings about the uniqueness of liberal democracy have always been strong in the United States, the era immediately preceding and following the end of the cold war brought increased attention to democratization as a focus of U.S. foreign policy. Beginning in the 1970s, a resurgence of democracy developed throughout the world, in what Samuel Huntington has described as the third wave of democracy.[3] From 1974 to 1990 more than thirty nations made the transformation to democratic rule. For many observers these transitions brought increased hope of a burgeoning new world order based on liberal democratic principles. The failure of communism, the exhaustion of caudillo rule throughout Latin America, and a combination of economic, environmental, and sociocultural challenges and changes facing many African and Asian countries prompted many people to reassess their system of governance and choose democracy as an alternative.

One significant aspect of this third wave is the illustration it provides concerning the origin and development of policy as a response to international events. Although specific policies are the product of interactions of policy makers, the necessity of policy development and the preclusion of policy options are often conditioned by shifts in the international setting. In short, the U.S. decision following the end of the cold war to promote democracy was not so much a policy put into motion by U.S. policy makers as it was a phenomenon brought about by this global wave of democracy.

Still, other events and concerns at the international level also played an important role in setting the stage for the U.S. pursuit of democratic enlargement. The changing distribution and composition of power described in chapter 1 also prompted the ascension of democratic enlargement to the forefront as a means of staving off some of the greater fears of a world fragmented along multipolar lines and characterized by new power relations. Writing in 1995 then Secretary of State Warren Christopher asserted that "we must support democracy and human rights to advance our interests and ideals."[4] Further, in outlining the benefits of democracy Christopher would note that

[d]emocratic nations are far less likely to go to war with each other and far more likely to respect international law. They are more likely to promote open markets and free trade, and to pursue policies that lead to sustained economic development. Democratic nations are critical to building a world where long-term stability is strengthened by accountable governments, not weakened by dictatorships; a world where disputes are mediated by dialogue, not by repression and violence; where information flows freely; and where the rule of law protects prosperity, contracts, patents, and the other essential elements of free-market economies.[5]

In the identification of these specific benefits Secretary Christopher was influenced by the burgeoning consensus among American academics concerning the advantages of wider democratization, as were others in the administration.[6] From this intellectual congruence, advocates of democracy concluded that if more democracies could be nurtured and developed around the globe many of the security problems of the United States and other countries would wither away. This led to the view of democracy as synonymous with peace and to the conclusion that democratic enlargement was the proper response to minimize the security threat from developing "zones of turmoil" thought to characterize many of the nations described in chapter 1 as members of the "second tier."

This view was also coupled with arguments that free markets and democracy formed a symbiotic and reciprocal relationship that produced free, stable, and prosperous societies. The contention was that the development of a free market for economic decisions would lay the groundwork for a free market for ideas and ultimately democracy. What was important, from the U.S. perspective, was that the existence of one increased the probability of the existence of the other, and that both produced benefits for the United States.

Following the end of the cold war, the decision by the Bush and Clinton administrations to pursue the enlargement of the democratic community can be viewed almost as an instinctive and involuntary reversion to the very core values of America. The *liberal, democratic, universalist* cultural characteristics described in chapter 1 molded the decision to promote democratization not just as a means for pursuing broadly defined international security interests but also as a means for satisfying societal demands. From the time of the founding, Americans have viewed themselves and their mode of government in a special light. The Winthropian metaphor of America as a shining "City upon a Hill" has held great meaning for countless Americans throughout time.

In what is perhaps the most famous dictum in the history of American foreign policy, President Woodrow Wilson argued that the primary aim of the United States during and after World War I was to make the world "safe for democracy." Similarly, in response to the query "If the United States had never existed, what would be the status in world affairs of democracy today?" Tony Smith responded, "We can have no confidence that, without the United States, democracy would have survived."[7] This leads Smith to argue that the promotion of democracy in the post–cold war world is "America's Mission."

America's history, however, has also created another cultural value that has long permeated society, that of staying out of the affairs of others. Isolationists sentiments are not something exogenous to the U.S. character; they are as natural and instinctual as any value. Yet, for many internationalists who were convinced of the necessity of continued U.S. leadership after the cold war this isolationist impulse was the one part of the American character that was to be most feared. If this meant remedial action was necessary to combat such isolationism then it was endorsed.

In fact, through the last two years of the Bush administration, references were increasingly made about the promotion of democracy as a way of reorganizing domestic consensus and enabling the United States to continue to pursue world order. The new Clinton administration would share this anxiety about neoisolationist tendencies on the part of the American public. In a series of speeches in the fall of 1993 by President Clinton, Secretary Christopher, National Security Adviser Anthony Lake and U.N. Ambassador Madeleine Albright that outlined the doctrine of engagement and enlargement, reference was commonly made to the loss of consensus and the fear of U.S. withdrawal from the world stage. As Lake put it a "disquieting rise in nativist, protectionist, and isolationist voices" in America threatened the ability of the United States to take advantage of the "vast, new opportunities" in the developing world.[8] Thus, it was necessary to develop a foreign policy framework that clearly explained to the American public the opportunities available to the United States after the end of the cold war while simultaneously devising a strategy that would appeal to American values. The solution, as perceived at the time, was a policy designed to enlarge the community of market democracies.

Thus, one of the most important reasons for the identification of a policy of the enlargement of democracy was as a means for rebuilding a foreign policy consensus among internationalists that could withstand a countervailing sentiment for returning to America's isolationist roots. Yet, to meld together these internationalists required a policy that promoted the values liberals cherished while pursuing the national interest that conservatives identified. Many conservative internationalists accepted the basic thesis that democracies rarely go to war with each other. This lead them to advocate democracy's spread because democracies are friendlier, more peaceful, and ultimately create fewer security problems for the United States. Many liberal internationalists, while accepting the view of democratization as consistent with the national interest, further justified such a policy on grounds of moralism or responsibility. These supporters, such as Ben Wattenberg, argued that America is duty-bound to follow its twentieth century visionary, Woodrow Wilson, by "waging democracy first-class."[9]

Yet, the impulses of internationalism and isolationism have long meant that any foreign policy effort risked encountering ambivalence from the American public. This reservation has constrained the amount of effort devoted to any policy. Moreover, this ambivalence has meant that successful results are necessary to sustain the foreign policy effort. Further, this lack of a firm consensus also meant that institutional actors in the foreign policy realm were also more likely to take up the invitation to struggle.

### The Formulation of Policy amid Shifting Constellations

The backdrop for the enlargement strategy included a series of efforts in support of democracy undertaken by the Bush administration. Coupled with movements toward democracy around the globe, the end of the cold war led the Bush administration to identify democratization as a key foreign policy goal. The White House, conditioned by the societal setting and in reaction to the changing international setting, took the lead in forging this agenda.

Throughout his tenure, President Bush would take numerous actions indicative of his support for democracy. These actions included: the December 1989 U.S. invasion of Panama to remove a military regime that was viewed as the only impediment to Panamanian democracy; the December 1989 threat of U.S. air power to defend the Aquino presidency against an attempted coup in the Philippines; endorsement of the Support for East European Democracy (SEED) Act (authorizing aid to Poland and Hungary, and then other East European countries in 1990 to "promote political democracy and economic pluralism" in recipient nations); endorsement of the FREEDOM Support Act of 1992 (geared toward providing assistance for the strengthening of a panoply of liberal democratic norms and institutions in the newly independent states of the former Soviet Union);[10] an Agency for International Development-led "Democracy Initiative"; pressure on the Organization of American States (OAS) to adopt Resolution 1080, which pledged democracies in the Western Hemisphere to act jointly in the case of an interruption of the democratic process in a member state.[11]

These events were also precursors of things to come. Yet, the level of support by the U.S. government for democratization should not be overstated. Even during the Bush administration, U.S. democratization policy would be forced to compete with other interests on the executive branch foreign policy agenda and would increasingly be caught up in a battle between the White House and an emboldened Congress over control of foreign policy.

*Engagement and Enlargement: The Clinton Effort of 1993–1994*
Following six months of relative inattention to foreign policy, the Clinton administration eventually elevated democracy promotion to the forefront of its policy effort. According to a recent account, in the summer of 1993, the administration began a "Kennan Sweepstakes" to devise "a strategic vision with an accompanying catch phrase."[12] Under the leadership of National Security Adviser Anthony Lake and the NSC staff, the White House developed a "strategy of enlargement" to replace the containment strategy that had guided the United States through the cold war. This term—which was offered by NSC staff member Jeremy Rosner—rested on four points: strengthening existing market democracies; consolidating new market democracies; containing aggressor states and encouraging their shift toward market democracy; and promoting market democracy in areas of great humanitarian turmoil.[13] This initiative was launched in a series of speeches by President Clinton and his top foreign policy advisers in September 1993.

In the public relations campaign that followed, President Clinton and his top foreign policy advisers laid out this vision for the engagement and enlargement of the world's democratic community as a means for also promoting U.S. security and economic prosperity. In this campaign, the Clinton administration very clearly attempted to use the informal powers of the presidency to set the foreign policy agenda for both the Congress and the American public. This White House leadership met with a good measure of success in setting the terms of debate throughout the first two years of the Clinton presidency as many executive officials, leaders in Congress, and a host of writers on foreign policy in both the academic and more general press engaged in a great debate over this issue. With the July 1994 release of the "National Security Strategy of Engagement and Enlargement" document it became even more obvious that democratization was a central pillar of Clinton's foreign policy.

The Clinton administration took additional steps to promote this agenda. The selection of adamant supporters of democratization to fill important positions in the foreign policy bureaucracy was an indication that Clinton meant to exert control over specific departments and agencies that would play an important role in his enlargement strategy. For example, in selecting Brian Atwood to head the United States Agency for International Development (USAID), Clinton tapped someone with experience in democracy promotion. Reflecting his background as head of the National Democratic Institute for International Affairs, a private institute primarily charged with promoting democracy abroad, Atwood made democracy promotion one of the four primary goals of USAID's strategy of promoting sustainable development.[14] The selection of Morton Halperin for the newly-created position of assistant secretary for democracy and peacekeeping within the Department of Defense also demonstrated this emphasis. In an article written prior to being nominated for this position Halperin argued that "when a people attempts to hold free elections and establish a constitutional democracy, the United States and the international community should not only assist but should 'guarantee' the result."[15]

Still, perhaps President Clinton's most important contribution to democratization was his effort to institutionalize the promotion of democracy. This effort included the creation within the State Department of deputy assistant secretary of state positions for the promotion of democracy within each regional bureau, the renaming of the Bureau of Human Rights and Humanitarian Affairs of the State Department as the Bureau for Democracy, Human Rights, and Labor, and the creation of the Center for Democracy and Governance within the United States Agency for International Development (USAID). Other steps were also taken to promote interagency coordination, although these efforts seemed to have accomplished little more than preventing turf wars.[16]

Additionally, in February 1994, the administration submitted a plan for overhauling the foreign aid laws. The intent of this rewrite was to shift emphasis away from traditional country-to-country aid programs toward the pursuit of more broadly defined categories of foreign policy goals. Included in the six goals identified in the proposed legislation was promoting democracy. The argument made in support of this new legislation was that it would strip away much of the specific and arcane regulations placed on USAID, thereby allowing the foreign aid programs greater flexibility to respond to shifting needs while also adjusting to the continued decline in foreign aid funding. Long criticized for its numerous statutory requirements, the 1961 Foreign Assistance Act with all of its amendments became a vehicle for promoting individual legislator's and interest group's parochial interests. The process of earmarking most of the foreign assistance budget was problematic in the eyes of the executive branch during most of the preceding decades, but, with the mid-1990s curtailment of funding exceeding the curtailment of earmarking, the problem had become acute, thus making greater flexibility more necessary.

In sum, these Clinton administration efforts can be viewed as an attempt on the part of the White House to take control of the foreign policy agenda concerning democracy promotion. The public relations campaign was designed to garner support among the American public and Congress for this goal. The reorientation of sectors of the executive branch and the placing of democratization supporters in important positions was designed to insure that Clinton's enlargement agenda would be implemented, at least in part. Last, the effort to rewrite foreign aid laws allowing USAID greater control was clearly an attempt to reduce congressional influence over foreign policy. Yet, as with most efforts in the federal government to wrest power from other actors these actions were resisted.

Almost from the outset, the Clinton administration faced a Congress hesitant about following his lead in foreign policy. Almost every attempt of Clinton's to steer foreign policy toward promoting democracy was resisted. Following the nomination of Halperin for assistant secretary of defense for democracy and peacekeeping, many of the more conservative Republican senators began a campaign to prevent his confirmation. Owing to Halperin's background as a former member of President Nixon's Defense Department and National Security Council staff who had resigned in protest over the U.S. invasion of Cambodia, his denunciation of Nixon-Kissinger wiretaps of NSC officials, and his outspoken criticism of U.S. actions concerning the general policy of the Vietnam war and of intelligence agency covert activities, these conservative senators would brand Halperin untrustworthy and a threat to national security. Finally, after confrontational hearings in November 1993 and other indications that his nomination would not be confirmed Halperin withdrew his name in early 1994.[17]

The Clinton administration's effort to reform foreign assistance legislation also met with opposition, this time led by members of his own party. In the period surrounding the presentation of the February 1994 proposed rewrite of the foreign aid bill, the administration lobbied heavily for its adoption. As the year went on, however, President Clinton, Secretary Christopher, and other top members of the administration became distracted by domestic concerns such as health care reform and foreign policy crises, such as those surrounding Bosnia, Haiti, and North Korea. This situation left the lobbying effort primarily to USAID, one of the executive branch agencies least respected on Capitol Hill.[18]

The attempt to eliminate earmarks in the legislation, to strip the bill of specific prohibitions, and to orient aid away from country programs toward broad categorical objectives met with hostility as individuals and small groups of members fought to protect their pet projects. Indicative of the response to many of the proposed initiatives was the reaction to the elimination of the Development Fund for Africa, a program designed to promote economic reform in African countries. This proposal was resisted by the Congressional Black Caucus. As Congressman Donald M. Payne (D-N.J.) said, "We feel that the administration is turning its back on an area that should get more consideration."[19] In more generic terms, this reform effort was seen as an attempt to reduce congressional control over foreign policy. Summarizing the view of many in Congress, David Obey, the chairman of the House Appropriations Foreign Operations Subcommittee (which had become the most important subcommittee overseeing foreign assistance) remarked that "[w]e will not give to an unelected bureaucracy federal authority to spend dollars any way they want, so long as they call it 'pursuit of democracy' or 'expanding economic development'. There will be no blank check."[20] Due to this resistance by many in the Democratic party, and also to a crowded congressional calendar, little serious action was taken on the Clinton initiative and the legislation died at the end of Congress.

Another issue illustrating the hesitance and growing antipathy about democracy promotion was the 1993 struggle over funding for the National Endowment for Democracy (NED). Born in fiscal year 1984 with an appropriation of $18 million, the NED was the culmination of several years of thinking by labor union leaders, business leaders, and members of the major political parties, and based on the recommendation of the American Political Foundation that a publicly funded, but privately administered development foundation was advantageous for promoting democracy abroad. The Clinton administration, valuing the work of the NED, sought funding for fiscal 1994 of $50 million, an increase from $30 million in fiscal 1993. In the House of Representatives, however, an amendment to kill the NED entirely was added to the State Department authorization bill. In the Senate, the proposed budget was trimmed to $35 million. After an extended conference and further discussion in the House a final appropriation of $35 million was made. Yet, divisions over this issue exemplified the growing disenchantment with democracy promotion.

The NED came under fire from many quarters, including the left-leaning publication *The Nation*, the conservative Cato Institute, moderate Democratic Senator Dale Bumpers (D-Ark.), conservative Senator Hank Brown (R-Colo.), and an overwhelming majority of House freshmen from both parties. For some, the NED was viewed as a meddlesome private entity conducting U.S. foreign policy with taxpayers' funds. This, essentially, was Senator Bumpers's criticism of the NED, which he accused of trying to undermine President Arias of Costa Rica in 1990. In Senator Bumpers's words, Arias was "the only sane voice" at the time in Central America.[21] Other critics charged that this private entity was ineffective and had wasted taxpayer funds. Noting that most of the NED funds were then awarded to private foundations affiliated with the Democratic and Republican parties, the Chamber of Commerce, and the AFL-CIO, Senator Brown contended that the NED was little more than a slush fund. In his words, "To talk about this as a debate about democracy is absurd. This is special treatment for the big boys."[22] For others, criticism of the NED was motivated more by a concern for cutting perceived unnecessary expenditures during a budgetary crisis. These criticisms, coupled with the lack of standing ties to the NED and its grantee foundations, led many of the freshman House members to vote against the program. Said first-term representative Marjorie Margolies-Mezvinsky (D-Pa.), the NED "was an idea whose time had come and gone."[23]

In sum, the attempt to kill the NED, the resistance to the rewriting of the foreign aid bill, and the refusal to confirm the Halperin nomination were indicative of the institutional competition that developed over many of the specifics of democracy promotion. While many reasons existed for this conflict, two deserve special mention. Using data taken from various Chicago Council of Foreign Relations surveys, table 10.1 displays the level of support among the general public and among foreign policy leaders for the goal of "helping to bring a democratic form of government to other nations." The percentages are those who responded "very important." In each of the years this goal ranked lowest or next to lowest for both the public and leaders. What is even more striking is that the level of support went down from 1990 to 1994 despite, or in relation to, the Clinton effort to fashion democratic en-

Table 10.1   Support for Promoting Democracy Abroad

| % responding Very Important to "Helping to Bring a Democratic Form of Government to other Nations" | 1982 | 1986 | 1990 | 1994 |
|---|---|---|---|---|
| Public | 26 | 30 | 28 | 25 |
| Leaders | 15 | 29 | 26 | 21 |

*Source:* Chicago Council of Foreign Relations.

largement as a central pillar of his foreign policy. Although the White House attempted to use its power of persuasion to rally support for its enlargement effort, it clearly met with limited success. This failure to rally the general public made it easier for the Congress to challenge White House leadership.

Further, this failure was compounded by the lack of sustained leadership from the White House in the effort to rewrite the foreign assistance legislation. Although foreign aid is never popular, and certainly is less so in an election year, the Clinton administration was backed by Democratic majorities in both Houses and showed enough willingness to compromise to entice several Republicans to line up in support of the rewrite. Yet, the legislation withered because of lack of support from the Democratic leadership in Congress and in the White House. Still, in this era, President Clinton and his program for enlarging democracy did achieve several successes. With the congressional elections of November 1994, the apogee of the policy of democratic enlargement seemed to pass.

### Divided Government: 1995–1996
In the third and fourth years of the Clinton administration, the policy of democratic enlargement met a different fortune. The new, Republican-controlled Congress rejected the basic premise that the chief executive was the symbolic leader of the American public, and set its sights on slashing much of the international affairs expenditures. In addition to the indirect challenge from Congress, enlargement also found its primacy slipping in the White House. In sum, the result was a deemphasis on democracy almost by default—the debate was not so much over the actual policy of enlargement, but at controlling the very sweep of foreign policy.

Many of the new Republican House members elected in 1994 carried an enmity toward all things associated with President Clinton. Following the Clinton administration's 1993 campaign promoting democratic enlargement, it was only natural that the congressional effort to redefine America's foreign policy agenda did not take special steps to exempt democratization. During the 1995 debates over the provision of fiscal 1996 funding for international affairs programs, almost all departments and agencies faced cuts. Foreign assistance, the NED, the United States Information Agency (USIA), and the general budget for the State Department were all slashed. In this effort, Congress issued no specific instructions identifying democratization programs as distinct. Hence, democracy promotion typically absorbed the 10 percent to 20 percent cuts aimed at general foreign policy.

In addition to anti-Clintonism, the motivation for this congressional resurgence was also related to the Republican-held belief that they were more in touch with the wishes of the American public. In many instances, believing deeply that the congressional victories in November 1994 were a mandate to pursue their vision, this new Congress set out to right what they perceived as a listing ship. Among the most important steps was the placing of domestic needs ahead of foreign policy wants. This meant not only diverting resources from foreign affairs, but also being less supportive of free trade, favoring less U.S. involvement in the United Nations, and restricting action in other foreign affairs realms. And in many ways this new congressional attitude was reflective of the American public which has long been hesitant to support foreign assistance efforts, agreeing to a large extent with Senator Jesse Helms (R-N.C.) that most foreign aid is poured down a "rathole." Efforts to promote democracy abroad were seen in a similar light. Public opinion polls evince the fact that Americans had not rallied around democratization as the guiding principle for foreign policy. Without broad societal support the likelihood of derailment by other players in the shifting constellations increased.

The White House therefore adapted its strategy to the domestic climate. This resulted in three key adjustments to the strategy of enlargement. First, consistent with polls that indicated the public liked to hear about the merits of democracy, even while it was unwilling to commit resources to its promotion and establishment, the administration ceased to push its strategy and opted to rely on rhetoric praising democracy and those states opting for it. Simply put, much of the public effort to establish a democratization strategy was jettisoned. Of course, this occurred in part because the Congress was unwilling to go along, and because other issues occupied center stage.

Second, the administration seemed to shift its emphasis to market promotion rather than democracy promotion per se. As a consequence, administration efforts focused mainly on expanding U.S. economic relations with a series of countries it deemed particularly promising for their potential to contribute to U.S. economic expansion. This refocusing on U.S. economic interests was substantially more defensible in Congress and the public. The predominance of economic issues was best exhibited by Clinton's handling of most-favored-nation (MFN) status with China and the U.S. reluctance to speak out against Indonesian human rights violations. With the 1994 decision to renew China's MFN status and to separate its renewal from human rights and democracy concerns the U.S. "sent a signal to other countries that they could hang tough on U.S. demands for participatory democracy and still benefit from American investment."[24] Following Secretary Christopher's eight-day trip to Asia in the summer of 1995, an American official who accompanied him remarked: "At the beginning of this administration, there were two key goals of U.S. foreign policy: promoting trade and promoting human rights; unfortunately, one goal often completely contradicted the other."[25]

Hence, although the Clinton administration identified democratic enlargement as one of the pillars of its foreign policy, there was no requirement that each pillar sustain an equal amount of weight. Writing in 1995, Secretary of State Warren Christopher noted that the support of democracy and human rights was one of the four principles of present foreign policy. As quoted earlier, he also expounded on the benefits to the United States of the enlargement of democracy. Yet, in surveying the areas of foreign policy opportunities for 1995, Secretary Christopher made only scant and indirect references to the opportunities for promoting democracy.[26] This suggested that the administration was not willing to place democratization above other goals. As one USAID official remarked, there was "still a cold war, geostrategic mentality where security and economic issues predominate."[27]

Third, despite the controversy swirling around the struggles between the White House and the Congress to control the foreign policy agenda and within the executive branch over prioritizing the importance of democratization, the formulation and implementation of specific policies designed to promote democracy continued. However, those efforts took on a lower profile—an almost "underground" approach. Although specific agencies within the executive branch increasingly faced tightened spending limits they continued to modify and refine democratization policy, chiefly relying on their control over the implementation

Table 10.2   USAID Objectives and Major Strategies, 1991–1995

| | | | | |
|---|---|---|---|---|
| 1991 | *Support Respect For Human Rights*<br>promote basic human rights | *Strengthen Democratic Representation*<br>elections and electoral systems<br>strengthen legislative institutions<br>strengthen local government<br>free flow of information | *Promote Lawful Governance*<br>legal and judicial reform<br>accountability of executive branch<br>reduce role of military | *Encourage Democratic Values*<br>civic education<br>leadership training |
| 1993 | *Strengthen Fundamental Rights*<br>promote basic human rights<br>legal and judicial reform | *Improve Representative Process for Resolving Conflicts*<br>elections and electoral systems<br>strengthen legislative institutions<br>strengthen local government<br>accountability of executive branch | | *Improve Democratic Environment*<br>reduce role of military |
| 1994 | *Strengthen Rule of Law and Human Rights*<br>promote basic human rights<br>legal and judicial reform | *Citizen Participation in Competitive Politics*<br>elections and electoral systems<br>strengthen legislative institutions | *More Accountable Governance*<br>accountability of executive branch<br>strengthen local government<br>reduce role of military | *Promote Active Civil Society*<br>free flow of information<br>civil associations |
| 1995 | *Strengthen Rule of Law and Human Rights*<br>promote basic human rights<br>legal and judicial reform | *Promote Competitive, Free, Fair Elections*<br>elections and electoral systems | *Foster Transparent/Accountable Government*<br>accountability of executive branch<br>strengthen legislative institutions<br>strengthen local government<br>civic education<br>reduce role of military | *Promote Active Civil Society*<br>free flow of information<br>civil associations |

Objectives are indicated in italics.
*Source:* Information compiled from various years of U.S. Agency for International Development, *Annual Program and Performance Report.*

of policy. While this has not occurred uniformly (and has been largely ignored by some agencies, including those of the "economic complex" discussed in chapter 4), this more low-key effort is clearly seen in the work of the Agency for International Development.

*Promoting Democracy outside the Public Eye: A Focus on USAID*
The U.S. Agency for International Development, like other parts of the executive branch, felt the attempts of the Clinton administration to make the promotion of democracy a more important part of U.S. foreign policy. Under the guidance of Brian Atwood, USAID elevated democratization to one of the four pillars of the agency strategy for sustainable development. Approved in 1995, this strategy for sustainable development reflected USAID's belief that long-term economic and social advancement depends on meeting four basic requirements: economic sustainability, demographic sustainability, environmental sustainability, and democratic sustainability. According to USAID, democratic sustainability means: "All members of a society must be able to participate in economic and political activity, contribute to decisions affecting their lives and be assured of equal protection under law. Exclusion of particular groups on the basis of social class, ethnicity, or gender is inherently destructive."[28]

The roots of USAID's vision of democratization extend back to December 1990 when they began a "Democracy Initiative." This initiative evolved over time through a series of objectives and strategies as shown in table 10.2.[29] As this table suggests, USAID's basic ideas of the building blocks of sustainable democracy have been packaged and repackaged so that, by 1995, four basic objectives had come into focus that more clearly reflected the fundamental goals of U.S. efforts to promote democracy. In the process, the strategies grouped under each heading came to have more in common. For instance, those programs designed to promote structural reforms and institutional strengthening came to be grouped under one objective, fostering transparent and accountable government.

In the eyes of many observers, free and fair elections are a primary benchmark of democracy. Elections, especially the first and second elections in a new democracy, are more likely to garner the attention of the world media and with it the attention of casual supporters of democratization in the United States. This interest carries with it both a positive and a negative side. Because of the deep-seated understanding of the importance of elections to democracy, Americans are very likely to be supportive of efforts to ensure their fairness. Further, funding for electoral processes developed as a corollary to U.S. efforts to promote human rights in other countries. In 1982 the El Salvadoran elections were one of the first instances where USAID was called upon to provide technical support (voter rolls, ballots, indelible inks for stamping voters' hands) for ensuring a fair election.[30] Following this effort, USAID ventured into other countries in support of elections and eventually USAID efforts to promote free and fair elections evolved into a stand-alone mission. By 1995, emphasis was still placed on providing advice concerning the legal and administrative framework for elections, on educating voters about the electoral process and the necessity to vote, and on the training of election monitors as a means of increasing the pressure for free and fair elections. The outcome of such elections is the enhancement of legitimacy of the political system. Additionally, under this category USAID was involved in enhancing the ability of political parties to be viable, competitive representatives of their constituents.

Yet, this extreme focus on elections would distract from efforts to promote the other objectives of democratization. Elections can be viewed as just a preliminary act in the effort to build sustainable democracy. The more important aspects of deepening democracy came after the election, when the new government was challenged to fulfill the promises of democracy. In the opinion of one USAID official, elections, although important as the signal event of democracy, were a distraction from the ongoing effort to promote democracy.[31] Their irregular nature tended to divert financial and other resources from endeavors aimed at sustainable democracy.

The second area of USAID actions was aimed at promoting the rule of law. One of the problems that became increasingly evident in many Latin American countries following democratic elections during the 1980s and early 1990s was the inability of civilian governments to hold accountable for crimes all elements of society, including former military officials and members of the aristocracy. Thus, in order to prevent the undermining of the new democratic regimes it became necessary for USAID to concentrate on the promotion of the administration of justice. By 1993 a host of programs had been launched that were aimed at the depoliticization and professionalization of the police force and the judiciary. To accomplish this, USAID provided support for the establishment of public prosecutors and public defenders offices as well as jury trials and constitutional reforms that protect the civil rights of citizens. This effort at the administration of justice was joined by programs to promote human rights to encompass an objective often referred to as rule of law. As indicated by the budget figures in table 10.3, rule of law

Table 10.3   USAID Democracy Obligations by Objective and Region, FY 1995

| Bureau | ELECTORAL PROCESSES Total | % | RULE OF LAW Total | % | GOVER- NANCE Total | % | CIVIL SOCIETY Total | % | Total |
|---|---|---|---|---|---|---|---|---|---|
| Africa | 15,894 | 19 | 12,661 | 15 | 12,667 | 15 | 43,463 | 51 | 84,685 |
| Asia and the Near East | 440 | 1 | 8,925 | 22 | 13,603 | 33 | 18,175 | 44 | 41,143 |
| Eastern Europe and NIS | 2,484 | 2 | 26,701 | 17 | 76,297 | 49 | 50,727 | 32 | 156,209 |
| Latin America and the Caribbean | 13,433 | 12 | 48,135 | 42 | 34,160 | 30 | 19,528 | 17 | 115,256 |
| Global Bureau | 5,686 | 17 | 5,148 | 16 | 3,434 | 11 | 18,409 | 56 | 32,677 |
| Bureau for Humani- tarian Affairs | 0 | 0 | 0 | 0 | 1,184 | 100 | 0 | 0 | 1,184 |
| Program and Policy Coordination | 0 | 0 | 246 | 24 | 162 | 16 | 629 | 61 | 1,037 |
| Total | 37,937 | 9 | 101,816 | 24 | 141,507 | 33 | 150,931 | 35 | 432,191 |

All figures estimated USD thousands.
*Source:* U.S. Agency for International Development, Center for Development Information and Evaluation.

continued to garner a significant share of democratization spending in this region as late as 1995 (see also table 10.4). More recent thinking, however, indicated that perhaps USAID overemphasized rule of law in the pre-1995 era. This view holds that judicial reform can only occur to the extent that host governments are willing to allow it. In fact, the experiences of several Latin American countries seemed to show that excess spending garnered diminishing returns.[32] Thus, USAID began to downplay this category in favor of other objectives.

The third category of democratization efforts was devoted to the promotion of more accountable and transparent governments. Among the specific aims of programs in this area was improving the honesty and accountability of the executive branch by improving financial management and fighting corruption; the improvement of the material, technical, and decision-making capabilities of legislatures; assisting in downsizing the military, reintegrating its members into civilian society, and training civilians as military specialists to act as watchdogs; and the pro-

Table 10.4  USAID Obligations for Democracy, 1990–1996

| Bureau | 1990 | 1991 | 1992 | 1993 | 1994 | 1995 | 1996 |
|---|---|---|---|---|---|---|---|
| Africa | 5,329 | 30,570 | 55,330 | 72,289 | 103,240 | 84,685 | 77,815 |
| Asia and the Near East | 20,807 | 27,728 | 22,015 | 30,405 | 25,712 | 41,143 | 77,422 |
| Eastern Europe and NIS | | 22,037 | 43,117 | 68,595 | 156,353 | 156,209 | 147,906 |
| Latin America and the Caribbean | 73,864 | 83,506 | 101,257 | 132,819 | 75,580 | 115,256 | 75,342 |
| Global Bureau | 6,456 | 1,372 | 2,364 | 9,626 | 9,353 | 32,677 | 25,265 |
| Bureau for Humanitarian Affairs | | | 179 | 145 | 475 | 1,184 | 1,363 |
| Program and Policy Coordination | 910 | | 607 | 1,598 | 515 | 1,037 | 1,601 |
| Total | 107,366 | 165,213 | 224,869 | 315,477 | 371,228 | 432,191 | 406,714 |

All figures USD thousands; figures for 1995 are estimates, and figures for 1996 are based on FY 1996 Congressional Presentation.
*Source:* U.S. Agency for International Development, Center for Development Information and Evaluation.

motion of open hearings and the publication of public documents.[33] This focus on reforming political institutions was seen as one of the most important factors in assuring that the benefits of democracy were delivered to the citizens. Without effective, transparent, accountable governments, public confidence in democracy will erode. Anticorruption efforts were a good example of the evolution of this objective. At the time of Clinton's inauguration both USAID and many new democracies were ill-equipped and hesitant to combat corruption. Increasingly as democracy deepened in these countries and USAID grew more skilled and confident, increased emphasis was placed on rooting out corruption. As a part of this, USAID also promoted the decentralization and devolution of power to local and municipal governments on the supposition that such actions lead to more citizen participation and the emergence of new leaders in the political process. Ultimately, increased participation, new leaders, and dispersed power increase the range of political debate and the number of proposed solutions to problems while reducing the ability of a national government to turn to corruption or opt for repression.[34]

Finally, USAID would contend that "[a] strong and pluralistic *civil society* is an indispensable ingredient of democracy."[35] To this end USAID would fund projects aimed at promoting civil society that could be further divided into several strategic programs. Support for free, democratic labor unions were viewed as a means for increasing the organizational ability of actors that were often suppressed in the past and that stood as a check on state power. Further, efforts within this program to improve labor-management relations can pay dividends by decreasing the likelihood that ruling elites would view labor demands in zero-sum terms, thereby reducing one incentive for the displacement of democracy. Additional programs in this area included efforts to promote independent media outlets; educational programs that advocate community participation and encourage tolerance; support for professional associations, women's groups, and other indigenous nongovernmental organizations; and a host of other general civil society organizations.

The basic thrust of civil society programs was to promote citizenship. Writing in 1995, USAID's Bureau for Latin America and the Caribbean argued that

> Latin Americans need to become citizens who participate in the democratic process and transform democratic forms into democratic substance. Citizenship is a concept that challenges Latin American societies, which historically have subjugated individual rights to enable elites to maintain political and economic power. Latin Americans must act as citizens to ensure that government institutions become more transparent, decentralized, accountable, effective, and accessible. This civic consciousness can be developed through judicious selection of projects and other development activities that encourage participation, especially by women, indigenous peoples, ethnic minorities, and other groups that traditionally have been hindered from full participation.[36]

Over the life of the sustainable democracy effort, civil society was the objective that grew the most in stature. This growth in stature was associated with, and partially the result of, the influence of a reevaluation of civil society by academicians.[37] Over the last few years, civil society has increasingly been viewed as the key to promoting both governmental accountability and citizen participation.

Table 10.3 displays spending patterns across the four objectives for fiscal 1995. As is evident, USAID diversified its effort at building sustainable democracy. Indeed, the lowest funded area was electoral processes, and almost one-third of that spending was devoted to the Haitian elections. Increasing emphasis was placed on what can be referred to as second-generation efforts to promote democracy through the governance and civil society objectives. This diversification reflected a maturation over time of thinking about the promotion of democracy. The realization that increased levels of funding for administration of justice programs in Latin America outstripped the capacity and willingness to reform was just one example of a lesson learned. Increasingly, USAID would identify and understand that the democratization process goes through a series of stages and that specific programs were more likely to meet with success if coordinated with the proper stage. For instance, programs aimed at rooting out corruption were more likely to be successful in the later, consolidation stage of democracy than in the earlier transition stages.

Questions should be asked, however, about the effectiveness of these programs. Although USAID learned many lessons, it still did not identify, in the words of one USAID official, any "silver bullets" that always work. This USAID official contends that, following a 1995 conference analyzing legislative strengthening programs, no one walked away with a clear impression that specific ideas and programs work across the board. The solutions were still situation-specific.[38] This was a primary reason for the ad hoc appearance of USAID efforts. Specific strategies for achieving sustainable democracy were developed on an individual-country basis. Thus, the mix of programs targeted toward individual countries appeared to be muddled. Yet, the study of the process of democratization has yielded few cardinal rules. International democratization indeed appears to be a laboratory in which to experiment, that is *if* the United States wishes to continue experimenting.

### Conclusion: Democratization amid Shifting Constellations

Clearly, the policy of the enlargement of the democratic community did not replace containment as broad-based U.S. foreign policy. In spite of the fact that considerable agreement about the benefits of democratization existed across parties and among the elites and attentive public, this agreement was not as encompassing nor as deeply felt as containment, and it fell short of becoming a guiding light for restructuring and reorienting foreign policy. This shortcoming does not arise just from the hesitance of the American public, the distracted vision of Congress, or the lack of leadership from the Clinton White House. Despite the well-worn mantra of democratization's supporters concerning all the purported benefits, this was simply a policy goal that lacked the depth of national security interests and ideological appeal to form a consensus rivaling that which surrounded containment. This chapter, with its focus on the evolution of democratic enlargement as one of the pillars of American foreign policy in the post–cold war world, serves to highlight at least six important points about foreign policy making after the end of the cold war.

1. *Foreign policy consensus is as much the result of the international setting as it is of institutional actors.* The introductory chapter in this book depicts an image of shifting constellations among various domestic political actors struggling to enact or block policies. This image was accurate for the democratization effort. Although the White House played the largest role in identifying democratization as a leading foreign policy pillar, the responses from other actors within the political environment played an important role in the development and implementation of this policy. Congress would show increasing reluctance to fund democratization programs, the American public exhibited hesitance about rallying around this policy, and the White House traded a concern for democracy for economic security. Why, if there was a deeply held belief on the part of most in the mainstream of the Democratic and Republican parties that all of the benefits Secretary Christopher ascribed as resulting from democratization are true, did this policy fail to rally majority support from all the political actors in the constellation? The answer, at least in part, is located in the international setting and its interaction with the societal setting.

Recall that in 1947, it was only following the British decision to stop supporting the Greek government, then engaged in a struggle with communist rebels, that the United States agreed to initiate the Truman Doctrine. Further, without the expansionism of the Soviet Union and the growing intransigence in relations between the Soviets and Americans, it is not at all certain that the United States would have accepted an obligation in 1947–48 that it refused in 1919–20. Today, without similar pressure from the international environment to make difficult and lasting decisions concerning future foreign policy, each individual actor within the constellation is free to pursue its own end. The result: multiple policy objectives with only minority constituencies.

2. *Policies without the support of the public are susceptible to becoming contested areas within the shifting constellations of actors.* A lack of firm support among the American public, coupled with high visibility, increases the likelihood that struggles within and between branches of government for control of policy will occur. In the case of the enlargement of democracy the Clinton administration's decision to

place this issue at the forefront of its foreign policy meant that it met with more circumspection than other policies. When public support failed to materialize for this endeavor in 1993–94, it meant that elements within the Democratic Party were free to challenge White House leadership on this issue, even if the challenges were focused on the specifics. With the change in control of Congress, however, the challenge to democratization, as the challenge to almost all of foreign policy, would be characterized by President Clinton as "nothing less than a frontal assault on the authority of the President."[39] Yet, without the public's ambivalence, the willingness to challenge would not have been so keen.

3. *Absent the necessity of bowing to White House leadership, Congress will seek to maintain and expand its influence.* During the early part of the cold war, foreign policy was characterized as consensual, in part, because of congressional deference to executive leadership. The fear of the Soviet Union and the crisis mentality that gripped the United States meant that most in Congress acquiesced to surrendering authority to the White House. Following Vietnam this would change. With the end of the cold war, the willingness of Congress to challenge, even the most prominent president-led issues, seemed to have increased. During 1993–1994, congressional Democrats led the assault on Clinton's democratization effort. The new Republican Congress took even more initiative. In all of these battles the standard congressional argument was that they, more so than an unelected bureaucracy or a minority president, knew what was in the best interest of the United States.

4. *New policies may originate in one institutional actor but evolve in other institutional actors.* The decisions in both the Bush and early Clinton White House to focus on democratization led several actors within the executive branch to adopt enlargement as one of their goals. USAID, USIA, the State Department, the Defense Department, and the Justice Department all developed programs designed to promote democracy abroad. The executive branch had only moderate success coordinating efforts across these departments. Indeed as a GAO report notes "there is no central U.S. government-wide democracy program, no overall statement of U.S. policy regarding U.S. objectives and strategy for democratic development, no specific and common definition of what constitutes a democracy program, and no specificity regarding the roles of foreign affairs and defense agencies in promoting democratic processes."[40] After the 1994 congressional elections coordination and direction from the White House or any other single source became less likely. Yet democratization policy was not forced to a standstill. Individual actors, as exemplified by USAID, adjusted their policies according to an

evolving conception of democracy and its requisites. Many of the details of policy formulation and implementation are addressed at the agency level, and this bureaucratic leadership at this level of policy making continued despite the struggles between the White House and Congress.

*5. New policies require presidential leadership.* The most important actor in developing new foreign policies that require a concerted and coordinated effort to be successful is still the White House. Although governmental funding for democratization policy is the lifeblood of the effort, only the president can give adequate voice to the endeavor. The lack of an overall statement of U.S. policy regarding U.S. objectives and strategy for democratic development, the failure of democratization to not be considered more important by top officials in the executive branch, and the degree of reluctance shown by Congress and the American public to support this policy are directly linked to the president. Although presidents cannot force policies to be embraced by all, they can alter the decision calculus through the formal and informal powers of their office.

*6. The ability of presidents to lead has been diminished.* Although it is my argument that the nature of the dyadic relations between the Office of the President and the other major foreign policy actors has changed only in degree, the interaction of these adjustments have potentially led to a change in kind concerning foreign policy making. The basic facts of this case, as they point to impediments and outright challenges to the enlargement strategy are really not new. Since at least the Nixon era, Congress has shown a substantial willingness to challenge presidential preeminence in foreign policy. The opposition from both the Democratic and Republican-led Congresses to Clinton's enlargement strategy was not unique. Neither was the hesitance of the American public to support such policies. Yet, the whole of these developments, coupled with the fundamental changes in the international system, potentially led foreign policy through a change in phase of matter.

If one accepts, at least in part, Fukuyama's "end of history" thesis, one can believe that presidents have been provided with unique opportunities for creative foreign policy making now that they are no longer bound by rigid cold war ideological thinking.[41] Yet, a fractured policy-making process coupled with the acceptance, even if unwitting, of many in the United States that the "end of history" means that the major foreign policy challenges are resolved and all that remains is the sorting out of the victory leads to an even more restrictive policy-making environment. In short, although constraints on creative thinking may have been removed, the shackles that accompany this victory are even more encumbering, at least from the perspective of the president. The implications of this changed policy environment point to an increased emphasis on consensual policy making. Ironically, in addition to allowing the enlargement of the global democratic community, the end of the cold war has also led to the increased "democratization" of U.S. foreign policy.

## Notes

1  Anthony Lake, "From Containment to Enlargement," *Dispatch* 4, no. 39 (1993): 659.

2  But see Douglas Brinkley, "Democratic Enlargement: The Clinton Doctrine," *Foreign Policy* 106 (Spring 1997): 111–127, who argues that the strategy of enlargement remains at the heart of the Clinton administration's foreign policy.

3  Samuel P. Huntington, "Democracy's Third Wave," in Larry Diamond and Marc F. Plattner, ed., *The Global Resurgence of Democracy* (Baltimore, Md.: Johns Hopkins University Press, 1993).

4  Warren Christopher, "America's Leadership, America's Opportunity," *Foreign Policy* 98 (Spring, 1995): 8.

5  Christopher, "America's Leadership," p. 15.

6  See Larry Diamond, "Promoting Democracy," *Foreign Policy* 87 (Summer 1992): 30–31, for a similarly identified list of advantages of democracy.

7  Tony Smith, *America's Mission: The United States and the Worldwide Struggle for Democracy in the Twentieth Century* (Princeton, N.J.: Princeton University Press, 1994), p. 9.

8  Anthony Lake, "A Strategy of Enlargement and the Developing World," *Dispatch* 4, no. 43 (1993): 748.

9  Quoted in Paul E. Gottfried, "Sovereign State at Bay," *Society* (September/October 1992): 24–25.

10 United States General Accounting Office, *Promoting Democracy: Foreign Affairs and Defense Agencies Funds and Activities, 1991 to 1993* (Washington, D.C.: GAO, 1994).

11 Strobe Talbott, "Democracy and the National Interest," *Foreign Affairs* 75, no. 6 (November/December 1996): 53.

12 Brinkley, "Democratic Enlargement," p. 114.

13 See, for example, Lake, "From Containment to Enlargement." On the development of the "vision," see Brinkley, "Democratic Enlargement."

14 Thomas Carothers, "Democracy Promotion under Clinton," *Washington Quarterly* 18 (Autumn 1995): 20.

15 Morton H. Halperin, "Guaranteeing Democracy," *Foreign Policy* 91 (Summer 1993): 105.

16 Carothers, "Democracy Promotion under Clinton," pp. 19–20.

17 Underneath the personal dynamics involved in this case was a more substantive issue. This new position was designed to oversee U.S. involvement in interna-

tional peacekeeping efforts. The Bush administration's talk of a new world order, the then occurring nation-building effort in Somalia, and this new Clinton rhetoric of enlarging democracy led many in Washington to see this assistant secretary position as a further attempt to expand the role of the United States in United Nations.

18  "Foreign Aid Reform Plan Scrapped," *Congressional Quarterly Almanac* (1994), p. 452.

19  "Foreign Aid Reform Plan Scrapped," p. 453.

20  "Foreign Aid Reform Plan Scrapped," p. 453.

21  Elizabeth Palmer, "Slush Fund vs. Path to Freedom: A Fight over Democracy Fund," *Congressional Quarterly Weekly Report* 51, no. 40 (October 9, 1993): 2760.

22  "Slush Fund," p. 2759.

23  "Slush Fund," p. 2759.

24  Michael Dobbs, "U.S. Shifts Goals in Markets of Asia: Failing to Sell Its Brand of Democracy American Now Promotes Its Merchandise," *Washington Post*, 9 August 1995, p. A:14.

25  Dobbs, "U.S. Shifts Goals," p. A:14.

26  Christopher, "America's Leadership, America's Opportunity."

27  Author interview with USAID official, Center for Democracy and Governance, December 12, 1996.

28  U.S. Agency for International Development. *The Strategic Role of U.S. Assistance in the Americas* (Washington, D.C.: USAID, 1995), p. 2.

29  The table ends in 1995 because the 1996 annual review had not been published at the time this chapter was written. Other USAID documents from 1996 indicate that no changes in the 1995 objectives have occurred.

30  Joshua Muravchik, *Exporting Democracy: Fulfilling America's Destiny* (Washington, D.C.: AEI Press, 1992), pp. 182–83.

31  Author interview with USAID official, Bureau for Latin America and the Caribbean, December 12, 1996.

32  Author interview with USAID official, Center for Democracy and Governance, December 12, 1996.

33  U.S. Agency for International Development, *Annual Report on Program and Performance* (Washington, D.C.: USAID, 1995).

34  Author interviews with USAID officials, Bureau for Latin America and the Caribbean, March 16, 1995; December 12, 1996.

35  U.S. Agency for International Development, *The A.I.D./Latin American and Caribbean Bureau Democratic Initiatives Program* (Washington, D.C.: USAID, 1993), p. 3.

36  U.S. Agency for International Development, *The Strategic Role of U.S. Assistance in the Americas*, p. 13.

37  See Larry Diamond, "Toward Democratic Consolidation," *Journal of Democracy* 5 (1994), pp. 4–17; and Michael W. Foley and Bob Edwards, "The Paradox of Civil Society." *Journal of Democracy* 7 (1996), pp. 38–52, for a further discussion of the benefits of civil society.

38  Author interview with USAID official, Bureau for Latin America and the Caribbean, December 12, 1996.

39  Editorial, *New York Times*, May 25, 1995, p. A28.

40  United States General Accounting Office, *Promoting Democracy: Foreign Affairs and Defense Agencies Funds and Activities, 1991 to 1993* (Washington, D.C.: GAO, 1994).

41  See Francis Fukuyama, "The End of History?" *National Interest* 16 (1989): 3–18.

## 11.

## Between a Rock and a Hard Place:

## Assertive Multilateralism and Post–Cold War

## U.S. Foreign Policy Making

*Jennifer Sterling-Folker*

During the cold war, the United States and the Soviet Union dealt with "second-tier" fragmentation through the prism of their relationship with one another. For the United States, the end of the cold war has meant that the traditional guidelines for dealing with such fragmentation no longer apply and that new criteria must be established. This chapter examines the rise and fall of "assertive multilateralism," which was the Clinton administration's early attempt to grapple with second-tier fragmentation and to establish a new policy for dealing with these conflicts in a post–cold war world. The case study demonstrates that, given the international environment, American political culture, and the institutional context of the early post–cold war period, assertive multilateralism was not a viable strategy for dealing with second-tier fragmentation.

### The Background for Assertive Multilateralism

The end of the cold war eclipsed Third World rivalries between the two superpowers and provided an opportunity to initiate new approaches with regard to second-tier fragmentation. Many foreign policy analysts suggested that, in the absence of great power rivalry, the United Nations would now be able to fulfill its originally intended collective-security function. The U.N. Security Council's initial post–cold war behavior looked promising in this regard, since five of the seven situations of armed conflict in which it has voted to take enforcement action have been since 1990.[1]

The 1991 Gulf War was the first post–cold war initiative directed at second-tier conflicts, and it appeared to set a precedent for multilateral, collective security efforts under the auspices of the United Nations. The compatibility of great power interests during the Gulf War was taken as evidence that more collective security under U.N. auspices would occur in the future. As Karen Mingst and Margaret Karns suggest, Security Council cooperation during the Gulf War "opened up a new era in UN activities" which included "proposals to create a standing UN peace force [and] anticipate the use of such forces for both traditional peacekeeping functions and enforcement."[2] The post–cold war peacekeeping vision described in Secretary General Boutros Boutros-Ghali's 1992 Plan for Action called for the U.N. to engage in actual "peacemaking."[3] Boutros-Ghali recommended that a peace-enforcement unit be created out of troops volunteered from member states, which would be at the disposal of the Security Council and under the secretary general's command. A new U.N. command and control center would also be created as a "24-hour-a-day warroom," which would monitor U.N. peacekeeping operations around the world while relying on access to intelligence and troops from member states.[4]

What became known as the policy of "assertive multilateralism" (so labeled by the administration's U.N. representative, Madeleine Albright) initially found a receptive American audience because it sought to combine traditional yet contradictory impulses from American political culture itself. In the abstract, the policy had something to please everyone. As a means of pulling back from America's consistent global interventionism during the cold war, the policy sought to rely upon others to shoulder some of the burden of global leadership. Its proponents argued that solutions to second-tier fragmentation could be reached through pragmatic global problem solving because a consensus of interests now existed within the Security Council.

American idealism, its sense of a global mission, and the societal tendency to assume that American values and interests are universal informed the policy. If the United States could afford to be less active globally while others picked up the mantle, it was because American political culture tended to encourage the belief that the cold war had sufficiently transformed great powers in America's own image. Pragmatic problem solving could occur precisely because America had produced a world of like-minded states who now agreed with Anthony Lake's assertion that "to the extent democracy and market economics hold sway in other nations, our own nation will be more secure, prosperous and influential."[5] Thus the policy's presumptions of global consensus and collective intervention provided a foreign policy rhetoric that allowed for multiple interpretations in a societal context that already tended to breed contradictory impulses in foreign policy.

While the tenets of assertive multilateralism seemed appealing to a broad range of voters, problems were bound to arise. Not only did the policy rely upon contradictory American impulses, but it also ignored (intentionally or unintentionally) the international reality that other states had differing interests and values. An international coalition of like-minded states willing to support U.N. efforts consistent with America's own specific interests and preferences simply did not exist. The potential for trouble was clear to many foreign policy observers who questioned the policy's practical viability. John Gerard Ruggie noted in 1993, for example, that the policy "lacks any corresponding expression in military doctrine and operational concepts,"[6] and Evan Thomas argued that it would tend to produce "goals that are at best fuzzy. Rhetoric that is not matched by results. Open-ended commitments to nations with no strategic value to the United States."[7] Yet within the context of American political culture, it is easy to see why its fuzzy open-endedness may have made assertive multilateralism an attractive policy choice during the first post–cold war presidential campaign.

### The Rise and Fall of Assertive Multilateralism

It was against this background that assertive multilateralism was formulated, implemented, and subsequently abandoned. When Clinton took office in January 1993, he inherited several second-tier conflicts which appeared to require some policy response (Bosnia, Somalia, and, to a lesser degree, Haiti). Assertive multilateralism was the administration's broader policy approach to each of these specific conflicts. As the ensuing discussion suggests, the broader policy and the specific conflicts had reciprocal effects on one another. In each case there was already U.N. involvement, but Bosnia and Somalia (Somalia is discussed in chapter 13) would eventually emerge as the crucibles within which assertive multilateralism would be tested and transformed.

*Toward a Policy—Spring 1993*
As a presidential candidate, Clinton had argued that the United States needed to be more assertive in second-tier conflicts and to develop and rely upon multilateral mechanisms to deal with them. These mechanisms, it was argued, would allow the United States to reduce the resources it devoted to acting as the "world's policeman." Reliance upon

the United Nations specifically was a pivotal piece of the new approach. Many of Clinton's foreign policy advisers argued that in dealing with second-tier conflicts, the United States should "expand U.N. peace operations and the U.S. role in them."[8] In an April 1992 campaign speech, Clinton called for the creation of a permanent U.N. rapid deployment force which would be "standing at the borders of countries threatened by aggression, preventing mass violence against civilian populations, providing humanitarian relief and combating terrorism."[9]

Initial administration efforts to formulate a second-tier conflict policy were consistent with Clinton's 1992 campaign position. The new secretary of defense, Les Aspin, said at his confirmation hearings that the administration was considering the creation and deployment of both permanent and ad hoc U.N. forces. In February President Clinton signed Presidential Review Directive 13 (PRD-13), which called for the development and articulation of just such a strategy. As Evan Thomas put it at the time, "In their search for a coherent policy—not to mention someone else to share the burden and the blame—the Clintonians have seized on multilateralism. No longer will the United States go it alone; increasingly, it will turn to the United Nations to help keep the peace."[10]

Efforts to articulate assertive multilateralism occurred simultaneously with the administration's first attempts to resolve the ongoing Bosnian crisis. Fighting between Croatia and Serbia had begun in mid-1991 and had shifted to Bosnia by that fall. In September 1991 the U.N. Security Council imposed a NATO-enforced embargo on all weapons deliveries, which essentially left most of the former Yugoslavia's weapons in the hands of the Serbs. Former secretary of state Cyrus Vance was also dispatched to convince the contestants to allow the deployment of a U.N. peacekeeping mission. The U.N. Protection Force (UNPROFOR) mission began in March 1992 with a mandate to serve as a neutral arbiter for cease-fires and humanitarian relief efforts. It was not initially instructed to enforce flight bans, and Serbian violations became the norm throughout 1992. In October the Security Council approved NATO enforcement of no-fly zones over the region, although NATO did not formally accept this role until April 1993. NATO's southern command was asked to take overall control of U.N. military operations throughout the former Yugoslavia, but was expected to answer to the Security Council through Boutros-Ghali.

As a presidential candidate Clinton had criticized Bush for not being tough enough with the Serbs.[11] Based on Clinton's campaign vows to take a more activist approach in Bosnia, the president's top-level foreign policy team, the NSC Principals Committee, began to discuss Bosnia in early February 1993.[12] Vance and former British foreign secretary Lord David Owen had been in the process of negotiating a peace plan in January 1993. The Principals Committee immediately and publicly disavowed it by announcing that they would not pressure the Muslims to accept the plan on the basis that it rewarded Serbian gains at the expense of the Muslims.[13]

The problem with this rejection was that no alternatives had been developed within the committee. A list of possible options had been drawn up, which included humanitarian airdrops, U.N. enforcement of the no-fly zone, tightened economic sanctions, dispatch of an envoy to further study the Vance-Owen plan, and a peacekeeping force if all parties would commit to a cease-fire. Yet there was disagreement among Clinton's foreign policy advisers over which options were preferable.[14] Vice President Al Gore, National Security Adviser Anthony Lake, and Albright favored more aggressive action and the use of force. Defense Secretary Les Aspin, Chairman of the Joint Chiefs of Staff Colin Powell, and Christopher were skeptical of military action and agreed that the introduction of American ground troops into the conflict with limited, unclear options would be undesirable. Powell wanted an all-or-nothing approach, while Christopher warned that getting involved might lead to another Vietnam. Although subsequent administration statements implied that it was on the verge of taking more forceful action, the Principals Committee and the president postponed a decision. Instead, they adopted a wait-and-see strategy and continued to revisit and discuss the list of options in what one participant referred to as "the world's most elegant seminar."[15]

The one option Clinton had definitely ruled out was unilateral action. There was consensus within the administration that Bosnia should not become an "American problem," a view supported by public opinion poll data collected by Clinton's consultants which showed "that there was increasing support for action by the United States in Bosnia in conjunction with the U.N., but there was no support for unilateral action."[16] This meant, consistent with assertive multilateralism, that multilateral interests would influence whatever option would eventually be pursued.

The administration's indecisiveness dragged on until mid-April when Srebrenica came under siege, and nightly news reports of the fighting finally provided the impetus for a decision. At a press conference on April 16, Clinton expressed outrage over the fighting, and stated that he thought the time had come "to consider things which at least previously have been unacceptable."[17] The impression he gave was that use of force against the Serbs was imminent. The Principals Committee met over the weekend of April 17–18 and decided to recommend two options from their February list: to lift the arms embargo against the Muslims and to use air power to punish Serb artillery and cease-fire violations. Yet despite repeated statements supporting greater actions throughout the end of April, Clinton did not officially sign the "lift-and-strike" option until May 1.

Christopher immediately left for Europe to discuss the lift-and-strike option with the other Security Council members. However, it quickly became apparent that they would not support the proposal.[18] Great Britain and France had volunteered troops to UNPROFOR as a means of dealing with the Bosnian situation without having to intervene forcefully to stop the war. Lifting the arms embargo would have meant expanding the conflict with their own troops caught in the cross-fire. They also feared that the Bosnian Serbs would target their troops if the no-fly zone was enforced. Serbia was a traditional Russian ally, and so Russia had no interest in supporting tougher action against them. The final disincentive for supporting lift-and-strike was that the Bosnian Serb leaders signed the Vance-Owen peace plan just as Christopher was arriving in Europe, thus fueling hope that further action would be a moot point.

Consistent with the emerging policy of assertive multilateralism, Christopher was not instructed to sell lift-and-strike to the other Security Council members. He had been dispatched to Europe to "consult" and maintain "maximum flexibility," not to insist, cajole, or even lead.[19] Despite conveying public impressions that U.S. action was imminent, Clinton and his advisers never intended to take unilateral actions inconsistent with the interests of U.S. allies. When Christopher returned on May 8, he informed the president and the committee that, unless the president personally convinced the allies to pursue the option, European support would not be forthcoming. But Clinton had begun to have misgivings about lift-and-strike even before Christopher had returned home, and there was agreement among the advisers that the president should not take the lead.

Clinton's response was exactly what one would expect given the parameters of assertive multilateralism. Without consensus on more forceful intervention in the former Yugoslavia, the lift-and-strike option was put on hold indefinitely. As Jane Sharp put it, "Clinton invoked a lack of consensus as an excuse not to act."[20] Instead, the U.N. began to plan for an expanded peacekeeping force to oversee the Vance-Owen peace plan if it held, and the Clinton White House agreed that it would contribute 25,000 troops to the mission. In a mid-May referendum, the

Bosnian Serbs rejected the plan, but since the lack of consensus among Security Council members continued, Clinton did not send Christopher back to Europe to press for lift-and-strike.

The administration also agreed to sign off on a European plan to establish "safe zones" for Muslims inside Bosnia, despite having earlier rejected the idea because, as Clinton had argued, such zones could become "shooting galleries."[21] Lake was skeptical of the plan as well, yet the administration's capitulation to European preferences was consistent with assertive multilateralism, which depended on a collective consensus not necessarily determined by American preferences. The policy in turn supported Clinton and Christopher's preferences for seeing the entire issue go away so that Clinton could concentrate on domestic policy again. When meeting with European allies in early June, Christopher brought no American proposals to the table and was sent simply to see what the United Nations and other Security Council members had decided on safe zone logistics.[22]

*Mounting Criticism—Summer to Early Fall, 1993*
The parameters of assertive multilateralism and its application in both the Bosnian and Somalian cases came under increasing scrutiny by mid-1993. The Pentagon let it be known throughout the spring that it had reservations about U.S. involvement in Bosnia. During congressional testimony in April, Powell voiced his misgivings with plans for U.S. participation in a peacekeeping mission.[23] And, even as the Principals Committee was meeting to decide the lift-and-strike option, the vice chairman of the Joint Chiefs of Staff, Admiral David Jeremiah, was publicly expressing his skepticism of the strike option as an effective deterrent to Serb aggression.[24]

Moreover, while the Defense Department accepted its assigned role in Somalia, from the start it expressed concerns over command and control issues, as well as the mission's objectives (see chapter 13). In addition, congressional concerns over the Somalia mission began to mount, especially after June, when American troops were reinserted into the conflict and the United Nation's attempt to capture General Aidid dragged on. Senator Sam Nunn, chairman of the Senate Armed Services Committee, voiced a common congressional fear that the administration had no real exit strategy for Somalia.[25] Republicans also frequently referred to Boutros-Ghali's comment earlier in the year that U.S. troops would be withdrawn from Somalia only "when *I* say they can come out'."[26]

The early results of PRD-13 made Congress even more skeptical of

Clinton's second-tier conflict policy.[27] Pursuant to the orders in PRD-13, the participants of the interagency review, which included representatives from State, Defense, the Joint Chiefs, and others under the leadership of the National Security Council (NSC) staff (with staff member Richard Clark coordinating the review), had completed a draft "presidential decision directive" in which the assertive multilateralism strategy was laid out. This draft, which was approved in mid-July by the NSC's Deputies Committee (chaired by Deputy National Security Adviser Samuel Berger), leaked in August and caused an immediate sensation because it called for expanding the role of U.N. peacekeeping missions and for placing U.S. troops under the operational command of foreigners on a case-by-case basis. This was consistent with the goals of assertive multilateralism, but not with Pentagon command and control structures. Powell and the Defense Department were particularly uneasy with the draft, while Christopher and State were highly ambivalent. Stories of divisions among Clinton's advisers began to surface in the press by September.[28]

In response to these divisions and to the draft directive itself, a House Appropriations Committee voted on September 23 to impose conditions before Clinton could deploy U.S. troops in peacekeeping missions, including notification of the appropriate committees about mission expense, budget plans, projected duration, and goals of the mission.[29] By this time, Congress was also mounting more pressure on Clinton's Somalia policy. The Senate approved a nonbinding resolution calling on the president to report his Somalia objectives to Congress by October 15 and seek congressional approval by November 15 to keep the troops there. The House was about to adopt similar resolutions. Congress also disliked the United Nation's reliance on U.S. troops, equipment, and supplies to conduct its missions, and refused to approve the Clinton administration's request over the summer for $400 million in peacekeeping and another $400 million in unpaid dues.

Both the public and the media were in step with (and perhaps driving) congressional concerns. In the last week of September, a Time/CNN poll found that only 43 percent of respondents approved of keeping U.S. troops in Somalia, while 46 percent disapproved.[30] The news media expressed dissatisfaction with the United Nation's reliance on American support because it suggested, as Michael Gordon put it, "that the United Nations was not capable of taking forceful action unless the Americans carried most of the weight," leading one "to wonder whether it should always be the Americans who wield the hammer."[31] What was being questioned, in essence, were some of the fundamental assumptions upon which assertive multilateralism was based.

There was also considerable congressional and public criticism of the White House's handling of Bosnia, but here the emphasis was less the content of the policy and more the president's policy-making style. Congress had generally been supportive of a tougher stance toward Serbian cease-fire violations and had also wanted the arms embargo lifted for Bosnian Muslims. However, there was no strong preference within Congress, the media, or the public for an escalated or unilateral intervention in the Bosnian conflict. In fact, during an April meeting between the president and congressional leaders, many of the latter had expressed deep reservations about becoming more directly involved in the conflict.[32]

Criticism focused instead on the way in which Clinton and his foreign policy team had handled the lift-and-strike option. In May 1993, for example, Joe Klein argued that Clinton's public threats to get tough with the Serbs followed by his inability to secure allied support meant "the message—to the allies, to the Serbs, to every lobbyist and politician in Washington and to troublemakers around the globe—was irresolution."[33] Descriptions of Clinton's foreign policy–making style in the summer of 1993 regularly referred to his indecisiveness, his tendency to hold consultative seminars instead of strategy sessions, and his eagerness to compromise.[34]

The impression of indecisiveness was reinforced when Clinton and the Principals Committee revisited the issue of tougher action in response to the Serbian siege of Sarajevo in early July. For the first time the Principals Committee considered the need to sell the strike plan to the European allies and the possibility of taking unilateral action if they refused.[35] France and Britain agreed to go along with a NATO air strike option if Boutros-Ghali called for them. But when the United Nations proved reluctant to do so in August and September, the administration did not take unilateral action on the grounds that it was "unwise for the U.S. to go it alone," according to various U.S. officials.[36]

Criticism of Clinton's foreign policy irresolution in Bosnia cut across both political parties. Democrats agreed with the press that Bosnia was, as one Senate Democrat put it, "not so damn difficult as they keep saying it is." Another commented on Clinton's policy-making style: "It is pathological. He just can't make a choice."[37] Republican Richard Lugar pressured Clinton during a May meeting to define his Bosnian policy, arguing that his record had created the "perception of drift" and that he should do more to lead the European allies.[38] Lugar also complained that the administration regularly failed to consult or adequately brief Congress on its foreign policies.

These mounting public, media, congressional, and the Pentagon concerns began to have an impact on the president and his advisers by the fall. On September 17, the Principals Committee met to discuss the draft directive.[39] Albright remained the strongest advocate for the assertive multilateralism approach, Powell was strongly opposed to it, and both Christopher and Aspin remained ambivalent. Lake was most concerned with public perception, arguing that the focus on peacekeeping was damaging the president's standing. Because the committee could not agree on the directive, it ordered the original interagency working group to redraft the sections dealing with the role of multilateral peace operations in overall U.S. foreign policy.

The draft directive was subsequently revised so that the centrality of multilateral peace operations to U.S. second-tier conflict efforts would be reduced. Guidelines on U.S. support for and participation in peace operations, as well as the use of U.S. troops in operations involving combat, were also made more restrictive, per the Pentagon's insistence. The new draft improved U.S. control over dangerous, large-scale peacekeeping operations, although it still allowed the ceding of control to U.N.-designated foreign commanders in safer or small-scale missions.[40]

In addition to redrafting the directive, the administration went on a public offensive in mid-September in an attempt to alleviate some of the foreign policy-making concerns expressed by its critics. For the first time since taking office, Clinton told reporters on September 23 that he would seek congressional approval before sending U.S. troops to a Bosnian peacekeeping mission, and he stressed that the troops would be under NATO and not U.N. control.[41] In a September 25 meeting, Christopher, Aspin, Lake, Powell, and White House Chief of Staff Thomas F. McClarty, hammered out criteria for U.S. involvement in a Bosnian peacekeeping mission that clearly reflected congressional and Pentagon concerns about U.N. control, exit strategies, and mission goals.[42]

In the week prior to Clinton's first address to the U.N. on September 27, Lake, Christopher, and Albright spoke at various forums about the administration's participation in U.N. peacekeeping. A common theme in these speeches was that a workable basis for determining when to send troops had been developed and that it took into account the need for public and congressional approval.[43] In his own address to the United Nations, Clinton acknowledged that congressional support for U.S. participation in U.N. peacekeeping missions was limited. He argued that a reduction in the U.S. assessment for peacekeeping missions and a more discerning criteria for selecting such missions would "make it easier for me as president to make sure we pay in a timely and full fashion."[44]

Yet despite Clinton's cautions, his speech at the United Nations also gave support to the U.N. "warroom" headquarters and logistical standby units for use in peacekeeping situations. Although the White House was becoming increasingly sensitive to bureaucratic, congressional, and public skepticism of assertive multilateralism and its application in Bosnia and Somalia, the White House still subscribed to the policy in the early fall.

*Reactions to the Somalian Debacle—October 1993*
Both the broad strategy of assertive multilateralism and its application to Bosnia were dramatically affected by early-October events in Somalia. When supporters of General Aidid retaliated against the continued U.N. man-hunt, several days of fighting resulted in the deaths of eighteen American soldiers. This proved pivotal in the subsequent abandonment of assertive multilateralism and in the administration's Bosnian policy thereafter. If the Pentagon, Congress, the news media, and the public had expressed reservations about the administration's Somalian policy before October 1993, the death of U.S. Marines led to a concerted attack on the policy in October.

The Somalia debacle appeared to confirm the Pentagon's worst fears with regard to the command and control structure of U.N. peacekeeping missions. When American relief forces had attempted to get to the ambushed marines, logistical difficulties coordinating with other U.N. troops prevented U.S. forces from reaching them until nine hours after the ambush had taken place. Although Les Aspin put most of the blame on the U.N. command structure, the Pentagon also had reason to reproach him specifically, since only the week before he had denied a request for additional equipment that might have been used to reach the Marines sooner. Aspin's justification for the refusal, that greater commitment to the Somalian mission might have jeopardized support for U.S. participation in the Bosnian mission, reinforced the Pentagon's opinion that assertive multilateralism was a deeply flawed policy.[45]

Congressional leaders were similarly outraged, and a Capitol Hill brief by Aspin and Christopher given just after the Marines were killed made relations between Congress and the White House even worse. Aspin mistakenly asked lawmakers what *they* thought should be done, which "managed only to convince congressional leaders that the administration had no clue as to what policy to pursue."[46] In summing up the congressional perception of Clinton's foreign policy in October, Lugar argued that there had been a "virtual collapse of Presidential leadership," and that there was "no significant congressional support for the President's policy . . . and it's his own fault."[47] The public tended to agree with Congress. In the week after the marines were killed, a Time/CNN poll found that only 36 percent of those polled approved of U.S. troops in Somalia and 89 percent wanted to bring the troops home as soon as possible.[48] The same poll also found that 51 percent of those surveyed did not think Clinton was doing a good job handling foreign policy.

By huge majorities, both Houses of Congress called for a rethinking of administration policy on Somalia in particular and multilateral peace operations in general. Congressional proposals were circulated that sought to place restrictions on U.S. troop deployments in Haiti and to prohibit U.N. payments if U.S. troops were put under U.N. command.[49] Any congressional support Clinton may have had for his multilateral approach fizzled. In fact, in February 1994, Congress refused to approve a $670 million supplementary appropriations bill meant to pay for outstanding American peacekeeping bills, beginning a trend that would only get worse when the Republicans later won control of Congress. Hostility toward the administration's failure in Somalia remained so high during the early part of 1994 that House Foreign Affairs Committee chairman, Democrat Lee Hamilton, could emphatically state in March, "If the Bosnians signed an agreement today, and the president came up tomorrow to ask us for troops, he wouldn't get them."[50]

*Abandoning Assertive Multilateralism—October 1993 to May 1994*
With his Somalian policy under vehement attack from all quarters, Clinton probably had little choice but to abandon assertive multilateralism if he wished to accomplish anything else in foreign or even domestic affairs. Certainly it would have been unlikely that Clinton could have obtained congressional approval for U.S. involvement in the Bosnian peacekeeping mission. Christopher noted within days of the Somalia crisis, for example, that, "[i]t inevitably casts a shadow on Bosnia. It shows the relative impatience of the American people for the involvement of American troops in situations where our vital national interests are not so directly engaged."[51] According to President Clinton, the Somalia debacle made him "more cautious about having any Americans in a peacekeeping role where there was any ambiguity at all about what the range of decisions were which could be made by a command other

than an American command with direct accountability to the United States here."[52]

Based on proposals from the Pentagon and the U.S. Central Command in Somalia, the White House immediately ordered more armor and reinforcements to Somalia and set a hard deadline of April 1 for their withdrawal. When his political consultants questioned the wisdom of setting an exit date, Clinton told them he was in no position to deny the military what it deemed necessary.[53] The new U.S. troops would be under American, not U.N., command, and U.S. troops were ordered to stop the pursuit of Aidid. In addition, the White House dispatched retired ambassador Robert Oakley to organize a peace conference among rival Somalian clan leaders, and Oakley was instructed to act as a representative for the U.S. government, not the United Nations. This new hard-line toward the United Nations was greeted with congressional approval, as Dole noted that Clinton's Somalia orders were finally about "what *we* were going to do, not Boutros-Ghali."[54]

Developments in the Somalia mission would also affect the administration's policy toward Haiti a week later. The United States was scheduled to send military engineers and medical specialists as part of a U.N. peacekeeping contingent, but Clinton unilaterally canceled the scheduled landing when a Haitian demonstration against their arrival was staged. Despite the fact that Canadian troops were also on board, neither the United Nations nor the Canadian government was consulted. The new White House attitude was summarized by a White House official, who argued: "I don't think we will give up trying to use the UN to leverage our involvement to do things that are worth doing, but not worth doing alone. But I think we will be far more skeptical about the ability of the United Nations to operate without vigorous involvement of the United States. Ultimately the UN is us. You can't hand off to an entity that is a bunch of bureaucrats who have never done this before."[55]

Events in Somalia also had a direct impact on the redrafting of PRD-13. In late October, Secretary of Defense Aspin contacted Lake to urge "a complete revision of the draft."[56] In November, the interagency working group completed a fresh draft, which was then subjected to a series of legislative-executive consultations. Finally, on May 3, 1994, President Clinton signed Presidential Decision Directive 25, which laid out the administration's policy vis-à-vis multilateral peace operations. The directive declared that the United States would participate in U.N. peacekeeping missions only if doing so would maximize U.S. interests, and then only under U.S. command. Before the United States would agree to support U.N. peacekeeping missions, strict conditions would have to be met including clear U.S. interests, congressional support, availability of personnel and funds, explicit objectives, an exit strategy, and an acceptable command and control structure.[57]

The directive also stated that the administration did *not* support the creation of a U.N. standing army and that it would *not* contribute American troops to such a force. In preparing the final draft, the administration had bowed to congressional and Defense Department preferences and insisted that "[a]ny large scale participation of us forces in a major peace enforcement mission that is likely to involve combat should ordinarily be conducted under us command and operational control or through competent regional organizations such as NATO"[58] (see also the list of conditions and discussion in chapter 13).

Public statements were supported by public deeds. Albright reported that the administration was already following many of the directive's guidelines in the Security Council and had blocked requests for U.N. peacekeeping operations in Burundi, Georgia, Angola, and Rwanda because they looked more like peace enforcement missions with goals that could not be easily achieved. Tougher U.S. standards were necessary, Albright argued, because, "[t]he UN has not yet demonstrated the ability to respond effectively when the risk of combat is high and the level of local cooperation is low."[59] Ten days later, Albright refused to authorize the immediate dispatch of U.N. troops to Rwanda, telling a House foreign affairs subcommittee, "We want to be confident that when we do turn to the UN, the UN will be able to do the job."[60]

When the Republicans took control of Congress in January 1995, it demanded greater restrictions on U.S. support for U.N. peacekeeping missions. Based on provisions in the "Contract with America," the House passed the National Security Revitalization Act in February, which sought among other things to limit U.S. contributions to U.N. peacekeeping operations and to restrict the placement of U.S. troops under U.N. command. Yet the White House had already substantially complied with these demands in the spring of 1994, including unilaterally reducing U.S. contributions to U.N. peacekeeping from 31.7 percent to 25 percent as provided for in PDD-25.[61] Despite Republican declarations to the contrary, by early 1995 the policy position between the White House and Congress on peacekeeping interventions had become a difference of degree and not kind.

A similar convergence of interests had occurred between the White House and the Department of Defense (DOD). PDD-25 had not only agreed that U.S. peacekeeping participation would only occur under Pentagon-preferred command structures, but had also given the Pentagon control over the management of allocated peacekeeping funds involving U.S. combat units. Clinton also decided to replace Aspin as secretary of defense in late 1993. He was careful to choose a nominee whom the military would approve, eventually deciding on Deputy Defense Secretary William Perry. As a former under secretary of defense for research and engineering responsible for military acquisitions under Carter and a leading advocate of defense industrial policy, Perry was a Pentagon insider. This tended to placate Pentagon criticisms of the administration, particularly since Perry proved to be a strong advocate of DOD interests in subsequent Bosnian policy.

Thus by mid-1994, the administration had essentially abandoned assertive multilateralism: it would no longer attempt to work through the United Nations and with its command structures in order to deal with second-tier fragmentation. There was a growing understanding, as State Department spokesman Nicholas Burns described it, that the United Nations "can keep the peace, but in terms of applying force, it's not a good instrument."[62] Recognizing that the dream of enhanced U.N. peacemaking was dead by 1995, a former U.S. representative to the United Nations noted, "We now realize how difficult certain peacekeeping operations are and that they should be restricted in scope."[63] The administration's new attitude toward the United Nations and its peacekeeping missions had direct ramifications for its policy toward the ongoing Bosnian conflict.

*Multilateralism the Old-Fashioned Way — Bosnian Policy between 1994 and 1995*

By early 1994 it was clear that the administration had become markedly less deferential to U.N. and allied concerns in Bosnia. Rather than take its cues for action from allied hesitancy and back away from the option of more robust force, the administration began to exert continual pressure on the United Nations to get tough with cease-fire violations. The first NATO engagement in the Bosnian conflict occurred on March 1 and was not an air strike but an enforcement of the no-fly zone. NATO had a mandate to enforce these zones at will and had not consulted the United Nations prior to its actions. U.N. officials were surprised and upset by the lack of notification, as well as by the aggressiveness of the action itself, but the Clinton White House was said to be "jubilant" that U.S. fighter jets had finally had the opportunity to take action.[64] Congressional leaders were supportive as well, and Dole gave "strong bipartisan support" to these air strikes saying, "I think it would certainly send a strong message to Belgrade."[65]

In subsequent months, the relationship between the United Nations and NATO began to deteriorate over when and how much retaliatory force to use. U.N. officials were predisposed to let violations pass, while NATO officials became increasingly frustrated at their inability to respond to violations with air strikes.[66] Even when the United Nations did call for air-strikes, NATO tended to want to pound Serb military installations, while the United Nations wanted attacks on isolated artillery pieces. Given DOD's experience with U.N. preferences and command structures in Somalia, it overwhelmingly supported NATO in these disagreements. Defense Secretary Perry spoke on behalf of both NATO and the Pentagon when he argued in the fall of 1994, "When we go in, I want to go in with compelling force. Force not necessarily just proportionate to the act at stake, but enough to make it clear that there's a heavy price to pay for violating the rules that NATO has established."[67] Because the new Republican Congress supported DOD's preferences, it also preferred NATO action over U.N. inaction in these disagreements.

Clinton and his other foreign policy advisers remained responsive to DOD and congressional concerns through early 1994. Administration officials consistently stressed that the United States would participate in a Bosnian peacekeeping mission only if it were NATO-led, which essentially meant under an American commander. In March the administration refused to support an expanded U.N. peacekeeping mission in Bosnia on the grounds that it would be unable to secure financial support from Congress. When the Security Council officially extended the UNPROFOR's Bosnian mission for another six months later in April, Albright vetoed a U.N. supplementary plan to send an additional ten thousand peacekeepers. She reiterated the administration's position that no American troops would be sent to Bosnia under a U.N. command and that a durable peace would have to be established.[68]

During the summer of 1994, administration officials also convinced the Security Council to turn over responsibility for Bosnian negotiations to a joint U.S.-European-Russian contact group, which would effectively exclude Boutros-Ghali and other U.N. officials. Responsibility for air strike decisions still resided with U.N. officials, but the White House was not satisfied and in 1994 consistently worked to push the United Nations out of the way so that it could pursue its preferred solutions in Bosnia through NATO. As a nod to continual congressional pressure, and over the objections of the United Nations and its allies, the administration ended U.S. participation in the NATO-enforced weapons embargo to Bosnia in November. U.N. officials later accused the United States of participating in, or at least turning a blind eye to, arms deliveries to Bosnian Muslims.[69]

A tenuous U.S.-negotiated cease-fire held into the spring of 1995, but by that summer the situation in Sarajevo had deteriorated again as Bosnian Serbs stole back weapons and began shelling the city. When the Serbs overran two U.N. "safe zones" in July, the Clinton administration reopened the U.N.-NATO debate regarding force levels. Because U.S. negotiators were now dominating negotiations to the exclusion of the United Nations, they informed Bosnian Serbs that NATO would react to Serb provocations with "disproportionate" and wide-ranging force. When the Serbs bombed a Sarajevo market at the end of August and killed thirty-eight people, the United States arranged for NATO air bombardment of Serbian positions. A two-week bombing campaign ensued to break the siege of the city and force the Serbs to negotiate.

The combination of a major offensive launched by Croats and Muslims between August and October and the NATO bombardment in September finally brought all three sides to the negotiating table. U.S.-brokered talks in the fall led to the Dayton Accords in November 1995 and the signing of a formal peace agreement in December. The accords outlined an American-envisioned, unified, and democratic Bosnian state, and called for a multinational peacekeeping force to oversee the transition. The administration's plan for this international peacekeeping force (IFOR) was designed to preempt congressional criticisms and alleviate Pentagon anxieties, and its parameters were precisely the opposite of those in the Somalian mission.

At a November 21 news conference, Clinton argued that only NATO could oversee the Dayton Accords, "and the United States, as NATO's leader, must play an essential role in this mission."[70] He pointed out that NATO's military mission would be clear and limited, that U.S. troops would only take orders from the American NATO commander, that they would follow NATO rules of engagement (which meant shoot first if necessary), and that there was a one-year timetable for their withdrawal. The United States insisted that NATO command was to be clear and unambiguous, and that U.N. officials would have no ability to interfere with NATO forces once IFOR went into effect. The United Nations was to play no part in what amounted to a U.S. NATO-led peacekeeping mission.

Although the House immediately voted to block money to send U.S. troops to Bosnia until hearings could be held, Clinton insisted from the moment he announced the IFOR plan that full consultation with

Congress would have to occur. In addition, congressional critics were greatly undercut by DOD's acceptance of the mission. The Pentagon was satisfied with the terms of IFOR because, as Eric Schmitt pointed out, "the agreement meets virtually every condition the American military insisted on for success."[71]

It is only within the context of failed assertive multilateralism in Somalia that it is possible to understand why the administration organized IFOR as it did. It did not wish to abandon multilateralism entirely, since IFOR expected and relied upon other NATO members to contribute troops and supplies to the effort. However, the Clinton administration had come to understand that in order to retain control over international outcomes while also meeting the particular interests of other American foreign policy institutions, the United States would have to be willing to accept a disproportionate share of the burden. While its greater share could be measured in terms of expense and personnel, it also involved taking a more forceful leadership position if it had a preference for particular solutions to second-tier conflicts. International consensus consistent with American preferences was not a given and continued to require encouragement, cajoling, and even imposition.

The multilateralism of IFOR, as well as its structure and command chain, had more in common with allied occupational strategies employed by the United States just after World War II than it did with the type of U.N. missions envisioned by assertive multilateralism. Thus by 1995 there was consensus within the administration that returning to a more traditional model of American-style multilateral intervention was preferable. This meant that the criteria for U.S. intervention in second-tier conflicts would be based solely upon American interests.

## Conclusions

The initial desire and subsequent inability of the Clinton administration to implement assertive multilateralism between 1993 and 1995 reflects both the possibilities and limitations of developing new policies toward second-tier fragmentation in the post–cold war period. The origin of the policy derived from a variety of sources including a changed international context, contradictory societal impulses, and Clinton's own preferences and inexperience in foreign policy making. Yet other elements of the foreign policy community had different preferences. As a result, these institutions had reasons to be skeptical of the policy. The broader foreign policy community mounted increasing pressure on assertive multilateralism throughout the summer of 1993 and, when the policy actually produced a crisis, congressional, military, public, and media displeasure coalesced into a concerted attack. In October 1993, the president was confronted with united opposition to his second-tier policy, which made his ability to achieve other foreign and domestic policy goals highly unlikely. In the face of these attacks, the White House reversed its course.

By 1995 the divisive relationship between the White House and the rest of the foreign policy community over post–cold war second-tier fragmentation policy had largely been resolved. A consensus had developed among the relevant policy-making circles that American policy toward such situations would not be assertive multilateralism but would instead continue to put American international and institutional interests first. While the president tended to hold the initiative in subsequent decisions, policy was informed by and responsive to other institutional circles. Because policy reflected the interests of multiple actors and institutions, it also represented a modicum of foreign policy democratization. Both the failure of assertive multilateralism and its implications for the making of post–cold war U.S. foreign policy in general need greater exploration in this regard.

### Post–Cold War U.S. Foreign Policy and the Failure of Assertive Multilateralism

The shift from "gung-ho" optimism over the possibilities of multilateral peace operations to skepticism over their desirability, feasibility, and utility is best explained as a function of the interaction among the White House, Congress, and foreign policy bureaucracy, whose actions were affected by both international and societal forces. Given the international environment, American political culture, and the institutional context of the early post–cold war period, assertive multilateralism was not a viable strategy for dealing with second-tier fragmentation. It sought to modify the intense U.S. internationalism of the cold war by relying upon collective decision making and burden sharing, yet it was based upon erroneous assumptions and contradictory aims. Moreover, it failed to account for diverging interests in Congress and the foreign policy bureaucracy, whose opposition forced the abandonment of the approach.

Internationally, assertive multilateralism suffered from a number of weaknesses that produced contradictions and limitations in policy. These contradictions also affected the preferences and decisions of U.S. policy makers, especially those who opted to oppose the initiative. Among these weaknesses, four warrant special mention. First, assertive multilateralism failed to account for weaknesses in U.N. organization and command structures, both for broad decision making and for actual military operations. Although the U.N. commands actual field operations, its peacekeeping missions are logistically reliant upon U.N. member states for both approval and manpower/supplies. The United Nations cannot lead in any tangible sense when it comes to the determination of missions, commitments to action, or application of resources. Moreover, U.N. field command structures are unwieldy, inefficient, and poorly equipped to manage complex military combat operations involving volunteer troops with incompatible equipment, training, operational guidelines, intelligence, and languages.

Second, assertive multilateralism was predicated on the highly questionable assumption that the Security Council had reached a consensus on the need for and parameters of second-tier intervention in general. Sharp differences continued to exist within the Security Council and among non–Security Council states over which conflicts deserved the U.N.'s attention, how this attention should be manifest, and what the precise formula would be for member-state responsibility. Other states proved either unwilling to provide leadership in order to arrive at solutions, or they sought solutions which the United States did not necessarily favor or perceive to be in its own interests. While the belief that assertive multilateralism would work only in support of U.S. interests was consistent with America's own societal impulses, it continued to be unrealistic within the context of the international environment.

Third, assertive multilateralism also foundered on the potential disparity between the costs of resolving second-tier fragmentation and the "national interest" in doing so. For assertive multilateralism to work, the United States either had to accept that in some situations no U.N. solutions would be forthcoming, or that it would have to support missions where it did not necessarily have a pressing national interest. By definition, the policy involved (at best) secondary issues for the United States, yet it expected the type of resource commitment normally reserved for issues of great threat and at a time when threats in the international environment had been dramatically reduced. This anomaly found voice in the objections and opposition from the U.S. Defense Department, members of Congress, and the broader public. The policy's overestimation of commitment extended to other countries as well. Despite the Gulf War and its accompanying consensus rhetoric, other states were also unwilling to make the necessary physical, financial, and command sacrifices in order to impose collective security in situations where their own national interests and security were not directly threatened.

Finally, for all its promise as a way for the United States to remain engaged and share the costs of engagement at a time in which pressures toward neoisolationism were growing, assertive multilateralism failed to account for the loss of control and the apparent encroachment of U.S. sovereignty implicit in the notion that such U.N.-led peacemaking would entail. Given the penchant for exceptionalism, and perhaps unilateralism, rooted in the American experience, this failure proved costly as it generated opposition and suspicion from various quarters within the government and in the public. As the new Clinton administration attempted to operationalize this policy, its inherent contradictions would have a significant impact on particular American foreign policy institutions. Many of these institutions were already experiencing new pressures as a result of the cold war's end and had reasons for resisting this new post–cold war policy toward second-tier conflict. If the international environment created a hard place where consensus was not readily available, the interests of particular American foreign policy institutions were the rock upon which the policy would eventually founder.

Having little foreign policy experience, the president was initially neither comfortable with nor interested in foreign affairs.[72] During his campaign Clinton had made it clear that foreign policy would be a lower priority in his administration than domestic issues. Polling data acquired by his political consultants seemed to confirm the public's relative lack of interest in foreign policy and so reinforced his own disinclination to address it. According to Christopher's description of the foreign policy process in February 1993, the president would lay down "the broad guidelines of foreign policy, expecting his State Department and national security advisers to implement them as a team, working together, and holding them accountable if they don't carry it out in a fairly straightforward way."[73] Clinton expected to delegate foreign policy formulation to his advisers, whom he assumed would work out solutions for him to approve or reject and thus free him to concentrate on domestic issues. As one foreign policy official put it, "He is there to do things when asked, but that is the extent of it."[74] Given the president's own preferences, assertive multilateralism appeared to be a relatively low-cost strategy for dealing with what were already considered low-priority issues. If a situation warranted action, the Security Council would collectively agree to intervene, otherwise a situation could safely be ignored. On paper, at least, it was the kind of approach that Clinton as candidate had argued "will permit us the freedom to focus on America's problems at home."[75]

The president's lack of experience in foreign affairs was coupled with a distinct unease over issues of military force. This was partly a function of Clinton's own personal history during the Vietnam War, which had done little to prepare him to be commander in chief or to earn him the Pentagon's respect. In fact, relations between the White House and Pentagon were so bad in that first year that, as one high-ranking Pentagon official later described it, "I had the feeling the White House wanted the Department of Defense to cease to be a part of the US Government. We had terrible relations with the White House."[76] In this context, assertive multilateralism appeared to provide Clinton with a convenient means to avoid making tough decisions about when to use military force. By depending on allied consensus for collective intervention in situations of Third World unrest, the president could shift responsibility for the use (or nonuse) of military force onto an external U.N. collective.

Among the foreign policy bureaucracies most affected by the end of the cold war *and* the implementation of assertive multilateralism, DOD must be singled out. To say, based on DOD's own institutional interests in the early post–cold war period, that it was highly skeptical of assertive multilateralism would be an understatement. Within the context of a shrinking budget and reassessments of war strategies, assertive multilateralism could not have come at a worse time for the Pentagon. Part of the problem with peacekeeping was that it required a different type of military training from that traditionally given to American soldiers who, as Evan Thomas points out, "are trained to maneuver and pour on the firepower, not to stand and obey fuzzy rules of engagement."[77] Exactly how the Pentagon was expected to pay for peacekeeping training, troops, and supplies was another problem.

Yet perhaps the greatest weakness of the new policy from DOD's perspective was its implications for battlefield command and control. Within the U.S. military, there is no tradition of or support for turning over command to an independent international actor such as the United Nations. Responsibility for American troops on the battlefield resides in a chain of command which begins with the constitutional provision for president as commander in chief and is then subsequently determined by and lodged in the military itself. If DOD was expected to work with troops from other countries in battlefield conditions, it preferred doing so through NATO because it had a clear and precise command structure dominated by the U.S. military, and it gave American commanders control over member state troops, equipment, and intelligence on the battlefield. In addition, NATO forces had experience conducting military exercises with one another, had developed intelligence and battlefield procedures in a variety of contingencies, and had already addressed logistical compatibility and language problems.

Other elements of the foreign policy bureaucracy were less opposed to the policy, at least initially. As might have been expected, the State Department—particularly the U.N. mission and the Bureau for International Organization Affairs—were the strongest advocates for the approach. Thus, for example, Madeleine Albright was the most assertive high-level official to argue in favor of the initiative. The NSC staff also supported the strategy prior to the fall of 1993. However, even those agencies that benefited from the policy did not develop vested interests in its continuation. This may have been because many of Clinton's early foreign policy advisers were more concerned with protecting the president than with the prerogatives of their respective agencies. Despite policy disagreements, Christopher, Lake, and Aspin all agreed that protecting the president was their first priority and that disagreements should be kept private.[78] Thus they may have been more willing to abandon assertive multilateralism when its implementation began to negatively affect the president's popularity.

If assertive multilateralism lacked an advocate among the foreign policy bureaucracies, it had an outspoken critic in the form of the U.S. Congress, largely because of its negative impact on the military and its reliance on the United Nations. Many members had long accused the U.N. bureaucracy of being bloated and inefficient and insisted that the U.S. share of the U.N. budget be reduced. Beginning in the mid-1980s, Congress began to regularly delay its payment assessments to the U.N. operating budget, though it continued to approve voluntary payments that it could earmark for particular U.N. programs. By 1993, however, it was not only refusing to pay its portion of the operating budget but the separate assessment for peacekeeping as well.[79] Furthermore, skepticism over the policies stemmed from the painful budget contractions DOD was experiencing. If money was to be reallocated within DOD's budget, members of Congress had little interest in funding a U.N. standby force or more U.N. peacekeeping missions in place of programs that more directly benefited their own constituents.

One of the arguments used by some members of Congress to justify their skepticism over assertive multilateralism was that public opinion would not support U.S. involvement in U.N. peacekeeping missions. There was actually little evidence for this argument. During the early 1990s, the American public was generally more supportive of the United Nations and its functions than was Congress. Depending on how questions were phrased, most respondents to polling questions about post–cold war international events consistently tended to favor multilateral international efforts over unilateral ones.[80] However, this support never translated into active pressure for U.N. peacemaking. As one observer pointed out, the minority who contact Congress about the United Nations tend "to have more concerns about the U.N. being too powerful," and are "more verbal about it, more active, and belong to organizations that mobilize people."[81] This would certainly prove to be the case when the reality of assertive multilateralism involved the loss of American soldiers.

*Assertive Multilateralism and the Making of U.S. Foreign Policy*
The institutional and societal factors discussed above reflect more general post–cold war features in U.S. foreign policy making, including a lack of consensus, an expanding congressional assertiveness, and a public ambivalence about U.S. leadership in the world. These forces combined to generate a policy process that defeated assertive multilateralism, and several aspects of this process should be highlighted. First, the White House retained the advantage of initiative, but then gradually peeled away its tenets in response to various criticisms from within the executive branch and Congress (both of which drew on public sentiment). Second, the White House faced multiple pressures between formulation and implementation which arose from the bureaucracy (DOD), Congress, the public, the international community, and President Clinton's own interests. Within the United States bureaucratic and congressional actors allied themselves to pressure or thwart the White House and eventually managed to force a policy reversal. Third, without utilizing substantive legislation, Congress effectively shaped U.S. policy through the use of legislative threat, nonbinding resolutions and hearings, other attempts at signaling and framing opinion, and collusion with other actors. Through it all, members seemed emboldened in their challenges by public opposition or, in some cases, lack of public approval of President Clinton. In the end, opponents in Congress, with allies elsewhere in the government, provoked a series of "anticipated reactions" that brought White House policy in line with broad congressional preferences. Finally, and perhaps most obviously, the executive branch did not speak with one voice. In fact, it may be argued that it was executive disagreement that generated increasing congressional intervention and, in the end, policy reversal.

This case study suggests that the fate of assertive multilateralism was the result of *interbranch leadership*, in which interactions among

White House, congressional, and bureaucratic actors led to changes (and finally consensus) in the broader second-tier fragmentation policy and its application to Bosnia specifically. Moreover, at different times during the period examined, policy making followed the institutional competition, confrontation and stalemate, and constructive compromise variants, depending on the extent to which the White House responded to the objections raised by its challengers in Congress and the bureaucracy.

The policy-making patterns suggested by this case imply a difficult foreign policy arena for the post–cold war world. The failure of assertive multilateralism says much about fragmenting interests and lack of consensus over the role, purposes, and costs of the U.S. foreign policy. It also implies that in times of uncertainty over role and interests in the world, policy making widens to include actors outside the executive branch, even as those actors inside the executive branch become increasingly divided. This indicates that U.S. foreign policy after the end of the cold war is likely to emerge from a complicated process involving both branches of government.

## Notes

1 Karen Mingst and Margaret Karns, *The United Nations in the Post-Cold War Era* (Boulder, Colo.: Westview Press, 1995), p. 23.
2 Mingst and Karns, *United Nations*, p. 76.
3 See Boutros Boutros-Ghali, "An Agenda for Peace," in Adam Roberts and Benedict Kingsbury, eds., *United Nations, Divided World: The UN's Roles in International Relations*, 2d ed. (New York: Oxford University Press, 1993).
4 Paul Lewis, "UN Is Developing Control Center to Coordinate Growing Peacekeeping Role," *New York Times*, March 28, 1993, p. A10.
5 Quoted in Christopher Layne, "Minding Our Own Business: The Case for American Non-Participation in International Peacekeeping/Peacemaking Operations," in Donald C. F. Daniel and Bradd C. Hayes, eds., *Beyond Traditional Peacekeeping* (New York: St. Martin's Press, 1995), p. 93.
6 "Wandering in the Void: Charting the UN's New Strategic Role," in Charles W. Kegley Jr. and Eugene R. Wittkopf, eds., *The Global Agenda: Issues and Perspectives*, 4th ed. (New York: McGraw-Hill, 1995), p. 206.
7 Evan Thomas, "Playing Globocop," *Newsweek*, June 28, 1993, p. 21; See also Michael Elliott, "High Hurdles and Low Moans," *Newsweek*, October 11, 1993, p. 39.
8 Ivo Daalder, "The Clinton Administration and Multilateral Peace Operations," *Pew Case Studies in International Affairs*, 462A and 462B (Washington: Institute of the Study of Diplomacy Publications, 1994), 462A, p. 3.
9 *New York Times*, May 6, 1994, p. A1.
10 Thomas, "Playing Globocop," 22–23.

11 Thomas L. Friedman, "Clinton's Foreign Policy Agenda Reaches across Broad Spectrum," *New York Times*, October 4, 1992, pp. A1+.

12 The committee consisted of National Security Adviser Lake, Secretary of State Christopher, Defense Secretary Les Aspin, Joint Chiefs of Staff Chairman Colin Powell, U.N. Ambassador Madeleine Albright, CIA director James Woolsey, Lake's deputy Samuel Berger, and Gore's representative on the NSC staff Leon Fuerth. When Clinton attended the meetings, Chief of Staff "Mac" McLarty and Gore would also be present. Drew, *On the Edge*, p. 145.

13 Thomas L. Friedman, "US Will Not Push Muslims to Accept Bosnia Peace Plan," *New York Times*, February 4, 1993, pp. A1+; Friedman, "Clinton Keeping Foreign Policy on Back Burner," *New York Times*, February 8, 1993, p. A9.

14 Elizabeth Drew, *On the Edge: The Clinton Presidency* (New York: Simon & Schuster, 1994), ch. 10; Tom Post, "The Road to Indecision," *Newsweek*, May 24, 1993, pp. 20–21; Charles A. Stevenson, "The Evolving Clinton Doctrine on the Use of Force," *Armed Forces and Society* 22 (1996): 522–523.

15 *Newsweek*, May 24, 1993, p. 17.

16 Drew, *On the Edge*, p. 150.

17 Drew, *On the Edge*, p. 151.

18 Lawrence Freedman, ed., *Military Intervention in European Conflicts* (Cambridge, Mass.: Blackwell, 1994); Drew, *On the Edge*, pp. 155–57.

19 *Newsweek*, May 24, 1993, p. 18; Drew, *On the Edge*, p. 156.

20 "Appeasement, Intervention and the Future of Europe," in Lawrence Freedman, ed., *Military Intervention in European Conflicts*, p. 53.

21 *New York Times*, June 9, 1993, p. A6.

22 Elaine Sciolino, "Christopher in Europe to Discuss Plan to Create Havens in Bosnia," *New York Times*, June 9, 1993, p. A6.

23 Stevenson, "The Evolving Clinton Doctrine," pp. 522–523.

24 Drew, *On the Edge*, p. 154.

25 *New York Times*, September 24, 1993, p. 11.

26 *Time*, October 18, 1993, p. 50.

27 Steven A. Holmes, "Clinton May Let US Troops Serve under UN Chiefs," *New York Times*, August 18, 1993, pp. A1+.

28 Irvin Molotsky, "Administration Is Divided on Role for US in Peacekeeping Efforts," *New York Times*, September 22, 1993, p. A8; Elaine Sciolino, "US Narrows Terms for Its Peacekeepers," *New York Times*, September 23, 1993, p. A8.

29 Sciolino, "US Narrows Terms," p. A8.

30 *Time*, October 4, 1993, p. 40.

31 "New Strength for UN Peacekeepers: US Might," *New York Times*, June 13, 1993, p. 24.

32 Drew, *On the Edge*, p. 154.

33 "Slow Motion," *Newsweek*, May 24, 1993, p. 18.

34 E.g., Klein, "Slow Motion," p. 18; Thomas, "Globocop," pp. 20–24.

35 Drew, *On the Edge*, pp. 275–77.

36 Drew, *On the Edge*, p. 279.

37 *Newsweek*, May 24, 1993, pp. 16–17.

38 *Newsweek*, May 24, 1993, p. 20. See also *New York Times*, March 22, 1993, p. A3.

39  This account of the NSC Principals Committee meeting is drawn from Daalder, "Multilateral Peace Operations," pp. 462A, 10, and 462B, 1–2.

40  On these changes, see Daalder, "The Clinton Administration and Multilateral Peace Operations," 462A, p. 10; and Molotsky, "Administration," p. A8.

41  Sciolino, "US Narrows Terms," p. A8.

42  Elaine Sciolino, "Clinton Aides Agree on Terms for US Bosnia Role," *New York Times*, September 26, 1993, p. L21.

43  Elliot, "High Hurdles," p. 39; *Time*, October 4, 1993, pp. 40–41; *New York Times*, September 24, 1993, p. 1.

44  *New York Times*, September 28, 1993, p. 1.

45  George J. Church, "They Beat Me Violently with Their Fists and Sticks," *Time*, October 18, 1993, p. 49.

46  Church, "They Beat Me," p. 49.

47  *New York Times*, October 13, 1993, p. A1.

48  *Time*, October 18, 1993, pp. 42, 49.

49  Thomas L. Friedman, "Clinton Vows to Fight Congress on His Power to Use the Military," *New York Times*, October 19, 1993, pp. A1+; Adam Clymer, "Democrats Study Amending War Powers Act," *New York Times*, October 24, 1993, p. L11.

50  *Congressional Quarterly*, March 26, 1994, p. 752.

51  *Time*, October 18, 1993, p. 46.

52  William J. Clinton, press conference, Washington, D.C., October 14, 1993, p. 7.

53  Drew, *On the Edge*, p. 329.

54  *Time*, October 18, 1993, p. 50.

55  *New York Times*, October 10, 1993, p. E3.

56  Daalder, "The Clinton Administration and Multilateral Peace Operations," 462B, p. 4.

57  See *The Clinton Administration's Policy on Reforming Multilateral Peace Operations*, Publication 10161 (Washington, D.C.: Department of State, Bureau of International Organization Affairs, May 1994).

58  *The Clinton Administration's Policy on Reforming Multilateral Peace Operations*, p. 2.

59  *New York Times*, May 6, 1994, p. A1.

60  *New York Times*, May 18, 1994, p. A1.

61  Sciolino, "De-emphasizes," p. A1.

62  *New York Times*, July 7, 1996, p. E5.

63  *New York Times*, March 3, 1995, p. A3.

64  Thomas, "Globocop," pp. 22–23.

65  *Boston Globe*, February 7, 1994, p. A1.

66  "Bosnia UN Aides Faulted," *Boston Globe*, March 15, 1994, p. 1; Michael R. Gordon, "Air Strikes on Serbs Are a Show of Resolve, *New York Times*, April 12, 1994, p. A10; Tom Post, "Mission Accomplished—Barely," *Newsweek*, August 15, 1994, p. 55; Roger Cohen, "At Odds over Bosnia," *New York Times*, October 2, 1994, p. A14; Roger Cohen, "NATO and the UN Quarrel in Bosnia As Serbs Press On," *New York Times*, November 27, 1994, p. A20.

67  *New York Times*, October 2, 1994, p. A14.

68  Sean Kay, "The Future of European Security: Institutional Enlargement or Realist

Realignment," Ph.D. dissertation, University of Massachusetts-Amherst, 1996, p. 39.

69  Roger Cohen, "NATO Disputes UN Reports of Possible Arms Airlift to Bosnia," *New York Times*, March 1, 1995, p. A5.

70  *New York Times*, November 22, 1995, p. A11.

71  "Commanders Say US Plan for Bosnia Will Work," *New York Times*, November 24, 1995, p. A1.

72  Friedman, "Clinton's Foreign Policy Agenda Reaches across Broad Spectrum"; Thomas L. Friedman, "Clinton Keeping Foreign Policy on the Back Burner," p. A9; Post, "The Road to Indecision," p. 21; Thomas L. Friedman, "Clinton's Foreign Policy: Top Adviser Speaks Out," *New York Times*, October 31, 1993, p. A8.

73  *New York Times*, March 22, 1993, p. A3; See also Drew, *On the Edge*, pp. 125, 138, 144.

74  *New York Times*, February 8, 1993, p. A9.

75  *New York Times*, April 24, 1994, p. 14.

76  *New York Times*, October 28, 1996, p. A1.

77  Thomas, "Globocop," p. 24.

78  Drew, *On the Edge*, pp. 140–141; Joe Klein, "The Hidden Lake," *Newsweek*, July 19, 1993, p. 21; Gwen Ifill, "Security Official Guides US Aims at Conference," *New York Times*, July 5, 1993, p. L5; Friedman, "Clinton's Top Adviser," p. A8.

79  See Robert Gregg, *About Face? The United States and the United Nations* (Boulder, Colo.: Lynne Rienner, 1993), ch. 4. By September 1996 the United States would owe the United Nations $1.7 billion in back dues, peacekeeping fees, and special assessments.

80  E.g., Randolph Ryan, "Is the US Public Bolder Than Its Leaders?" *Boston Sunday Globe*, July 23, 1995, pp. 63+; Barbara Crossette, "Poll Finds American Support for Peacekeeping by UN," *New York Times*, April 28, 1995, p. A17; Barbara Crossette, "Does America Love or Hate the UN?" *New York Times*, September 23, 1996, p. A6.

81  *New York Times*, September 23, 1996, p. A6.

# 12.

## The White House, Congress, and the Paralysis

## of the U.S. State Department after the Cold War

*Steven W. Hook*

As the previous chapters in this volume have described, the cold war's abrupt collapse forced the United States to redefine its role in the transformed international system. In the absence of the Soviet threat, the bipolar balance of power, and the ideologically charged regional rivalries of the cold war era, the containment doctrine pursued by nine presidential administrations had suddenly become obsolete. The new era demanded a new grand strategy.

This task, of course, would have tangible consequences for the U.S. foreign policy bureaucracy, whose structures and standard operating procedures were built around the overriding goal of communist containment. Consequently, each institution of foreign policy—the diplomatic corps, armed services, and intelligence agencies—was required to clarify and justify its relevance in the new systemic environment. And the White House, which oversaw these institutions, required support from the legislative branch in implementing their reform. This institutional interdependence was crucial in the mid-1990s because, in peacetime, Congress historically has assumed a more assertive role in foreign policy than it has when the United States is at war. Thus, as Robert Lieber recently observed, "the disappearance of the Soviet threat has been conducive to an erosion of presidential and executive power, and a reassertion of the Madisonian features of the American political system."[1]

This chapter explores the practical effects—and adverse consequences—of this pattern. It builds on the general discussion in chapter 3 by examining the protracted struggle between the Clinton administration and Congress over a primary arm of the foreign policy bureaucracy—the U.S. State Department and its affiliated agencies. Critics of the State Department had been calling for its restructuring since the heyday of the cold war, but their charges of bureaucratic inertia and inefficiency were overshadowed by the superpower rivalry. Their critiques received more attention in the cold war's aftermath, which came at a time when concerns over budget deficits and the need to downsize the federal bureaucracy had become a national preoccupation. But the State Department's version of *perestroika* would not follow a steady course. To the contrary, Bill Clinton would bring his own normative agenda to the restructuring process, very different from than that of his predecessors, along with a revised mission for the State Department that would require more refinements than simply downsizing along previously established lines. Far from the wholesale cutbacks advocated by its critics, Clinton called on the State Department to assume a central role in pursuing his new foreign policy.

As we will discover in the pages to follow, Clinton's policy proposals and their attending structural reforms were not widely accepted within Congress. National ambivalence about the emerging international climate and the global responsibilities of the United States, reflected in public opinion polls, fueled a bitter political confrontation between Congress and the White House—and between the Republican and Democratic parties that controlled the respective branches of government after the November 1994 midterm elections. In contrast to Clinton's call for a new era of liberal internationalism, powerful members of Congress sought a more modest role for the United States based upon tangible national self-interests. They demanded not only dramatic reductions in the State Department's budget, but also the abolition of its three primary affiliates—the U.S. Agency for International Development (USAID), the U.S. Information Agency (USIA), and the U.S. Arms Control and Disarmament Agency (USACDA).

Clinton rejected these calls on both substantive and institutional grounds. He defended his proposed strategy as best suited to the transnational problems of the post–cold war era. Further, he asserted that the congressional demands went far beyond structural issues and attempted to set the general tone of U.S. foreign policy—an authority that he argued was firmly lodged in the White House. The resulting stalemate, openly visible to a world audience, led to the gradual erosion of the State Department's budget, forced temporary disruptions within several foreign embassies and consulates, demoralized the foreign service, and left dozens of diplomatic appointments and international agreements in limbo—all at a time when the United States might otherwise have been exploiting its status as the cold war's champion and the world's lone superpower.

This impasse, just the latest in a series of legislative-executive confrontations that spans the country's history, symbolizes the practical and often disabling consequences of "shifting constellations" within the U.S. government during a period of systemic transformation. The new international environment clearly demanded a shift in both policy and bureaucratic structures. But across the United States and in Washington, no consensus emerged to replace the broad-based support for communist containment that had sustained that strategy for more than four decades.[2] Lacking public and elite support for his new grand strategy, Clinton could not translate his new policy into practice, and the foreign policy bureaucracy entered a period of prolonged disarray. Rarely has the "invitation to struggle" created by the Constitution been so apparent, and so disabling, in the conduct of U.S. foreign policy.[3]

This episode thus illustrates the sources and consequences of *clashing* executive and legislative constellations that result when the global objectives of the United States are cast into doubt. As the two branches of government hardened their positions over post–cold war policy, the foreign affairs bureaucracy was held captive to their institutional rivalry. Itself an arm of the executive branch, the State Department was openly allied with the White House during this struggle. Meanwhile, the proposed shift in U.S. foreign policy was welcomed by many foreign governments, particularly in developing areas, and by international organizations such as the United Nations, the World Bank, and the Organization for Economic Cooperation and Development (OECD). Nevertheless, Clinton's ability to implement his policy initiatives required the consent of Congress, which maintained the "power of the purse" and thus could effectively thwart any new policies proclaimed by the president.

This chapter begins by reviewing Clinton's early effort to change the course of U.S. foreign policy and to provide a new mission for the State Department and its key agencies. Particular attention is given to the struggle over USAID, an independent arm of the State Department that serves as the primary source of U.S. foreign aid. The chapter then describes the frontal assault on Clinton's proposals—and on USAID itself—by the Republican-led Congress after the 1994 midterm elections. Finally, it places these events in the context of the "shifting constellations" framework used throughout this volume and considers their implications for the formulation and conduct of U.S. foreign policy in the future.

## Clinton's Policy Initiatives, 1993–1994

Bill Clinton entered the White House in January 1993 with a mandate to emphasize domestic concerns such as U.S. economic competitiveness, deficit reduction, education, and crime—issues that had been neglected to varying degrees as the United States engaged the Soviet Union in nearly half a century of superpower competition. Clinton claimed neither expertise nor an overriding interest in U.S. foreign policy, and his erratic performance in response to a wide range of regional crises in 1993 and 1994 reflected this disposition.

Clinton, however, still hoped to make his mark in foreign policy. Just as social problems within the United States had been neglected during the cold war, he believed transnational problems deserved a concerted response that was long overdue. Specifically, Clinton embraced the ongoing global campaign of "sustainable development," a loosely knit concept encompassing such issues as environmental protection, population control, democratization, and broadly based, market-driven economic growth. Clinton's support for sustainable development recalled certain aspects of John F. Kennedy's Alliance for Progress and Jimmy Carter's world order politics, which emphasized cooperative North-South relations, human rights, and the "complex interdependence" of all countries in a rapidly integrating global system.[4]

The impetus for sustainable development came in the summer of 1992 during the United Nations Conference on Environment and Development, at the time the largest single gathering of world leaders in history. Political leaders acknowledged their responsibility at this Earth Summit for promoting long-term development sensitive to environmental, demographic, and political concerns. The United Nations encouraged this effort by establishing a Commission on Sustainable Development, and forty countries established their own such agencies in 1992 and 1993.

Unlike most other world leaders at the Earth Summit, George Bush opposed many of these proposals, claiming they would unduly restrict American sovereignty and impose excessive burdens on its industries and public resources. But after his victory over Bush in the 1992 presidential election, Clinton endorsed the provisions of *Agenda 21*, the Earth Summit's concluding statement that would later inform his own policy proposals.[5] Vice President Albert Gore, a proponent of environmental preservation, was directed to lead the effort, and a new position was created, under secretary of state for global affairs, which symbolized the new thrust of American policy.[6] The Clinton administration looked forward to ongoing support from a U.S. Congress then controlled by the Democratic Party.

In addition, the Clinton administration initiated a reorganization of USAID, whose aid programs had previously been tailored to facilitate the containment effort. Rather than Soviet subversion, USAID would address perceived new threats to American security: the growth of the world's population to nearly 6 billion, environmental problems such as global warming and deforestation, political repression in many Third World countries that threatened democratic reforms, and the continuing obstacles to economic growth in many developing countries. Secretary of State Warren Christopher defended the continuing need for U.S. aid and testified before Congress that "we must now target our assistance to address today's priorities." Spending categories for USAID were reorganized under such titles as Promoting Sustainable Development, Building Democracy, Promoting U.S. Prosperity, and Advancing Diplomacy. Finally, USAID proposed shifting the Economic Support Fund, which had pursued security-oriented concerns, out of the development assistance program and into a new functional category entitled "Promoting Peace."[7]

As noted above, Clinton supported the general idea of reorganizing the State Department in general and USAID in particular, an idea previously endorsed by former secretaries of state Lawrence Eagleburger, James A. Baker, George Shultz, Alexander Haig, and Henry Kissinger.[8] Many of these reforms—including the elimination of more than a thousand positions, the streamlining of the department's hierarchy, and the closure of several overseas missions and consular posts—had previously been accepted by the State Department and were endorsed by Christopher when he took office.[9] Clinton assigned Gore to examine the State Department as part of his National Performance Review, and Gore's subsequent restructuring proposals were also widely accepted by Congress. Beyond the proposed cutbacks, however, Clinton insisted that the remaining workforce at State and USAID be assigned to fulfilling his new foreign policy goals.

Clinton's pursuit of sustainable development, of course, must not be viewed in isolation from his other foreign policy priorities. Among others he also sought to raise the profile of foreign *economic* policy, primarily the promotion of U.S. exports, which served as an extension of his domestic agenda. Toward this end Clinton actively supported the process of regional economic integration in North America, the creation of the World Trade Organization, and a more cooperative relationship between the federal government and the private sector. In all of these efforts, designed to make U.S. industries more competitive and create a more market-friendly global marketplace, he received broad congressional support and enjoyed considerable success.

In addition, the Clinton administration adopted a high profile in the effort to "enlarge" and consolidate democratic rule overseas. Echoing George Kennan, containment's intellectual founder, National Security Adviser Anthony Lake pledged that the United States would "seek to isolate [nondemocratic states] diplomatically, militarily, economically and technologically." Further, he declared, "The successor to a doctrine of containment must be a strategy of enlargement—enlargement of the world's free community. . . . We must counter the aggression—and support the liberalization—of states hostile to democracy."[10]

Secretary of State Christopher cited U.S. support for democratization programs in southern Africa, Southeast Asia, and Latin America as evidence of the administration's determination to match its words with deeds. Indeed, large annual commitments of economic aid to Russia and its neighbors—at a time when the popularity of foreign aid had descended to record lows—was viewed as a critical component of this effort. Christopher justified the continuing priority of the United States in promoting democratization, both as a means to enhance its own security and as a moral imperative:

> At bottom, support for democracy and human rights, setting an example, and standing up for what we believe in are vital parts of U.S. leadership. Other nations have long followed America's lead in part because our nation has a proven willingness to stand for something larger than itself. From the time of the American Revolution, people everywhere have looked to the United States for inspiration in their struggle for freedom and a better life. We are committed to carrying on that tradition because it is right and because it is our greatest source of strength in the world.[11]

The democratization campaign was explicitly linked to Clinton's broader effort to promote sustainable development. Only in a representative government, it was presumed, could broad-based and ecologically responsive development occur. Many of these policy proposals were tied together in the Peace, Prosperity, and Democracy Act of 1994, which repealed the Foreign Assistance Act of 1961. The bill, supported by Clinton and a U.S. Congress then dominated by the Democratic Party, called for an aggressive U.S. role in confronting global problems that transcended narrowly defied U.S. "national interests." For a brief time in 1994, it appeared that the ideals of Clinton's policy shift, which Lake labeled "pragmatic neo-Wilsonianism," would be realized and enacted into law.[12]

But this was not to be. As the next section of this case study illustrates, the Clinton administration's window of opportunity slammed shut in November 1994 after midterm congressional elections reversed the political tides and brought an entirely different agenda to Washington.

### The Congressional Challenge, 1995–1996

It was not foreign upheavals that launched the challenge to the Clinton administration's worldview. To the contrary, the challenge began at home, for reasons only marginally related to foreign policy. Despite reductions in the federal deficit and improved economic growth during this period, public opinion polls revealed widespread distrust of the federal government. This pervasive skepticism was accompanied by the revival of the Republican Party in many state governments, particularly in the South, where a historic realignment in state legislatures and congressional representation had been under way for more than a decade. While many expected Republican Party gains in the midterm elections of 1994, few predicted its sweeping victories and its capture of majority rule in both houses of Congress.

The congressional elections of 1994 witnessed a historic resurgence of the Republican Party—its first claim to majority status in both houses since 1954. The Republicans, who held just 204 of the 435 House seats before the elections, won 235 seats to capture majority control. On the Senate side, the Republican Party increased its share from 46 to 53 of the 100 seats—a solid if not veto-proof majority. The Republican gains were strengthened by several retirements among Democratic members of Congress shortly before the election, and by the switching of parties by five former Democrats shortly afterward. Thus the final two years of Clinton's first term would feature a reversal of the pattern of divided government experienced by former presidents Ronald Reagan and George Bush: now a *Republican* Congress would offset a *Democratic* White House.[13]

The political sea change was keenly reflected in the composition of congressional committees involved in foreign policy. Most notably, Senator Jesse Helms (R-N.C.), the senior Republican member of the Foreign Relations Committee, asserted his right to assume the role of chairman. Although some members of Congress preferred other candidates for this powerful position, particularly Senator Richard Lugar of

Indiana, Majority Leader Bob Dole allowed Helms to assume control of the committee. Given Helms's track record as a committee member, it surprised few when Helms, dubbed "Senator No" for his consistent opposition to an activist U.S. foreign policy, adopted his confrontational tactics early in 1995.

Helms required little time to propose his overhaul of the State Department after the midterm elections. He announced his proposals on March 15, 1995, which included the elimination of USAID, USIA, and USACDA, along with the creation of a "new" State Department, much more streamlined and centrally controlled than under the existing system.[14] Finally, he recommended increases in U.S. military spending as a more appropriate means to achieve these interests in the post–cold war world.

Among the institutions of U.S. foreign policy that Helms believed had outlived their usefulness, USAID was his primary target. "At the heart of the matter is his longstanding disdain for foreign aid," one journalist observed. "His reorganization proposal strikes at the core of foreign aid."[15] For decades, Helms condemned the foreign aid program as an expression of naive American idealism and as a "rathole" for squandered taxpayer dollars. Further, he argued that USAID, the primary source of U.S. foreign aid, operated as a "rogue" agency without oversight and had become beholden as much to its own bureaucratic self-interests as to the needs of developing countries. Upon taking control of the Foreign Relations Committee, he openly dismissed USAID's effort to promote sustainable development in foreign countries of marginal strategic relevance to the United States.

Well before Clinton's election, the effectiveness of U.S. foreign aid had come under intensified scrutiny. The bipartisan Hamilton-Gilman Task Force concluded in 1989 that USAID had become overburdened and ineffective. Among many other subsequent studies, a July 1993 report by the General Accounting Office concluded that "USAID had entered the 1990s unprepared to meet the management challenges facing it." According to its authors, USAID "lacked a clearly articulated strategic direction," maintained too many overseas missions with inadequate resources, and had a poor system in place to train USAID officers and evaluate their performance.[16] Analyses in the early 1990s were replete with suggestions for fundamental reform of U.S. foreign assistance. Other critics called upon the Clinton administration to "scuttle America's bilateral aid program and begin anew with a concise, clearly defined initiative to promote environmentally sound forms of economic growth."[17]

Within USAID, administrators scrambled to satisfy congressional demands and to avoid the agency's abolition. In addition to their proposals to align U.S. foreign aid with the global program of sustainable development, Christopher and USAID administrator J. Brian Atwood called for reducing the number of U.S. bilateral aid programs and reducing the number of staffed overseas missions. Twenty-one of these missions were identified for possible closure by fiscal year 1996.[18] Atwood proposed to lower the ratio of Washington-based USAID employees to those serving overseas and pledged to reform the system by which USAID procured domestic goods and services, a system which many critics argued had been tainted by corruption.

These measures were designed to streamline USAID and to limit its mission to sustainable development while other objectives of U.S. foreign policy were pursued elsewhere. While many welcomed these reforms, they suggested that the American public and federal government would be asked to provide funds for purposes indirectly related to national self-interests. In an era of growing fiscal austerity, and of continuing doubts about the ability and responsibility of the United States to play a proactive role in resolving global problems, it became increasingly doubtful that sufficient support could be achieved to sustain U.S. foreign aid at even these greatly reduced levels.

Faced with opposition by the White House and the foreign affairs bureaucracy, Helms indefinitely adjourned the Foreign Relations Committee and effectively held much of U.S. foreign policy hostage—including nearly four hundred foreign-service promotions, thirty ambassadorial nominations, more than a dozen treaties and international agreements, and many routine functions of the State Department. Nearly three-quarters of the department's Washington-based staff was furloughed as it operated under stopgap funding, and the handling of nearly thirty thousand daily visa applications was temporarily suspended. The U.S. government stopped paying utility bills at many foreign embassies, and funds to operate the State Department's computer and cable services were suspended. "As a result," the *New York Times* reported, "the day-to-day foreign policy business on Capitol Hill has ground to a halt."[19]

The Senate Foreign Relations Committee completed the Helms legislation, entitled the Foreign Relations Revitalization Act of 1995, on May 17, 1995, and sent it to the full Senate for debate on July 28. The bill, which called for the abolition of all three agencies, was designed to reduce the scope of U.S. foreign policy activities as part of an overall effort to reduce the national debt and to balance the federal budget. "Seldom before has such a comprehensive foreign policy reorganization effort been undertaken by a Congressional committee," the bill proclaimed.

"The opportunity to achieve enormous cost savings through streamlining and eliminating duplication of functions is unparalleled."[20]

Given the large number of Democrats still in the Senate, Republicans were unable to prevent a filibuster and force a vote on the issue. Thus after several months of negotiation, Democrats led by Senator John Kerry (D-Mass.) reached a compromise with Republicans. On December 14 the full Senate approved a bill by a vote of 82 to 16 to reduce foreign affairs spending by $1.7 billion over five years without requiring the abolition of USAID, USIA, and USACDA. The budget reductions, though, would cut deeply into the operating expenses of all three agencies. Program funds, such as USAID's development assistance, could only account for 30 percent of the cutbacks, meaning that most of the downsizing would involve Washington-based staff.

Meanwhile, the House of Representatives considered its own measure to reform the State Department, entitled the Foreign Affairs Agencies Consolidation Act of 1995. Its International Relations Committee, chaired by Representative Benjamin Gilman (R-N.Y.), took the lead in this effort. In many ways the House version, introduced by Gilman on May 3 and approved by the full House June 8 by a vote of 222 to 192, was stronger than the Senate version. In the House version the three agencies were to be abolished, with their reduced functions supervised by State Department officials. Under the existing framework, the heads of the three agencies merely operated under the foreign policy "guidance" of the secretary of state. The bill further required that the spending of the consolidated agencies be reduced by 20 percent in each of the two years after their merger.

The Clinton administration remained opposed to the congressional reforms, and Helms promised to keep the Foreign Relations Committee in indefinite recess, an unprecedented step in its long history, until Clinton agreed to his demands. "These people are playing hardball and dirty pool at the same time, and I'm not going to cave in," Helms declared in September 1995. "But all the President has got to do is say, 'Senator, let's talk,' and we'll talk. It'll end on the day the President says we'll make a deal and we bust up that little fairyland."[21]

The stalemate was finally relieved—if temporarily—after the Senate agreed to a compromise in December 1995. Under the agreement, the Foreign Relations Committee agreed to vote on eighteen ambassadorial nominations. Once the members reconvened, each of the nominees was confirmed within two days. Consequently, after months of confusion and drift, the United States again had high-level representation in such strategically important countries as China, Pakistan, Indonesia, and Panama. Helms also allowed the committee to consider several tax treaties and two major arms control treaties—the second Strategic Arms Reduction Treaty (START II) between the United States and Russia, and the multilateral Chemical Weapons Convention. After Helms relinquished the START II treaty, it was quickly approved by the committee and sent to the full Senate, where it was approved by an overwhelming margin of 87 to 4.[22]

With the exception of these measures, the deadlock over the management and scope of U.S. foreign affairs continued. The compromise merely cleared the most urgent matters for action; the broader conflicts between the Republican-led Congress and the Clinton administration were far from resolved. As a result, the State Department cut deeper into its already reduced operating budget and the three embattled agencies further scaled back their activities. The U.S. remained in arrears to the United Nations for previous financial commitments it had failed to honor, and its reduced funding for bilateral and multilateral development programs placed greater pressure on other industrialized states to increase their contributions.

For obvious reasons, the congressional assault on the State Department further dampened the already low morale among its personnel. "It's hard to have an effective foreign policy when 72 percent of your employees can't come to work by law, when nobody is receiving a full paycheck, and when most of the people that we normally depend on to do the work cannot come to work," State Department spokesman Nicholas Burns lamented in January 1996.[23] As for U.S. representation overseas, it quickly became clear that U.S. credibility was eroding in foreign capitals where key diplomatic posts were left vacant. "The chief of mission is the President's personal representative and it is he or she who makes the embassy run efficiently," stated USAID Richard Moose, under secretary of state for management. "Our Government is not highly regarded if there is no ambassador there."[24]

Faced with the threat of their outright abolition, officials in USAID, USIA, and USACDA complained that long-term planning and the implementation of many approved programs had become impossible. And in many developing countries, where the United States had coordinated aid programs and other activities for decades, the political deadlock in Washington raised doubts about their future support from the United States. Finally, leaders of the United Nations and OECD questioned why they should shoulder the burden of sustainable development if the United States, with its vast economic resources, withdrew from the process.

## Legislative Action and a Presidential Veto

The showdown over the U.S. State Department was only one of several areas of contention after the midterm elections, but one which struck at the core of the president's ability to manage foreign affairs. Not only was Clinton deprived of his ability to execute his policy shift, but in the final months of 1995 his foreign policy team was unable to manage effectively many routine functions of the State Department. To many Republicans, including Helms, the resulting gridlock within the State Department was justified after years of bureaucratic inertia.

On March 7, 1996, a House-Senate conference committee reached agreement on an authorization bill (known by its House designation, H.R. 1561) that would enact many of the Republicans' restructuring plans. The Foreign Relations Committee then moved forward on the Foreign Relations Authorization Act, fiscal years 1996 and 1997, which called for cuts of nearly $500 million in the State Department's $3-billion operating budget. The bill called for the abolition of USAID, USIA, and USACDA by March 1, 1997, with their restricted roles to be overseen by the secretary of state. In the case of USAID, a new position—undersecretary of state for development, economic and commercial affairs—would be created to manage the smaller allotments of development aid originating in the United States. All aid would be terminated under the bill except for programs explicitly approved by Congress, such as the massive aid programs for Israel and Egypt ($5.1 billion annually), the Peace Corps ($435 million over two years), and narcotics control ($426 million). The operating budget for administering U.S. economic aid would fall from $515 million in fiscal year 1995 to $435 million by fiscal year 1999.

Under the congressional bill, Clinton would be granted a waiver which would allow him to preserve two of the three threatened agencies of his choosing. According to the committee, this would "put the onus on the President to actually prevent their shutdown." In applying for the waiver, however, Clinton would be required to satisfy several requirements. First, he would have to submit a State Department reorganization plan to Congress by October 1, 1996. Second, he would have to document that his plan would achieve savings of at least $1.7 billion between fiscal years 1996 and 1999. Finally, he would have to demonstrate that the two remaining agencies were "important to the national interest of the United States."[25]

The conference committee's final legislation went far beyond reorganizing the State Department. The wide-ranging bill included amendments covering several unrelated policy areas that were of interest to Republican leaders. Among others, these provisions included:

- prohibiting U.S. assistance to "international organizations espousing world government";
- denying passports to parents for nonpayment of child support;
- linking normalized U.S.-Vietnamese relations to progress in accounting for prisoners of war;
- authorizing the president to appoint a special envoy for Tibet; and
- establishing a $100 million Bosnian "self-defense fund" to arm and train Bosnian-Croat forces in their war against Serbia.

The bill further called for limiting U.S. contributions to U.N. peace-keeping efforts to 25 percent of their total costs, down from their existing level of nearly one-third. Finally, it required the United States to withdraw from such organizations as the U.N. Industrial Development Organization, the World Tourism Organization, the Inter-American Indian Institute, and the International Tropical Timber Organization. Few areas of U.S. foreign policy were left untouched by the legislation.

After being approved by the conference committee on March 28, 1996, the bill was sent to the floor of both houses of Congress. It passed the Senate 52 to 44 and the House of Representatives 226 to 172, largely along party lines in both cases. As one journalist observed, "The measure was one of the most partisan foreign policy bills enacted by Congress at least since the end of World War II."[26] Shortly before the vote, the White House issued a Statement of Administration Policy that warned, "If the conference report on H.R. 1561 is presented to the President in its current form, the President will veto the bill. While steps have been taken to improve the bill, it still contains numerous provisions which do not serve U.S. foreign policy or U.S. national interests." The White House argued that the forced consolidation of the agencies "interferes with the President's prerogative to organize the foreign affairs agencies in a manner that best serves the Nation's interests and the Administration's foreign policy priorities."[27]

The warning did not prevent congressional passage of the bill. And as expected, Clinton vetoed the Foreign Relations Authorization Bill on April 12. "This legislation contains many unacceptable provisions that would undercut U.S. leadership abroad and damage our ability to assure the future security and prosperity of the American people," Clinton declared in his veto message.[28] With Clinton's veto, the State Department continued to operate under a stopgap bill passed earlier. But the veto did not put to rest the impasse over U.S. foreign policy. To the contrary,

Helms vowed to continue his campaign and warned USAID, USIA, and USACDA that "the writing is on the wall; the question is not if they will be eliminated, but when." As Helms further argued, "The President has made a most regrettable mistake in vetoing this bill. In doing so, he chose to stick his head in the sand and avoid confronting the reality that the foreign aid budget is shrinking and that he must choose priorities—spending American taxpayers' money on the programs the President tells us are important, or spending on keeping unnecessary bureaucrats on the dole."[29]

At the same time, the Clinton administration expanded its effort to make sustainable development a key feature of U.S. foreign policy. Just as the battle with Congress was reaching its climax, Christopher launched a major environmental initiative at four levels—global, regional, bilateral, and "partnerships" with multinational corporations and other nongovernmental organizations. "Environmental forces transcend borders and oceans to threaten directly the health, prosperity, and jobs of American citizens," Christopher declared.[30] Once again, his proposals would require new resources, further changes to the foreign policy bureaucracy, and approval by the U.S. Congress.

As part of its platform completed in August 1996, the Democratic Party renewed its pledge to change the course of U.S. foreign policy and accused Republicans of ignoring global problems in their pursuit of narrow national self-interests. Clinton's acceptance speech at the Democratic Convention, which otherwise focused on problems at home, called for continued efforts to implement a more "enlightened" foreign policy. Beyond their rhetorical flourishes, however, both sides put the debate to rest as all the parties to the conflict—Republicans and Democrats, the White House and Congress—turned their attention to the November 1996 presidential elections. Both sides would cite their actions during the deadlock to support their cases, and both would continue to promote their divergent visions of U.S. foreign policy in the post–cold war period. Clinton, whose main foreign policy concern during the campaign was being perceived as "soft on defense," conceded to Republican demands and approved a $257 billion budget for fiscal year 1997 that was more than $11 billion greater than the level recommended by the Joint Chiefs of Staff. Tellingly, many of the new funds were directed toward struggling military-industrial sectors of the U.S. economy and justified largely on the basis of their impact on local and regional economic growth; their connection to the Pentagon's overall strategy of "preventive defense" was obscure at best.

The presidential elections of November 1996 returned Clinton to the White House and a Republican majority to Congress. While the Democratic Party gained several seats in the House of Representatives, Republicans widened their advantage in the Senate, although they fell far short of the sixty-seven seats necessary to produce a veto-proof majority. As a result, the pattern of divided government established two years earlier remained intact, as did the prospects for continuing competition between the White House and Congress over the structure and scope of U.S. foreign policy.

### External and Internal Sources of the Political Impasse

As we have seen, Clinton's ability to chart a new course for the State Department, based on his conception of the emerging international system, was greatly constrained by the political realities of the post–cold war era. The political sea change led to a two-front assault against Clinton's policy: from the emboldened Republican Party, which reflected and exploited deepening public distrust of the federal government, and from Congress, whose leaders skillfully utilized their constitutional prerogatives to disrupt the executive branch's initiatives and the routine functions of the foreign policy bureaucracy.

The shifting constellations image used throughout this volume correctly presumes that the conduct of the three institutional actors is to a large extent bounded by the external environment in which they operate (see figure 1.2). The image's causal chain begins with these international and societal forces, then moves downward to the White House, Congress, and foreign policy bureaucracy. This concluding section will first consider the impact of these external forces on the showdown over the U.S. State Department and then examine their interaction with the domestic policy debate in Washington. As we will find, the showdown between the White House and Congress not only reflected national ambivalence about America's post–cold war role, but also demonstrated the limits of presidential power in foreign policy when the United States is not at war or faced with an imminent foreign threat or crisis. In more tranquil periods, Congress historically holds sway, primarily through its "power of the purse" that prevents new foreign ventures sought by the president from being implemented. In this climate the political balance of power *within* the United States becomes a key determinant of its foreign policy.

*International and Societal Forces*

The starting point for this analysis was the transformed nature of world politics in the wake of the cold war. This period witnessed a shift from bipolarity to an uncertain global balance of power, the dissolution of the Soviet Union into fifteen republics, the de facto liberation of its satellites in Eastern Europe, the reunification of Germany and the consolidation of the European Union, and, to a large degree, a resolution of the ideological rivalry that had contaminated the post–world war II period. Although history clearly did not end, the Western model of liberal democracy prevailed over a wider terrain than ever.

These changes opened the door for other systemic forces to assert themselves. The market-based world economy integrated rapidly during this period, ushering in an era of *geoeconomics*. Nearly every nation-state agreed to the creation of a World Trade Organization to regulate international commerce. Economic blocs in Western Europe, North America, and the Asia-Pacific region became more cohesive. Multinational corporations obtained greater sway than ever, in government policy as well as economics. And in the United States, foreign economic policy was promoted to "high politics" and made a cornerstone of Bill Clinton's foreign policy. At the same time, international governmental organizations (IGOs) assumed a more prominent role. The United Nations expanded its peacekeeping role, which had been impossible during the cold war. And it aligned itself with other IGOs in calling attention to global problems and pledging to correct them through a worldwide campaign of sustainable development. The number of international nongovernmental organizations (NGOs) also increased dramatically during this period and outnumbered IGOs in the 1990s by a margin of about 4,500 to 300. These NGOs imposed new demands on state actors and frequently served as institutional links between states and IGOs.[31]

In the euphoria surrounding the cold war's collapse, these international forces were collectively expected to produce a "new world order" in which multilateral cooperation would replace interstate conflict. Global competition would be channeled peacefully through economic markets, and the spread of democratic government would produce a more just world and discourage future wars. In the United States, many welcomed the opportunity to address social problems that were neglected during the cold war, and to seize the opportunities posed by geoeconomics. Further, the ability of the United States to lead a United Nations coalition against Iraq in the Persian Gulf demonstrated the extent of its political influence and the overwhelming strength of its military forces, which surpassed all expectations in the Gulf War. This high level of self-confidence led the Bush administration to assume a lead role in supporting economic and political reforms across the former Soviet bloc and in launching a humanitarian intervention in Somalia.

Beyond these new ventures, however, the general public in the United States seemed ambivalent about the country's role in the new global climate. Public opinion polls consistently revealed that domestic issues had become primary and foreign policy secondary.[32] Since the latter was most associated with George Bush, he was vulnerable to the agenda put forward by Bill Clinton, who promised to make lower budget deficits and the revival of American economic competitiveness his primary objectives. For these and other reasons Clinton defeated Bush in the 1992 elections, and once in office he focused primarily on his domestic agenda, turning much of his foreign policy into an extension of his domestic priorities.

In this context, Clinton's embrace of sustainable development ran counter to the prevailing national sentiment as reflected in opinion polls. Clinton's approach was, in fact, more consistent with world opinion and the goals espoused by major international organizations. But Clinton sought to draw on another side of domestic opinion, one which historically favored a proactive role by the United States in spreading its national values to other societies. Based upon the traditional self-image of the United States as the "city upon a hill," this idealistic aspect of the national character was implicit in widespread presumptions of "manifest destiny" that legitimated American expansion in the nineteenth century and that, to a large extent, animated its approach to the two "hot" wars of the twentieth century and the cold war.[33] Thus the optimism of the immediate post–cold war period lent itself to the liberal internationalism espoused by Bill Clinton when he took office in January 1993. For the next two years, he refined his new program and looked forward to support, when the time came, from a Congress then dominated by the Democratic Party.

Developments overseas, however, raised serious doubts about the new order. Specifically, the collapse of the multilateral relief effort in Somalia and the inability of the United Nations to bring the Balkan conflict under control revealed serious deficiencies in the cooperative framework that was supposedly in place to resolve regional conflicts. At the same time, ethnic divisions in other areas erupted in large-scale violence and new questions were raised about the future of Russia, China, and the Middle East peace process. Global fragmentation became as central to the new order as integration. Far from a harmony of global interests, a darker world view emerged, reflected in the pessimistic text of Samuel Huntington's article, "The Clash of Civilizations."[34]

*Governmental Forces*

It was in this deteriorating international context that the Republican Party unexpectedly captured control of the U.S. Congress and opposed Clinton's effort to pursue a policy of liberal internationalism. The Republican challenge was based in large measure upon deep-seated public antipathy toward the U.S. government and a preference for a more limited federal role in domestic affairs. As for foreign policy, public opinion surveys revealed growing opposition to an activist role by the United States in the absence of a direct threat to U.S. vital interests. Given that the transnational concerns drawn together under the rubric of sustainable development related to broad, often imperceptible threats that related only indirectly to U.S. self-interests, their failure to register among the general public was consistent with past patterns. The divided government produced by the congressional elections of 1994 thus served as a metaphor for the societal ambivalence of the United States regarding its world role.

When profound differences exist regarding the country's global responsibilities, as they have in the aftermath of the cold war, bureaucratic rivalries intensify and actors within the executive and legislative branches have many institutional levers at their disposal—the power of the purse, committee action or inaction, manipulation of the federal bureaucracy, the veto power—to prevent action they oppose. Both sides in this struggle turned to these instruments, leading to an institutional stalemate, the estrangement and demoralization of the State Department, and more broadly, the failure of Clinton's policy shift.

The most important power of the president in U.S. foreign policy is also the most abstract, involving his or her ability to set the general tone and direction of policy. Clinton drew on this informal power in proposing his reforms in 1993 and 1994. After the midterm elections, however, Congress was able to prevent his new principles from being put into practice. Aside from the power to declare war, a congressional power that was irrelevant to this debate, the most important tool for the legislative branch is its authority over the expenditure of U.S. funds, or the "power of the purse." In restricting funds for the State Department, or more precisely, in reducing its operating budget by nearly 50 percent, Congress effectively suffocated the Clinton initiatives.

Importantly, the congressional assault against the White House was channeled through the committee system, which it dominated after the midterm elections. The Senate Foreign Relations Committee, with primary responsibility in this area, is required to approve high-level diplomatic appointments and ratify international treaties signed by the president before subjecting them to consideration by the full Senate. During its recess, the most crucial matters placed before this committee were suspended. In this manner the full force of congressional authority was brought to bear on the executive branch.

Clinton, of course, utilized his most direct authority *vis-à-vis* Congress in 1996, the veto power, which prevented the sweeping reforms approved by both houses from taking effect. But in some respects this was a hollow victory. In trying to salvage USAID, Atwood emasculated the agency and canceled many programs to promote environmental preservation, population control, and poverty relief in the world's most troubled regions. By 1995 the United States had fallen to fourth among donors of development aid, behind Japan, France, and Germany. Of its $7.4 billion in aid allocations, the largest bilateral packages were destined for Israel and Egypt, strategic allies of the United States and hardly the most hard-pressed of developing countries. U.S. development aid represented one-tenth of one percent of U.S. GNP in 1995, the lowest share among all industrialized societies and a figure that would be still lower if the large transfers to Israel and Egypt were not included.[35]

It must be recalled that the White House was supported by the State Department bureaucracy throughout this struggle. But the unfolding events revealed the limits of the department's ability to protect its interests in the face of congressional opposition and public skepticism. To some extent, this was due to the relatively small size of the State Department, whose 1996 staff of fifteen thousand and $2.5-billion operating budget were dwarfed by that of the Pentagon, with nearly 1.5 million officers in uniform, a massive Washington-based civilian staff, and an annual budget more than one hundred times that of the State Department. In this respect the disproportionate size of the defense bureaucracy, and its relatively large share of both federal spending and U.S. economic output, gave it a decisive advantage in its competition with the State Department for congressional support and federal funding.

The State Department's support for the expansive mission outlined by Clinton was predictable, however, given its institutional self-interests that would have been served by the new policy. Rarely do bureaucracies favor their own dismemberment, and rarely do they oppose measures that would broaden their mandates. Consistent with the model of bureaucratic politics, however, multiple bureaucratic actors are generally at play in a complex governmental structure and their interests frequently collide.[36] This leads either to government action that moves in several directions at once, or, in cases when policy must be guided by a cohesive overriding strategy, it leads to the demise of a policy favored by overmatched bureaucratic actors. In advocating a foreign policy based on liberal internationalism, the State Department was largely isolated within the broader foreign policy bureaucracy including the armed forces, other executive agencies, and Congress. State's relatively shallow power base thus contributed to its failure to implement the policy advanced by the president and endorsed by its own secretary.

The impotence of the State Department further reflected its lack of influential constituencies from which to derive domestic support for its programs. Congressional advocates of greater military spending could always cite "national security" as a compelling rationale for their budget proposals, even if they were in part motivated by the need to secure federal funds for key congressional districts. In this effort they could rely upon support from high-level Pentagon officials who were also driven by institutional as well as strategic considerations. In the mid-1990s, the Defense Department sought a reversal of cutbacks which began just after the cold war; it proposed a security strategy based on "preventive defense" that would maintain a strong U.S. military presence throughout the world.[37]

This pattern demonstrated how military leaders may emphasize foreign threats "to convince society to grant them the size, wealth, autonomy, and prestige that all bureaucracies seek—not to provoke war."[38] Ambiguous warnings of a "new cold war" with China or Russia resonated deeply across the country while calls for increased spending on sustainable development, whose immediate benefactors would be citizens and leaders of foreign countries, generally fell on deaf ears. This reality forced USAID officials to increasingly cite U.S. self-interests in seeking congressional support, whether in the form of creating overseas markets for U.S. exports or in the designation of aid programs to be tied to domestic goods and services.[39] But even these appeals failed to exact concessions from congressional leaders.

For his part, Clinton was conspicuously detached from the struggle over the State Department after the 1994 congressional elections. While this study has focused on the rivalry between the White House and Congress, in practice there was little personal follow-up from the president himself. To the contrary, Clinton left the defense of his policy shift to his subordinates in the State Department and USAID. As Clinton devoted his energies to domestic policy and to more immediate problems in foreign policy—the faltering Middle East peace process, the failed Somalia mission, the intervention in Haiti, the Bosnia war—he did not fight aggressively to rescue these institutions from the severe budget cuts that ensued in 1995 and 1996. His lack of personal attention to sustainable development, which contradicted his rhetorical appeals, left the field open to congressional critics of the proposed shift.[40]

Clinton's inattention to the deadlock over the State Department clearly reflected his general emphasis on domestic policy, particularly economic development. Further, it resulted from his growing concern over reelection in 1996, something that was by no means assured after the Republican resurgence in 1994. In many other issue areas, the president abandoned or reversed previous positions and supported policies championed by Republican leaders, such as welfare reform and a larger defense budget. His attempt to capture the "vital center" of American politics dismayed many liberals who felt abandoned by the president. But his strategy, combined with a strong economy and the lackluster performance of his Republican challenger, former Senator Bob Dole, proved successful in gaining his reelection. Furthermore, Clinton could be satisfied that another thrust of U.S. foreign policy—the expansion of U.S. exports and overseas competitiveness—had clearly borne fruit.

As Clinton began his second term, the impasse over the U.S. State Department continued. While Congress approved most of Clinton's nominees for top-level foreign policy posts—including Secretary of State Madeleine Albright and Defense Secretary William Cohen—it remained opposed to the shift in grand strategy proposed by Clinton. Calls for a shrunken State Department and the elimination of USAID, USIA, and USACDA remained in force, but the institutional framework that was built during the cold war remained largely intact. Albright predictably called for a restoration of the State Department's funding and an increase in foreign aid expenditures, primarily for Russia and Eastern European states. The United States, she argued, should take an assertive role in world politics; it should be an "author of history" rather than a bystander. But it remained doubtful that Congress, which had been so effective in restraining Clinton, would reverse itself in his second term.

The deadlock between the White House and Congress was broken, however, early in April 1997 when the two sides reached a compromise agreement that covered several foreign policy issues, including foreign aid. On the very day that Helms allowed a Senate vote on the Chemical Weapons Convention, a top priority of the Clinton administration, the White House announced its support for a modified version of the State Department restructuring plan proposed by Congress.[41] As the White

House proclaimed, the agreement "puts matters of international arms control, sustainable development, and public diplomacy where they belong, at the heart of our foreign policy within a reinvented Department of State."[42] Under the compromise, the Clinton administration agreed to abolish the USACDA and USIA and fold them into the State Department. The directors of USACDA and USIA would be given new titles of under secretaries of state under the plan. The United States would maintain many of the functions provided by the two agencies, albeit at a much smaller scale.

As for USAID, Congress agreed to retain the agency's independent status, a principle demand of the White House. Clinton agreed, however, to merge several USAID and State Department functions, such as press relations, and to bring USAID's administrator under the "direct authority and foreign policy guidance of the Secretary of State." The International Development Cooperation Agency, created in 1979 and considered by many as duplicating other USAID functions was abolished. And in the future, the secretary of state and USAID administrator were required to "recommend what further steps might be taken to eliminate duplication."[43]

More generally, however, the institutional struggle over U.S. foreign policy was far from resolved, and the casualties of the long impasse were clearly visible. Contrary to the Clinton administration's public statements, sustainable development had been effectively eliminated from the U.S. foreign policy agenda while further cutbacks in the Pentagon's budget and a new round of base closings previously endorsed by Clinton were blocked by Congress. For his part, Senator Helms renewed his offensive against the White House by opposing—and eventually killing—the nomination of former Massachusetts governor William Weld—a moderate Republican—to be U.S. ambassador to Mexico. The United States pressed forward on NATO expansion and extended the NATO-led mission in the former Yugoslavia, efforts that were more consistent with the congressional foreign policy agenda.

In the years to come, the liberation of U.S. foreign policy from the protracted political impasse of the post–cold war era will likely require the restoration of consensus regarding the country's appropriate role in foreign affairs. In the absence of such a consensus, the likelihood remains that U.S. policy will continue to be driven by crises overseas—whether in southern Europe, the Middle East, central Africa, or Latin America. In the immediate aftermath of the cold war the United States was forced to respond defensively, and often inconsistently, to crises in these regions, which diverted attention from long-term problems such as the need for sustainable development. Given the volatile nature of the international system in the late 1990s and the continuing clash over an appropriate U.S. grand strategy, this pattern will likely continue. If so, it would be a logical, if not reassuring, outcome of the constitution's "invitation to struggle" over U.S. foreign policy.

## Notes

1 Robert Lieber, "Eagle without a Cause: Making Foreign Policy without the Soviet Threat," in Robert Lieber, ed., *Eagle Adrift* (New York: Longman, 1997), pp. 3–25, quote at p. 3.

2 See Barry R. Posen and Andrew L. Ross, "Competing Visions for U.S. Grand Strategy," *International Security* 21, no. 3 1996–1997: 5–53.

3 Cecil V. Crabb Jr. and Pat M. Holt, *Invitation to Struggle: Congress, the President, and Foreign Policy*, 4th ed. (Washington, D.C.: CQ Press, 1992).

4 See Robert O. Keohane and Joseph N. Nye Jr., *Power and Interdependence*, 2d ed. (Glenview, Ill.: Scott, Foresman/Little, Brown, 1989); and Stanley Hoffmann, *Primacy or World Order* (New York: McGraw Hill, 1978).

5 See the United Nations Department for Policy Coordination and Sustainable Development, *Agenda 21* (New York: United Nations, 1993).

6 Gore outlined his environmental proposals in *Earth in the Balance* (New York: Plume, 1993).

7 For details see U.S. Agency for International Development, *Strategies for Sustainable Development* (Washington, D.C.: USAID, January 1994).

8 These critiques are reviewed in Lawrence S. Eagleburger and Robert L. Barry, "Dollars and Sense Diplomacy," *Foreign Affairs* 75 (July–August 1996): 2–8.

9 See U.S. State Department, Office of Management Task Force, *State 2000: A New Model for Managing Foreign Affairs* (Washington, D.C.: U.S. State Department, 1992).

10 Anthony Lake, "From Containment to Enlargement," *Department of State Dispatch*, September 27, 1993, pp. 658–664.

11 Warren Christopher, "America's Leadership, America's Opportunity," *Foreign Policy* 98 (Spring 1995): 26.

12 See Thomas L. Friedman, "Clinton's Foreign Policy: Top Advisor Speaks Up," *New York Times*, October 31, 1993, p. 8A.

13 Whereas before the midterm elections Democrats held eleven of twenty seats on the powerful Senate Foreign Relations Committee, Republicans held twelve of the seats afterward. Another important Senate committee, Armed Services, was occupied by eleven Republicans and nine Democrats after the election.

14 As of April 1996 USAID operated aid programs in 111 countries with a staff of 2,929 American employees, along with 5,140 American and foreign-national contractors. USIA, whose mission is to "understand, inform, and influence foreign publics in promotion of the national interest," employed 8,202 people, of whom about 3,000 were foreign nationals. And USACDA, whose mission involves advocating, negotiating, implementing, and verifying arms-control agreements,

maintained a relatively small staff of about 250. See Congressional Research Service, *Foreign Policy Agency Reorganization* (April 16, 1996): 3.

15  Leslie Phillips, "'Senator No' Puts U.S. Foreign Policy on Hold," *USA Today*, December 5, 1995, p. 7A.

16  U.S. General Accounting Office, "Reforming the Economic Aid Program," July 26, 1993, pp. 1–2.

17  James C. Clad and Roger D. Stone, "New Mission for Foreign Aid," *Foreign Affairs* 72 (Fall 1993): 196.

18  These included the African countries of Burkina Faso, Botswana, Cameroon, Cape Verde, Chad, Côte d'Ivoire, Lesotho, Togo, and Zaire; the Asian states of Afghanistan, Pakistan, Thailand; nine small states in the South Pacific; the Latin American states of Argentina, Belize, Chile, Costa Rica, Uruguay; seven small Caribbean states; and the Near Eastern states of Oman and Tunisia.

19  Elaine Sciolino, "Awaiting Call, Helms Puts Foreign Policy on Hold," *New York Times*, September 23, 1995, p. A1.

20  U.S. Senate, Committee on Foreign Relations, "Foreign Relations Revitalization Act of 1995" (S. 908), 104th Cong., 1st Sess. (5 June 1995), p. 6.

21  Quoted in Sciolino, "Awaiting Call," A1.

22  The START II treaty required the United States and Russia to reduce the number of their long-range nuclear warheads to 3,500 by the year 2003. In addition, it banned long-range nuclear weapons with multiple warheads.

23  Jim Lobe, "U.S. Diplomacy, Foreign Aid Caught in Budget Limbo," *Inter Press Service*, January 4, 1996.

24  Quoted in Sciolino, "Awaiting Call," A4.

25  House of Representatives, Conference Report 104-478 (H.R. 1561), "Foreign Relations Authorization Act, Fiscal Years 1996 and 1997," 104th Cong., 2d Sess. March 8, 1996.

26  Norman Kempster, "Clinton Vetoes GOP's Bill to Overhaul Foreign Policy," *Los Angeles Times*, April 13, 1996, p. A1.

27  Executive Office of the President, Office of Management and Budget, "Statement of Administration Policy," March 11, 1996.

28  Quoted in Kempster, "Clinton Vetoes GOP's Bill," A18.

29  Jesse Helms, "Clinton Must Back Up Downsizing Talk with Action," *Roll Call*, April 29, 1996.

30  Warren Christopher, "American Diplomacy and the Global Environmental Challenges of the 21st Century," speech at Stanford University, April 9, 1996.

31  See Michael Maren, *The Road to Hell: The Ravaging Effects of Foreign Aid and International Charity* (New York: Free Press, 1997).

32  See Chicago Council on Foreign Relations, *American Public Opinion Report, 1995* (Chicago: Chicago Council on Foreign Relations, 1995).

33  See John Spanier and Steven W. Hook, *American Foreign Policy since World War II*, 14th ed. (Washington: CQ Press, 1998).

34  Samuel Huntington, "The Clash of Civilizations," *Foreign Affairs* 72 (Summer 1993): 22–49.

35  Organization for Economic Cooperation and Development, *Development Co-*

*operation: Efforts and Policies of the Members of the Development Assistance Committee* (Paris: OECD, 1997), pp. A7–A8.

36  Graham Allison, *Essence of Decision: Explaining the Cuban Missile Crisis* (Glenview, Ill.: Scott, Foresman, 1971).

37  See William Perry, speech to John F. Kennedy School of Government, Harvard University (Washington, D.C.: Department of Defense, May 13, 1996). He elaborated on this strategy in "Defense in an Age of Hope," *Foreign Affairs* (November–December 1996): 64–79.

38  Stephen Van Evera, "Primed for Peace: Europe after the Cold War," *International Security* 15 (Winter 1990/1991): 7–57.

39  For an illustrative example of such appeals, see U.S. Agency for International Development, *U.S. Foreign Assistance Means Business* (Washington, D.C.: USAID, 1992).

40  See Marvin S. Soroos, "From Stockholm to Rio and Beyond: The Evolution of Global Environmental Governance," in Norman J. Vig and Michael E. Kraft, eds., *Environmental Policy in the 1990s: Reform or Reaction?* (Washington, D.C.: CQ Press, 1997), pp. 294–295.

41  See Steven Lee Myers, "State Department Set for Reshaping, Pleasing Helms," *New York Times*, April 18, 1997, p. A1.

42  The White House, Office of the Press Secretary, "Reinventing State, ACDA, USIA, and USAID," April 18, 1997.

43  The White House, "Reinventing State."

## 13.

## From Ally to Orphan: Understanding U.S. Policy

## toward Somalia after the Cold War

*Peter J. Schraeder*

On October 3-4, 1993, eighteen U.S. soldiers were killed and dozens were wounded in a fierce firefight in Mogadishu, Somalia. Their deaths were the direct result of U.S. leadership in a series of United Nations–sanctioned military interventions in Somalia that are popularly referred to as Operation Restore Hope.[1] With the Cable News Network (CNN) providing almost instantaneous transmission to audiences in the U.S. and abroad, the victorious Somali forces not only paraded a captured U.S. helicopter pilot, Corporal William Durant, through the streets of Mogadishu, but also dragged the naked corpse of a U.S. soldier past mobs of Somali citizens who vented their anger by spitting on, stoning, and kicking the body.

These media images triggered a firestorm of public debate that asked, in the words of one journalist: "How did an operation that began with American soldiers feeding starving Somalis wind up with an American soldier's corpse being dragged through the streets of Mogadishu by Somalis starving only for revenge?"[2] The visceral response of the American public was to demand an immediate withdrawal of U.S. military forces. "It's really very simple," explained Tony Bright, an emergency health care administrator who captured the public wave of protest against any further U.S. involvement in Somalia. "If I have to choose between pictures of starving Somalian babies or dead American soldiers being dragged through the streets of Mogadishu, well, I don't want to see any more dead Americans. Sorry. It's time to bring the boys home."[3]

The Somalia case presents a splendid opportunity to examine U.S. decision making in the post–cold war period. The implementation of Operation Restore Hope constituted the first time that the U.S. had supported a peacemaking (as opposed to a peacekeeping) operation under the auspices of the U.N. and without the approval of the sovereign government of the target country. The case is also unique in that the U.S. experience had a negative impact on the way U.S. policy makers perceived the viability of future U.S. involvement in peacemaking operations in Africa and the other regions of the Third World, most notably the U.S. ability to resolve ethnic strife and the practicality of launching joint U.S.-U.N. military operations.

This chapter examines the evolution of the U.S. intervention in Somalia during the Bush and Clinton administrations. In particular, it highlights two key, high-level decisions—the Bush decision to intervene militarily and the Clinton decision to withdraw U.S. forces—both of which were preceded by periods of inattention and bureaucratic drift.[4] In combination, these four phases reveal some interesting patterns concerning the formulation and implementation of U.S. foreign policy toward Africa in the post–cold war era.

### Background: Cold War Security Ties and Civil Conflict

The context of the 1992–93 U.S. intervention stretches back into the cold war. In the late 1970s, the Carter administration began to consider a relationship with the Siad Barre regime in Somalia. This decision followed a Marxist revolution in Ethiopia (1974–77) which placed a pro-Soviet regime in power under the leadership of Mengistu Haile Mariam. A U.S. security relationship with Somalia, some administration officials argued, offered a possible regional counter to growing Soviet and Cuban influence in the Horn of Africa. White House initiatives were largely put on hold, however, due to Somalia's invasion of Ethiopia's eastern region (largely inhabited by ethnic Somalis), which touched off the 1977–78 Ogaden War between Ethiopia and Somalia.

In 1979, when an Islamic revolution swept the pro-U.S. Shah out of power in Iran (replacing his regime with a virulently anti-American regime), and the Soviet Union invaded Afghanistan, the die was cast. A White House decision to seek military access agreements with friendly powers in southwestern Asia and northeast Africa touched off a debate within the executive branch over seeking a security relationship with Somalia. Administration "globalists," who viewed the Horn of Africa as a strategic region in the superpower conflict,[5] opted to establish a relationship with Somalia to counter what was perceived as Soviet "pincers" closing in on Middle Eastern oil. On December 4, 1979, the National Security Council (NSC) formally directed the State Department and the Pentagon to seek a military access agreement with Somalia.

According to the U.S.-Somali agreement signed in August 1980, the

Siad regime granted the U.S. access to air and seaport facilities in return for economic and military aid that eventually exceeded $750 million during the decade of the 1980s. The U.S. maintained this essentially cold war–driven relationship despite the growing authoritarianism of the Siad regime and the emergence in 1981 of a guerrilla insurgency that pitted various clans against the regime. The primary protagonists in this guerrilla insurgency were the Isaak-dominated Somali National Movement (SNM) and other clan-based insurgent groups, including the Hawiye-dominated United Somali Congress (USC) and the Ogadeni-dominated Somali Patriotic Movement (SPM).[6]

The escalation of the guerrilla insurgency into a full-blown civil war in the late 1980s coincided with the end of the cold war and prompted U.S. policy makers to reconsider the maintenance of security ties with Somalia. By 1991, the United States had terminated all foreign aid to the Siad regime. What in essence constituted the gradual abandonment of Somalia reflected two trends within the policy-making establishment: rising congressional concerns with the growing atrocities of the Siad regime, and the State Department's decreased interest in undertaking bureaucratic battles for a country of "little importance" in the post–cold war era. At the beginning of 1991, the United States by default was pursuing a "muddle through" policy in Somalia; while opponents were unable to completely sever the relationship, proponents were also constrained in what they could do. In short, the United States maintained an uneasy middle ground that neither completely supported nor opposed the Siad regime, while hoping that political conditions in Somalia would work themselves out.

### The U.S. Intervention in Somalia, 1991–1993

The Siad regime was overthrown on January 26, 1991, when the USC guerrilla army overran the Somali capital of Mogadishu. The tenuous power-sharing agreement among the victorious guerrilla groups that followed soon collapsed when one—the USC—unilaterally named a Hawiye, Ali Mahdi Mohammed, president of the country. This move heightened the already tense relations between the Isaak-dominated SNM, the Hawiye-dominated USC, the Ogadeni-dominated SPM, and scores of other less organized clan groupings. As a result, the SNM announced on May 17, 1991, that northern Somalia (the territory controlled by the SNM) was seceding from the Republic of Somalia and henceforth would be known as the Somaliland Republic. In short, the loose coalition of guerrilla groups fell apart once its common enemy was defeated, leading to the complete collapse of the Somali state and the intensification of an increasingly brutal civil war.[7]

*Phase 1: High-Level Neglect in the Bush Administration*
The first phase of U.S. policy lasted from January 1991 to December 1992. With presidential and congressional attention focused first on the Gulf War and then elsewhere, this phase involved leadership from the traditional foreign policy bureaucracy, especially the State Department's Africa Bureau. The decline of cold war tensions ensured that neither the Somali civil war nor the impending overthrow of the Siad regime attracted the ongoing attention of the White House, despite the fact that President Bush had to authorize the emergency evacuation of U.S. embassy personnel in Mogadishu. Unlike the 1970s, when the region had become an East-West flashpoint, the Soviet Union was pursuing a policy of disengagement that underscored the importance of superpower cooperation in settling local conflicts.[8] A significant example of how superpower cooperation was replacing superpower conflict in a rapidly developing post–cold war era was the evacuation of the Soviet ambassador and thirty-five members of his staff by the aforementioned U.S. rescue mission. As aptly summarized by the assistant secretary of state for African Affairs, Herman Cohen, superpower competition had become a "thing of the past" in the Horn of Africa.[9]

The State Department's Africa Bureau presided over a reactive policy that emphasized the internal roots of the Somali civil war and the need for national reconciliation through diplomatic means. This stance was reinforced by the simple reality that the guerrilla groups opposed to the Siad regime professed strong desires to maintain, and in fact enhance, Somalia's relationship with the United States. "In short," explained a former member of the Africa Bureau, "a kind of 'win-win' situation prevailed in which risk-averse bureaucrats could count on maintaining U.S. influence regardless of whether the Somali government or the guerrilla opposition emerged victorious."[10]

Somalia's changing fortunes within a rapidly changing post–cold war international system were best demonstrated by growing criticism within the Pentagon, one of the staunchest proponents of providing support to the Siad regime during the early 1980s. Colonel Alfred F. Girardi, who served as a military attaché at the U.S. embassy in Mogadishu from 1987 to 1989, argued in congressional hearings against any further aid on the basis that the Somali armed forces were "poorly motivated" and "poorly led by inept officers."[11] This testimony was matched by a growing respect in some quarters for the military successes and the pro-Western leanings of some guerrilla leaders, such as Omar Jess, the renegade military leader of the SPM. Such arguments notwithstanding, few, if any, career officers within the Pentagon foresaw an end to the internal fighting in Somalia that could lead to a beneficial relationship with any future government. As Colonel Girardi presciently warned in 1989, the most likely outcome of a post-Siad Somalia was continued "turmoil and instability" as opposing clan factions vied for control.[12]

The worst-case scenario feared by Somalia experts was realized in September 1991, when a further round of fighting broke out in southern Somalia. Less than two months later the fighting turned into an all-out struggle for control of Mogadishu. Unlike the first round (to overthrow Siad) and the second round (interclan fighting) of the Somali civil war, this round constituted a brutal intraclan power struggle within the Hawiye-based USC guerrilla army between forces loyal to interim President Mahdi, a member of the Abgal subclan of the Hawiye, and those led by General Mohamed Farah Aidid, a member of the Habar Gedir subclan of the Hawiye. Despite the efforts of outside mediators to establish a series of cease-fires, nearly thirty thousand Somalis died during this round of the Somali civil war, and the total collapse of the Somali state ensured Somalia's continued division into dozens of fiefdoms controlled by clan-based military movements.[13]

With White House and congressional attention focused elsewhere, the State Department's Africa Bureau oversaw a two-track policy that sought to limit U.S. involvement in what one Foreign Service officer (FSO) described as a "clan-based quagmire destined to last years, if not decades."[14] First, the Africa Bureau argued that the United States should support the efforts of Secretary General Boutros Boutros-Ghali to place the United Nations in the forefront of a multilateral effort designed to meet the humanitarian needs of the Somali people. In keeping with Africa Bureau desires to avoid direct U.S. military involvement in the ongoing clan warfare, the United States voted on April 24, 1992, for Security Council Resolution 751. This resolution authorized the sending of a small number of unarmed observers to monitor a cease-fire as part of what became known as United Nations Operation in Somalia I (UNOSOM I). Second, the Africa Bureau suggested that Britain and Italy should take the lead in resolving the interclan fighting and the attempted secession of Somaliland Republic. According to the Africa Bureau, the United States should follow the European lead and refrain from taking positions that diverged from or exceeded the preferences of either Italy or Britain. Hence, the bureau supported the preservation of the Republic of Somalia as constituted in 1960 in part because "that is what the Europeans wanted."[15]

The Africa Bureau's strategy of limiting U.S. involvement in Somalia's intensifying clan conflicts was slightly altered on August 14, 1992. On that day, the White House announced the launching of Operation Provide Relief—a short-term humanitarian airlift of food aid that would be carried out under the auspices of UNOSOM I. Two weeks later on August 28, a contingent of five hundred U.S. soldiers oversaw the first flight of four C-140 transport planes from their bases in Mombasa, Kenya, to a variety of drop-off points in Somalia. White House authorization of Operation Provide Relief followed in the aftermath of a U.N. agreement with Aidid, the USC militia leader who controlled access to the port, which in turn permitted the deployment of a U.N. force of five hundred Pakistani soldiers to protect food supplies and relief workers in Mogadishu.

The launching of Operation Provide Relief represented neither a basic change in U.S. policy nor the ongoing attention of the highest levels of the Bush administration. The end of the cold war had relegated Somalia and the African continent to an arena that did not figure in the hierarchy of regions deemed important in the post–cold war era, and the Bush White House was clearly in favor of an Africa Bureau policy that sought to make the United Nations and the former colonial powers responsible for resolving crises on the African continent. Nonetheless, an expanding humanitarian crisis threatened to enter the 1992 presidential campaign and, more important, to tarnish the Republican nominating convention, as Democrats began criticizing the Bush administration for abandoning Somalia in its hour of greatest humanitarian need. Operation Provide Relief therefore became a short-term solution to deflecting potential partisan criticism, while at the same time reinforcing the notion that long-term responsibility for curing Somalia's clan-based ills rested with the United Nations, the former European colonial powers, and the Somali peoples themselves.

*Phase 2: Humanitarian Crisis and Military Intervention under Bush*
In the late fall of 1992, the second phase of U.S. policy began, involving high-level attention to what was perceived to be an accelerating crisis in Somalia. With images of a humanitarian disaster displayed daily in practically every media outlet, and with congressional and public criticism increasing, White House attention focused on Somalia shortly after the 1992 election. As a consequence of high-level White House reviews in

November 1992, President Bush and his top advisers devised a plan to deal with the events in Somalia.

In sharp contrast to the limited objectives associated with Operation Provide Relief, Bush announced on December 4, 1992, that his administration was prepared to lead a massive multilateral military operation to "create a secure environment" for the distribution of famine relief aid. Five days later the first contingent of U.S. troops led by three teams of navy SEALS (sea-air-land commandos) landed on the beaches of Mogadishu and secured the airport and the port. The U.S. military operation, popularly referred to as Operation Restore Hope and known in U.N. circles as the United Task Force (UNITAF), was sanctioned by U.N. Security Council Resolution 794. In the weeks that followed, over 38,000 foreign troops from twenty countries (including approximately 25,000 U.S. military personnel) occupied various cities and towns throughout central and southern Somalia, and began the task of opening food supply routes, as well as creating distribution networks.[16] The UNITAF ground forces were under the direct command of Lieutenant General Robert Johnston, chief of staff to General Norman Schwarzkopf during Operation Desert Storm, who reported to General Joseph P. Hoar, commander of the U.S. Central Command (CENTCOM).

Bush's decision to undertake a massive U.S. military intervention in Somalia was surprising to both policy analysts and policy makers for two reasons. First, Bush chose the most interventionist of three options that were prepared over a period of three weeks by the Deputies Committee of the NSC, and subsequently presented to him on November 25 at a full meeting of the NSC devoted to Somalia. Whereas a minimalist option called for U.S. air and sea support for a reinforced U.N. military force, and a compromise position—nicknamed the "ball-peen hammer" option—called for limited U.S. ground forces as a prelude to an expanded U.N. military force, the maximalist approach—the so-called sledgehammer option—called for at least one U.S. combat division to lead an allied military intervention under U.N. auspices.[17] The White House's selection of the sledgehammer option was especially noteworthy in that an interagency consensus favored the ball-peen hammer option, and clearly would have accepted the minimalist approach.

The range of choices presented to Bush was also surprising, due to the lack of truly minimalist options of nonintervention or, at least, nonmilitary intervention. Moreover, several weeks earlier all three options were almost unanimously opposed by Africa specialists within the foreign policy bureaucracies. In the State Department's Africa Bureau, FSOS strongly opposed direct U.S. military intervention, and instead favored a more proactive diplomatic approach that centered on resolving clan differences, as well as pressuring the U.N. Security Council to take a more active role in military operations if deemed necessary. The CIA and the Pentagon also initially opposed the introduction of U.S. combat troops into Somalia. In a view characteristic of that adhered to by CIA analysts of the Horn of Africa, Robert M. Gates, Director of Central Intelligence, warned that "anarchy" was "so sweeping" and "the warring factions so firmly entrenched" that the United States was potentially setting itself up for the unintended long-term responsibility of maintaining stability in Somalia.[18] As for the Pentagon, officials were described as having "resisted *any* direct American military involvement" (emphasis added) in Somalia. The Pentagon only embraced the "sledgehammer option" once it became clear after Bush's defeat in the 1992 presidential elections that the president was committed to some form of U.S. military intervention.

One of the harshest critics within the foreign policy bureaucracies was Smith Hempstone Jr., the U.S. ambassador to Kenya, who warned that Somalia could become a quagmire for U.S. foreign policy. "Somalis, as the Italians and British discovered to their discomfiture, are natural-born guerrillas," explained Hempstone in a December 1 diplomatic cable that was leaked and reprinted in *U.S. News & World Report*. "They will mine the roads. They will lay ambushes. They will launch hit and run attacks. They will not be able to stop the convoys from getting through. But they will inflict—and take—casualties." Taking such a risk, according to Hempstone, was ill advised for the simple reason that Somalia does not constitute a country of vital interest to the United States. "Aside from the humanitarian issue—which admittedly is compelling (but so is it in the Sudan)—I fail to see where any vital interest is involved." In an often quoted phrase underscoring the dangers of sending U.S. combat troops to Somalia, Hempstone warned his colleagues: "If you loved Beirut, you'll love Mogadishu."[19]

The primary reason for the dramatic shift in policy was rising domestic and congressional pressures to "do something" about what James R. Kunder, the head of the U.S. Office of Foreign Disaster Assistance, labeled the "world's worst humanitarian disaster."[20] By August 1992, nine months after the start of fighting between factions of the USC, as many as 1.5 million of an estimated Somali population of 6 million were threatened with starvation, with approximately 300,000 Somalis already dead, including roughly 25 percent of children under the age of five. As media reporting of this humanitarian crisis increased beginning in July 1992, particularly with live satellite broadcasts that portrayed images of starving Somali children, criticism of executive branch inaction from a variety of quarters increasingly was taken more seriously by the White House.[21]

In addition to being "bombarded with appeals" from private relief organizations, the White House found itself being criticized by prominent newspaper columnists, some of whom were calling for a "shoot-to-feed" policy.[22] In the case of Congress, this criticism reached new levels on August 3, 1992, when a bipartisan resolution cosponsored by Senators Paul Simon (D-Ill.) and Nancy Kassebaum (R-Kans.), and calling for a more activist response on the part of the White House, overwhelmingly passed the Senate, followed by passage of this same bill in the House of Representatives on August 10. Public opinion also strongly favored the military option. According to a poll conducted prior to the beginning of Operation Restore Hope, 81 percent of public opinion believed that Bush was "doing the right thing in sending troops to Somalia to make sure food gets to the people," and 70 percent believed that sending troops was even "worth the possible loss of American lives, financial costs and other risks."[23]

A complete explanation of this dramatic shift in Bush administration policy must also take into account the role of presidential politics once the Somali crisis had caught the public eye. As criticism by both Democrats and Republicans threatened to tarnish the successful foreign policy image that the Bush administration wanted to project, Bush's defeat in the 1992 election led to the not uncommon desire of outgoing presidents to ensure that the history books remember him as a "decisive leader" as opposed to a "vanquished politician" unable to secure a second term in office.[24] It is noteworthy that the NSC Deputies Committee began drawing up serious options for direct U.S. military intervention only *after* a defeated Bush made it clear to his senior advisers that some form of direct U.S. military intervention would be undertaken during the transition process. It is precisely for this reason that some critics claim that Bush would never have approved the introduction of U.S. combat forces into what Ambassador Hempstone characterized as the Somali "quagmire" if he had won a second term. According to these critics, Bush would have been warier about the long-term political risks associated with committing the U.S. to a full-scale military operation in a country of little if any strategic importance to the U.S. in the post–cold war era.[25]

*Phase 3: "Mission Creep" and White House Inattention*

In the third phase of the U.S. intervention in Somalia, which began with Bill Clinton's inauguration and lasted into the fall of 1993, White House attention to Somalia again waned. During the transition to the new administration, and subsequently during its initial focus on domestic and economic issues, the foreign policy bureaucracy again assumed leadership over the ongoing policy with White House and congressional attention directed to other matters. Although the newly inaugurated Clinton administration had the opportunity to review and, if desired, alter the basic principles of U.S. foreign policy toward Somalia—as is the case with all presidential transitions—the Clinton White House did not assert itself in this way.

Clinton had firmly supported Bush's decision to commit U.S. forces to Somalia during the 1992 presidential campaign. A routine NSC review of policy during February 1993 confirmed the general consensus among senior policy makers that "things were proceeding rather well": famine and factional fighting were under control, public support remained high, and "no one" in the White House "foresaw any major problems" in the transfer of responsibility for military operations to a U.N. peacekeeping force.[26] Most important, Clinton had won the 1992 presidential elections based on the campaign pledge to focus like a "laser beam" on the domestic economy, subsequently putting together a White House policy-making team focused on an aggressive domestic agenda.

The combination of positive assumptions concerning Operation Restore Hope and the central focus on the domestic economy promoted a laissez-faire environment in which Clinton and his senior foreign policy advisers, most notably National Security Adviser Anthony Lake and Secretary of State Warren Christopher, largely ignored U.S. foreign policy toward Somalia during their first eight months in office. As admitted by Christopher, the fact that policy was largely being handled by the NSC's Deputies Committee ensured that Cabinet-level officials "were not sufficiently attentive."[27]

This lack of high-level attention was not unique to Somalia, explains Dick Morris, Clinton's former chief strategist for the 1996 presidential elections. It was characteristic of a president "determined to make a priority of domestic affairs" who only "reacted, more or less reluctantly, to global concerns when they intruded so deeply into American politics that he had to do something."[28] The White House's early tendency to downgrade foreign policy in favor of an unprecedented focus on domestic policy was succinctly captured in a December 1992 interview in which Clinton underscored that foreign policy could "only unmake" presidencies (as opposed to domestic policy which "made" them) and therefore should be approached as "a damage limitation exercise."[29]

As was the case during the early months of the Bush administration, the net result of White House inattention to Somalia was the delegation of responsibility for the formulation and the implementation of policy to the foreign policy bureaucracies, with three important consequences for the evolution of U.S. intervention in Somalia.

1. *Promotion of Status Quo–Oriented Policies.* The first consequence was the administration's acceptance and continuation of the policies established by the Bush administration. The foreign policy bureaucracies continued to support the delegation of long-term responsibility for resolving Somalia's economic and political problems to other powers. This translated into support for a short-term, U.S.-led military operation that was to be quickly replaced by U.N. peacekeeping forces directly responsible to the U.N. Security Council. In the aftermath of the Bush administration's token but highly symbolic withdrawal of approximately 550 U.S. troops from Somalia on January 19, 1993 (the day before Clinton's inauguration), the foreign policy bureaucracies publicly maintained the necessity of replacing U.S. combat forces with their U.N. counterparts.

An important dilemma revolved around the fact that the Bush administration never formulated a precise "exit strategy," detailing how and when U.S. troops should be withdrawn and replaced by their U.N. counterparts. According to Colin Powell, chairman of the Joint Chiefs of Staff during the Bush administration (and the first year of the Clinton administration), both he and Secretary of Defense Richard B. Cheney made it clear to Bush that a significant disengagement dilemma accompanied the decision to launch Operation Restore Hope.[30] "The famine had been provoked not by the whims of nature but by internal feuding," explains Powell. "How do we get out of Somalia without turning the country back to the same warlords whose rivalries had produced the famine in the first place?"[31] This view was reiterated by Robert B. Oakley, the former ambassador to Somalia, who served as special envoy to Operation Restore Hope and remained during the early months of the newly elected Clinton administration. Oakley cautioned that disengagement would be neither as easy nor as quickly attained as originally assumed by Bush, and projected the necessity of maintaining a long-term presence of at least twenty thousand U.N. troops, including several thousand U.S. combat troops who could be held in reserve in case they were needed. Oakley also recommended the long-term stationing of between five thousand to eight thousand U.S. logistical troops.[32]

The principal problem associated with the lack of a detailed exit strategy was that a U.N. military force without U.S. troops would be incapable of maintaining order. According to this logic, the complete withdrawal of U.S. forces might cause the lawlessness and famine conditions that existed in Somalia prior to the beginning of Operation Restore Hope to resume. As stated by Michael Mandelbaum, taking such a risk was unacceptable to the newly inaugurated Clinton White House, in that the return of chaos "would have meant, in effect, that we spent $1 billion and sent 28,000 troops to prevent Somalia from starving in 1992 so they could starve in 1993"—only this time under the leadership of a Democratic president, who surely would be vilified by Republican opponents as incapable of managing foreign policy.[33]

Risk-averse bureaucrats therefore promoted a policy that responded to the challenges of Operation Restore Hope, but which also ran counter to the public pronouncements of the Bush and Clinton administrations. Although the majority of U.S. combat forces would be withdrawn and a U.N. commander and military force would assume long-term responsibility for maintaining order in Somalia, the United States would maintain eight thousand logistical troops and a thousand-strong "Quick Response Force" from the U.S. army's 10th Mountain Division for buttressing the military capabilities of U.N. forces should the need arise. This agreement was the cornerstone of U.S. support for U.N. Security Council Resolution 814 that was adopted on March 26, 1993, and implemented in Somalia on May 4.

Largely written by the Pentagon and supported by the State Department's Bureaus of African and International Organization Affairs, Resolution 814 marked the official end of Operation Restore Hope and its replacement by U.N. Operation in Somalia II (UNOSOM II), otherwise known in U.S. military circles as Operation Continue Hope. In UNOSOM II, despite the assumption that the U.S. military force would be controlled by a U.N. commander for the first time in U.S. military history, the troops remained under the operational control of U.S. commanders. Most important, Operation Continue Hope still lacked a timetable for the complete withdrawal of U.S. troops, in essence maintaining an open-ended commitment to the stationing of U.S. military forces in Somalia.

2. *Bureaucratic Incrementalism.* A second result of White House delegation of responsibility to the foreign policy bureaucracies was a process of bureaucratic incrementalism: the natural organizational tendency to promote gradual growth in the scope and intensity of U.S. involvement in another country. Sometimes referred to as "mission creep," a critical element of bureaucratic incrementalism is the promotion of unintended and often self-defeating outcomes bearing little if any resemblance to the originally conceived policy. In the preceding case, for example, U.S. policy had shifted from rhetorical support for the withdrawal of U.S. troops (although no concrete exit plan existed) to the open-ended deployment of a reduced number of combat and logistical troops.

The most important example of bureaucratic incrementalism often cited by supporters of Bush and critics of Clinton was the supposed shift in the mission of Operation Restore Hope from a humanitarian operation designed to avoid any involvement in Somali politics (the publicly stated goal of the Bush administration) to the significant involvement of U.S. troops in the political reconstruction of a Somali polity—the so-called nation-building imperative in Resolution 814, adopted during the Clinton administration. In the broadest sense, some would argue that there is "no such thing as a humanitarian surgical strike," and that, whether it wanted to be or not, the Bush administration was involved in Somali politics the moment U.S. Marines landed on the beaches in Mogadishu. "When U.S. troops intervened in December 1992 to stop the theft of food, they disrupted the political economy and stepped deep into the muck of Somali politics," explains Walter Clarke, the deputy chief of mission at the U.S. Embassy in Somalia during Operation Restore Hope. "By reestablishing some order, the U.S. operation inevitably affected the direction of Somali politics and became nation-building because the most basic component of nation-building is the end of anarchy."[34] Sharply critical of the conventional wisdom that assumes that one can draw distinctions between apolitical humanitarian interventions and politically motivated military interventions, Clarke concludes by posing the following question: "How could anyone believe that landing 30,000 troops in a country was anything but a gross interference in its politics?"[35]

From the moment of the intervention, the seeds were already being sown for a long-term commitment to nation building. Almost immediately, U.S. forces became involved in the clan fighting, first by defending themselves against attacks, then by efforts to isolate Aidid's clan faction in favor of his opponents, most notably Ali Mahdi.[36] As early as

January 7, 1993, four hundred Marines conducted an attack on an Aidid military camp. As the intervention wore on, the U.S. military became more and more involved in nation building despite the lack of any official policy guiding such action. "The initial understanding or intent for our part was just to create a security committee that would work with us to take care of any internal problems that might interfere with our operations," explained Colonel Werner Hellmer, a U.S. military officer described as one of the "new Marine politicians" who became responsible for creating civilian local government in the Somali town of Baidoa. "All of a sudden we got involved a little bit more with the community because the community was interested in working with the military. Everything's been spontaneous."[37] Officially supported or not, nation building was taking place during the Bush administration.

As nation-building activities gradually increased throughout spring 1993, a turning point in the incremental growth of U.S. involvement occurred on June 5, when twenty-four Pakistani soldiers of UNOSOM II were killed in a series of clashes orchestrated by Aidid's military forces. The very next day, the State Department's Bureau of International Organization Affairs coordinated U.S. support for the adoption of U.N. Security Council Resolution 837 that authorized UNOSOM II to undertake "all necessary measures" (i.e., military action) against those responsible for the attack. This marked the beginning of an "official" war between UNOSOM II forces and those of Aidid. Once again responsible for the initial drafting of the U.N. resolution, the Pentagon not only authorized the involvement of the Quick Reaction Force in a series of retaliatory strikes against Aidid, but on August 26 deployed an elite force of U.S. Army Rangers and Delta Force commandos known as Task Force Rangers, which undertook a series of failed missions to capture Aidid in the weeks that followed. The most telling aspect of this decision is that it was "taken without any serious discussion among senior policymakers."[38]

The tendency of U.S. field commanders to become advocates for the commitment of greater resources from Washington served as the critical driving force behind the incremental expansion of U.S. military involvement in the war against Aidid. The most noted and controversial figure was retired Admiral Jonathan Howe, the deputy national security adviser when the Bush administration made the decision to launch Operation Provide Relief and Operation Restore Hope, and the U.N. special representative in Somalia as of March 7, 1993, when the Clinton administration was beginning the transition phase to Operation Continue Relief.[39] According to former Secretary of Defense Les Aspin, Howe engaged in "frenetic and obsessive lobbying," using his extensive ties within the foreign policy bureaucracies to promote greater U.S. military involvement, particularly against Aidid's forces.[40] These actions were reinforced by the equally persuasive lobbying efforts of U.S. military commanders, most notably Major General Thomas Montgomery, deputy commander of UNOSOM II forces, who finally convinced Powell to dispatch an elite military force to capture Aidid. "In late August, I reluctantly yielded to the repeated requests from the field and recommended to Aspin that we dispatch the Rangers and the Delta Force," explains Powell in his autobiography. "It was a recommendation I would later regret."[41]

3. *Fragmentation of Policy.* The overriding influence of U.S. citizens as senior political envoys and military commanders was the cornerstone of Operation Restore and its later permutations. During the initial stages of the operation, Ambassador Oakley clearly emerged as the preeminent political strategist and Lieutenant General Johnston was deemed responsible for military operations. After March 1993, these responsibilities were increasingly taken up by Admiral Howe and Major General Montgomery. Theoretically more subject to U.N. priorities than their predecessors, Howe and Montgomery in reality served as the principal conduits and initiators of enhanced U.S. political and military efforts.

Unfortunately, the undue influence wielded by these and other American officials in the field did not contribute to a well-coordinated policy approach. Indeed, an important consequence of de facto White House delegation of authority to these Americans in the field was rising bureaucratic competition and conflict. Rising tensions were evident among the representatives of various bureaucracies in Washington as each jealously guarded their respective bureaucratic "turfs." The most notable outcome of this bureaucratic infighting was a highly fragmented policy in which separate bureaucracies pursued different, often contradictory goals.

The primary example of policy fragmentation, often cited by critics of Operation Restore Hope, was the uneasy tension between the State Department and the Pentagon. At the same time that the State Department sought in August 1993 to rejuvenate a diplomatic approach promoting negotiated outcomes and political reconciliation, the Pentagon was reinforcing military operations designed to defeat and capture Aidid. This trend was demonstrated on August 26, 1993, by the dispatch of the Delta Force one day before Secretary of Defense Aspin made a speech detailing the administration's decreased emphasis on military force in favor of diplomatic initiatives.

According to critics of U.S. policy, the emphasis on political reconciliation was at best contradicted and at worst superseded by an exclusionary military approach favored by military officials in the field. "How can one expect the opposition to negotiate," complained a representative of Aidid's militia, "when, at the same time, one is carrying out military policies resulting in the deaths of Somalis and the attempted capture of their leaders?"[42] These critiques were echoed by Oakley, who claimed that the military operation jeopardized any hope of achieving the political reconciliation of Somalia's warring clans. "It sends the wrong signal—to the American people, to the U.N. and to Aidid."[43]

*Phase 4: Renewed Crisis and Clinton's Decision to Withdraw*

As the fourth phase began in early October 1993, more than eight months after the inauguration of the Clinton administration and roughly ten months after the launching of Operation Restore Hope, the cumulative impact of high-level inattention and delegation of authority to the foreign policy bureaucracies was a drifting, fragmented, and deepening U.S. involvement with no clear end in sight. The dramatic events of October 3–4, 1993, in which ninety-six U.S. soldiers were killed and wounded, a U.S. helicopter pilot was taken hostage, and the naked corpse of a U.S. soldier was desecrated and dragged through the streets of Mogadishu, dramatically altered the Clinton administration's approach to Somalia. These events—another perceived crisis in Africa and for U.S. policy—again attracted high-level White House and congressional attention.

After three days of high-level meetings with the NSC and senior members of Congress, Clinton made a nationally televised address on October 7 in which he disavowed U.S. responsibility for nation building and called for a permanent halt in U.S. involvement in seeking military solutions, effectively ending the hunt for Aidid. "It is not our job to rebuild Somalia's society or even to create a political process that can allow Somalia's clans to live and work in peace," explained Clinton. "The Somalis must do that for themselves."[44] Clinton also set a definite deadline of March 31, 1994, for the complete withdrawal of U.S. military forces, "except for a few hundred support personnel in noncombat roles." In order to ensure the protection of these forces during the six-month interim period in which the U.N. was to prepare for the U.S. departure, Clinton authorized the immediate, short-term strengthening of U.S. combat capabilities by sending an additional 1,700 army troops, 104 armored personnel carriers, an aircraft carrier group, and 3,400 Marines from two amphibious groups.[45]

The primary reason for the dramatic shift in administration policy was rising public and congressional pressures to withdraw U.S. forces from Somalia regardless of the consequences. During the ten months preceding the events of October 1993, polling data measuring popular approval of the president's handling of the Somali crisis declined from a high of 77 percent at the beginning of the Clinton administration, to 51 percent in June and 41 percent in September.[46] Declining public approval ratings not surprisingly were matched by rising congressional criticisms and inquiries into administration policies during this same period. According to Harry Johnson, chairman of the House Subcommittee on Africa, at least fifteen bills and resolutions were brought to the floors of the House and Senate demanding the withdrawal of U.S. troops from Somalia.[47] These actions culminated in House passage on September 7, 1993, of a nonbinding amendment to the Defense Authorization Bill (HR 2401), followed two days later by a Senate version that called upon the White House to submit a report of U.S. activities in Somalia by October 15, and to seek congressional authorization for the continued deployment of U.S. troops by November 15.[48]

Rising popular discontent turned into popular outrage in the aftermath of the events of October 3–4. According to the polling data, Clinton's approval rating for his handling of the Somali crisis fell to a low of 31 percent, with only 33 percent of those polled favoring the continued deployment of U.S. troops.[49] "From here on, we shouldn't do any more than get back our dead and our prisoners and get out safely," explained Carl Kamp, a retired bank official from Atlanta. "If that takes a few more troops and a few more weeks, then O.K. But absolutely no escalation and don't drag it out. I don't like this."[50]

Popular outrage prompted congressional demands for the immediate withdrawal of U.S. troops, especially after Secretary of State Christopher and Secretary of Defense Aspin sought on October 5, 1993, to calm congressional criticisms by providing what turned out to be a very disjointed overview of policy toward Somalia. "It's Vietnam all over again," exclaimed Senator Ernest F. Hollings (D-S.C.), one of the most strident opponents of administration policy. "There's no education in the second kick of a mule."[51] "I learned nothing I didn't already know," noted Senator John McCain (R-Ariz.) in a strident rebuke of the administration's briefing. "Anyone who watches the local and national news would get more information."[52] The harshest criticism, however, came in response to the media images of desecrated U.S. soldiers. "The people who are dragging American bodies don't look very hungry to the people of Texas," explained Senator Phil Gramm (R-Tex.). "Support for the president in the country and Congress is dying rather rapidly."[53]

An important element of popular outrage was the continued relevance of the "Vietnam syndrome"—a clear and pervasive reluctance on the part of a public no longer automatically willing to accept arguments promoting direct U.S. military intervention (and thus U.S. casualties) in foreign lands. In 1991, the dramatic levels of popular support for Operation Desert Storm seemed to indicate the emergence of a new interventionist consensus in which the public increasingly is willing to perceive the United States as the guarantor of peace and stability throughout the world. In a shift that began with popular support for the 1983 invasion of Grenada that was similarly forthcoming for the 1989 military invasion of Panama, the massive U.S.-led military operation against Iraq indicated the reemergence of a trend that during the cold war era had led to U.S. involvement in the highly costly and divisive Vietnam War. Yet it is important to remember that U.S. intervention in Grenada, Panama, and Iraq, as opposed to the Clinton administration's handling of U.S. intervention in Somalia, conformed to the central dictum of the Vietnam syndrome that is still very prevalent in the popular psyche: military intervention must be short in duration and low in the number of casualties.

The dual media images of a captured U.S. helicopter pilot, Corporal Durant, being paraded through the streets of Mogadishu, and that of a naked corpse of a U.S. soldier being desecrated by Somalis, clearly played a critical role in transforming rising discontent into public perceptions of an extended crisis in U.S. foreign policy.[54] Once again turning to the polling data, it is striking to note that 84 percent of those polled saw at least one of these media images, while only 18 percent had heard Clinton's speech of October 6 in which he outlined changes in U.S. foreign policy.[55] "When I saw those pictures, I knew there was no turning back, that we had to get out," explained Robin Elliott, a hospital worker from Cincinnati. "Nothing the president can do will change my mind on that. We don't have any real interest in Somalia beyond humanitarian aid and that's begun to cost us lives."[56]

A complete explanation of the dramatic shift in Clinton administration policy must also take into account the role of presidential politics once the Somali crisis had caught the public eye. In the aftermath of what constituted the first extended, high-level review of U.S. foreign policy toward Somalia that actively engaged Clinton and his senior foreign policy advisers, the NSC presented the president with three broad sets of foreign policy options, from which a more specific policy could be developed: (1) *immediate withdrawal:* a complete, quick withdrawal of all U.S. combat forces as demanded by the U.S. public and a significant portion of Congress; (2) *assertive multilateralism:* the reinforcement of U.S. military forces to defeat Aidid and to establish political order as promoted by Secretary General Boutros-Ghali; and (3) *phased withdrawal:* a middle-range option based on the short-term reinforcement of the U.S. military presence to create a stable environment for the pursuit of political negotiations, while at the same time preparing for the complete withdrawal of U.S. forces.[57]

Whereas a careful reading of Clinton's campaign statements, most notably his early support for greater U.S. involvement in peacemaking exercises, suggested a worldview conducive to the selection of the assertive multilateralism option,[58] a purely domestic politics explanation would have ensured adherence to the immediate withdrawal option. From a presidential politics perspective, however, both options boded ill for Clinton's future popularity and his ability to avoid being labeled a failure in the realm of foreign policy. Adherence to assertive multilateralism, although principled, would further inflame public opinion and most likely lead to congressional opposition strong enough to terminate U.S. involvement against the will of the executive branch. However, immediate withdrawal threatened a quick return to anarchy in Somalia, complete with partisan critiques that Clinton, like most Democratic presidents, mismanaged a perfectly managed foreign policy operation established by his Republican predecessor.

The obvious solution for Clinton was to choose a middle ground —phased withdrawal—that would silence both popular and congressional critiques and forestall future partisan attacks. As demonstrated by strong congressional and public support in the aftermath of Clinton's pronouncement of policy changes on October 7, critics were mollified by the establishment of the precise deadline of March 31, 1994, by which all U.S. troops would be withdrawn from Somalia. "Not only does the president deserve our support, the American forces deserve our support," explained Senator Robert Dole (R-Kans.), who eventually would run against Clinton in the 1996 presidential elections. "The president has now given a timetable and the mission has been drastically contracted."[59]

As further demonstrated by Somalia's almost complete exclusion from mention in the 1996 presidential election campaign, Clinton's short-term expansion of the U.S. military commitment in preparation for a full withdrawal equally mollified partisan critics who ideally would have liked to blame the administration for Somalia's return to anarchy. Even Clinton's staunchest opponents, such as presidential candidate Dole, found it difficult to accuse Clinton of abandoning Somalia after his administration provided six additional months of breathing space to work out political accords under the auspices of U.S. military protection and political negotiators.

In the aftermath of Clinton's decision to significantly alter U.S. involvement in Operation Continue Relief, subsequent U.S. foreign policy was anticlimactic. Six days prior to the withdrawal deadline of May 31, 1994, the remainder of U.S. combat forces were withdrawn. Except for Clinton's authorization to send U.S. troops one year later to protect the withdrawal of remaining U.N. military forces in Somalia, the U.S. withdrawal signaled the end of high-level attention to Somalia as policy once again was relegated to the foreign policy bureaucracies. Whereas the State Department's Africa Bureau emerged again as the lead agency for overseeing policies designed to promote national reconciliation, and the State Department's Bureau of International Organization Affairs remained influential in coordinating international relief efforts, the Pentagon largely receded in importance once U.S. troops had been withdrawn. Diplomatic strategies based on local realities had clearly replaced military initiatives as the guiding element of greatly reduced U.S. involvement in the Horn of Africa.

### Understanding Policy Making in the Post–Cold War Era

The irony of nearly two decades of U.S. involvement in Somali politics is that literally billions of dollars—whether in the form of bilateral aid during the 1980s or multilateral aid associated with military intervention during the 1990s—were not enough to prevent the collapse of the Somali state or the continued division of Somalia into dozens of fiefdoms controlled by clan-based politico-military movements. Although the famine of 1991–92 has not recurred, thousands of Somalis have died in the periodic intensification of clan-based conflict since the withdrawal of U.S. and other U.N.-sponsored forces. Interestingly, the U.S. media rarely mention this conflict now that U.S. military forces have been withdrawn, potentially leaving Americans with the erroneous assumption that peace has returned to the Horn of Africa. As in the case of other former U.S. clients in Africa that had once supported U.S. containment policies during the cold war, Somalia has become a "neglected orphan" of the post–cold war international system.[60]

The U.S. experience in Somalia had a tremendous impact on the future evolution of U.S. foreign policy in the post–cold war era. On May 5, 1994, a long awaited policy directive, Presidential Decision Directive 25 (PDD-25), outlined conditions that had to be met before the Clinton administration would agree to any further U.N.-sponsored military operations, including in Africa, regardless of whether U.S. troops were taking part:

1. threat to international security, including an urgent need for relief aid after widespread violence or rioting;
2. a sudden interruption of a democracy, or a gross violation of human rights;
3. clear objectives;
4. the availability of enough money and troops;
5. a mandate appropriate to the mission;
6. a realistic exit strategy; and
7. consent of the parties before the force is deployed.

The most important result of PDD-25, which in essence rejected future U.S. involvement in U.N.-sponsored peacemaking operations designed to militarily impose peace among warring parties, was an extremely cautious approach to ethnically and religiously based conflicts in Africa and elsewhere. In the case of Rwanda, for example, extremists among the Hutu ethnic group unleashed a reign of terror against the Tutsi minority (as well as against Hutu deemed sympathetic to the plight of the Tutsi) that, according to a U.N. report issued in December 1994, had resulted in the execution of between 500,000 and one million unarmed civilians. Fearful of being drawn into "another Somalia," the Clinton administration not only initially blocked the dispatch of 5,500 troops requested by Secretary General Boutros-Ghali, but also instructed administration spokespersons to avoid labeling the unfolding ethnic conflict as "genocide" (lest such a label further inflame U.S. public sympathy and demand U.S. intervention, as happened in the case of Somalia).[61]

The U.S. experience in Somalia also significantly affected the Clinton administration's approach to conflict resolution in Africa. Entering office at a period in which internal civil conflicts were multiplying throughout the African continent, the Clinton administration was expected to formulate and to adopt a comprehensive policy of conflict resolution that went beyond the sporadic policies of previous administrations. However, the Clinton White House was in reality split between two currents of thought as concerned conflict management in Africa.

The first emphasized the classic belief that African issues would unnecessarily distract the administration and potentially plunge the White House into unwanted domestic political controversies. According to this viewpoint, U.S. involvement should be restricted to avoid entanglement in "future Somalias."[62] A second, more activist point of view also was derivative of the Somali experience, but underscored that the massive costs associated with Operation Restore Hope could have been avoided by earlier, preventive action. "The choice is not between intervening or not intervening," explained a Clinton administration official. "It is between getting involved early and doing it at a cheaper cost, or being forced to intervene in a massive, more costly way later."[63] As witnessed by the Clinton administration's cautious approach to the initial stages of the Rwandan conflict, the events of October 1993 in Somalia clearly strengthened the position of those warning against getting too closely involved in "intractable" conflicts in Africa.

The U.S. experience in Somalia also allows us to draw some tentative conclusions about U.S. foreign policy making in the post–cold war era. The first conclusion suggests that the foreign policy bureaucracy tends to exercise leadership in the formulation and implementation of foreign policy toward Africa during routine (i.e., noncrisis) periods.[64] The primary reason for this tendency, which has been reinforced by the end of the cold war, is that historic White House neglect of African issues ensures the delegation of responsibility for the formulation and implementation of policy to the foreign policy bureaucracies. What in essence constituted bureaucratic dominance within the policy-making process clearly characterized Bush administration policy toward Somalia prior to December 1992, and Clinton administration policy toward Somalia from January to October 1993. The first eight months of Clinton administration policy are especially instructive in that they clearly demonstrate how the combination of high-level inattention and delegation of authority can lead to the promotion of unintended and often self-defeating outcomes bearing little if any resemblance to the originally conceived policy relationship.

The case study of U.S. foreign policy toward Somalia also suggests that sustained presidential involvement in the policy-making process occurs only during crisis situations on the African continent.[65] During the cold war era, the real or imagined involvement of the European allies and the communist bloc countries was critical to White House attention to African conflicts. In conflicts marked by high levels of European involvement and low levels of communist bloc involvement, such as the Nigerian civil war of the late 1960s, the White House ignored the situation and deferred the proper policy response to the European allies. In sharp contrast, conflicts marked by little if any European involvement and high levels of communist bloc involvement, such as the Angolan civil war of the mid-1970s, were almost automatically perceived at the level of the White House as crises demanding the sustained attention of the president and his closest advisers.

The case study of Somalia demonstrates that the decline of the cold war has significantly altered how presidents and their closest advisers perceive the evolution of conflict in Africa. At the end of the 1970s, the Carter administration developed a security relationship with the Siad regime in response to the cold war crises associated with the Soviet invasion of Afghanistan and the Iranian revolution. In sharp contrast, the decline of cold war tensions by the beginning of 1991 ensured that neither the Somali civil war nor the impending overthrow of the Siad regime were perceived as crises by Bush and his closest foreign policy advisers. Simply put, the lack of a global communist threat suggests a dramatic decline in the number of African conflicts relative to those of the cold war era that will be capable of achieving sustained presidential attention. Although it has been hypothesized that other perceived threats, such as the rise of Islamic fundamentalism, may possibly become the triggers of sustained presidential attention in the post–cold war international system, the Somali case does not bear this out.

The case study of Somalia also demonstrates the important link between the unfolding of extended humanitarian crises and the role of domestic politics in prompting changes in U.S. foreign policy toward Africa.[66] The longer a crisis with a significant humanitarian component remains unresolved, the greater is the possibility that U.S. involvement (or lack of involvement) will become the concern of increasing numbers of congresspersons and other interested individuals outside of the executive branch. This is especially true if an issue becomes the focus of popular opinion. In this regard, neither Bush's decision to launch Operation Restore Hope nor Clinton's decision to withdraw U.S. troops were decided in a vacuum. In each of these cases, public opinion had become increasingly critical and disenchanted with established policies over several months.

The media has played a unique yet often neglected agenda-setting role in creating public awareness of humanitarian crises on the African continent. In numerous cases, such as the Reagan administration's decision to extend famine relief to Ethiopia during 1983–85 despite the avowedly pro-Marxist, pro-Soviet tilt of the ruling regime, changes in policies were principally due to media-driven protests. The importance of media-driven policies was especially relevant to the evolution of U.S. policy toward Somalia. "Americans were horrified by the sight of a dead American being dragged through the streets of Mogadishu," explains Powell in his autobiography. "We had been drawn into this place by television images; now we were being repelled by them."[67]

It is important to note, however, that reference to domestic politics was not sufficient to explain either Bush's decision to launch Operation Restore Hope in December 1992 or Clinton's decision to withdraw U.S. troops after the tragic events of October 1993. In both cases, White House recognition of growing popular discontent with existing policies allowed a certain degree of latitude in fashioning an appropriate policy response. Although domestic discontent formed the backdrop of policy and in some sense restrained the range of choices available to Bush and Clinton, both White House decisions nonetheless demonstrated the importance of presidential politics in understanding the final policy choice. This constraint was perhaps more evident in the Clinton decision due to the president's desire to ensure his reelection in November 1996, whereas Bush's decision was geared more toward how his administration would be remembered, given the fact that he had lost the 1992 presidential elections.

The preceding analysis therefore suggests that two different "constellations" of policy-making leadership will characterize the future evolution of U.S. foreign policy toward Africa. As already suggested, the *bureaucratic leadership constellation* was indicative of early Bush (prior to December 1992) and Clinton administration (January to October 1993) policies toward Africa, and the bureaucracy will constitute the dominant constellation of U.S. Africa policies in the post–cold war era. The bureaucratic constellation will be periodically displaced by the *interbranch leadership constellation* during periods of crisis or extended crisis, in which the established policies of the bureaucracies will be altered by an institutional give-and-take between the White House and Congress. As demonstrated by Bush's decision to commit U.S. military troops (December 1992) and Clinton's decision to withdraw them (October 1993) amidst intense domestic pressures, a combination of domestic politics and presidential politics will coincide to create a policy reflective of constructive compromise. Although neither side will be completely free to act as they please, each will nonetheless be able to cite some margin of victory in promoting their preferred future course for U.S. foreign policy toward Africa in the post–cold war era and beyond.

## Notes

1   In order to avoid confusion, the official U.S. (and parallel U.N.) titles of these interventions, each of which is more specifically described within the text, are as follows: (1) Operation Provide Relief (August–December 1992) (United Nations Operation in Somalia I—UNOSOM I); (2) Operation Restore Hope (December 1992–April 1993) (United Task Force—UNITAF); (3) Operation Continue Relief (May 1993–March 1994) (United Nations Operation in Somalia II—UNOSOM II).

2   Thomas L. Freidman, "U.S. Pays Dearly for an Education in Somalia," *New York Times*, October 10, 1993, sec. 4, p. 1.

3   Quoted in B. Drummond Ayres Jr., "A Common Cry across the U.S.: It's Time to Exit," *New York Times*, October 9, 1993, p. A1.

4   For overviews, see John L. Hirsch and Robert B. Oakley, *Somalia and Operation Restore Hope: Reflections on Peacemaking and Peacekeeping* (Washington, D.C.: United States Institute for Peace Press, 1995); Walter Clarke and Jeffrey Herbst, eds., *Learning from Somalia: The Lessons of Armed Humanitarian Intervention* (Boulder, Colo.: Westview, 1997); and Mohamed Shanoun, *Somalia: The Missed Opportunities* (Washington, D.C.: United States Institute for Peace Press, 1994).

5   For discussion, see Charles F. Doran, "The Regionalist-Globalist Debate," in Peter J. Schraeder, ed., *Intervention into the 1990s: U.S. Foreign Policy in the Third World* (Boulder, Colo.: Lynne Rienner, 1992), pp. 55–74.

6   Daniel Compagnon, "The Somali Opposition Fronts: Some Comments and Questions," *Horn of Africa* 13, nos. 1–2 (January–March, April–June 1990): 29–54.

7   For an overview, see Terrence Lyons and Ahmed I. Samatar, *Somalia: State Collapse, Multilateral Intervention, and Strategies for Political Reconstruction* (Washington, D.C.: Brookings Institution, 1995), pp. 1–24; and Anna Simons, *Networks of Dissolution: Somalia Undone* (Boulder, Colo.: Westview, 1995).

8   Robert G. Patman, *The Soviet Union in the Horn of Africa: The Diplomacy of Intervention and Disengagement* (Cambridge: Cambridge University Press, 1990). See in particular the revealing remarks of Anatoly Dobrynin, *In Confidence: Moscow's Ambassador to America's Six Cold War Presidents, 1962-1986* (New York: Times Books, 1995), esp. p. 407.

9   Quoted in Jane Perlez, "Heavy Fighting Erupts in Somali Capital," *New York Times*, January 1, 1991, p. A3.

10   Interview.

11   Quoted in Perlez, "Heavy Fighting," p. A3.

12   Perlez, "Heavy Fighting," p. A3.

13   For discussion, see Said S. Samatar, *Somalia: A Nation in Turmoil* (London: Minority Rights Group, 1991).

14   Interview.

15   Interview.

16   For details, see Hirsch and Oakley, *Somalia and Operation Restore Hope*, pp. 49–79.

17   For a good summary, see Ken Menkhaus and Louis Ortmayer, "Key Decisions in

the Somalia Intervention," *Pew Case Studies in International Affairs,* Instructor Copy 46, 1995, p. 7.

18 Quoted in Elaine Sciolino, "Bush Offered Troops to Aid Somalis Despite C.I.A.'s Doubts," *New York Times,* December 3, 1992, p. A8.

19 Portions of the cable were printed as "An Ambassador's Warning: Think Three Times before You Embrace the Somali Tarbaby," *U.S. News and World Report,* December 14, 1992, p. 30. See also Smith Hempstone Jr., *Rogue Ambassador: An African Memoir* (Sewanee, Tenn.: University of the South Press, 1997).

20 Quoted in Jane Perlez, "Somali Warlord Agrees to Allow U.N. to Protect Its Relief Supplies," *New York Times,* August 13, 1992, p. A1.

21 See Carolyn J. Logan, "U.S. Public Opinion and the Intervention in Somalia: Lessons for the Future of Military-Humanitarian Interventions," *The Fletcher Forum of World Affairs* 20, no. 2 (Summer/Fall 1996): 155–80.

22 See, for example, Anthony Lewis, "Action or Death," *New York Times,* November 20, 1992, p. A15.

23 Quoted in Peter Applebome, "Seared by Faces of Need, Americans Say, 'How Could We Not Do This?'" *New York Times,* December 13, 1992, p. A8.

24 Quoted in Michael Wines, "Aides Say U.S. Role in Somalia Gives Bush a Way to Exit in Glory," *New York Times,* December 6, 1992, p. A12.

25 See, for example, Carroll J. Doherty, "The Question at the Hearing: 'How Do We Get Out?'" *Congressional Quarterly* 50 (December 19, 1992): 3890. Another, largely cold war–derivative explanation cites U.S. strategic interests, most notably the desire to maintain access to military bases in preparation for future U.S. military contingencies within the region. However, in an interesting conclusion to a long-simmering policy debate over Somalia's strategic importance, the U.S. naval facility at Berbera turned out to be completely unnecessary for the massive deployment of U.S. troops and matériel associated with Operation Desert Storm. A "worldview" perspective is also initially appealing in that Operation Restore Hope clearly reflected the globalist worldview of Bush and his two closest foreign policy advisers—Secretary of State James A. Baker III and National Security Adviser Brendt Scowcroft—specifically in terms of their collective desire to fashion a "new world order" based on active U.S. involvement within the international system as the sole remaining superpower. Despite the lofty rhetoric, however, this interpretation of events fails to explain why the Bush administration ignored domestic and international appeals to aid Somalia during 1991, as well as the timing and nature of White House responses during 1992. In other words, why did Bush decide to launch Operation Provide Relief during August 1992 as opposed to July 1992 (or earlier), and why did he decide to launch Operation Restore Hope only after (as opposed to prior to) the presidential elections of November 1992?

26 Hirsch and Oakley, *Somalia and Operation Restore Hope,* p. 152.

27 Quoted in Michael R. Gordon (with John H. Cushman Jr.), "U.S. Supported Hunt for Aidid; Now Calls U.N. Policy Skewed," *New York Times,* October 18, 1993, p. A6.

28 Dick Morris, *Behind the Oval Office: Winning the Presidency in the Nineties* (New York: Random House, 1997), p. 245. An exception to this trend was ongoing White House attention to events in Russia.

29 Quoted in Tim Hanes, "Searching for a New World Order: The Clinton Administration and Foreign Policy in 1993," *International Relations* 12, no. 1 (April 1994): 112.

30 See Colin L. Powell (with Joseph E. Persico), *My American Journey* (New York: Random House, 1995), p. 565.

31 Powell, *American Journey*, p. 566.

32 Cited in Francis A. Kornegay Jr., "Africa in the New World Order," *Africa Report* 38, no. 1 (January–February 1993): 13–17.

33 Quoted in Donatella Lorch, "Somalis, Mired in War, Torn by Feelings about Americans," *New York Times*, October 17, 1993, p. A6.

34 Walter Clarke and Jeffrey Herbst, "Somalia and the Future of Humanitarian Intervention," *Foreign Affairs* 75, no. 2 (March/April 1996): 74.

35 Clarke and Herbst, "Somalia," p. 74.

36 See Kenneth B. Noble, "400 U.S. Marines Attack Compound of Somali Gunmen," *New York Times*, January 8, 1993, pp. A1, A4.

37 Quoted in Alison Mitchell, "Marines in Somalia Try to Rebuild a Town Council," *New York Times*, January 18, 1993, p. A3.

38 Powell, *My American Journey*, p. 584.

39 Indeed, it is Admiral Howe who was responsible for the much ridiculed decision to hand out "wanted posters" in Mogadishu offering $25,000 for Aidid's capture.

40 Quoted in Michael R. Gordon, "U.S. Supported Hunt for Aidid."

41 Powell, *My American Journey*, p. 584.

42 Interview.

43 Quoted in Elaine Sciolino, "Somalia Puzzle: What Is the American Strategy?" *New York Times*, October 5, 1993, p. A3.

44 Transcript of Clinton's televised address on October 7, 1993. Reproduced in "Clinton's Words on Somalia: 'The Responsibilities of American Leadership,'" *New York Times*, October 8, 1993, p. A9.

45 "Clinton's Words on Somalia," p. A9.

46 Logan, "Public Opinion and U.S. Intervention in Somalia," p. 158.

47 Harry Johnston and Ted Dagne, "Congress and the Somali Crisis," in Walter S. Clarke and Jeffrey Herbst, eds., *Learning from Somalia* (Boulder, Colo.: Westview, 1997), pp. 191–206.

48 Johnston and Dagne, "Congress and the Somali Crisis," p. 14.

49 Logan, "Public Opinion and U.S. Intervention in Somalia," p. 156.

50 Quoted in Ayres Jr., "A Common Cry," p. 6.

51 Quoted in Clifford Krauss, "White House Tries to Calm Congress," *New York Times*, October 6, 1993, p. A6.

52 Krauss, "White House Tries to Calm," p. A6.

53 Krauss, "White House Tries to Calm," p. A6.

54 See Jacqueline Sharkey, "When Pictures Drive Foreign Policy," *American Journalism Review* (December 1993): 14–19; and Frank J. Stech, "Winning CNN Wars," *Parameter: U.S. Army War College Quarterly* 24, no. 3 (Autumn 1994): 37–56.

55 Logan, "Public Opinion and U.S. Intervention in Somalia," p. 161.

56 Quoted in Ayres Jr., "A Common Cry," p. A6.

57 Thomas L. Friedman, "Clinton Reviews Policy in Somalia as Unease Grows," *New York Times*, October 6, 1993, p. A1.

58 See Peter J. Schraeder, "The Clinton Administration's Africa Policies: Some Comments on Continuity and Change at Mid-Term," *L'Afrique politique 1995: le meilleur, le pire, et l'incertain* (Paris: Editions Karthala, 1995), pp. 57–60.

59 Quoted in Clifford Krauss, "Clinton Gathers Congress Support," *New York Times*, October 8, 1993, p. A8.

60 See Michael Clough, *Free at Last? U.S. Policy toward Africa and the End of the Cold War* (New York: Council on Foreign Relations Press, 1992).

61 See Douglas Jehl, "Officials Told to Avoid Calling Rwanda Killings 'Genocide,'" *New York Times*, June 10, 1994, p. A8.

62 See Jim Cason and Bill Martin, "Clinton and Africa: Searching for a Post–Cold War Order," *ACAS Bulletin*, no. 38–39 (Winter 1993): 2.

63 Cason and Martin, "Clinton and Africa," p. 2.

64 For a summary, see Peter J. Schraeder, *United States Foreign Policy Toward Africa: Incrementalism, Crisis, and Change* (Cambridge: Cambridge University Press, 1994), pp. 12–25.

65 Schraeder, "U.S. Foreign Policy," pp. 26–37.

66 Schraeder, "U.S. Foreign Policy," pp. 37–48.

67 Powell, *My American Journey*, p. 588.

## 14.

## NAFTA and Beyond: The Politics of Trade

## in the Post–Cold War Period

*Renee G. Scherlen*

A key aspect of the post–cold war era is the growing primacy of economic issues. In this context, the fight surrounding the North American Free Trade Agreement (NAFTA) and its extension offers a preview of future foreign policy decision making. The NAFTA case epitomizes the messy, complicated process that is beginning to characterize post–cold war foreign policy, which has—particularly in the economic realm—grown ever more complex. Foreign economic policy making involves shifting constellations of leadership with a variety of participants that operate in an ever changing environment. As the exploration of NAFTA reveals, after the end of the cold war there was no consensus over the goals and instruments of foreign economic policy. Not surprisingly, this reduced presidential dominance and increased congressional activism. Furthermore, NAFTA expanded the bureaucratic agencies beyond the usual players: at one time or another, the Office of the United States Trade Representative, the State and Commerce Departments, as well as the Environmental Protection Agency and Labor Department were key bureaucratic participants. As is to be anticipated in this post–cold war era, a broad spectrum of interests and perspectives were intertwined in NAFTA. Consequently, the foreign policy process proved difficult for either President Bush or President Clinton to control. Moreover, the high degree of congressional participation both reflected and stimulated heightened public awareness over the foreign policy issue. This, in turn, probably contributed a more prominent role played by nongovernmental actors including labor unions, environmental organizations, and business groups.

Thus, this case study should shed light on the shifting constellations of decision making and the unanticipated alliances that will most likely govern foreign economic policy making in the years to come. It begins with a brief synopsis of U.S. foreign economic policy before the end of the cold war. It then turns to an examination of NAFTA and subsequent efforts at its expansion, broken down into key phrases: the "fast track" negotiation period (March 1991–October 1992); the elections of 1992 and the side agreement negotiations (July 1992–August 1993); the ratification process (summer and fall 1993); and the postimplementation plans for NAFTA expansion (1994–97). The conclusion evaluates NAFTA's lessons about post–cold war U.S. foreign policy making.

### U.S. Foreign Economic Policy before "the End"

Historically, economic concerns have underpinned much of U.S. foreign policy—especially prior to World War II. In the years immediately following U.S. independence, struggles over the rights of neutral ships (a major factor leading up to the War of 1812) developed out of economic necessity: the importance of maritime commerce demanded that the U.S. government guard this economic livelihood. As the United States emerged as a global power, its blueprint for action emphasized economic issues. Its "Open Door" policy asserted that open markets and U.S. commercial access were the goals of U.S. foreign policy.[1] Moreover, the "return to isolationism" following World War I referred primarily to military and political entanglements. The United States maintained a vigorous and active global economic interaction until the Smoot-Hawley Tariff Act of 1930 raised duties to protect domestic producers, thus contributing to a downward spiral in international trade.

U.S. involvement in World War II marked a transition. Initially, geopolitical perspectives dominated economic issues in the postwar years. Foreign policy was controlled by the White House and State Department; the economic bureaucracy was generally excluded from the process. For instance, the Marshall Plan—a gigantic economic aid package —was developed and implemented primarily by noneconomic foreign policy actors. Over time, this domination subsided. As the economies of U.S. allies grew and the overwhelming power of the United States diminished, purely economic concerns grew. The era of U.S. preeminence in the world economy ended, bringing about an increase in the importance of an economic perspective on foreign policy. Correspondingly, there was a change in bureaucratic control over foreign economic policy; the Commerce Department was drawn into the process and the Office of the United States Trade Representative became more powerful. However, as long as the cold war lasted, the challenge of the Soviet Union meant that economic priorities would always give way to geopolitical concerns. An example of this was the grain embargo imposed by the United States in response to the Soviet invasion of Afghanistan in 1979. U.S. economic interests argued against such a move—the vital U.S. agricultural sector would be harmed. However, geopolitical concerns necessitated a strong signal of U.S. displeasure.

Many signs indicate that after the end of the cold war, U.S. foreign policy is regaining its economic focus. For instance, assessments conducted in 1986, 1990, and 1994 show that protecting U.S. jobs was either the first or second most cited foreign policy goal for the public. Protecting U.S. business abroad has steadily risen as a policy goal as well: in 1986 it ranked tenth, while by 1994 it had emerged as the third most common foreign policy goal.[2] Economic diplomacy is currently seen as key component of domestic prosperity: as Joan E. Spero, undersecretary for economic and agricultural affairs, noted "[the U.S.] foreign economic program . . . [is] part and parcel of [the] larger [U.S.] strategy to revitalize the domestic economy."[3] Without a single, overwhelming military threat to divert attention, economics dominates the foreign policy agenda. Under such circumstances, the issues involved in the NAFTA case may be the dominant concerns of U.S. foreign policy makers in the future.

### Foreign Economic Policy after the Cold War: NAFTA and Beyond

Initially, the passage of a North American Free Trade Agreement appeared assured. With bipartisan support and foundations in an economic accord with Canada that had generated little controversy (in the United States), its approval seemed automatic. However, the passage of NAFTA grew into a long, multidimensional, and multiactor process involving the White House (under both Republican Bush and Democrat Clinton), Congress, several executive departments (the Office of the USTR, Commerce, Treasury, Labor, etc.), the two main political parties, an independent presidential candidate (H. Ross Perot), and a number of interest groups (labor unions, environmental groups, and others).

*Roots of NAFTA*

Most analysts agree that NAFTA resulted from several trends in Mexico, the United States, and Canada. Years earlier, the concept of a continental economic union similar to Europe's emerged as a possible policy option for the United States. It failed to gain momentum beause of the lack of enthusiasm on the part of Mexico and Canada—not the United States.[4] By the late 1980s, the situation had changed enough for Canada and the United States to sign a bilateral free trade agreement. However, the key to constructing a North American agreement lay with events inside Mexico.

Beginning in 1982—in response to its debt crisis—Mexico started to transform its economic relationship with other nations. For example, after years of nonparticipation, Mexico joined the General Agreement on Tariffs and Trade (GATT) in 1985. Long-held protectionist policies that underpinned Mexico's import-substitution industrialization strategy began to give way to open-market, low-tariff policies. This neoliberal perspective held by President de la Madrid was reinforced by his successor, Carlos Salinas, who entered office in 1988. In an effort to further strengthen neoliberal economic policies, President Salinas sought trade agreements and foreign investment from a number of nations—the European Union and Japan in particular.[5] However, these countries were primarily interested in Eastern European and the Pacific Rim nations respectively, as areas for expanding economic ties. Given the importance of the United States to Mexico, as well as the reluctance of other economically powerful countries, a trade agreement with the United States became the logical focal point of Mexican efforts.

The movement on the part of Mexico to create a new economic agreement did not necessarily entail a three-way treaty. Canada was informed in early 1990 of a possible U.S.-Mexican trade accord. Initially, Canadian officials were unenthusiastic about joining in the process; the free trade agreement with the United States had generated much domestic opposition in Canada, and Mexico was not a very important Canadian trading partner (it ranked seventeenth at the time).[6] However, the prospect of more preferential trading terms with Mexico and the desire to develop Canadian-Latin American trade led Canada to join in the negotiation to draft a North American free trade agreement.

Consistent with its traditional support of free trade, the United States had previously tried to develop more open trade with Canada and Mexico. With the completion of the Canadian Free Trade Agreement (CTFA), U.S. acceptance of the Mexican proposal for a bilateral free trade agreement was therefore unsurprising. Within the government, different actors gave different priority to the agreement, though. While the National Security Council and the Departments of State and Commerce advocated pushing ahead, the Office of the USTR and the Department of Agriculture were more lukewarm.[7] In particular, the relative importance of the Uruguay Round of GATT were of concern: would negotiation of NAFTA sidetrack the United States from its efforts in the GATT negotiation? Strategic political considerations balanced this economic concern. The United States has always been preoccupied with Mexican stability—both economic and political—and a free trade agreement was viewed as a way to shore up both. Advocates thought it might enhance the Mexican economy while lessening the potential for political turmoil. Indeed, there were those who argued that without NAFTA, Mexico would be heading toward both financial and political crises.[8] The White House decided to pursue NAFTA; on March 1, 1991, President Bush requested fast-track authorization for the NAFTA negotiation and the first foreign policy battle began.

*The Fast-Track Request and Initial Negotiations*
The "fast-track" procedure is a mechanism for foreign economic policy making using the shared powers of Congress and the president. According to the Constitution, the president has the power to negotiate treaties (subject to Senate ratification). Yet, the Constitution also empowers Congress to regulate foreign commerce. In the twentieth century, the president and Congress have tried a couple of strategies to make sure that this constitutional "check" did not hinder international economic relations and trade. With the Reciprocal Trade Agreements Act of 1934, Congress delegated to the president all authority for trade negotiations. Specifically, U.S. tariff reductions (within certain specified limits) that were matched by reductions by other nations could be implemented by presidential proclamation—without congressional involvement. This process became increasingly challenged in the 1960s; as tariffs were lowered, nontariff barriers became the most significant obstacles to free trade. Yet, there was no agreed upon method to develop treaties to combat nontariff barriers. Often, one person's "nontariff barrier" was another's legitimate health or safety regulation. Seemingly, the United States would be in a position where the executive would negotiate a treaty, and then Congress would alter it. This clearly hurt the executive's ability to devise an agreement; negotiating partners would wisely be wary of devoting time and energy to a document that could be changed unilaterally through amendments by the legislative branch. The "fast-track" mechanism was born out of this situation with the Trade Reform Act of 1974. Fast track allows the executive to negotiate a treaty while consulting with the legislature. Then, after the text is complete, Congress must accept or reject it—without changes.

Fast track worked well for many years. When President Bush announced he was seeking fast-track approval, problems were not anticipated. Yet, the changing post–cold war environment was already influencing Congress. Legislators were concerned about the usurpation of legislative power via fast track: while key members of Congress were to be consulted during the negotiations (the House Ways and Means and Senate Finance Committees), often the input of rank-and-file members was limited to a vote for or against an entire treaty. Clearly, as opinion polls and election results indicated, foreign economic policy was a growing issue for voters; therefore, it was an increasingly vital subject for legislators as well. Furthermore, the substance of the proposed agreement worried representatives. Would fast track force them to vote down a treaty with several good aspects because of flaws in the labor and environmental areas? President Bush, anticipating congressional opposition to granting fast track, pledged to be timely with congressional consultations during the negotiations. Interest in the labor and environmental aspects of the agreement was also noted. Indeed, the Bush administration pledged to have environmental organizations consult with the USTR on measures contained in the treaty. Thus, NAFTA demonstrated, even before it was negotiated, a new twist in U.S. foreign economic policy. No longer would the fast-track mechanism be taken for granted by the executive branch, and nongovernmental organizations gained recognition as players in the negotiating process.

Negotiations between Canada, Mexico, and the United States began on June 12, 1991, resulting in a draft initialed by the lead negotiators—in front of Presidents Bush and Salinas and Prime Minister Mulroney—on October 7, 1992. Despite the difficulty in attaining fast-track status, for the most part the negotiating phase of NAFTA involved constructive compromise between the White House and Congress. The White House, operating through high-ranking members of the Cabinet, particularly the USTR, dominated the drafting of NAFTA within the United States. The actual "nuts and bolts" of the treaty were developed by eighteen working groups comprised of bureaucratic experts in the different functional/technical areas: agriculture, automotive, dispute settlement, energy and petrochemicals, financial services, government procurement, insurance services, intellectual property, investment, land transportation, rules of origin, safeguards, services, subsidies/trade remedies, standards, tariffs/nontariff barriers, telecommunications, and textiles.

This domination by the executive branch was slightly offset by discussions between the USTR and business and environmental groups. For instance, Industry Functional Advisory Committees (IFACs) and Industry Sectoral Advisory Committees (ISACs) were consulted. In particular, then-U.S. Trade Representative Carla Hills sought out the advice of CEOs of large, export-oriented companies, as well as those from potentially endangered firms in the glass and textile area.[9] Likewise, the USTR made sure that Congress continued to be apprised of the scope and direction of the talks. One method was to submit drafts of the text to the offices of concerned legislators. Specifically, the USTR made sure that the eighteen House and Senate Committees with jurisdiction over trade were regularly updated. This was supplemented by informal talks to congressional members and their staffs.[10] According to Trade Representative Carla Hills, "[T]he number of congressional and private sector consultations . . . held since the talks began . . . amount[ed] to more than three per day."[11]

Though the primary focus of the NAFTA talks was reconciliation of Canadian, Mexican, and U.S. positions, the U.S. negotiators often had to mold their position based on U.S. private industry, labor, environmental, and congressional suggestions. These consultations were both legally required and politically prudent; failure to do so would result in an unratified treaty. Legislative input was often quite direct. For instance, in March of 1992, seven senators, representing energy-producing states, sent a letter to U.S. negotiators, proposing certain "guiding principles" for the U.S. position in the energy section of the treaty. The suggested U.S. negotiating stance was in direct conflict with Mexico's position on the oil industry, which stated that a significant opening of the oil industry (nationalized in 1938) to foreign participation was not possible. State control over this vital resource was viewed as a mainstay of Mexican sovereignty and nonnegotiable.[12] Thus, the U.S. negotiators had a senatorial suggestion that clashed with a firm Mexican stance. The team had to find a way to address congressional concerns while developing positions acceptable to both Canada and Mexico.

Nongovernmental actors shaped the negotiations as well. In a letter sent to the U.S. negotiating team in September 1991, the three major U.S. automakers "proposed increasing exports of autos and trucks to Mexico [and] push[ed] for measures preventing the use of Mexico as a 'trampoline' for auto industries in non-pact nations"[13] among other items. Sometimes, interest groups intervened directly at the presidential level. In February 1992, the U.S. Coalition for Trade Expansion, an umbrella group of twenty U.S. business organizations, sent a letter to President Bush threatening to withdraw support for the NAFTA if U.S. negotiators fail to secure the desired level of trade liberalization sought by U.S. business. The signatories included the U.S. Chamber of Commerce, the Business Roundtable, the Council of the Americas, the Association of Chemical Manufacturers, and the National Association of Manufacturers, among others.[14] However, some interest groups encountered some difficulty in influencing the negotiations. For instance, delays in the appointment of environmentalists to an advisory board limited their input until the fall of 1992.[15]

At times, interest group members and members of Congress talked directly with Canadian and Mexican officials. In February 1992, an eleven-member congressional delegation, accompanied by twenty-seven private sector representatives, traveled to Mexico. They spoke with President Salinas, members of the Mexican cabinet, and Mexican business leaders about NAFTA. They used the opportunity to express their positions about the terms of the proposed trade agreement. After returning from Mexico, Representative Jim Kolbe (R-Ariz.) noted the areas of continued disagreement between the United States and Mexico and stated that "the US [would] not accept Mexican demands for modifying anti-dumping clauses and compensatory taxes for the displacement of US workers resulting from Mexican imports."[16]

Not surprisingly, given the detail of the treaty, it took many meetings and countless revisions to draft a document acceptable to the negotiators representing the three nations. As 1992 progressed, the U.S. team was under increasing pressure to complete the draft. With a view toward election year politics, President Bush believed that a finalized treaty would gain votes for the Republican party in Texas and California—two key electoral prizes. Standing in the way of a completed treaty were a host of issues such as dispute resolution, rules of origin, government procurement, and subsidies and trade remedies. A series of marathon negotiating sessions resulted in a treaty acceptable to all three negotiating teams. The final text provided for unrestricted trade of goods, services, and capital among the three nations implemented over a fifteen-year period (barriers are lowered at different rates and different times depending on the area). Key aspects of the treaty included provisions for protecting intellectual property (i.e., respect for copyrights), opening the Mexican financial services sector to United States and Canada, partial opening of the energy sector in Mexico, and creating a three-tiered procedure for the resolution of trade disputes between the three nations. President Bush was able to oversee the initialing of a draft agreement in San Antonio about one month before the election.[17]

*The Side Agreements and Ratification*
The signing of the treaty marks the beginning of a new phase and the ascendancy of a new policy-making constellation. Confrontation and the possibility of stalemate best describes the process of developing side agreements and gaining ratification. The change in the policy-making constellation came about for two reasons: the presidential elec-

tion and the constitutional requirement of congressional approval for trade agreements. That is to say, submitting a treaty for ratification always opens up the policy-making process—to a greater or lesser degree depending on the circumstances. However, NAFTA underwent a sea-change in policy-making structure not only because the ratification stage had been reached but also because of the 1992 presidential election. NAFTA became a campaign issue. Mobilized interest groups and concerned legislators scrutinized the text. Debate over the treaty grew so heated that its fate was not quite secure up until the time of the vote in the House of Representatives. Between the signing of the treaty in 1992 and its ratification in 1993, interbranch leadership—shifting between constructive compromise and confrontation/stalemate—turned NAFTA policy making into a highly contentious issue.

Only one of the three main candidates for president in 1992 campaigned as an unconditional supporter of NAFTA. President Bush, not surprisingly, supported the treaty as written. He campaigned on the theme of the benefits of free trade and the promise of NAFTA for the U.S. economy. Democratic candidate Bill Clinton conditionally supported the treaty. His position reflected the realities of a Democratic candidate seeking office. Numerous organizations—such as key labor unions and environmental groups—opposed the treaty. Many of these were stalwart supporters of the Democratic party. Yet, the candidate himself, as well as other elements within the Democratic Party—particularly influential "centrists"—favored a free trade agreement. Thus, the candidate developed a compromise position. As he stated in a campaign speech in North Carolina: "Although it is unpopular with some people and organizations I admire and who represent the very Americans I am fighting so hard for in this election, I think we should go forward with NAFTA because it advances our interests, the interests of ordinary Americans, more than it undermines them—if we also do the other things needed to deal with the deficiencies in this agreement."[18] The mechanism to deal with these "deficiencies" was the creation of supplemental agreements on labor and the environment. In this speech, Bill Clinton pledged to sign NAFTA implementation legislation only if side agreements accompanied the treaty.

A mainstay of the campaign of the other key presidential candidate, H. Ross Perot, was complete opposition to NAFTA. Among the most memorable "sound bites" of the campaign is Perot's famous prediction of the "giant sucking sound" that would be heard as U.S. industries and well-paying jobs went south if NAFTA were ratified. The election campaign marked the beginning of strange alliances that would characterize the latter part of the NAFTA policy-making process. The grouping together of a populist Texas billionaire businessman with labor union activists and environmental groups was a new phenomenon. Similarly, the emergence of a more isolationist, protectionist element in the Republican Party (demonstrated by the candidacy of Pat Buchanan) was new.

The presidential election—and the bid for the presidency by Perot especially—proved a rallying point for anti-NAFTA forces. Critical voices gained volume, and public opinion started to shift. In 1991, almost immediately after negotiations over NAFTA began, a Gallup poll revealed that 83 percent of those expressing an opinion favored a North America–wide free trade agreement similar to the one the United States had with Canada. By September 1992, as the presidential election entered its final phase, a Gallup poll showed that 57 percent of those expressing an opinion opposed NAFTA.[19] The lens of the campaign focused attention on NAFTA, and criticism dominated the debate.

The election of Bill Clinton in November 1992 signified a new round of negotiations between Canada, Mexico, and the United States. Additional agreements over the environment and labor were to be created in order to address deficiencies in the treaty. Numerous comments by legislators made it clear that NAFTA would not pass if changes were not made. For instance, prior to a September 16, 1992, Senate foreign trade subcommittee hearing, the subcommittee chair, Senator Max Baucus (D-Mont.), suggested that NAFTA include sanctions, such as temporary reimposition of tariffs, if a NAFTA partner failed to comply with environmental requirements. His concerns were echoed by Senator Lloyd Bentsen (D-Tex.), chair of the Senate finance committee, who said "important environmental topics must be included in the treaty."[20] Senators Baucus, Donald Riegle (D-Mich.), Thomas Daschle (D-S.D.) and John Breaux (D-La.) all insisted on the need to include provisions guaranteeing enforcement of environmental conservation standards in Mexico.[21] It is not surprising, then, that President Clinton insisted on negotiating parallel agreements to NAFTA.

The side agreement negotiations differed from the NAFTA negotiation. More agencies were involved, and interest groups were targeted as key players. For instance, suggestions about key issues were solicited from environmental groups.[22] As with NAFTA, the USTR directed the side agreement negotiations. However, the economic agencies of the U.S. bureaucracy were not the main participants. Rather, the USTR was joined by the State Department, the Environmental Protection Agency, and the Departments of Commerce, Justice, Labor, and Health and Human Services. The opinions of interest groups funneled in through a number of channels. One of the most important was the vice president, who had close ties to the environmental movement. Certain members of the State Department (such as Richard Smith and Counselor Timothy Wirth) and the EPA administrator, Carol Browner, also had tight links to environmental groups.[23]

Divisions existed within the U.S. negotiating team. Should trade sanctions be used to punish violations of environmental and labor standards? While the USTR, EPA, and Treasury Department supported sanctions, the Department of State opposed such an action. What type of mechanism would hear complaints and settle disputes? Could standards be identified and procedures created that would safeguard the environment and labor without undermining national sovereignty? In a report to President Clinton's National Economic Council, the State Department warned that the creation of a supranational enforcement agency would "run up against serious Constitutional concerns in the United States."[24] Finally, could additional agreements be reached that would be acceptable to Mexico and Canada as well as satisfactory to U.S. critics? The answers to most of these questions were compromises: positions that garnered the widest support (or the least opposition) while attacking—at least partially—the environmental and labor flaws in the NAFTA text.

The side agreement on the environment is the more rigorous of the two. A Commission for Environmental Cooperation governed by a council made up of environmental ministers (the director of the EPA in the United States) is the centerpiece of the environmental side agreement. There is also a secretariat that gives technical, administrative, and operational support to the commission. The secretariat hears complaints from any person or organization on noncompliance with existing domestic environmental laws. The secretariat is assisted by a joint advisory committee, whose members come from nongovernmental organizations as well as the governments of member nations. The committee offers technical and scientific information to the secretariat, as well as suggestions on budget and program matters.[25]

These characteristics reflect the preferences of U.S. environmental groups, which advocated the establishment of a trilateral commission as well as the long-term participation of nongovernmental organizations with expertise in this area.[26] Yet, efforts to insulate the commission from domestic political pressure failed. Not only did Mexican and Canadian negotiators reject a strongly independent, essentially "supranational" commission, other voices in the United States opposed such a move. In a letter to the president, House Minority Leader Robert H. Michel (R-Ill.) and House Minority Whip Newt Gingrich (R-Ga.) stated that they would work against an implementing bill that created "multilateral environmental and labor bureaucracies with little accountability and sweeping mandates."[27] Since Republican congressional support was needed to ratify NAFTA, the U.S. team had to find a path between environmental groups (part of the president's constituency, as well as a loud voice to be reckoned with in the upcoming battle for the hearts and minds of the public during the ratification process) and House Republicans. The side deal reflects these compromises.

Action on the environment begins with a complaint lodged with the secretariat concerning a "persistent pattern of failure to effectively enforce an environmental law."[28] The violation must be linked to the production of goods or services traded between the member nations. The complaint may come from any source. The secretariat proceeds to investigate the charge. If the complaint is found to have merit, and if the dispute cannot be resolved by the council, an arbitration board may be created. Two out of the three council members must vote for such a board. If the arbitration panel agrees that the member persistently failed to enforce its laws, a number of events may occur. A mutually agreed upon plan of action (reviewed by the panel) may be implemented. Fines may be assessed. In extreme cases (involving the United States and Mexico), the complaining party/parties may suspend NAFTA benefits. The process is designed, though, to avoid this last option.[29]

In the design of the dispute settlement procedure, the desires of U.S. environmental groups are balanced out by congressional Republican leadership concerns. This effort to gain broad support can be seen in the plan to give the trilateral commission broad powers while at the same time attempting to limit its scope so that the commission could not be used for protectionism. The testimony of U.S. trade negotiator Rufus Yerxa before the Senate Finance Committee on May 19, 1993, reflects this balancing act. He addressed the concern of Democrats (and environmentalists) by emphasizing the U.S. plan to seek strong enforcement mechanisms for the environmental commission. However, Yerxa assuaged the concern of Republicans by noting that sanctions would only be applied in cases where there was a "clear and consistent problem."[30]

The negotiation process for and the agreement signed on labor differed from that on the environment. Mexico and Canada sharply opposed any significant international intervention into labor issues. For both nations—albeit for different reasons—the political costs of such foreign intrusion were substantial. Thus, the U.S. team faced constraints with their partners. Unlike the situation with the environment, nongovernmental organizations were not highly mobilized and involved in the negotiation. The AFL-CIO, the major U.S. labor union, did not articulate a "wish list" for the side agreement, unlike U.S. environmental interest groups. The other private actors interested in NAFTA—businesses— were opposed to opening management-labor relations to international scrutiny. As stated above, Republican leaders in the House were opposed to any type of multilateral institution that might countermand the authority of the U.S. government, particularly Congress. Nevertheless, labor displeasure with NAFTA, as well as public opinion concerns about the future of U.S. jobs, necessitated some sort of labor side deal. However, the context in which the deal was negotiated resulted in a less stringent agreement. In many ways, the policy-making process for this segment reflected constructive compromise. The White House dominated the process, primarily because of labor's disinclination for participation and business's desire not to subject labor issues to outside review.

In several institutional respects, the labor side agreement is similar to that on the environment. A council made up of labor ministers/secretaries oversees the Commission for Labor Cooperation. It has an international coordinating secretariat that manages the implementation of the side deal. However, unlike that stipulated for the environmental agreement, there is no formal mechanism for the participation of nongovernmental organizations. Rather than an international advisory commission, labor disputes are channeled through a national administrative office (each nation has one), whose structure and operation is determined by each nation. It serves as the main sources of information and review for complaints. In the case of disputes between member countries over labor issues, the enforcement mechanisms are the same as for environmental violations.[31]

Complaints concerning persistent failure to enforce national labor standards are heard by the national administrative office. The NAOs are charged with investigating the labor conditions in the other NAFTA countries. They must also provide information about labor codes and practices within their own borders. Each NAO has its own procedures for investigation. Likewise, each NAO determines whether or not to follow through on a complaint.[32] The mechanism developed emphasizes "exchanging information, discussing issues, and resolving problems through [consultation]."[33] This high degree of national discretion limits the scope of the labor accord. It also mirrors the relative autonomy enjoyed by the U.S. labor accord negotiators in comparison to the environmental negotiation. Unlike numerous environmental groups, the

AFL-CIO did not actively participate in designing the labor agreement. Its main contribution was to have a single representative on the Labor Advisory Committee which monitored the negotiations but did not draft any articles.[34]

## The Ratification Debate

With the creation of side agreements, the Clinton administration was prepared to start the NAFTA ratification process, which, of course, involved interbranch interaction. The Clinton White House argued that the side agreement represented a constructive compromise that addressed key concerns of legislators and rectified deficiencies in the NAFTA text. Opponents of NAFTA, unsatisfied by the side agreements, pushed for confrontation and stalemate, hoping that NAFTA implementation legislation would not pass the House of Representatives.

Opponents of NAFTA initially gained the upper hand in the public debate because of divisions within the White House. Proponents of other priorities—such as health care reform—battled with supporters of NAFTA implementation for the attention and political capital of the President. Hillary Rodham Clinton, Ira Magaziner, Bob Boorstein, and George Stephanopoulos focused on health care and were allied with labor unions (who supported medical reform and opposed NAFTA). In contrast, Secretary of Treasury Bentsen, U.S. Trade Representative Kantor, and Presidential Counselor Gergen pushed for full-scale presidential lobbying for NAFTA. By late summer 1993, President Clinton sided with those calling for whole-hearted support of NAFTA.[35]

While the White House originally intended for the side agreements to quiet most opponents of NAFTA, the debate over ratification caused another round of constructive compromise. Again, the administration used the tactic of drafting legislation aimed at calming specific fears. Unlike the side agreements, these were unilateral efforts covering topics such as financing NAFTA, border clean-up, and worker assistance. For instance, a plan for retraining laid-off workers and a detailed border clean-up plan were highlighted in the last month before NAFTA came for a vote.[36] The White House also coordinated a push from pro-NAFTA groups such as businesses organized under the USA*NAFTA umbrella and the Hispanic American community, to counterbalance anti-NAFTA activity on Capitol Hill. This process of compromise extended to making deals with specific representatives addressing specific problems. For instance, the administration agreed to support efforts to protect domestic textile firms, at the request of Representative Lewis Payne Jr. (D-Va.) and to consider spending money earmarked for environmental clean-up outside of the border region, as proposed by Representative Esteban Torres (D-Calif.).[37] Thus, although NAFTA was technically on a "fast track" with Congress to vote either for or against implementation, an informal process of "amending" NAFTA through complementary legislation and executive agreement developed in order to assure ratification.

Many opponents of NAFTA did not seek constructive compromise. Rather, they sought to defeat NAFTA, following the confrontation and stalemate pattern of Constellation 3, interbranch leadership. The old saying that "politics makes for strange bedfellows" was fulfilled in the anti-NAFTA coalition: Jesse Jackson, Jerry Brown, Ralph Nader, and AFL-CIO leader Lane Kirkland joined with Ross Perot and Pat Buchanan to voice their opposition to the treaty. This group, therefore, included both conservatives and liberals, establishment political figures and political renegades. Economic nationalism (protection of U.S. jobs and the U.S. economy), environmental safety, and democracy were invoked as reasons to oppose NAFTA. The battle lines were drawn for a showdown in the House of Representatives linked to a drive to capture the hearts and minds of the American public.

Both sides of the NAFTA fight sought to influence public opinion as leverage to swing congressional votes. The White House used the prestige of expert opinion, such as Nobel-winning economists, as well as additional legislation, to convince people that NAFTA was in the best interest of the United States. Opponents—primarily the blue-green combination of labor, environmentalists, and consumer advocates—countered with traditional lobbying tactics (spearheaded by labor unions) and grassroots mobilization. The pitched battle caused both sides to exaggerate. Economists generally agreed that NAFTA would have little impact on the U.S. economy (aside from a long-term benefit); the size of the U.S. economy (relative to Mexico), the low percentage of U.S. trade flows accounted for by trade with Mexico, and Mexico's already open market access to the United States meant that NAFTA would—at best or at worst—have only a modest effect.[38] At the time, though, the threat of economic disaster and the promise of economic miracles were attributed to NAFTA.

Anti-NAFTA forces appeared to be poised for victory. Even though NAFTA enjoyed high-ranking, bipartisan support, key figures were allied with opponents. For instance, two of the top three Democratic leaders in the House (Majority Leader Gephardt (D-Mo.) and Majority Whip Bonior (D-Mich.), openly opposed implementation of NAFTA. This left the pro-NAFTA faction without strong leadership in the House. The relatively large number of House freshmen (100 to 63 of whom were Democrats) also favored the anti-NAFTA coalition. These newcomers were relatively beholden to labor, which contributed significantly through its political action committees (PACs) to their victories (averaging 44 percent of the total value of contributions).[39] Coupled with the ambitious legislative agenda of the president (which would require help from Democratic representatives opposed to NAFTA), it seemed that confrontation and stalemate would dominate the policy-making process and win the day.

On the other side, as the day of the vote drew closer, the White House marshaled its forces. It called upon the influential business lobby to make the pro-NAFTA case on Capitol Hill, while simultaneously addressing, via public forums, ads, and addresses, the benefits of the treaty. This combined with the above-mentioned efforts at legislative compromise. The White House also began to emphasize the more traditional "foreign policy" component of NAFTA, hoping to regain control over the debate. For example, Secretary of State Warren Christopher met personally with fifty-seven congressional representatives and made four speeches in favor of NAFTA. He stressed the importance of NAFTA for U.S. foreign policy. Other voices joined in on the effort to highlight the political and national security basis of the treaty. Defeat, they prophesied, would wreak political and economic chaos on America's southern border. Attempts were made to shift the context of the debate from its contentious, intermestic economic focus to a less threatening, more international perspective.[40] President Clinton himself stated that NAFTA was "essential to (U.S.) leadership in this hemisphere, in the world."[41] All the living former U.S. presidents endorsed the treaty.

The final push for the treaty also included some "log-rolling." For example, Representative Martin Meehan (D-Mass.) received a commitment from Vice President Gore to attend a fund raiser in his district just prior to the NAFTA vote. In another case, Representative Clay Shaw (R-Fl.) agreed to vote in favor of NAFTA after the Clinton administration persuaded the Mexican government to extradite a man.[42] These last-minute efforts contributed to the eventual victory for pro-NAFTA forces.

The implementation of NAFTA narrowly passed the House of Representatives (234 to 200), on November 17, 1993. Conventional partisan lines broke down in the final tally: more Republicans supported the bill favored by the Democratic president (75 percent of total Republicans in the House) than Democratic representatives (40 percent of the total Democrats in the House). Both opponents and supporters had made alliances with nongovernmental organizations and interest groups and used public opinion to gain adherents to their cause. Both sides overstated the benefits or flaws of the treaty in their quest to control the policy-making process. The battle over ratification involved both constructive compromise and confrontation. The Clinton administration, certain members of Congress, and some interest groups were willing to craft legislation that broadened support for NAFTA. Others, such as certain public interest groups, the AFL-CIO, and members of Congress worked hard to prevent NAFTA's passage. The ratification process clearly modeled interbranch leadership.

*Post-NAFTA Regional Free Trade Expansion*
With the implementation of NAFTA, new plans were envisioned that would spread free trade even further throughout the Western Hemisphere. A December 1994 meeting in Miami of all the leaders of the Western Hemisphere (save Cuba)—termed the Summit of the Americas—marked the next phase in the unfolding of post–cold war U.S. economic policy. In the heady days of December 1994, during the Summit of the Americas, NAFTA appeared to be the initial step toward a hemispheric free trade zone. Pledges were made to expand economic cooperation and create a Free Trade Area of the Americas (FTAA); a timetable was established to move the hemisphere forward. The first expansion of NAFTA was also announced; Chile was selected as the first new, non–North American member of NAFTA. Even before NAFTA went into effect, it was presented as the mechanism for greater economic development in the Americas. The day after NAFTA was approved by Congress, President Clinton pledged to "reach out to the other market-oriented democracies to ask them to join in this great American pact."[43]

The White House initially took the lead as high-ranking officials from the three NAFTA nations met together and with Chilean officials to outline the accession process. The Office of the USTR again led the U.S. effort to enlarge NAFTA; the consultations and pretreaty negotiations occurred entirely within the executive branch, with little congressional or interest group input.[44] Yet this expansion of NAFTA became the victim of external circumstances. Mexico was beset by economic and political crises. In January 1994 a rebellion broke out in the Mexican state of Chiapas. Then, in March 1994, the leading Mexican presidential candidate was assassinated. The end of 1994 was marked by a massive devaluation of the Mexican peso. These crises in Mexico raised doubts in the United States about the wisdom of NAFTA. In 1995, a bill was introduced in the House (H.R. 2651, the "NAFTA Accountability Act") that called for an assessment of the agreement, its potential renegotiation, and provisos for the withdrawal of the U.S. from NAFTA if certain conditions were not met. The bill had 110 cosponsors.[45] Thus, rather than a move forward toward an ever expanding free trade area, there was a growing chorus to withdraw from the existing agreement.

Public attention focused primarily on the economic relationship between Mexico and the United States. Little was heard about the Chilean accession. A review of the National Newspaper Index reveals a total of only twenty-two articles about Chile and NAFTA. No nightly newscasts devoted time to a story on the accession.[46] As criticism of NAFTA grew, accession for Chile lost momentum.

In part, there was a deliberate retreat on the part of the White House, as well as those favoring NAFTA expansion in the legislative branch.[47] The fight over NAFTA implementation taught a number of valuable lessons to those advocating NAFTA expansion in 1995 and 1996. Three were particularly important: (1) silence (in terms of media coverage) was golden; (2) lower prominence was preferable; and (3) emphasis on the international elements, minimizing the intermestic impact, made the expansion more palatable. In addition to these lessons from the NAFTA experience, two other factors further encouraged a deliberate policy of downplaying NAFTA enlargement: the 1996 presidential campaign (no one wanted it to be an issue, except those who opposed—a minority of the presidential hopefuls), and the Mexican crisis, which called into question the legitimacy and validity of the original NAFTA promises, thus—by extension—compromising the reasoning behind NAFTA's expansion and the vision of the FTAA.

In order to avoid possible derailing of NAFTA's expansion, the Clinton administration developed a multifaceted strategy to overcome possible obstacles. In particular, the administration worked strenuously to prevent a shift to the confrontation/stalemate version of Constellation 3, interbranch leadership. The first move was the selection of Chile: a nation far away from the United States (less immigration threat), with a smaller economy (less competition). Overall, in comparison to Mexico, Chile was less "threatening" to domestic interests. In addition, Chile's economic record supported its selection as one of the "Four Amigos." As U.S. Secretary of Commerce Ron Brown noted, Chile had "moved further along with economic reform, with an open economy, than other countries in the region."[48]

Yet in the months after the selection of Chile, little official attention was paid to NAFTA expansion. There was an official "quiet." From January 1995 to May 1995, Canada, Chile, Mexico, and the United States had several informal, technical-level meetings. Beginning in June 1995, formal rounds began. The first meeting included the trade ministers from each of the countries, who established the calendar of negotiations, which lasted until December 1995.[49] These negotiations, though, did not generate much attention.

What little was said about Chile tended to reemphasize the symmetrical, non-zero sum benefits of expansion, as well as its more international components. For example, in a statement before the Subcommittees on the Western Hemisphere and on International Economic Policy and Trade of the House International Relations Committee (October 25, 1995), the Clinton administration's first assistant secretary for inter-American affairs, Alexander F. Watson, focused on the benefits accruing to the United States from expansion. He stated bluntly that "[t]he U.S. has far more to gain than to lose from a mutual opening of markets in the hemisphere."[50] In addition, Assistant Secretary Watson signaled an international challenge that must be met by U.S. support for NAFTA expansion: "Remember, too, that we are not the only actors in the drama. In addition to the momentum of sub-regional integration, Latin America is forming links outside the hemisphere, with the Asia-Pacific Economic Cooperation—APEC—and with the EU. . . . *Without U.S. leadership in structuring a liberalization process, the balance of interest and commitment in Latin America may well start to shift away from us*" (emphasis added).[51] The latter part of the statement clearly raised traditional international concerns; as such, it tried to place the debate over NAFTA expansion into a more international rather than intermestic context, invoking an up-dated version of the Monroe Doctrine.

But the strategy adopted—the lack of public attention and the international emphasis—did not translate into greater control over the accession process. The failure of the fast-track bill doomed Chilean accession. In essence, the "silent treatment" strategy resulted in paralysis and, ultimately, abandonment of Chilean accession prior to the 1996 presidential election. Thus, while it appeared to adhere to Constellation 1 (the executive branch has continued informal talks on Chilean accession),[52] in reality NAFTA expansion encountered confrontation and stalemate. The White House could not move forward without congressional acquiescence to fast-track authority, and Chile would not enter into formal accession talks without such negotiating authority.[53]

Senator Gramm (R-Tex.) introduced bills into the 103d and 104th Congresses providing fast-track authority. This was countered by a resolution presented by Representative Kaptur, which limited fast-track negotiating authority for NAFTA expansion solely to talks with the European Union and the creation of a Trans-Atlantic Free Trade Agreement (H. Res. 547).[54] A provision of the NAFTA Accountability Act noted above prohibited the renewal of fast-track authority for NAFTA expansion unless the conditions of the bill were met. These official challenges by opponents of NAFTA were coupled with congressional confrontation by accession supporters. The House Ways and Means Committee approved a limited fast-track authority in September 1995 that excluded provisions granting the president the power to negotiate parallel accords on environmental protection and labor rights, similar to those already negotiated with Mexico and Canada under NAFTA. The Clinton administration opposed the limitation approved by the Ways and Means Committee,[55] thus, the vote against Clinton's fast-track request in October 1995 did not completely disappoint the White House. This experience suggests that the quest to promulgate foreign economic policy with a minimal number of actors is quixotic. The days of relative administration autonomy in foreign policy is over—particularly in the realm of economics.

The end of 1996 marked the renewal of plans for Chilean accession. The presidential campaigns ended. Mexico repaid its emergency loan early and in full, assuaging concerns about the viability of Mexico's economy—and, by extension, Latin American economies in general. Jeffrey Davidow, the newly appointed (August 1996) assistant secretary for inter-American affairs, stated that "Chile's entrance to NAFTA [is] again on the administration's priority list."[56] Chile also concluded an economic agreement with Canada in November 1996, viewed by many as "a stepping stone to Chile's NAFTA membership."[57]

In the fall of 1997, the Clinton administration mounted a new effort to achieve fast-track authority. In striking contrast to its earlier low-profile strategy, the new push replicated the strategies and tactics of the fight for NAFTA implementation. President Clinton gave a formal speech detailing the importance of fast-track to overall U.S. economic interests. Negotiations between the White House and the Congress attempted to find a compromise position that would not alienate either Democrats or Republicans. Outside forces joined in the fray. Business groups supportive of fast track linked together and mounted a public relations campaign with ads meant to sway voters (and Congress). Countering this were labor and environmental groups who again utilized more grassroots tactics to marshal opposition to fast-track authority. As with NAFTA, the post-NAFTA expansion had elements of constructive compromise as well as confrontation and stalemate. In the end, this effort failed as well.

## Conclusion

So, what do NAFTA and FTAA teach us about post–cold war foreign policy making, especially with regard to foreign economic issues? First, it is clear that both old and new players are central to the process. The president and White House leadership are still important. Most analysts agree that the "full court press" mounted by the Clinton administration in the last days before the implementation vote were essential for its passage.[58] For much of the negotiation process with Canada and Mexico, constellation 3—interbranch leadership with constructive compromise—accurately describes the situation. While Congress has always been a key player in foreign policy, NAFTA demonstrates that this role has been enhanced. Likewise, the traditional actors of the bureaucracy and the media were prominent. Bureaucrats wrote NAFTA and its side agreements and began to fashion the expansion process. Media coverage served as a conduit for the flow of information and leverage between different players in the policy-making process.

Proponents of NAFTA—despite their overwhelming numbers within the ranks of official Washington—lost control over the process. Indeed, it devolved to the point where passage was uncertain right until the moment of the vote. Thus, in spite of relatively strong and broad bipartisan support at the elite level (encompassing two administrations from different political parties as well as prominent congressional supporters from both parties), NAFTA was a near defeat. Supporters were overwhelmed as the number of participants increased, particularly as negative public attention grew. The policy-making process shifted from constructive compromise (during bargaining between Canada, Mexico, and the United States) to confrontation and near stalemate (during the election and ratification period). This stands in marked contrast with the experience over the agreement to create a free trade area with Canada, which passed without debate or controversy in the United States.

Why was passage of NAFTA so contentious? There are many possible explanations. Essentially, economic union with Canada was perceived as nonthreatening. Some may attribute this to the relative economic parity between the United States and Canada—as compared to the great disparity between the United States and Mexico. The agreement marked the first time the United States had entered into such a comprehensive accord with a developing country. The per capita GNP in both Canada and the United States at the time of NAFTA negotiations was about $20,000. In contrast, Mexico had a per capita GNP of about $2,200. This meant that there was roughly a ten-to-one difference between Mexico and its two other partners.[59] Others may argue that while many in the United States are ignorant about both Canada and Mexico, Canada is viewed much more positively than Mexico (based on similarities in language, ethnicity, racial composition, etc.). All of these may be true and may have contributed to the environment surrounding the passage of NAFTA. But part of the explanation lies in the change in the decision-making context.

The economic agreement between Canada and the United States was perceived in the United States as more international than intermestic and enjoyed low public prominence. The domestic stakes were thought to be minimal; the situation was perceived to be a noncrisis, status quo–oriented one, generally beneficial and without any losers. In contrast, perceptions of NAFTA were almost completely the opposite. The domestic stakes were thought to be high, and the prominence was also high, given that perceptions developed that viewed the agreement as *not* mutually beneficial or without any losers.

One can argue that over the course of time the passage of NAFTA shifted from constellation 3, "constructive compromise," to constellation 3, "confrontation and stalemate," as perceptions of the domestic impact increased, and fears about adverse and unequal results grew. As the intermestic character of NAFTA assumed greater importance, its prominence swelled. A review of articles about NAFTA between 1980 and 1993 illustrate this rising attention paid to the treaty. In that thirteen year span, 932 articles were written about NAFTA. Of those, 630 (roughly 68 percent were written after October 7, 1992, when the draft of NAFTA was initialed in front of Presidents Bush and Salinas and Prime Minister Mulroney.[60] A review of television news coverage is even more telling. There were no TV news stories about NAFTA prior to 1992. In 1992, there were three stories; this blossomed into eighty-four stories on the nightly news in 1993. Likewise, there were no TV news specials dedicated to NAFTA prior to 1993. In 1993, though, there were nine special reports.[61] This clearly demonstrates the "spiking" interest about NAFTA that concentrated around the time of passage. Media coverage both reflected and added to public interest in NAFTA: it got media attention because of public concerns, yet at the same time, high media prominence fueled public fears. The number of actors involved in the passage increased dramatically; at the same time—and related to this growing number of participants—certainty about passage decreased.

NAFTA also demonstrated that relatively new actors were emerging in the foreign economic policy-making arena. And, established—albeit previously marginal—participants gained importance. A type of democratization of the foreign policy process occurred. Nongovernmental organizations and interest groups were particularly vital in shaping NAFTA policy. The Sierra Club, the National Wildlife Federation, the Natural Resources Defense Council, and the Environmental Defense Fund all participated in the policy-making process. They were joined by consumer advocate groups, the AFL-CIO, and other grassroots organizations who had rarely (except for labor unions) been part of the foreign economic policy-making matrix in Washington, D.C. Business interest groups, normally circumspect in their public bargaining on Capitol Hill, mounted a national media campaign under the auspices of USA*NAFTA. Another relatively new element in the policy process was the introduction of foreign lobbying: Mexico especially transformed its typical pattern of behavior (focusing on the White House) into a new interaction with Congress and the media. Clearly, Mexicans were aware that the White House no longer governed NAFTA decision making.

A strategic ploy by interest groups and nongovernmental organizations was to engage public opinion in order to influence congressional votes. Thus, public opinion assumed a larger than normal role in policy making. Both proponents and opponents struggled to win the battle over public opinion. The rhetoric escalated: the public received "an entirely unrealistic view of the role of trade, . . . either a solution for every problem or a cause of every problem, when in fact it [wasn't] either."[62]

NAFTA revealed a change in the alliances that operate in the policy-making constellation. Rival alliances with governmental and nongovernmental actors abounded. Republican and Democratic free-traders within both the executive and legislative branch partnered against Republican and Democratic supporters of "fair trade." Bipartisanship existed on both sides of the issue. Labor, previously an active supporter of expanded trade, shifted positions. Environmental groups, usually focused on domestic issues and associated with "liberal causes" joined forces with conservatives such as Pat Buchanan—linked solely by their opposition to the treaty.

Another key feature of the NAFTA policy-making process was the heated tone of the debate. Most agree that the depth of feelings surrounding NAFTA concerned not the substance of the treaty but rather what the treaty stood for. According to one article, "[the] actual terms of the agreement have little to do with the emotional arguments over the trade accord's effect."[63] Some have likened it to the "free silver" debates of the 1890s, when the issue of the gold or silver standard for currency became the symbolic issue in the struggle between agricultural and industrial forces. Likewise, there are those who assert that NAFTA and international trade has become the symbolic center of gravity in the fight between those who are hurt by the emerging postindustrial, transnational economic environment and those who benefit from the new economic context. After the end of the cold war, the U.S. position in the world, including its economic role, became subject to debate. Growing economic competition from allies such as Japan and Germany, coupled with corporate down-sizing and the disappearance of high-wage manufacturing jobs created a group hostile to continued wide-open trade that seemed more "unfair" than "free." To counter this perception, President Clinton and others argued that the solution to these economic woes lay with more open trade, symbolized by NAFTA. In a speech to rally support for the treaty, he linked NAFTA to the cold war, stating that the agreement was an opportunity to "consolidate the victory of democracy and opportunity and freedom."[64] One might expect that free trade will continue to be a highly contentious arena, taking on symbolic importance regardless of the intrinsic weight of the specific agreement under consideration.

The North Atlantic Free Trade Agreement and its aftermath suggest that foreign economic policy making will be characterized by uncertainty and inconsistency. White House leadership does not appear to be a likely structure for decision making. Whatever its flaws, this array does provide for a high degree of coordination and certainty—for those negotiating with the United States. The experience of NAFTA suggests that policy making in the realm of foreign economic policy will most probably alternate between constructive compromise and confrontation/stalemate. While this process might be the most inclusive and might best mirror the divided opinion over continuing traditional free trade policies, it also poses problems for the future. Nations are unlikely to devote time and energy negotiating a treaty that will be unmade or remade in latter stages. Thus, it may be difficult to get other countries to engage in economic diplomacy with the United States.

Furthermore, the scope and pace of negotiations are likely to follow the electoral calendar. Given the contentious nature of trade, mainstream candidates (as opposed to third-party ones) will want to avoid the topic. The alliances generated defy tradition: Democrats might find themselves drawing on support from Republican constituencies and vice versa. Neither party can comfortably support or oppose trade agreements without alienating some part of their original core. Given the frequency of elections, this bodes ill for attempts to develop long-term trade policy.

Powerful forces are allied both for and against trade agreements.

NAFTA and FTAA demonstrate that both sides can influence the policy-making process. While "free trade" won NAFTA implementation, expansion of NAFTA into FTAA was stymied, despite White House goals. Clearly, consensus no longer exists over U.S. trade policy. Elements long simmering have come to a boil after the end of the cold war. And the experience of NAFTA and FTAA auger interbranch leadership—sometimes cooperative, sometimes confrontational—for the policy-making process in this arena. The number of voices involved in policy making will increase; the resulting cacophony will generate both uncertainty and inconsistency. The NAFTA debate was the opening movement of this new foreign policy-making symphony, not the finale.

## Notes

1  For an elaboration of this perspective, see William Appleman Williams, *The Tragedy of American Diplomacy,* 2d ed. (New York: Dell, 1972).

2  These findings are from John E. Rielly, "America's State of Mind," *Foreign Policy,* 66 (Spring 1987): 39–56, John E. Rielly, "Public Opinion: The Pulse of the '90s," *Foreign Policy* 82 (Spring 1991): 79–96, and John E. Rielly, "The Public Mood at Mid-Decade," *Foreign Policy* 98 (Spring 1995): 76–94.

3  "Economic Diplomacy: Key to Domestic Prosperity," *U.S. Department of State Dispatch* 4, no. 24 (June 14, 1993): 434.

4  See Herbert E. Meyer, "Why a North American Common Market Won't Work—Yet," *Fortune,* September 10, 1979, pp. 118–124.

5  George Grayson, *The North American Free Trade Agreement* (New York: University Press of America, 1995), p. 51.

6  Grayson, *NAFTA,* p. 58.

7  Grayson, *NAFTA,* p. 55.

8  See, for instance, Paul Krugman, "The Uncomfortable Truth about NAFTA: It's Foreign Policy, Stupid," *Foreign Affairs,* 72, no. 5 (November 1993): 13–19.

9  Grayson, *NAFTA,* p. 74.

10  Grayson, *NAFTA,* pp. 89–90.

11  Quoted in "North American Free Trade Agreement Debate: Where Domestic and Foreign Policy Meet," *Foreign Policy Bulletin* (November/December 1992): 28.

12  Grayson, *NAFTA,* p. 82.

13  "Summary: Free Trade Agreement Negotiations and Related Developments, October 11–November 1," *SourceMex—Economic News and Analysis on Mexico,* November 6, 1991.

14  "North American Free Trade Agreement (NAFTA): Summary of Events and Statements, February 24–28," *SourceMex—Economic News and Analysis on Mexico,* March 4, 1992.

15  Todd Eisenstadt, "Keep the 'Fast Track' Honest," *Christian Science Monitor,* August 21, 1991, p. 19.

16  "North American Free Trade Agreement (NAFTA): Summary of Developments, January 10–February 17," *SourceMex—Economic News and Analysis on Mexico,* February 19, 1992.

17  Amy Kaslow, "Bush Sees Campaign Boost from Free Trade," *Christian Science Monitor,* October 7, 1992, p. 1.

18  "Expanding Trade and Creating American Jobs," speech by presidential candidate Bill Clinton, North Carolina State University, October 4, 1992, quoted in *Foreign Policy Bulletin* (November/December 1992), p. 40.

19  John B. Judis, "The Divide," *New Republic,* October 11, 1993, p. 32.

20  "North American Free Trade Agreement (NAFTA): Summary of Developments, September 13–22," *SourceMex—Economic News and Analysis on Mexico,* September 23, 1992.

21  "Summary of Developments, September 13–22."

22  Grayson, *NAFTA,* p. 135.

23  Grayson, *NAFTA,* p. 136.

24  Quoted in Grayson, *NAFTA,* p. 134.

25  Government Accounting Office, *North American Free Trade Agreement: Structure and Status of Implementing Organizations* (Washington, D.C.: Government Printing Office, 1994).

26  *Inside U.S. Trade* (Special Report), 9 April 1993, S-6.

27  Quoted in *Inside U.S. Trade,* 28 May 1993.

28  Text of the Environmental Side Agreement appears in *NAFTA Supplemental Agreements* (Washington, D.C.: Government Printing Office, 1993).

29  See Government Accounting Office, *North American Free Trade Agreement.*

30  "U.S., Canada and Mexico Agree on Single Text for NAFTA Side Accords but Disagree on Trilateral Commissions," *SourceMex—Economic News and Analysis on Mexico,* May 26, 1993.

31  Government Accounting Office, *North American Free Trade Agreement.*

32  Government Accounting Office, *North American Free Trade Agreement.*

33  Grayson, *NAFTA,* p. 148.

34  Grayson, *NAFTA,* p. 147.

35  Grayson, *NAFTA,* pp. 195–201.

36  "Clinton Turns Up Volume on NAFTA Sales Pitch," *Congressional Quarterly,* October 23, 1993, pp. 2863–2864.

37  "Administration Pressed to Deal to Win NAFTA Converts," *Congressional Quarterly,* October 2, 1993, pp. 2620–2621.

38  The years since its implementation bear this prediction out. See, for instance, Paul Blustein, "In Retrospect, Both Fears and Promise of Pact Were Exaggerated," *Washington Post,* September 30, 1996, p. A1.

39  *Wall Street Journal,* October 25, 1993, p. A22, reported the Center for Responsive Politics PAC figures.

40  See, for instance, Paul Krugman, "The Uncomfortable Truth about NAFTA."

41  Quoted in *Congressional Quarterly Weekly Report,* September 18, 1993, pp. 2501–2502.

42  See Linda Feldmann, "Wheeling and Dealing Led to NAFTA Victory," *Christian*

*Science Monitor*, November 19, 1993, p. 2, for information on these "deals" and others.

43  Quoted in Amy Kaslow, "NAFTA's Sequel: Moving Free Trade Farther South," *Christian Science Monitor*, November 29, 1993, p. 1.

44  See Renee G. Scherlen, "Chilean Accession: The First Step from NAFTA to FTAA?" in David Davila Villers, ed., *The First Year of NAFTA: The View from Mexico* (New York: University Press of America, 1996), pp. 24–33.

45  "Bill Summary and Status for the 104th Congress," http://thomas.loc.gov.

46  This data is the result of a search of the Vanderbilt Television News Archive, which records the nightly news of the three major networks (NBC, ABC, CBS) as well as news specials presented by the major networks and CNN. The archive can be accessed at http://tvnews.vanderbilt.edu.

47  Howard La Franchi, "NAFTA Buffeted by US Politics," *Christian Science Monitor*, January 19, 1996, p. 6.

48  Quoted in "Nothing from NAFTA, Chilean Critics Say," by Christina Nifong, *Christian Science Monitor*, December 15, 1994, p. 7.

49  "NAFTA Members Open Negotiations to Admit Chile into Free Trade Accord," *Chronicle of Latin American Economic Affairs*, June 15, 1995, n. pag., online, Latin American Database.

50  Alexander F. Watson, "Statement before the Subcommittees on the Western Hemisphere and on International Economic Policy and Trade, U.S. House International Relations Committee," *U.S. Department of State Dispatch*, November 1995, p. 803.

51  Watson, "Statement before the Subcommittees," p. 803.

52  Clay Chandler, "U.S. Vows to Continue Trade Talks with Chile: NAFTA Inclusion Sought despite Opposition," *Washington Post*, March 18, 1995, p. C2, and "Chile Meets with NAFTA Negotiators," *Los Angeles Times*, April 20, 1995, p. D4.

53  "NAFTA Members Open Negotiations to Admit Chile into Free Trade Accord," *Chronicle of Latin American Economic Affairs*, June 15, 1995, n. pag., online, Latin American Database.

54  "Bill Summary and Status for the 104th Congress," http://thomas.loc.gov.

55  "U.S. Congressional Opposition to Fast-Track Authority Reduces Chances for Chile to Conclude NAFTA Accord in 1996," *Chronicle of Latin American Economic Affairs*, November 9, 1995, n. pag., online, Latin American Database.

56  Quoted in Howard LaFranchi, "NAFTA Membership for Chile May Be Back in the Offing after U.S. Election-Season Hiatus," *Christian Science Monitor*, November 20, 1996, p. 6.

57  LaFranchi, "NAFTA Membership for Chile."

58  See, for example, Grayson, *NAFTA*.

59  Sidney Weintraub, "NAFTA and European Situation Compared," *International Migration Review* 26, no. 2 (Summer 1992), pp. 507–508.

60  This data is the result of a search of InfoTrac Expanded Academic database. The database contains citations for newspaper, periodical, and journal stories from 1980 to the present.

61  This data is the result of a search of the Vanderbilt Television News Archive.

62 Quoted in Paul Blustein, "In Retrospect."

63 "Sound and Fury over NAFTA Overshadows the Debate," *Congressional Quarterly Weekly Report*, October 16, 1993, pp. 2791–2796.

64 Quoted in *Congressional Quarterly Weekly Report*, September 18, 1993, pp. 2501–2502.

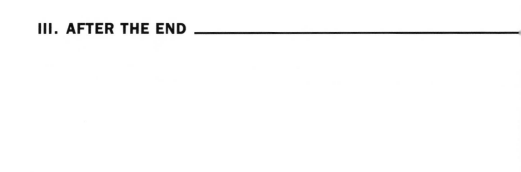

## III. AFTER THE END

# 15.

## Interbranch Policy Making after the End

*James M. Scott*

Not long ago, an observer of U.S. foreign policy predicted that, in the post–cold war era, "most foreign policy issues will confront a more divided, highly decentralized, and more partisan policy process, which can produce policies with multiple and conflicting objectives."[1] In the main, this volume supports and substantiates that speculation. In fact, the overall thrust of the preceding pages indicates that a "constellation shift" has occurred in the manner in which the foreign policy of the United States is formulated and implemented. Policy seems to emerge from a more decentralized foreign policy arena in which no single element of the shifting constellations image depicted in figure 1.2 dominates or even leads. If foreign policy is "adaptive behavior," this shift may be the most important adaptation to the post–cold war world: in a sense, it constitutes a shift from the cold war consensus to what might be best understood as the post–cold war dissensus. This concluding chapter considers the constellation shift and offers some observations on the post–cold war adaptations (and failures to adapt) in both the policy and process arenas. As it does so, it suggests that changes in the process arena have stalled the creation of a new policy paradigm to deal with the post–cold war world.

### Foreign Policy in the Post–Cold War World

This volume indicates that U.S. foreign policy makers are struggling to deal with two post–cold war developments. There are, first, *competing trends:* a "contest between forces of integration and fragmentation."[2] Of the various features discussed in chapter 1 and throughout, globalization and interdependence, ideological harmony, the growing security community, the processes of democratization and liberalization in many areas, and the formation of free trade areas clearly fall into the category of integrative forces. Conversely, the power diffusion associated with multipolarity, heightened economic (and potentially politi-cal) competition between the United States, its former partners, and others, increasing neonationalism and ethnic conflict, and reactions against the dominance of the United States and the West by members of the developing world constitute some of the forces of fragmentation. As important, however, there are *divergent worlds:* a "first tier" com-posed of the twenty-five to thirty liberal democracies of the world, who are generally wealthy, stable, and at peace with one another, and a "sec-ond tier" composed of all the rest, a diverse group that includes newly industrializing, transitional, developing, and very poor countries who are in the midst of a variety of developmental and identity problems.[3] These distinctions help to highlight the nature of the issue arena for U.S. foreign policy and constitute the nature of the post–cold war world to which U.S. foreign policy must try to adapt.

In this milieu, the contents of this volume indicate that U.S. foreign policy makers are adapting to the post–cold war world by wrestling with three broad policy concerns. First, U.S. foreign policy with the other members of the first tier seems to take the form of *the politics of peace and prosperity.* The level of threat among these powers has diminished significantly even while the international setting that shapes their com-petition has grown more complicated. American alliances with powers in the first tier, combined with the cultural and institutional linkages that the United States has developed with these nations, virtually en-sure that in this most critical dimension, post–cold war U.S. foreign policy will be fundamentally concerned with managing economic con-flict, sustaining economic cooperation, and maintaining the political and security community, as well as strengthening the rules, procedures, and institutions of the liberal democratic order. Because this tier is so deeply affected by interdependence, managing the intricate relationship is critical, and multilateralism of varying kinds is required. Thus the fundamental question facing U.S. foreign policy toward other members of the first tier is whether the "zone of peace" can be maintained in the face of the growing pressure generated by multipolarity and heightened economic competition.

Second, relations between the United States and nations in the sec-ond tier concern *the politics of dependency and transition.* In relations with members of the second tier, the U.S. faces significant security issues (e.g., terrorism, weapons proliferation), but few, if any, large-scale, centrally directed security threats.[4] Key to this dimension are the tasks of addressing the attempts of "transitional" countries (e.g., Russia and the former Soviet bloc) to join the ranks of the first tier, addressing rising powers such as China, isolating and containing/countering the "weapons states" or "rogue states" of the second tier, gaining and maintaining access to markets and resources, and dealing with the gap between rich and poor states. Hence, moderation, liberalization, and democratization are key interests, and equitable and sustainable development are important issues. However, U.S. foreign policy makers have a "hard sell" in advancing policies toward nations in the second tier: no institutional player in U.S. foreign policy making has any compelling interest in working with such nations, and the broader U.S. society has few reasons to want to invest U.S. resources and efforts in those countries.

The third dimension of U.S. foreign policy making "after the end" involves the U.S. role in influencing the relations among the members of the second tier, or *the politics of turmoil and development*. In large measure, what goes on in the second tier is less important to the United States. None of the international, cultural, or institutional influences on U.S. foreign policy making encourages the United States to participate in such relations to any great degree. Yet, as the forces of fragmentation—and even a "coming anarchy"[5]—play themselves out within and among second-tier states, the United States may be forced to respond, often through multilateral efforts and institutions. Coping with and containing these forces by promoting stability and order, advancing and supporting the forces of integration, and building and sustaining institutions are among the key issues for U.S. foreign policy in this dimension. Moreover, the United States will continue to have economic interests, perhaps even growing concerns in certain parts of the second tier, given the intensified economic competition of the post–cold war. Hence, the United States will likely devote considerable attention in the sphere of foreign economic policy in this dimension.

The essays in this volume indicates that the United States has, in some ways, already adapted to the post–cold war policy arena: policy makers are already contending with the host of new issues and challenges discussed in the first chapter. Consider the sample of policies discussed in this volume: dealing with changing states (Russia), rising powers (China), economic issues (NAFTA and China), new "grand strategies" and policy instruments (democracy promotion, "assertive multilateralism," sustainable development), and concerns with fragmentation and development in the developing world, or second tier (Somalia, NAFTA, China). American policy makers are clearly grappling with new problems; on the surface then, adjustment has occurred.

At another level, however, it is less clear that the U.S. response to a changing slate of issues and dynamics yet constitutes a fundamental policy adaptation to the changing world arena. In spite of the fact that U.S. policy makers are now contending with post–cold war problems, their efforts are, as yet, incomplete. For example, this volume suggests that attempts to refocus U.S. foreign policy (e.g., to promote democracy and pursue assertive multilateralism) have largely failed; even as policy makers took up these efforts, their attempts to forge a strategy to face the post–cold war world fell short. Additionally, attempts to reorient budgetary priorities (as discussed in chapter 3 and elsewhere) have proceeded sluggishly, apparently less directed by planning than by politics and compromise. Furthermore, while restructuring has certainly been attempted in efforts to establish a more apt institutional framework to deal with the post–cold war world (e.g., the creation of the National Economic Council discussed in chapter 4, the organizational adjustments in the bureaucracy and the White House discussed in chapters 2–3, and the struggle over the restructuring of the foreign affairs agencies discussed in chapter 12), these efforts have been ambiguous, incomplete, imperfect, and unsuccessful. Apparently, there has been as much effort to pour new wine into old bottles as to create new bottles. Overall, the authors suggest that there has been a shift away from the cold war and post-Vietnam era paradigms, but an as-yet-incomplete shift to a post–cold war paradigm.

The contributors to this volume describe an inability (thus far) to successfully adapt U.S. foreign policies and institutions to changing international features. The struggles to reorient U.S. foreign policy to better address the international politics of peace and prosperity, dependency and transition, and turmoil and development can, perhaps, be understood as a consequence of other "adaptations" in the foreign policy-making arena that have been triggered in the wake of the cold war.

### Foreign Policy Making in the Post–Cold War World

If it were possible for the current occupant of the White House to design and implement radical policy and organizational changes to meet the challenges of the post–cold war world, surely such changes would have occurred. Even the limited sample of policy cases contained in this volume indicates that some efforts at such reorientation have occurred in the Clinton White House. However, in addition to introducing new problems with which to contend, the end of the cold war also helped to complete a shift toward a more "democratized"[6] and decentralized policy-making arena. This "adaptation" is, thus far, probably the most significant of the changes associated with transition from cold war to post–cold war worlds. At the societal and institutional levels, the threat ambiguity, increasing ideological harmony among key powers, increasing importance for interdependence, globalization, and others post–cold war features previously discussed have spurred greater ambivalence in the public toward international leadership and foreign policy behavior, more fragmentation in interests and objectives, and more activity and involvement by a wider circle of voices. These factors have served to mitigate the ability of U.S. foreign policy makers (from any quarter) to shift policy to meet their understanding of post–cold war exigencies.

### Foreign Policy Democratization

The authors represented in both major sections of this volume argue that more voices (with more varied interests and preferences) are engaged in the making of foreign policy than during the cold war. This "democratization" can be considered along the lines of the elements of the shifting constellations image that has guided this entire inquiry.

*The White House.* In the post–cold war world, the president is central to U.S. foreign policy, but the White House is not always the center of policy making. By virtue of the executive power, the president fulfills a series of "chief" roles in the foreign policy-making arena that make the White House central. These include constitutional roles as chief executive, commander in chief, and chief diplomat, and the less formal, but still vital roles of chief communicator, chief legislator, and, perhaps, chief lobbyist. Together these place the president in a position to initiate and/or shape efforts to forge foreign policy. However, as Rosati and Twing explain, while the president has numerous opportunities and advantages in the foreign policy-making arena, there are also important constraints, most of which have grown since the end of the cold war.

A cluster of roles for the White House continue to place the president in a key position. First, the White House plays a vital role in foreign policy agenda-setting—the process of identifying problems, setting priorities, and so on. Ordering policy reviews, requiring the development of options on one issue and not another, and assigning responsibilities to certain executive branch structures and agencies rather than others, among other abilities, give the president the capability to influence heavily the "list of subjects or problems to which government officials, and people outside of government closely associated with those officials, are paying some serious attention at any given time."[7] Obviously this does not ensure the ability of the White House to enact its preferred option. Examples include:

- the White House decision to make aid to Russia a central issue of its 1993 foreign policy efforts, its establishment of a special planning group, and the presentation of that plan to Congress;
- the White House decision to concentrate on U.S.-China relations, the assignment of that responsibility first to a group led by the State Department, and then to the National Economic Council, and the emphasis on the economic and strategic elements of the relationship;
- the White House efforts to conduct a "Kennan sweepstakes" to elevate democracy promotion to the level of grand strategy;
- the White House–led efforts to develop a strategy of "assertive multilateralism" to deal with second-tier fragmentation;
- the White House–led focus on "sustainable development" and the retooling of parts of the foreign policy bureaucracy through budgetary and reorganization proposals;
- the White House decision to place the Somalia issue on the back burner for the first half of 1993; and
- the White House emphasis on NAFTA as a key element of its foreign economic strategy.

Obviously, in these and other examples, a key aspect of White House influence concerns its ability to structure initial efforts to formulate an option or options (also, obviously, influenced by those elements of the bureaucracy assigned the options development task). This is, perhaps, the limited meaning of "presidential preeminence" in the post–cold war world.

Second, a principal element of presidential influence in the post–cold war world, as well as in other periods, stems from the ability to initiate action, a function of the chief executive, chief diplomat, and commander in chief hats worn by the president. Although it is closely related to the agenda-setting power possessed by the White House, this capability to take action gives the White House the ability to force other elements of the shifting constellations to respond. However, policy instruments matter in this area: some are more obviously executive-dominated (allowing for White House initiation of action), such as diplomacy, executive agreements, some aspects of military action, etc.), while some are clearly more susceptible to influence by Congress (trade agreements, foreign aid requests, and perhaps the war power as well).[8]

The White House has "negative" power—the power to say no. While this does not mean the president can determine foreign policy, it may mean that the president has the ability to determine what will *not* be foreign policy. In this sense, the other elements in the foreign policy arena have a difficult, if not impossible, time making foreign policy without the White House. Perhaps the best of many illustrations in this volume is the ability of the White House to defy the 1995–96 attempt by Senator Helms and others to reorganize and reorient the foreign policy bureaucracy (chapter 12).

Nevertheless, the president does not make foreign policy alone. Other elements in the arena also have "negative" powers that enable them to obstruct or block presidential preferences. Moreover, presidential actions are clearly shaped and constrained by the preferences and actions of these other elements. Hence, the White House must persuade, bargain, compromise, and even accede to the preferences of other players. Furthermore, the actions or preferences of other elements of the foreign policy arena may be instrumental in White House choices regarding the agenda, and they may also structure initial formulation and actions. Such a situation is one of "anticipated reactions," through which the public, interest groups, members of Congress, and officials of the bureaucracy may exercise (enormous) influence. Hence, while the president is surely one force, perhaps even the most significant one, the foreign policy stage is shared with other actors.

*Nongovernmental Actors.* Together, the constraints and pressures provided by the public and by interest groups and the media in the post–cold war world create cross-pressures, higher political stakes, and expanded scrutiny from members of Congress, which reduce the leadership abilities of the White House and contribute to the diffusion and fragmentation of policy-making responsibilities and influence. Additionally, interest groups also provide allies for officials from the bureaucracy and Congress to join with to shape policy.

In the broad societal context of the American public, the post–cold war world helps to create a problematic setting. On the one hand, the absence of serious strategic threat reinforces an ambivalence and a lack of consensus in the American public. This ambivalence, which rests in part on the fundamental split between internationalist and isolationist impulses, manifests itself in several areas that complicate U.S. foreign policy making. First, as McCormick argued, the issues that present themselves in the post–cold war world tend to divide rather than unify. The result is a more fragmented environment of conflicting principles, beliefs, goals, and so on. Also, the American public (along with elites in and out of government) is dramatically less certain of the proper role for the United States to play in the post–cold war world, being particularly concerned with domestic issues and especially suspicious of new grand strategic visions. In addition, while generally supportive of U.S. leadership in world affairs (as indicated by Holsti's analysis), the U.S. public seems, at the same time, to be less concerned with foreign policy issues in general, significantly less willing to pay the costs of leadership in specific situations (where that cost might be time, treasure, and/or lives), and essentially less supportive of leadership ventures, where policy makers undertake actions to promote U.S. leadership in the post–cold war world. On this last point, public hesitance is especially acute on issues of involvement in the second tier. Clear examples of this were provided by the case studies on assertive multilateralism, Somalia, and democracy promotion.

Overall, these factors translate into a more difficult policy-making environment, and reduced opportunity to undertake and sustain policies. In sum, the public in the post–cold war world establishes a series of constraints that work against active, sustained, and coherent foreign policy. Such constraints were apparent in the policy cases examined in this volume, and include public uncertainty over, ambivalence toward, and opposition to the promotion of democracy, the attempt at assertive multilateralism, the U.S. involvement in Somalia, and the conclusion and extension of the North American Free Trade Agreement, among others. In each of these cases, public opinion seemed to play a dual role: constraining White House efforts, and encouraging other actors, especially members of Congress, to try to shape policy. Specifically on this last point, the cases in this volume suggest that the less popular a presidential policy becomes with the American public, the more assertive members of Congress become in their efforts to influence the policy.

At the same time, the post–cold war environment, which seems to support the public's inclination to reduce commitments and activity in the world arena and focus attention on "domestic" problems, also opens the foreign policy–making arena to interest group activity. As McCormick notes, cold war dynamics tended to dampen the role of interest groups, while most of the key features of the post–cold war world tend to expand opportunities for access and activity. While the post–cold war environment is far from the "hyperpluralism" of the domestic political scene, greater pluralism does exist, clearly illustrated in the case studies of China policy and NAFTA policy in this volume. This greater activity is due in part to three basic dynamics of the post–cold war era: (1) the rise of economics in foreign affairs (including issues of globalization and interdependence); (2) the rise of intermestic issues, which create domestic stakes for foreign affairs, and; (3) the rise of transnational issues. These factors contribute to a more active and interested interest group community whose access to executive branch agencies and official and members of Congress gives them opportunities to help shape foreign policy. In at least one category of cases—trade agreements and foreign economic policy, as exemplified in the NAFTA case—Congress actually required the executive branch to include interest groups as a part of the negotiating team and in the working groups through which government and nongovernment actors formulated the policy/agreement.

*Congress.* In general, members of Congress have been less deferential to the White House in foreign policy after the cold war than during. Moreover, they have more opportunities to affect foreign policy since the end of the cold war, and they continue to have many tools with which to shape policy. Additionally, public opinion and interest group activity provide greater political incentives for congressional involvement. Furthermore, as McCormick argues, the changing nature of the world after the end of the cold war provides incentives for members to strategize as well as "micromanage" in foreign policy. These factors, and the items discussed below point to a more vigilant, engaged, and influential Congress.

These cases reveal that the overall post–cold war environment works to increase, rather than restrain, congressional involvement and influence. For example, the rise of economic and intermestic issues entails domestic winners and losers, prompting more congressional involvement. The emphasis on aid and trade also hardwires members of Congress into the policy process. Moreover, since most military issues concern second-tier fragmentation, and since the use of troops in "nonstrategic" situations does not enjoy a great deal of public support (given the lack of threat and, perhaps, interest), members of Congress have tended to be less deferential on most such issues (e.g., Somalia, Bosnia/assertive multilateralism, etc.). Furthermore, fiscal constraints mean that any foreign policy issue that involves the expenditure of funds is potentially a budgetary issue as well as a foreign policy concern, subject to congressional disposal. The message is simple: the lack of consensus makes more difficult the task of determining when, why, and how to commit U.S. resources to which foreign policy objectives, a set of concerns over which members of Congress are increasingly active.

Moreover, it is equally clear from these cases that Congress does not have to act for members to influence foreign policy. Of course, the institution may go through its formal, legislative process and produce issue-specific legislation that shapes U.S. foreign policy. Such was the case, for instance, in the Russian aid case, in which the White House presented a proposal to Congress, whose members acted on it through the institution's procedures and produced legislation providing assistance (with conditions). Such was also the case in the NAFTA debate, although "fast-track" procedures streamlined the legislative process dramatically. In addition, members relied on the oversight responsibility to gain information, make policy statements, and generate momentum for further policy actions (e.g., in the cases of Somalia, Bosnia/assertive multilateralism, democracy promotion, and the restructuring of the State Department).

However, members of Congress exerted influence in all the cases through nonlegislative or other less direct means. First, members attempted to "frame opinion" to shape the policy debate and generate pressure for or constraints on the administration. These actions, which Carter describes as "institutional dissent" and "policy advocacy," played a role in structuring policy debate, shaping the climate of executive branch policy formulation, and establishing a basis for additional, more formal, congressional policy making. *Every* case included such activity, often to great effect.

In addition, members resorted to the *threat* of legislative action as leverage to bring administration proposals or actions into line with their preferences. Such actions—which occurred through such measures as simple public or floor statements, letters to the White House, nonbinding resolutions, and even the actual introduction of legislation—often persuaded the administration to adjust a policy. These "anticipated reactions" seem to take two forms. In *congressional signaling*, members offered signals about a desired course of action through informal statements, speeches and media appearances, letters, hearings, and so on. In effect, some members warned of the possibility of further legislative action, or actually began such action by proposing legislation. In *congressional conditioning*, the backdrop of previous congressional actions and/or preferences prompted the administration to try to preempt congressional activity by incorporating some features of member preferences into policy, placing the stamp of congressional influence on the policy. Examples abound, including the Russia aid case, in which the initial administration aid proposal was written with congressional preferences in mind, and the assertive multilateralism case, in which the administration's draft policy was subjected to a series of revisions caused in part by congressional objections, resolutions, etc.

Furthermore, interested individuals from Congress can exert a powerful influence on a foreign policy even if the institution fails to act collectively. The ability of various leaders, committee and subcommittee chairs, and policy entrepreneurs to utilize their positions and powers can be extremely significant (e.g., Senator Jesse Helms in the State Department restructuring case). Such individuals can block action, hold up legislation, and, in the case of the Senate, obstruct treaties, personnel appointments, and so on. In combination with legislation, framing, and anticipated reactions, such actions by these members can force policy adjustments (i.e., accommodation by the administration), stalemate, and/or wider institutional action.

Additionally, members of Congress have more negative power than positive power, but they are hardwired into the process by which foreign policy is made. These cases indicate that members of Congress are handicapped when it comes to making foreign policy on their own. This is, in part, because of the substantial negative power of the White House, and because no matter what Congress directs, the responsibility for executing foreign policy rests in the hands of the administration. Hence, *congressional leadership* is likely to be rare for the life of a policy, even if it occurs in a particular stage or cycle of the policy process. Yet, virtually all foreign policies must come to Congress for authorizing legislation, funding, or evaluation (in the oversight process). Thus, members have opportunities, and, after the cold war, they seem also to have greater incentives.

Also, even though members attempt to frame, signal, or condition initial administration choices, the cases presented here indicate that they tend to react to executive branch initiatives, agendas, and actions rather than initiate their own foreign policies. These cases suggest that members of Congress *initially* defer to the executive branch, preferring to try to channel, push, or shape *administration* approaches at first. It would appear that greater congressional assertiveness follows administration failures to act on an issue and/or to respond to congressional signals regarding its actions on an issue, as well as new developments or "crises" that call into question the administration's approach to an issue. Moreover members generally begin their attempts to shape foreign policy through nonlegislative and/or more indirect avenues (e.g., "framing," and signaling), moving to more direct, legislative approaches only if these fail to win a response (conversely, administration accommodation seems to preclude more formal activity). Just a few of the many examples from the cases nicely illustrate these points: the preference by Congress, even with a broad consensus, that the administration take the lead on plans to aid Russia in 1993; the ratcheting-up of congressional pressure on the "assertive multilateralism" strategy (from signals to legislation); the reaction of Congress to events in Somalia, which helped to shape a major policy change.

Moreover, members also rely on their ability to form "rival alliances" with individuals from the bureaucracy, the White House, and the public to shape foreign policy and the process by which it is made. For all alliance members, such networks enhance their own avenues of influence and provide access to different instruments and avenues. For members of Congress, the gains are particularly significant. Members of these alliances gain access to executive branch information and debates and are given a voice in the internal administrative debates through their executive branch allies. These rival alliances also constitute additional channels through which members of Congress can send signals, advocate options, apply pressure, or provide support. Such access also helps members of Congress to time their actions carefully to maximize their impact, and members can shape statements, letters, and legislative proposals in light of the "inside" information they receive from advisers and bureaucrats. The combination of these effects increase the influence of members of Congress and amplify their impact on policy.

*The Foreign Policy Bureaucracy.* The bureaucracy plays a role in both executive branch formulation and implementation of foreign policy, so it always matters. This volume argues that bureaucratic influence on post–cold war foreign policy is likely to become more complex, thereby further diminishing the opportunity for White House leadership (and, perhaps, congressional oversight as well). The combination of fiscal constraints and the need to redefine agency roles and missions generates complicated pressures and heightens both the probability of bureaucratic competition and scrutiny by members of Congress. Likewise, the rise of the "economic complex" in the bureaucracy contributes to dilemmas having to do with the relative roles and influence of different agencies, the broad goals and objectives of foreign policy, and greater links to domestic, economic, and congressional interests generated by such economic and intermestic concerns.

Consequently, the foreign policy bureaucracy is likely to be less "leadable" in the post–cold war world. The competition over the fiscal pie and new post–cold war missions gives every indication of being severe. In various ways, this is seen in the Bosnia case (Defense vs. State), the post–cold war restructuring case (State, USAID, etc., and the search for new purposes), the clash between the diplomatic, security, and economic complexes on China, and other cases. Additionally, the rise of the economic complex is critically important. During the cold war, as Destler suggests, the influence of this complex was generally insulated from security issues. Now, however, the economic complex influences many more issues, bringing in new actors and interests, and substantial domestic and congressional constituencies. This, too, creates a more fragmented and less manageable foreign policy bureaucracy.

Bureaucratic agencies continue to exert great influence over policy making. As indicated by these cases, (1) control over implementation allows the shaping of policy (e.g., USAID in the democracy promotion case, DOD in the assertive multilateralism and Somalia cases); (2) reliance on bureaucratic actors for information, advice, and options-planning allows great influence over policy (e.g., the assertive multilateralism and China cases); (3) bureaucrats also make rival alliances with members of Congress and others to shape policy (e.g., DOD in the assertive multilateralism case, economic agencies in the China and NAFTA cases). All told, these factors appear to be greatest when attention by the White House and Congress is at lower levels. In such situations, policy making tends to exhibit those classic characteristics of bureaucratic politics, including incrementalism, fragmented, agency-specific efforts, and others.

*Foreign Policy Decentralization*
From this cacophony of voices, U.S. foreign policy emerges. This expanded circle of actors and the variation in their role and involvement (i.e., policy democratization) create *policy decentralization,* which is, perhaps, the most important consequence—thus far—of the post–cold war policy-making environment. In terms of the shifting constellations image, there seems to have been a macro-level constellation shift: from the cold war's dominance by the White House Leadership constellation, the post–cold war appears to have completed a shift to an Interbranch Leadership constellation as the dominant form of U.S. foreign policy making, in which a wide array of policy makers from the White House, bureaucracy, and Congress interact to make policy.

Interbranch leadership appears to be the most significant adaptation to the post–cold war world. According to the contents of this volume, the shift to interbranch leadership as the base policy-making constellation of the post–cold war world seems to rest on several related factors. A changing agenda and increasing interdependence and transnational ties make foreign policy making more like domestic policy making: subject to conflict, bargaining, and persuasion among competing groups within and outside the government. As one observer has noted, "[T]he foreign policy environment is no longer the arena of con-

tending national interests."[9] One cause of this is the increasingly important link between domestic interests and international events, which
has given rise to the expansion of intermestic issues. This growing per-
meability between foreign and domestic issues reduces the role of the
president as the preeminent foreign policy maker, triggers a greater fragmentation of responsibility and control, and increases the competition
for influence.[10] As well, the international environment also contributes
to reduced interest in world affairs on the part of most Americans (an
isolationist tendency caused, in part by the much more benign international environment); reduced consensus over American goals and interests (caused, in part, by the more complex and subtle environment of
the post–cold war world); reduced emphasis on national security, with
the corresponding reduction in the role of the national security appara-
tus of the government; a rise in the importance of economics and issues
of prosperity and economic security; and multiplying interests, voices,
and agendas (caused by the preceding factors, and the impact of globalization and interdependence). In turn, the lack of consensus over U.S.
goals and interests (which generally triggers more legislative-executive
friction), the heightened importance of economic policy (an area of
congressional strength), and the increased involvement of nongovernmental actors (who have many avenues into policy through Congress,
the most public and open of the government's institutions) contribute
to the involvement of all three governmental circles, along with the
nongovernmental actors, accelerating both democratization and decentralization of foreign policy making. This, in essence, is the basis of the
Interbranch Leadership constellation.

In the making of U.S. foreign policy, these factors mean a reduction
in the instances of presidential preeminence or White House leadership. As Ralph Carter notes in this volume, presidential preeminence
depends as much on substantive agreement on the purposes and instruments of U.S. foreign policy as it does on institutional powers and
levers of influence. Moreover, post–cold war foreign policy is likely to
be more heavily influenced by societal forces (specifically, nongovernmental actors) than has been previously the case. As an observer has
noted, "policy across a broad array of regional and functional issues is
much more heavily affected by domestic factors. Many of these make
it harder to shape coherent policies and to achieve cooperation with
allies or even former adversaries."[11] Given the dual forces of competing
agendas/fragmented interests and growing indifference in the American
public, this complicates the making of foreign policy decisions. Furthermore, interbranch leadership means more assertive and more involved

members of Congress, and a wider, more varied "foreign policy bureaucracy" impacting foreign policy.

The dynamics of the post–cold war world therefore seem to ensure continued policy-making activity by the White House, foreign policy bureaucracy, Congress, and nongovernmental actors. For the White House, tradition, the role as chief executive, manager of the sprawling foreign policy bureaucracy, and the combination of other formal and informal roles guarantee presidential involvement, if not dominance. Members of Congress have a formidable set of tools and, if anything, have greater motives for foreign policy activity. The erosion of consensus over foreign policy goals and appropriate instruments signals the likelihood of congressional activism on substantive grounds, while expanding interdependence and growing "intermestic" policy issues reduce the gap between foreign and domestic policy, thus increasing the political incentives for activism. Furthermore, the post–cold war period indicates greater bureaucratic fragmentation as well: the foreign policy bureaucracy will increasingly include economic and other, more traditionally domestic, agencies, resulting in an increasingly broad spectrum of interests, perspectives, and bureaucratic missions to be defended.

All of this points to interbranch policy making. Overall, in such a situation, the White House has the initial advantage, seeming to enjoy initial leadership, in the context of various constraints established by Congress and nongovernmental actors such as public opinion and interest groups. Yet, members of Congress appear to become increasingly involved, either through the necessity of acting on White House proposals or requests, or by virtue of disagreement by various members over an administration's course of action. Hence, foreign policy resembles the "President proposes, Congress disposes" model even more closely in the post–cold war world. There are also more numerous points of contact for nongovernmental groups and individuals—whose incentive to engage in the kind of pressure politics more typically characteristic of domestic policy is greater. Therefore, this volume may mean that there is no true "policy leadership" at all, only leadership by different actors over certain parts or stages of the policy.

Even within this overall constellation, however, there is variation. As the cases of this volume indicate, all of the variants of the Interbranch Leadership constellation are likely to occur in post–cold war foreign policy issues. Of the variants, *cooperation* occurred in the Russia and China cases, which were of high prominence and relative strategic importance and clarity (perhaps the necessary ingredients for the cooperation variant of interbranch policymaking). *Confrontation and stalemate* clearly occurred in the struggle over State Department restructuring, and in the post-NAFTA expansion efforts (in which a White House preference was blocked by congressional opposition). *Constructive compromise* developed in the early cycles of the NAFTA case, and the later stages of the Somalia and assertive multilateralism cases, while *institutional competition* developed in the latter stages of the struggle over State Department restructuring, democracy promotion, Somalia, and assertive multilateralism cases.

Even as during the cold war and the post-Vietnam era, when the White House often gave way to the assertiveness and involvement of other actors, so too will the interbranch constellation, as the dominant, but not only policy-making constellation, give way to other constellations in certain circumstances. These micro-level shifts in constellations (i.e., shifts within or across policies and situations rather than historical periods) will continue. Here, in this volume, there are at least five factors that appear to be related to the nature and circumstance of such shifts (and which might serve as guides to further analysis).

1. *Policy situation* seems to matter: while interbranch leadership seems to be most likely in situations of normal and high priority/prominence, low priority/prominence situations seem to trigger bureaucratic leadership, while crisis situations seem to trigger White House leadership (not surprisingly). However, at least one case in this volume (Somalia, chapter 13) demonstrates that the longer a crisis extends, the more likely the leadership is to revert to the interbranch constellation. Another element of situation also seems important: while nonroutine situations seem to involve interbranch leadership, routine situations seem more likely to involve bureaucratic leadership, while, again, crisis situations (especially nonroutine) again prompt White House leadership.
2. *Process timing* also factors in these micro-level shifts: holding other variables constant, earlier stages and cycles in the policy-making process generally seem to involve a higher degree of White House and bureaucratic leadership, while later stages and cycles of the process widens the circle of relevant actors. This is a policy-specific shift in that, for the overall policy, all other things being equal, the dominant constellation is still likely to be the Interbranch Leadership constellation since non–executive branch actors get involved in later stages and cycles.
3. *Policy issue* constitutes a third factor: as policies move from foreign to intermestic to domestic issues, more and more actors become involved throughout all stages and cycles of the process.

4. *Policy type* also seems to play a role:[12] White House leadership appears to dominate in crisis policy, while strategic policy seems now to invoke interbranch leadership (as compared to the cold war when the White House dominated this policy type, too). Structural policy prompts more bureaucratic leadership and subgovernment leadership (which implies a congressional-bureaucratic-interest group network).

5. *Policy instrument* also has an effect: executive-dominated instruments (e.g., diplomacy, war) provide a better platform for White House or bureaucratic leadership than non-executive-dominated instruments (e.g., aid, trade). One caveat might be offered here as well, however: while the use of the military is generally executive-dominated (in practice if not by law), members of Congress have been increasingly assertive on "operations other than war" involving the U.S. military (e.g., in this volume, Somalia and Bosnia). This makes at least one traditionally executive-dominated instrument (especially during the cold war) subject to more interbranch policy making in the post–cold war period.

### Conclusion

According to Richard Melanson, the cold war consensus that drove U.S. foreign policy for the first two decades after World War II rested on three characteristics: a cultural or societal consensus on the need for international involvement and national sacrifice; a policy consensus around the strategy of containment; and a procedural consensus around presidential leadership of foreign affairs.[13] The contents of this volume suggest that the transition from cold war era to post-Vietnam era to post–cold war era has completed the dismantling of this consensus. In its place, there now seems to be a *post–cold war dissensus* predicated on societal disagreement on the nature and extent of U.S. leadership, policy disagreement on the proper role, strategy, goals, and instruments of U.S. foreign policy, and procedural decentralization away from presidential leadership to more widely diffused involvement of actors from a wider circle of bureaucratic agencies, members of Congress, and nongovernmental actors. For the purposes of this volume, the primary consequence of this dissensus has been foreign policy democratization and decentralization, leading to a shift to interbranch leadership as the dominant foreign policy-making constellation for the post–cold war world thus far. This shift, an "adaptation" of sorts, has contributed to the halting and incomplete policy and institutional transformations designed to deal with the dynamics and challenges of the post–cold war world. To the extent that the U.S. has "adapted" to the post–cold war world, thus far this would appear to be the key adaptation.

The post–cold war world is, at its heart, everything that the cold war was not. Threat is more ambiguous, priorities are more problematic, and policy making is more fragmented and decentralized. The constraints and opportunities of the post–cold war world, the attitudes and actions of the American public and other nongovernmental actors, and the role of influence of institutional actors all point to a more varied and less coherent foreign policy-making environment in which role, goals, and policies are harder to determine, develop, apply, and sustain. Compared to the cold war years, the post–cold war dissensus therefore means less clarity for problems, goals, policies, and instruments; less coherence in process; and expanded cross-pressures from the societal context, owing to the expansion of group pressure and the ambivalence of the American public. This policy of democratization and decentralization can act as brakes on ill-conceived policy and broaden the debate to include more interests and wider perspectives so that policy emerging from this environment is likely to be more sustainable and possess greater legitimacy. However, they also slow down the process and make it more difficult to produce policy. They seem to assure politicization, bargaining, persuasion, and to increase the likelihood of compromise, stalemate, conflict, and policy contradictions. In the fragmented, pluralist U.S. environment, consensus is necessary for coherent, sustained, White House–led foreign policy. Consensus, however, rests on clarity of threat, purpose, and interest, making it a rare commodity in the post–cold war world. This is the era of interbranch policy making.

## Notes

1 David A. Deese, "Making American Foreign Policy in the 1990s," in David A. Deese, ed., *The New Politics of American Foreign Policy* (New York: St. Martin's Press, 1994), p. 264.

2 John Lewis Gaddis, "Toward the Post–Cold War World," *Foreign Affairs* 70, no. 2 (March/April 1991): 103.

3 As noted in chapter 1, this distinction derives from Francis Fukuyama, "The End of History?" *National Interest* 16 (Summer 1989): 3–18; Barry Buzan, "New Patterns in Global Security," *International Affairs* 67, no. 3 (Fall 1991): 431–451; Max Singer and Aaron Wildavsky, *The Real World Order*, rev. ed. (Chatham, N.J.: Chatham House, 1996); and Donald Snow and Eugene Brown, *The Contours of Power* (New York: St. Martin's Press, 1996), who use the terms "first tier" and "second tier."

4 Snow and Brown, "Contours of Power," p. 32.

5 See Robert D. Kaplan, "The Coming Anarchy," *Atlantic Monthly* 273 (February 1994): 44–76.

6 Dario Moreno, *U.S. Policy in Central America: The Endless Debate* (Miami: Florida International University Press, 1990), p. 12.

7 John W. Kingdon, *Agendas, Alternatives, and Public Policies*, 2d ed. (New York: HarperCollins, 1995), p. 3.

8 On this point, see Robert A. Pastor, *Whirlpool: U.S. Foreign Policy toward Latin America and the Caribbean* (Princeton, N.J.: Princeton University Press, 1992), p. 112.

9 William Schneider, "From Foreign Policy to 'Politics As Usual,'" in Deese, ed., *New Politics*, p. xi.

10 Bert A. Rockman, "Presidents, Opinion, and Institutional Leadership," in Deese, ed., *New Politics*, p. 73.

11 Robert J. Lieber, "Eagle without a Cause: Making Foreign Policy without the Soviet Threat," in Lieber, *Eagle Adrift: American Foreign Policy at the End of the Century* (New York: Longman's, 1997), p. 5.

12 Here I rely on the policy typology utilized by Randall Ripley and Grace Franklin, *Congress, the Bureaucracy, and Public Policy*, 5th ed. (Pacific Grove, Calif.: Brooks/Cole, 1991); and Randall Ripley and James M. Lindsay, eds., *Congress Resurgent: Foreign and Defense Policy on Capitol Hill* (Ann Arbor: University of Michigan Press, 1993).

13 Richard Melanson, *American Foreign Policy since World War II: The Search for Consensus from Nixon to Clinton* (Armonk, N.Y.: M. E. Sharpe, 1996).

# Notes on Contributors

**Ralph G. Carter** is professor in the Political Science Department at Texas Christian University.

**Richard Clark** is a Ph.D. candidate in the Department of Political Science at the University of Connecticut.

**A. Lane Crothers** is assistant professor in the Department of Political Science at Illinois State University.

**I. M. Destler** is professor at the School of Public Affairs and director of the Center for International and Security Studies at the University of Maryland.

**Ole R. Holsti** is George V. Allen Professor of Political Science and director of Undergraduate Studies at Duke University.

**Steven W. Hook** is assistant professor in the Department of Political Science at Kent State University.

**Christopher M. Jones** is assistant professor in the Department of Political Science at Northern Illinois University.

**James M. McCormick** is professor in the Department of Political Science at Iowa State University.

**Jerel Rosati** is associate professor in the Department of Government and International Studies at the University of South Carolina.

**Jeremy Rosner** is a fellow at the Carnegie Endowment for International Peace, currently serving as special adviser to the U.S. State Department on NATO enlargement and ratification.

**John T. Rourke** is professor in the Department of Political Science at the University of Connecticut.

**Renee G. Scherlen** is associate professor in the Department of Political Science at Appalachian State University.

**Peter J. Schraeder** is associate professor in the Department of Political Science at Loyola University Chicago.

**James M. Scott** is assistant professor in the Department of Political Science at the University of Nebraska at Kearney.

**Jennifer Sterling-Folker** is assistant professor in the Department of Political Science at the University of Connecticut.

**Rick Travis** is assistant professor in the Department of Political Science at Mississippi State University.

**Stephen Twing** is visiting assistant professor in the Department of Political Science at Virginia Tech University.

# Index

Library of Congress Cataloging-in-Publication Data
After the end : making U.S. foreign policy in the
post–cold war world / edited by James M. Scott.
p.   cm.
Includes index.
ISBN 0-8223-2134-3 (cloth : alk. paper). —
ISBN 0-8223-2266-8 (pbk. : alk. paper)
1. United States—Foreign relations—1989–
I. Scott, James M., 1964–   .
JZ1480.A95   1998
327.73′009′049—dc21   98-27296   CIP